TEXTS AND STUDIES

CONTRIBUTIONS TO

BIBLICAL AND PATRISTIC LITERATURE

EDITED BY

J. ARMITAGE ROBINSON D.D.

HON. PH.D. GÖTTINGEN HON. D.D. HALLE

DEAN OF WESTMINSTER

VOL. VI.

No. 2. THE LAUSIAC HISTORY OF PALLADIUS. II

THE LAUSIAC HISTORY OF PALLADIUS. II

THE GREEK TEXT EDITED WITH INTRODUCTION AND NOTES

BY

DOM CUTHBERT BUTLER M.A.

BENEDICTINE MONK OF THE ENGLISH CONGREGATION
AND OF DOWNSIDE ABBEY

Wipf & Stock
PUBLISHERS
Eugene, Oregon

Wipf and Stock Publishers
199 W 8th Ave, Suite 3
Eugene, OR 97401

Lausiac History of Palladius
By Butler, Cuthbert
ISBN: 1-59244-828-3
Publication date 9/1/2004
Previously published by Cambridge, 1904

IN · MEMORIAM

FORBES · ROBINSON

AMICI · DESIDERATI

PREFACE.

Dr Ehrhard, in the theological section which he contributed to the second edition of Krumbacher's *Geschichte der byzantinischen Litteratur,* declared in 1897 that in the domain of Greek Hagiography "the most pressing need is a critical edition of the *Historia Lausiaca* of Palladius." After pointing out that the task would be a laborious one, he continued: "The labour, however, bestowed upon it would be amply repaid not only by the results for Byzantine Monasteriology, but also from the point of view of the history of civilisation, as we have here to do with a popular book of far reaching influence" (*op. cit.* p. 188). This estimate by so eminent a patrologist and hellenist is at once a justification for the appearance of this edition of the Lausiac History, and an explanation of the fact that so much longer a time than I had anticipated has elapsed since the publication of the volume of Prolegomena which formed the First Part of this Study (*Texts and Studies*, VI 1, 1898). The value of the work as one of the chief authorities for the beginnings of the Christian Monastic movement, itself one of the most important episodes in Christian history, is now recognised by all critics, as may be seen in § 1 of the ensuing Introduction. The partially unforeseen difficulties of the undertaking are the result of the popularity which the book at once obtained. So popular was it that no respect whatever was felt for its text: it was re-written, re-arranged, enlarged, shortened, paraphrased, combined with kindred works, without any scruple. Thus every known process of corruption—revision, interpolation, redaction, intermixture of texts—has had free play among the MSS. both of the Greek text and of the versions. It will be seen as we proceed that all printed copies of the Greek present a metaphrastic re-writing of the text, while those in current use are in addition interpolated with great masses of foreign matter; similarly all printed copies of the versions present them in advanced stages of deterioration. I do not think it is an illusion to suppose that the editor's task has been of quite extraordinary difficulty. In such circumstances all pretence to finality is excluded: what I do believe, however, is that now, for the first time, the Lausiac History is printed in a form that may justly claim to represent substantially what Palladius wrote. Thus for historical purposes the present text may be used with security, and for these purposes I do not think it will ever require substantial revision. For mere textual criticism there may yet be room; but that would depend on the discovery of new types of MSS. in the East, for I believe I have practically exhausted the material available in Western Libraries. The claims and limitations of the edition are set forth in § 10 of the Introduction. It may be well to state that no one will be in a position to pass judgment on the text here offered, who has not mastered the Introduction as a whole.

I venture to direct attention to the body of Notes. One of the objects kept in view in writing them has been to control Palladius' statements wherever they come in contact with external history, that so it may be possible to form a judgment of his character as a historian. I believe that he emerges from the trial with an enhanced reputation.

My best thanks are again due to the editor of this Series; his insight and experience in textual work have helped me materially in arriving at the practical conclusions, formulated on pp. lxxxiv and xcii, as to the proper mode of procedure in the selection of readings: also to Mr Edmund Bishop, for many criticisms and suggestions in Introduction, Notes, and Appendices: and to Dom Rylance for verifying a large number of my collations of Italian MSS., and for drawing the map of Monastic Egypt. Other obligations are acknowledged as they occur. But it would not be right to pass by without mention and thanks my debt to the Managers of the Hort Fund, who by their two grants made it possible for me to visit the Italian libraries: how much this edition of the Lausiac History owes to their assistance may be estimated by considering what it would have been without the Turin and Venice Greek MSS., the Roman and Cassinese Latin MSS., and the Vatican Syriac MS.

A note from the Librarian at Turin leaves little hope that the Palladius MS. is among those saved from the recent fire. There is therefore a double cause of satisfaction that its readings in the Lausiac History have been preserved:—both for their own intrinsic value, and because without them the determination of the relations between the textual sources would have been well nigh impossible.

CUTHBERT BUTLER.

CHRIST'S COLLEGE, CAMBRIDGE.
30 *April*, 1904.

CONTENTS.

INTRODUCTION ON THE SOURCES OF THE TEXT.

TEXT AND NOTES.

APPENDICES

(continued from Part I).

INDEX.

INTRODUCTION ON THE SOURCES OF THE TEXT.

Throughout this volume *Introd.* signifies the present Introduction, *Prol.* the previous volume of Prolegomena (*Texts and Studies* VI. 1).

§ 1. Present Opinion of Critics as to early Egyptian Monachism.

Within half a year of each other three works appeared dealing with the origins of Christian monachism in Egypt and the literary and historical criticism of the chief sources for that history:—*Palladius und Rufinus* by Dr Preuschen (Giessen, 1897), *Le Cénobitisme Pakhomien* by Abbé Ladeuze (Louvain, 1898), and the present writer's *Lausiac History of Palladius* (Cambridge, 1898). Though dealing with different aspects of the subject matter, the three writers had to a great extent to investigate the same problems, and on a large number of the more important points they independently arrived at substantially identical results. The three books were reviewed by scholars of competence and even of eminence, so that it is possible from the reviews to gauge the present attitude of expert opinion in regard to many questions raised by the early history of Egyptian monachism, a subject of much debate during the past thirty years. It will be in place here to put on record the verdict of the critics on the more fundamental of these questions.

(1) The first point that stands out with almost startling clearness is the absolute abandonment on all hands of the sceptical

attitude in regard to the traditional account and to the documents, which gained currency through Weingarten's articles a quarter of a century ago[1]. Nothing can bring out the change so strikingly as a comparison of Weingarten's article *Mönchtum* in the second edition of Herzog's *Realencyklopädie*, x (1882), with Grützmacher's article on the same subject in the third edition, xiii (1903); there is hardly anything in common between them. Preuschen in a Programme published after his *Palladius u. Rufinus* does not hesitate to say: "All the assertions which Weingarten put forward and defended, in a presentation full of suggestiveness and life, have been attacked and abandoned as exaggerated or unfounded[2]." Similarly Lejay: "Of the scepticism of Weingarten and his disciples nothing remains[3]"; and Grützmacher: "Weingarten's criticism went essentially wrong" over the *Historia Lausiaca* and the *Historia Monachorum*[4]; and again: "The time is past when anyone regards, like Weingarten, the sources of early monastic history as fantastic romances devoid of historical value[5]." And this, so far as my knowledge goes, is universally the tone of the critics.

(2) Of all Weingarten's speculations those concerning St Anthony are the best known, and they were popularised in an accentuated form in England. But in his review of my book Preuschen implied that the section wherein I argued the question was superfluous, for in Germany "there is no longer any doubt concerning the historical character of Anthony's personality[6]." In regard to the *Vita Antonii*, while avowing my own deficiency in the special knowledge requisite for a pronouncement as to the vexed question of authorship, I stated that "the tendency seems to be in the direction of connecting the *Vita* with St Athanasius" (*Prol.* 226). Since these words were written the following scholars have unreservedly declared for the Athanasian author-

[1] His views were sufficiently indicated in *Prol.* (*i.e.* Texts and Studies, vi. 1), pp. 3, 194—6, 215, 216.

[2] *Mönchtum und Sarapiskult*, 4 (Darmstadt, 1899; reprinted, Giessen, 1903).

[3] *Revue Critique d'Histoire et de Littérature* (1899), i. 150.

[4] *Theologische Literaturzeitung* (1898), 107. (The *Historia Monachorum* is a book of the same character as the *Historia Lausiaca* described in *Prol.* § 3.)

[5] *Theologische Rundschau* (1899), 99.

[6] *Theologische Literaturzeitung* (1899), 123.

ship: Preuschen[1], Stülcken[2], Bardenhewer[3], Holl[4], Völter[5], Leipoldt[6], and Grützmacher, who in his article in the *Realencyklopädie* says that "the *Vita* without any doubt goes back to Athanasius"; and adds: "As to the historical value of the source there can be no doubt, as Athanasius stood in close relationship with Anthony" (XIII., p. 218).

It will be instructive to summarise the opinions of Holl and Völter. The former says that he is inclined to give more credence to the *Vita Antonii* than it usually receives; "there is on all hands a reaction from Weingarten's doubt as to the genuineness of the work, but the tone in which he applied his criticism still remains. And yet it would be impossible more completely to mistake the spirit and character of the *Vita*, than by seeing in it, as Weingarten did, a kind of Christian romance": the writer, in common with his contemporaries, believed in the conflicts with demons which he relates: certainly it is not to be supposed that Athanasius reproduced the speeches from short-hand reports: no doubt his intention was to set forth an ideal; this ideal, however, he did not invent, but derived it from the reality (*loc. cit.*). Völter, a member of the Dutch critical school, pronounces the *Vita* to be partly history, partly legend, and partly idealisation; but even the legendary and idealised portions contain a kernel of good history, and "the general picture which the *Vita* gives of its hero makes the impression of being essentially true to nature and true to history" (*loc. cit.*).

(3) The *Hist. Laus.*, the *Hist. Mon.*, the *Vita Pachomii* and the other sources of the history were all alike discredited by Weingarten and his followers as mere romance and fairy-tale. A protest was made by a few scholars, and notably by Zöckler, who, all through the period in which extreme scepticism was dominant, steadily maintained that substantial historicity of the chief documents which the critics now unanimously recognise.

[1] *Mönchtum u. Sarapiskult*, 4.

[2] *Athanasiana*, Texte u. Untersuchungen N.F., IV. 4 (1899), 79. (The purpose of the first half is to determine the genuine works of Athanasius.)

[3] *Patrologie*, ed. 2 (1901), 225. [4] *Enthusiasmus u. Bussgewalt* (1898), 139, 140.

[5] *Ursprung des Mönchtums* (1900), 6—9.

[6] *Schenute von Atripe*, Texte u. Untersuchungen N.F., X. 1 (1903), 86.

It is needless to multiply quotations; only one sentence shall be cited from Dr Carl Schmidt's review of Preuschen's book and mine, by far the most important of all the critiques, and itself a notable contribution to the study of Egyptian monastic literature. He says: "The high historical value of both sources (*Hist. Laus.* and *Hist. Mon.*) is proved beyond all doubt[1]." What was said in §§ 15 and 16 of *Prol.* (especially pp. 188—196) on the sense in which this cycle of literature may be taken as historical, and on the presence in it of so conspicuous a miraculous element, often grotesque and "merely magical," sufficed to make my position clear to my foreign critics of whatever school of thought, though I was not equally successful with some critics in England. So I will here only say further that Völter's estimate of the author of the *Vita Antonii* is, in my judgment, equally applicable to Palladius and his compeers: "He intended nothing else than to record the truth. But he accepted whatever he heard or came across, and related it without doubting and without examination, and the more wonderful it was the better was he pleased" (*loc. cit.*). Mr Burkitt's estimate of the Lausiac History neatly characterises all this literature: "In Palladius we are reading neither romance nor scientific history....We seem to have before us the narrative of a contemporary who saw much and heard more, and whose testimony, if not always credible, is at least honest and useful[2]." Finally Zöckler closes his review of Preuschen's book by saying that "notwithstanding the superabundance of miraculous stories," the *Hist. Laus.* "is of the highest interest as a rich repertory of authentic sketches[3]."

Naturally all the documents relating to early Egyptian monachism do not stand on the same level of historical value: on the relatively highest level I would place the Lausiac History, the Greek *Vita Pachomii*, Cassian, and Schenoudi's writings; on a somewhat lower level, the *Vita Antonii*, the *Historia Monachorum*, the other Pachomian documents, the *Apophthegmata*, Schenoudi's Life, and the "subsidiary sources" (8—12) enumerated in *Prol.* 197; and on a much lower level—indeed in a different category—

[1] *Göttingische gelehrte Anzeigen* (1899), No. I., 27.

[2] *Cambridge Review* (1898-9), 143.

[3] *Theologisches Literaturblatt* (1898), 107.

the other *Vitae*, including those by St Jerome: several of this last group are not historical in any sense at all.

In view of the disrepute in which this whole cycle of literature stood ten years ago and even later, it has seemed desirable thus to bring together a body of testimony as to the change that has come over critical opinion. We may now pass to more technical points of mere textual criticism.

(4) Preuschen, Ladeuze and myself all combated the theory that the Greek documents describing Egyptian monachism are translations from Coptic. This theory is now, to the best of my knowledge, universally and absolutely rejected, the critics one and all regarding the Greek (or in one or two cases perhaps the Latin) as the original. (The Schenoudi literature is Coptic.)

(5) With almost equal unanimity is the theory abandoned that Rufinus, Palladius and Sozomen derived their materials independently from a lost Greek common source: Grützmacher seems to have some hesitation as to whether such a document may not have stood behind the Greek and Latin forms of the *Hist. Mon.*; but in regard to the *Hist. Laus.* he shares the common opinion that Palladius used no Greek source in compiling his history[1].

(6) As a consequence it is accepted that Sozomen's abridgments are based on the *Hist. Laus.* and *Hist. Mon.* (see *Prol.* § 8 and App. II),—a point of first importance for the textual critic. Preuschen indeed holds that Sozomen used not the works themselves, but a collection of excerpts: this, however, is a corollary of the view that the Latin, not the Greek, is the original of the *Hist. Mon.*,—a view shared by Zöckler[2], but opposed by the present writer with arguments accepted as convincing by the Bollandist reviewer, Burkitt, Chabot, Grützmacher, Lejay, Richardson, and by Carl Schmidt, who discusses the point with great care[3].

(7) Finally, Dr Preuschen and I, by means of an extended examination of the MSS. and versions, arrived independently at

[1] See Appendix VI.

[2] *Theologisches Literaturblatt* (1899), 306.

[3] *Analecta Bollandiana* (1898), 458; Chabot, *Revue de l'histoire des Religions* (1899), i. 491; Richardson, *American Journal of Theology* (1900), Jan.; for the others see *locc. citt.*

the conclusion that the currently received Lausiac History, the Long Recension (Migne and Hervet, Bk. VIII of Rosweyd's *Vitae Patrum*) is an interpolated redaction, in which some later editor has fused together the *Hist. Mon.* and the true *Hist. Laus.*, and that the genuine work is represented substantially by the Short Recension (Meursius and the Latin *Paradisus Heraclidis*). This conclusion has been accepted on all hands. Zöckler, indeed, expresses some doubt whether Palladius himself may not have made the fusion of the two books; but I have confidence that the last scruples will be removed when the curiously composite and mixed character of the Greek text of the *Hist. Laus.* as it stands in the Long Recension, has been exposed.

I may add that no doubt has been expressed as to Palladius of Helenopolis being the author of the Lausiac History.

The way has thus been made clear for a critical edition of the Greek text, and to this task I now address myself.

§ 2. The Greek MSS. of the Lausiac History.

The following is a list of the Greek MSS. of the Lausiac History with which I am acquainted.

The order is determined by textual, not by chronological, considerations. The dates assigned (in Roman figures) are commonly those of the Catalogues, but in the case of many of the Vatican MSS. I consulted Dr Mercati. Detailed descriptions of several are supplied by Dr Preuschen (*Palladius u. Rufinus*, 137—151).

1. **Vatican**, *Palatine* 41, X (ff. 8—222) [Preuschen μ].
   (The MS. printed by Meursius, Leyden, 1616.)
2. **Venice**, *Bessarion* 338, X (ff. 217—270).
3. **Paris**, *fonds grec* 464, XVI (ff. 95—176) [Pr. P4].
4. **Oxford**, Christ Church, *Wake* 70, A.D. 1107 (ff. 1—111).
5. **Paris**, *Coislin* 83, X (ff. 148—266) [Pr. C1].

5b. **British Museum**, *Arundel* 546, XV (ff. 120—214).
   (5b is closely akin to 5, and is probably a transcript of it.)

6. **Paris**, *fonds grec* 853, XI (ff. 56—149) [Pr. P1].
7. **Munich**, *graec.* 498, X (ff. 189—210) [Pr. M].
   (Extracts from *Hist. Laus.* and *Hist. Mon.*: of *Hist. Laus.* it contains cc. 35 (imperf.), 26, 32—34, 4, 47, 46, 54, 61, 63 (imperf.)[1]. This MS.

[1] The numbers of the chapters here, and always, are those of the present edition.

was formerly at Augsburg, and under the title *Cod. Augustanus* Rosweyd (*Vitae Patrum*), in the notes to the various Latin forms of the *Hist. Laus.*, cites a number of its readings from a copy apparently made for him and now at Brussels (cod. graec. 34). In this transcript c. 63 is complete and is followed by c. 65, which shows that some leaves of the Munich MS. have since been lost.)

8. **Venice**, *Nanianus* 92, XI | XII (ff. 1—71).
9. **Paris**, *fonds grec* 1596, XI (ff. 63—162) [Pr. P^6].
   (cc. 1—22 (med.) are lost.)
10. **Paris**, *fonds grec* 1597, XIII (ff. 1—95) [Pr. P^7].
11. **Paris**, *fonds grec* 594, XIII (ff. 357—476) [Pr. P^8].
   (Breaks off at c. 35, med.)
12. **Leyden**, *Vossianus in fol.* 46, X (ff. 1—78) [Pr. L].
13. **Paris**, *fonds grec* 1600, XI (ff. 19—141) [Pr. P^3].
14. **Vienna**, *hist. graec.* 84, XI (entire codex) [Pr. V^1].
15. **Vienna**, *hist. graec.* 9, XIV (ff. 163—230) [Pr. V^2].
16. **Paris**, *fonds grec* 1532, XII (ff. 173—411) [Pr. P^9].
17. **British Museum**, *Arundel* 519, A.D. 1568 (entire codex).
18. **Oxford**, Bodleian, *Cromwell* 18, XII | XIII (ff. 325—410).
   (Broken up into sections, see Bernard's *Catalogus Codicum Angliae* I. i. 39, 40.)
19. **Vatican**, *graec.* 2091, XII | XIII (entire codex).
20. **Venice**, *Nanianus* 42, X (ff. 102—192).
21. **Venice**, *Bessarion* 345, XV (ff. 89—159).
22. **Vatican**, *graec.* 863, A.D. 1301 (ff. 1—209).

Nos. 23—28 are only excerpts and fragments:

23. **Oxford**, Bodleian, *Baroc.* 240, XII (ff. 153, 154).
   (c. 32, in a vol. of *Vitae* for May.)
24. **Vatican**, *Palatine* 258 (passim).
   (Several extracts in a large collection of spiritual precepts.)
25. **Vatican**, *graec.* 375 (f. 169).
   (The Dedicatory Epistle Μακαρίζω, in a collection of Letters.)
26. **British Museum**, *Burney* 50, XIV (passim).
   (Several extracts in a large collection of *Apophthegmata*.)
27. **Paris**, *fonds grec* 635, XIV (ff. 232—237).
   (Extract from c. 17, and cc. 25, 26, 27, 70.)
28. **St Petersburg**, St Catharine
   (c. 32; printed by Pitra, *Anal. Sacra*, v. 112.)

---

29. **Oxford**, Christ Church, *Wake* 67, X (ff. 150, 193—251). **W**
   (To be described fully in § 9.)

29[b]. Same MS. (ff. 61—70). **W°**
   (cc. 22, 20, 21.)

30. **Paris**, *fonds grec* 1628, XIV (ff. 1—144) [Pr. P^2]. **P**
31. **Turin**, Università, *graec.* C. IV. 8 (*al.* 141), XVI (ff. 53—126). **T**

31[b]. Codex Venetus, used by Rosweyd, now lost (see § 9)

32. **Oxford,** Bodleian, *Laud. graec.* 84, XI | XII (ff. 223—227). **O**
(cc. 32, half 33, 22.)
33. **Paris,** *fonds grec* 919, XIV (ff. 29—46).
(cc. 17, 18, 32, 33, 34, 37, and some chapters of *Hist. Mon.*)
34. **Paris,** *fonds grec* 881, X (ff. 222—224).
(c. 32, in collection of *Vitae* and *Acta.*)
35. **British Museum,** *Addit.* 14066, XII (ff. 164, 165).
(Fragment out of c. 17.)
36. Fragment. inter Opera S. Nili (Migne, *P. G.* LXXIX. 1312).
(c. 23.)
36^b. **Vatican,** *Ottoboni* 436, XV (f. 186).
(c. 23.)

---

37. **Paris,** *fonds grec* 1626, XII (entire codex) [Pr. P^{10}].
38. **Paris,** *Coislin* 295, XIV (ff. 1—218) [Pr. C^4]. **A**
39. **Vatican,** *graec.* 864, XV (ff. 1—191).
40. **Vatican,** *graec.* 2092, X | XI (ff. 21—111).
41. **Grotta Ferrata,** B. β. 1, X (entire codex).
(Written by St Nilus, founder of the monastery; see Rocchi, *Codices Cryptenses*, pp. 100 and 137.)
42. **Vatican,** *Ottoboni* 377, XV | XVI (entire codex).
43. **Oxford,** Christ Church, *Wake* 78, XVII (ff. 572—688).
(Considerable lacunae.)
44. **Vatican,** *graec.* 2081, XI (ff. 96—134).
(cc. 1—31.)
44^b. **Paris,** *Coislin* 370, X (ff. 199—245).
(Proem., Ep., cc. 1, 2, 4, 7—12, 14, 16, 17, 37.)
44^c. **British Museum,** *Addit.* 10073, XV (ff. 253—258).
(c. 22.)
45. **Venice,** *Bessarion* 346, XI (ff. 127—173). **V**
46. **Paris,** *Coislin* 282, XI (ff. 100—137) [Pr. C^2]. **C**
47. **Paris,** *fonds grec* 1627, XIII (entire codex) [Pr. P^5].
[The MS. referred to on p. 8 as 50 is 36^b in the List.]

The following MSS. are known to me only from the entries in the Catalogues:

Madrid, Escurial Φ—III—4 (Miller).
Berlin, Royal Lib. 300, 322 (De Boor).
Palermo, Nat. Lib. I. D. 4 } (Martini).
Parma, fondo de-Rossi 4 } (Martini).
Rome, Vallicellana 68 } (Martini).
Moscow, H. Synod 340, 341 (Wladimir).
Athens, Nat. Lib. 228, 281 (Sakkelion).
Andros, Hagia 59 (Lambros).
Patmos, 176 (Sakkelion).

Athos, 333, 574, 578, 1088, 1163, 1321, 1571, 2031, 2060, 2095, 2096, 2280, 2560, 2589, 3172, 3714, 3768, 4294, 4328, 4808, 5627, 5995: and numerous extracts (Lambros).

Jerusalem, H. Sepulchre 112; S. Sabas 368, 369; H. Cross 77 (Papadopulos-Kerameus).

Sinai, 431, 432, 433, 435 (Gardthausen).

Bernard in the *Catal. Codicum Angliae* (II. p. 390) mentions among the Moore MSS. one "De Vita sanctorum Patrum et Paradisus de Eremitis &c. Ad Lausum Praepositum Palatii"; this is one of the MSS. that did not come to Cambridge, and I have been unable to trace it: it is impossible to say whether this was a Greek or a Latin MS., but more probably it was Latin.

The Bollandists in their Catalogues of Greek hagiographical MSS. have not included copies of the *Hist. Laus.*, though in the corresponding Latin Catalogues they did include copies of the Latin versions and of *Hist. Mon.* No doubt other extracts and fragments exist in the libraries in which I have worked; in the Vatican I had not time to examine all the MSS. in the list I made from the unprinted Catalogue. In no other library at Rome, nor at Naples, Florence or Milan, did I find any Greek MSS. of the *Hist. Laus.*

Out of the fifty-three MSS. and fragments in the numbered List, I have personally inspected and collated in test passages all except five. Of these five, the fragments 28 and 36 are in print: 31^b I have been unable to trace, but the readings given from it by Rosweyd show it to have been closely akin to 31: concerning 14 and 15 abundant information is available for their identification as members of the same sub-group as 16, 17, 18 (see Note 11). Information kindly supplied to me by the Librarian at the Escurial shows that the Escurial MS. (saec. XIV) is a member of the great class hereafter called B. The Berlin MSS. and the three Italian MSS. mentioned by Martini contain mere fragments: doubtless as the cataloguing of the Italian libraries progresses other MSS. will be revealed. But at the present time I may claim to have seen every Greek MS. of the Lausiac History in Western Europe, the existence of which is known to me after a diligent search in the printed catalogues, except only three (14, 15, and Escurial); and I possess adequate information as to the character of these three. I regret that I have been unable to extend my researches to the East[1].

I proceed to the classification and characterisation of the MSS. They fall into three main groups:

[1] See note on p. xcvi.

I. Nos. 1—28 are representatives of what may be called the *Textus Receptus,* the text found in all Greek editions hitherto printed. These MSS. contain the form of the *Hist. Laus.* designated B throughout the first volume of this study (*Prol.*); it is therefore natural to call this the B group, and these MSS. the B MSS., and the type of text which they contain the B text.

II. Nos. 29—36^{b} contain a text of a type quite distinct from B: it may be characterised as simpler, less rhetorical, and shorter than B. There are also differences of redaction, in that the structure of the later portion of the book differs from B. This group was called γ in *Prol.* 139; and therefore the letter G will be affixed to it, so that we shall speak of the G MSS. and the G text. In 33, 34, 36^{b} the G text has been freely subjected to literary revisions, independent of each other.

III. Nos. 37—47 contain composite texts, *i.e.* texts made up in various ways of portions of B and portions of G.

It is desirable to adhere, as far as possible, to the nomenclature employed in the former volume of this study (*Prol.*). There the main problem investigated was the question of *redaction*, and the symbol B was used to represent the uninterpolated form of the book, the type of text now designated as G being treated as a variety of B. Here it is assumed, in view of the common consent of the critics, that the question of redaction has been settled by Dr Preuschen and myself; so that the only problem to be investigated is the question of *text*. Thus it is now necessary to distinguish the two types of text in which the genuine uninterpolated *Hist. Laus.* has been transmitted. I do not think that any inconvenience will arise from continuing to use B to designate the numerically predominant type of text, which was practically always taken throughout *Prol.* as representing the uninterpolated work. In the discussions that follow, the text of the *Hist. Laus.* alone is considered, no account being taken of the fact that in certain groups of B MSS. (8-9-10-11 and 14-15-16-17-18) fusions of the *Hist. Mon.* with the *Hist. Laus.* have been effected distinct from that in the Long Recension (A), discussed in *Prol.* Thus B no longer primarily signifies a redaction; it signifies primarily a type of text.

The first problem that faces an editor of the Lausiac History is the relationship between the B and G texts; it is therefore important that a just idea of the magnitude and character of the differences between them should be formed at the outset. As might be expected, the degree of difference varies very much in different parts of the book. But it is necessary to establish at once the fact that in some places the divergence is so great that it cannot be due to ordinary errors in transmission, but is the result of a deliberate re-writing of the text on one side or the other. To exemplify this I take a passage out of the story of Eulogius and the Cripple (c. 21): the portions common to B and G are printed in Clarendon type, those peculiar to B in ordinary type: words found in G but not in B are enclosed in parenthesis. A few unimportant variants are not here noticed.

Μετὰ δὲ τὰ δεκαπέντε ἔτη δαίμων ἐνέσκηψεν εἰς αὐτὸν θέλων τάχα καὶ τὸν Εὐλόγιον τῆς ἐντολῆς καὶ τῆς προθέσεως στερῆσαι, καὶ τὸν λελωβημένον τῆς ἀναπαύσεως καὶ τῆς εὐχαριστίας κυρίου· **καὶ ἀποστασιάζει** οὗτος **πρὸς τὸν Εὐλόγιον· καὶ ἤρξατο** λέγειν κατ' αὐτοῦ πολλὰ δύσφημα (τοσαύταις δυσφημίαις) ὡς **καὶ λοιδορίαις** λοιπὸν **πλύνειν τὸν ἄνδρα, ἐπιλέγων** αὐτῷ· **Σχάστα,** γλούττων, **φυγοκύρι, ἀλλότρια χρήματα ἔκλεψας,** καὶ τάχα δοῦλος ὑπάρχων τὸν ἴδιον δεσπότην ἐσύλησας· καὶ τῇ ἐμῇ προφάσει βούλει λαθεῖν, ὡς ἐπὶ προφάσει δῆθεν εὐποιίας εἰς τὸ ξενίδιόν σου λαβών με, **καὶ δι' ἐμοῦ θέλεις σωθῆναι.** ὁ δὲ Εὐλόγιος παρεκάλει αὐτὸν θεραπεύων αὐτοῦ τὴν καρδίαν, λέγων· Μή, κύριε, μὴ λέγε τοιαῦτα· ἀλλ' εἰπὲ τί σε ἐλύπησα, καὶ διορθοῦμαι. ὁ δὲ ὅλος λελωβημένος ἔλεγεν ἐμβριθῶς· Οὐ θέλω σου ταύτας τὰς κολακείας· ἀπένεγκε, **ῥῖψόν με εἰς τὴν ἀγορὰν** παρὰ τὴν σήν μοι ἀνάπαυσιν. ὁ δὲ Εὐλόγιος· Παρακαλῶ σε, θεραπεύθητι, εἴ τι λυπῇ, κύρι ὁ μέγας. ὁ δὲ λελωβημένος ἀγριαίνων θυμῷ πρὸς αὐτὸν ἔλεγεν· Οὐκέτι ἀνέχομαι τῆς ὑπούλου σου καὶ εἰρωνικῆς κολακείας. οὐκ ἀρέσκομαι τῇ ζωῇ ταύτῃ τῇ τεταριχευμένῃ καὶ φειδωλῷ. ἐγὼ **κρέα θέλω** ἐσθίειν. ὁ δὲ μακρόθυμος Εὐλόγιος **ἤνεγκεν αὐτῷ κρέα.** ἰδὼν δὲ ταῦτα **πάλιν** (+οὖν) **ἀνέκραξεν** ὁ δυσπαθής· **Οὐ πληροφοροῦμαι** εἶναι μετὰ σοῦ μόνου· **ὄχλους θέλω.** λέγει αὐτῷ ὁ Εὐλόγιος· Ἐγώ σοι φέρω ἄρτι πλῆθος ἀδελφῶν. ὁ δὲ πάλιν ἀποδυσπετῶν λέγει· Οὐαί μοι τῷ ταλαιπώρῳ, τὴν σὴν ὄψιν οὐ θέλω ἰδεῖν, καὶ ἄγεις μοι τοὺς ὁμοίους σου ἀργοφάγους; καὶ σπαράξας ἑαυτὸν, ἀτάκτῳ φωνῇ ἀνέκραξε λέγων· Οὐ θέλω, οὐ θέλω· **εἰς τὴν ἀγορὰν θέλω**[1]. **ὦ βία· ῥῖψόν με ὅπου με εὗρες.** λέγω ὅτι (ὡς) **εἰ εἶχε χεῖρας τάχα** (+ἂν) οὐ παρῃτεῖτο **καὶ** ἀγχόνῃ χρήσασθαι (ἀπήγξατο) ἢ ξίφει ἑαυτὸν χειρίσασθαι, **τοῦ δαίμονος αὐτὸν οὕτως ἐξαγριώσαντος.**

This passage has been selected as a fair sample of the differences often found between B and G: sometimes, as in the chapters

[1] The Turin MS. (No. 31) here agrees with the B text; it reads as follows: ὄχλους θέλω· εἰς τὴν ἀγορὰν θέλω. λέγει αὐτῷ ὁ Εὐλόγιος· Ἐγὼ κ.τ.λ.... Οὐ θέλω, οὐ θέλω· εἰς τὴν ἀγορὰν θέλω. κ.τ.λ. (The words τῷ ταλαιπώρῳ...ἄγεις μοι are omitted, evidently by homoeoteleuton.) Elsewhere throughout this passage the Turin MS. agrees with the other G MSS. 29ᵇ and 30; the fact that the clause εἰς τὴν ἀγορὰν θέλω occurs both at the beginning and at the end of the passage in 31, shows clearly that the passage did not originally stand in the text represented by 31, but has been interpolated from a B MS.

on Olympias (c. 56) and the Calumniated Lector (c. 70), they are even more considerable; sometimes, as in the story of Pachon (c. 23; see § 5, where B and G are printed in full), they are comparatively trifling.

We must now speak of the third group of MSS. (37—47), those which contain composite texts.

By a *composite* text is meant one in which some sections are taken from a B MS. and others from a G MS.; the term *mixed* text is reserved for cases in which a B text or a G text has been contaminated by the introduction of readings from the rival type of text. Both phenomena are common in MSS. of the Lausiac History.

Of group III, Nos. 37—44^c are the MSS. which represent the Long Recension (that of Hervet, Du Duc, and Migne), called A in *Prol.* It may be remembered that the characteristic feature of A *as a redaction* was shown to consist in this: that it is an *interpolated* edition, containing a particular kind of fusion of the *Hist. Laus.* and *Hist. Mon.*, essentially different from the other fusions of the two works. The characteristic feature of A *as a text* consists in this: that the text of the *Hist. Laus.* which it contains is a *composite* text, being partly a B text and partly a G text, distributed as follows:

(The order is the order of A, but the numbers of the chapters are those of the present edition: the corresponding numbers in A may be seen in the List of Chapters preceding the Text: the question of order is dealt with in § 7. On the printed Greek text of A see § 3.)

B Prologue, 1—24, 29, 32—34,
G 18 (*med.*), 25—28, 30, 31, 35—37,

B 38, 39, 42, 48—52, 45, 66,
G 39 (*med.*), 47, 58, 40, 44, 43, 53,

B 68, [+][1] 41 (*init.*), 54 (*init.*), 61, 62, 41, 67, 63,
G 46, 54, 59, 60,

B 69, 70, 56, 57, 64, 65, [+][1], Epilogue.
G 55, 71,

[1] At the two points marked [+] occur respectively the chapters numbered 116 and 150 (the first half) in A, containing matter not found in any other redaction of the *Hist. Laus.*, nor as yet discovered elsewhere. No account is taken in the above Table of the interpolations from *Hist. Mon.*

It will be convenient to continue to apply the symbol A to the text contained in these MSS. (37—44[c]), distinguishing, however, as A^B the portions that contain a B text: so that hereafter A will signify a special sub-group of the G text, and A^B a variety of the B text which is not found elsewhere. The characteristics of both portions will be examined later.

The Vatican MS. 863 (no. 22) has the outward semblance of an A MS.; for the *Hist. Mon.* has been interpolated almost in the manner characteristic of the Long Recension. But the entire text of the *Hist. Laus.* is a B text of the type found also in MSS. 19-20-21, and quite distinct from A^B; the order, too, of the later portion of the book is that of B. It seems as if a scribe incorporated a MS. of the *Hist. Mon.* with a B MS. of the *Hist. Laus.*, making the product resemble an A MS. lying before him,—why he should not, rather, have copied the latter, it is impossible to surmise. In places, too, he introduced A readings into his B text: (see instances below in c. 18, p. 51, 1, and in c. 35, p. 101, 8—10, and p. 102, 9—11, where clauses omitted in all other known B MSS. stand in no. 22).

On Ottoboni 377 (no. 42) see § 3.

Nos. 45 and 46 are of great importance. They are so closely allied both in structure and in text as to be evidently collateral descendants of a single proximate ancestor; they are, indeed, twin manuscripts. Their text falls into three sections:—

(1) Proem (Ἐν ταύτῃ) and cc. 1—20; from an A^B text.

(2) cc. 23—28, 31, 35—39; from a G text.

(3) cc. 21, 22, 32—34, 71; from a B text, and a singularly interesting representative of the type.

The rest of the *Hist. Laus.* is wanting; there follow three chapters of the *Hist. Mon.* (1, 8, 16, ed. Preuschen).

No. 47 is the most anomalous MS. of all; (for description and contents see Preuschen, P^5, *op. cit.* 142—144). I have examined its textual affinities only here and there, but sufficiently to see that, though of considerable textual interest for the *Hist. Mon.* (see *Prol.* 269), it possesses little or no value for the *Hist. Laus.*

The following summary of its contents will suffice:

(1) Proem, Ep. Μακαρίζω (with title found elsewhere only in no. 19), Prologue (without fresh title).

(2) *Hist. Laus.* cc. 1—21: (cc. 8—10 are B text; c. 17 is the unique rewriting of G found in MS. 33; c. 18 is again B: cc. 17 and 18 both have a number of Apophthegmata interpolated).

(3) *Hist. Laus.* cc. 32—34: (the form of G found in MS. 33).

(4) John of Lycopolis from *Hist. Mon.* (c. 1) and *Hist. Laus.* (c. 35, incomplete).

(5) *Hist. Mon.* cc. 8, 9.

(6) *Hist. Laus.* cc. 22—31: (c. 22 is A^B; c. 27 is B).

(7) The bulk of *Hist. Mon.*: (as in (4) and (5), the text is that signalised as unique in *Prol.* 269; but the lives follow the certainly wrong sequence found elsewhere only as incorporated in the Long Recension—cc. 16, 21—24, (25, 26), 19, 32, 33, 17, 18, 20 (Hervet cc. 62—76).

(8) *Hist. Laus.* cc. 36, 37 (c. 38 is wanting): (B text).

(9) *Hist. Laus.* c. 39 onwards, in the sequence of the Long Recension, including the chapter on Bessarion, found only in that recension; but omitting a few chapters. I am unable to say whether in this portion the text exhibits the alternations of A and A^B found in the normal MSS. of the Long Recension.

How such a medley of texts ever came together into a single codex is inexplicable. The scribe must have had before him a copy of the Long Recension, and also a number of other MSS. and fragments of *Hist. Laus.* and *Hist. Mon.*, and, as appears evident from (7), must have tried to build up out of these heterogeneous elements a text on the general model of the Long Recension.

This will be the most convenient place to indicate the grouping and relationships of the great body of MSS. containing the B text. The annexed Table is based upon a full collation of c. 32 (Pachomius) made in all the MSS., supplemented by collations of other selected passages, and in many cases by external phenomena of structure, order, omissions, fusion with *Hist. Mon.*, and general contents of the codices: Note 32 affords a detailed sample of the phenomena which underlie the classification of the B MSS.

Mere fragments are not included in the Table. MSS. containing composite texts are enclosed in brackets; account is taken only of the portions of the B text which they contain. MSS. which are the offspring of a single proximate ancestor are linked by hyphens. Of all these B MSS. the sub-group 14-15-16-17-18 alone shows signs of a deliberate literary revision; their text differs notably from the normal B type (see Note 11). In all the rest the texts are, considering the circumstances, wonderfully in accord. In the sub-groups 8—11, 14—18, 37—44^c, and in 7, 22 and 47, the *Hist. Mon.* has been fused with the *Hist. Laus.* in various ways; and in the majority of the other MSS. it goes either immediately before or after the *Hist. Laus.*

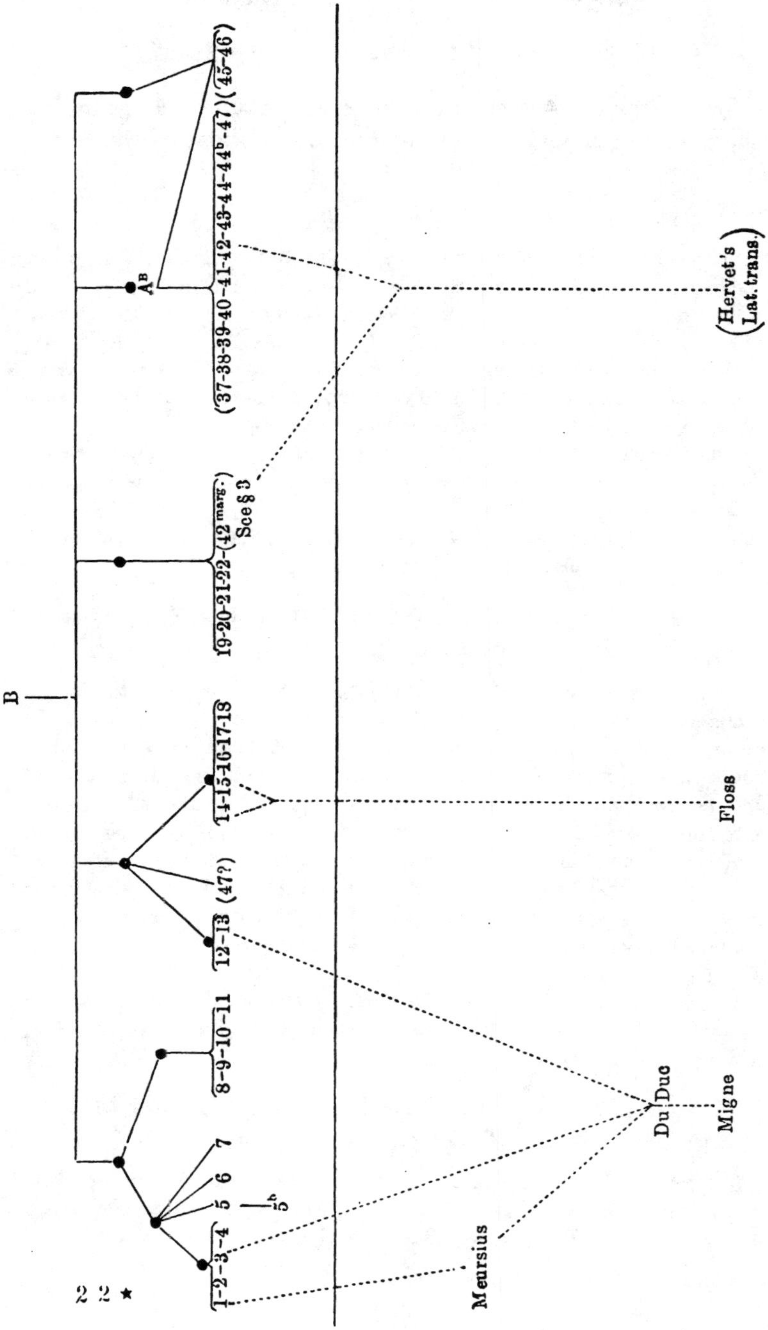

(The lower half of the Table belongs to § 3.)

§ 3. The Printed Editions of the Greek Text.

The foregoing Table prepares the way for a right understanding of the genesis and character of the previous editions of the Greek text. These are:

(I) Meursius, Leyden 1616.

This was based on the single MS. *Palatine* 41 (no. 1). Besides a page lost at the beginning (supplied from another MS., see Meursius' note p. 170) and one torn out in c. 17 (p. 40), the following lacunae occur in the text as compared with the normal B MSS.: the Letter Μακαρίζω; Didymus (c. 4); Evagrius (c. 38); and a passage at the end of the book (ἀλλὰ τοῦτον κατῄσχυνεν, to the end). The omission of cc. 4 and 38, shared by the whole subgroup 1—6, is unquestionably due to orthodox "Tendenz."

A comparison of Meursius' text with the MS. in c. 32 (Pachomius) revealed no fewer than twelve differences: a few are attempted emendations, but most are mere errors.

Meursius added at the end a number of historical and critical notes, which have not yet lost their value.

(II) Du Duc, Paris 1624 (in tom. II. of the *Auctarium* to La Bigne's *Bibliotheca Veterum Patrum*).

In the notes at the end of the volume (p. 4) Du Duc explains the nature and method of his work. He took Meursius' text as his basis, and used in addition two MSS., which he describes with sufficient detail for their identification with the present Paris MSS. 464 and 1600 (nos. 3 and 13), in both of which the *Hist. Mon.* follows the *Hist. Laus.* By means of these MSS. he was able to emend the text of the *Hist. Laus.*, and also to supply the portions of the *Hist. Mon.* found in Latin in Hervet's translation of the Long Recension. Du Duc tells us that he took Hervet and built up the Greek text, patching it together so as to agree in structure with Hervet's Latin. Certain lacunae remain, and various traces of the patchwork (see Migne, *P. G.* XXXIV. 1114 D and 1115 B).

Du Duc also added notes on the text, which were largely utilised by Rosweyd for the *Notatio* in the second edition of the *Vitae Patrum* (1628, reprinted in *P. L.* LXXIII.).

(III) and (IV) Reprints of Du Duc, Paris 1644 and 1654 (in tom. XIII. of the *Magna Bibliotheca Veterum Patrum*).

[In 1686 Cotelier (*Eccl. Graec. Mon.* III. 158--170) printed from the Paris MSS. 1626 and 1627 (nos. 37 and 47) the passages omitted in Du Duc's edition as compared with Hervet. But all such passages belong to the *Hist.*

Mon., with the exception of one piece in c. 18, and even this I have not admitted into the text (see p. 57, 12).]

(V) Lami, Florence 1746 (in tom. VIII. of his edition of the *Opera Omnia* of Meursius).

This is a reprint not of Meursius' edition, but of Du Duc's; but the fragments printed by Cotelier are placed at the end of the chapters in which they should occur. Meursius' notes are printed at the foot of the pages, and Lami has added at the end extracts from Cave, Oudin, Baronius and Fabricius; also a very few footnotes, of no value.

(VI) Migne, Paris 1860 (in tom. XXXIV. of the *Patrologia Graeca*).

This again is a reprint of Du Duc, but Cotelier's fragments are inserted in their places in the text, so that the lacunae no longer appear. The notes are the excellent critical and historical *Notatio* of Rosweyd's second edition of *Vitae Patrum*, and contain a number of valuable Greek readings from the lost MS. 31^b.

From what has been said it follows that, in spite of appearances, the Greek text of the Long Recension (A) has never been printed, Du Duc's text being based exclusively on B MSS.

In view of the importance which Hervet's Latin thus acquires, as the only printed representative of A, it will be in place here to utter a word of warning in regard to it.

Frequently it presents readings, and even considerable passages, proper to B, in places where the Greek MSS. of A adhere to G (*e.g.* c. 27, see Note 45). I was unable to account for this phenomenon until I saw the Vatican MS. *Ottobon.* 377 (no. 42 in the List). This MS. contains a text of the normal A type; but in the margins have been entered by the original hand a number of readings from a B MS. of the type of the sub-group 19-20-21-22, at times amounting to several lines (as in c. 27, referred to above). I examined these marginal entries in a large number of the places where Hervet departs from the A text, and in every case (with two exceptions, trifling and easily accounted for,—see Note 9) it appeared that this MS. supplied the explanation of the disagreement; so that it may be concluded that Hervet made his translation from the *Ottobon.* MS., or from a copy of it. Moreover Du Duc made many alterations in Hervet's Latin in order to bring it into conformity with the B MSS. from which he edited the text; and this adulterated form of the Latin is the one found in all later editions, including Rosweyd's ed. 2, 1628, and Migne, *P. L.* LXXIII. and *P. G.* XXXIV. Thus it comes to pass that Hervet's Latin, even in its primitive form, cannot for textual purposes be relied on as representing the A text.

Besides the complete editions a few chapters have been separately edited. In the Appendix to his edition of the *Epistolae etc. Macarii Aegyptii* (Cologne, 1851) Floss printed cc. 17, 18, 20, 21 (a few lines), 25, 26; (reprinted in Migne, *P. G.* XXXIV. 177—205): he relied wholly on the two Vienna MSS. (nos. 14-15), which, however, present an eccentric and almost worthless form of the B text (see Note 11). Pitra printed c. 32 from a B fragment at St Petersburg (no. 28). Finally Preuschen has quite recently edited critically four chapters, using a number of B and G MSS.: viz. c. 65 (the "Story from Hippolytus") in Achelis' edition of the *Kleinere Exegetische u. Homiletische Schriften* of Hippolytus (Berlin Series of Ante-Nicene Greek Writers, I. ii. 275—7); and cc. 35, 38, 10 in his own *Palladius u. Rufinus* (pp. 98—123). The Maurists had undertaken an edition of Palladius, and a volume of their collations of various Royal and Colbert MSS. (now at Paris) exists in the Bibliothèque Nationale (*Supplément Gr.* 277).

The genesis of the editions is indicated in the Table of B MSS. (p. xxiii). The exception to be made in the case of Preuschen (and Floss) is so inconsiderable, that it is still true to say broadly that since Du Duc there has been no recourse to MSS.; also that all editions of the Lausiac History have been based wholly upon B MSS.; so that this type of text is the only one that has hitherto been known.

The first step in preparing a new edition must be an endeavour, by tracing the history of the text, to discover which type, B or G, preserves the primitive form.

§ 4. HISTORY OF THE TEXT: CITATIONS BY LATER WRITERS.

The passage, cited *Prol.* 138, from the end of Socrates' chapter on the Monks (IV. 23), shows that he knew of the existence of the Lausiac History and was acquainted with its general character; still it is very doubtful whether he made any use of it as a source. Preuschen thinks that Socrates' account of Amoun the Nitriot may be derived from Palladius (c. 8), but nothing more (*op. cit.* 224—6); I cannot satisfy myself even on this point. The reader will find on pp. 26, 27 of the Text the materials for forming his own judgment. In any case, there is no textual agreement such as would indicate the type of text which Socrates may have used[1].

Sozomen.

There is practical agreement among the critics that Sozomen made frequent and copious use of the *Hist. Laus.* (see § 1; and, for the discussion of the point, *Prol.* § 8 and App. II). He however nowhere names or actually quotes it; when he uses it he ordinarily abridges and alters the text freely, though sometimes reproducing a clause or expression. Thus it is only occasionally possible to determine from Sozomen the readings of his copy. Furthermore, in many of these latter cases there is no difference between the B and G texts; or, again, at times the reading of one or other text is not certain: so that the passages are useless for the present purpose. The following is a full schedule of the passages that may be taken with security as throwing light, however faint, on the type of text (B or G) that Sozomen had before him: in § 10 are further cases wherein Sozomen's evidence is invoked on minor questions of variant readings. For the Sozomen text I have taken Hussey's edition and apparatus; for the Palladius readings of both types of text I have in every case examined a number of independent witnesses, and where any practical doubt exists as to either text, I do not adduce the passage at all.

In the following schedule the references are to page and line of the Palladius Text in this volume; the corresponding places in Migne (B) may easily be found by the references in the headlines; all the portions of Sozomen derived from the *Hist. Laus.* are printed in full beneath the Text.

p. 17, 7	B	ἤσθιε μὲν γὰρ οὐγκίας ἓξ ἄρτου καθ' ἑκάστην ἡμέραν	καὶ λεπτολαχάνων δέμα
	Soz.	τροφὴ δὲ ἦν αὐτῷ ἄρτου οὐγγίαι ἓξ	καὶ λεπτῶν λαχάνων δέμα
	G	ἤσθιε μὲν γὰρ οὐγκίας ἓξ ἄρτου	καὶ λεπτολαχάνων δέμα
9	B	οὐ καθευδήσαντα ἐξεπίτηδες ἢ ἐπὶ ψιαθίου ἢ ἐπὶ κλίνης	
	Soz.	(οὐδέ ποτε) ἐπὶ ῥιπὸς ἢ κλίνης καθευδήσας	
	G	οὐ καθευδήσαντα ἐπὶ ψιαθίου οὐκ ἐπὶ κλίνης	
14	B	ἐκ νεαρᾶς ἡλικίας	Soz. ἐκ νέου G ἀπὸ νεότητος

[1] Geppert's somewhat wild suggestion that Socrates may have had a different redaction of the *Hist. Laus.* from those that have come down to us deserves no consideration (*Quellen des Kirchenhistorikers Socrates*, 80).

p. 18, 1 B ἐὰν πείσῃς τοὺς ἀγγέλους κοιμηθῆναί ποτε, πείσεις ἐν τούτῳ καὶ τὸν σπουδαῖον
Soz. εἰ τοὺς ἀγγέλους πείσεις καθεύδειν, πείσεις καὶ τὸν σπουδαῖον
G ἐὰν πείσῃς τοὺς ἀγγέλους κοιμηθῆναι, πείσεις καὶ τὸν σπουδαῖον

p. 20, 16 B καθεζομένου Soz. καθεζόμενος G καθήμενον
17 B ἰδεῖν ἐν ἐκστάσει Soz. ἐν ἐκστάσει...ὁρᾶν G ἰδεῖν ἔκστασιν

p. 28, 11 B ὁ δὲ εὐχαριστήσας αὐτῇ καὶ δεδωκὼς δόξαν τῷ θεῷ λέγει αὐτῃ
Soz. ὁ δὲ χάριν ὁμολογήσας τῷ θεῷ...ἔφη
G ὁ δὲ εὐχαριστήσας τῷ θεῷ (al. κυρίῳ) λέγει αὐτῇ
13 B ἐγὼ δὲ ἀπελθὼν ποιήσω μοι ἕτερον οἶκον
Soz. ἐγὼ δὲ ἕτερον ἐμαυτῷ ποιήσω
G ἐγὼ δὲ ποιήσω (al. ποιῶ) ἐμαυτῷ ἕτερον οἶκον

p. 33, 9 B ἀδύνατόν με γενέσθαι λοιπὸν ὅπερ αὐτοὶ ἀναγκάζετε τοῦ νόμου κ.τ.λ.
Soz. λοιπὸν γὰρ οὐδὲ ἑκόντα με ὁ ἱερατικὸς νόμος συγχωρεῖ χειροτονεῖσθαι
G ἀδύνατόν μοι (al. με) γενέσθαι τοῦ νόμου κ.τ.λ.
14 B μόνον ἄξιον ὄντα τοῖς τρόποις
Soz. ἦν μόνον ἄρτιος ᾖ τοῖς τρόποις
G ἄξιον ὄντα τοῖς τρόποις

p. 35, 4 B πάσης ἀπηλλάττετο ἀρρωστίας ὁ ἐνοχλούμενος
Soz. πάσης ἀπαλλάσσειν νόσου τοὺς κάμνοντας
G πάσης ἀπαλλάττεσθαι (al. -τετο) ἀρρωστίας

p. 36, 3 B παρέβλαψε Soz. ἔβλαψε G ἔβλαψε
10 B κέλλης Soz. οἰκήματος G οἴκου

p. 37, 7 B ὅστις τελευτᾶν μέλλων
Soz. μέλλων δὲ τελευτᾶν
G ὃς τελευτῶν

p. 43, 5

B	Soz.	G
τὰ κατὰ τοὺς ἁγίους καὶ ἀθανάτους πατέρας Μακάριον τὸν Αἰγύπτιον καὶ Μ. τὸν Ἀλεξανδρέα τοὺς γενναίους ἄνδρας, καὶ ἀκαταγωνίστους ἀθλητὰς τοῦ ἐναρέτου βίου ἆθλα πολλὰ ὄντα καὶ μεγάλα κ.τ.λ............	ἄρξομαι δὲ ἐξ Αἰγύπτου καὶ Μακαρίων τῶν δύο τῶν ἀοιδιμωτάτων ἡγεμόνων τῆς Σκήτεως καὶ τοῦ τῇδε ὄρους.	τὰ κατὰ τοὺς δύο Μακαρίους τοὺς ἀοιδίμους ἄνδρας πολλὰ καὶ μεγάλα κ.τ.λ............
ὁ μὲν πρῶτος ἀθλητὴς τοῦ Χριστοῦ Μακάριος ὀνόματι Αἰγύπτιος τῷ γένει ὑπῆρχεν· ὁ δὲ δεύτερος ἡλικίᾳ, πρῶτος δὲ τοῖς προτερήμασι τῶν μοναχῶν, καὶ αὐτὸς Μακάριος καλούμενος τῷ ὀνόματι, Ἀλεξανδρέων πολίτης γέγονεν.	τούτοιν δὲ ὁ μὲν Αἰγύπτιος ὁ δὲ πολιτικὸς ὡς ἀστὸς ὠνομάζετο· ἦν γὰρ τῷ γένει Ἀλεξανδρεύς.	τούτων τῶν Μακαρίων ὁ μὲν εἷς ἦν Αἰγύπτιος τὸ γένος, ὁ δὲ ἄλλος Ἀλεξανδρεύς.

15 B νεώτερος τῇ ἡλικίᾳ Soz. ἔτι νέος ὤν G νέος

p. 48, 2
B εἴ τι ἀκήκοε πώποτέ τινα πεποιηκότα ἔργον ἀσκήσεως διαπύρως πάντως τοῦτο κατώρθωσεν
Soz. ἃ δὲ παρ' ἄλλοις ἤκουσεν ἐκ παντὸς τρόπου κατορθῶν
G εἴ τι ἀκήκοε πώποτε (τινα πεποιηκότα ?) πάντως τοῦτο κατώρθωσεν

p. 62, 20 B παρεκτὸς οὗ ἔμελλεν ἐν αὐτῇ τῇ ἡμέρᾳ (al. ὥρᾳ) ἐσθίειν
Soz. πλὴν ὅσον ἤσθιεν
G παρεκτὸς οὗ ἤσθιεν

p. 88, 4 B ἄγγελος κυρίου Soz. θεῖος ἄγγελος G ἄγγελος

p. 89, 10 B (μηλωτὴν)...ἧς ἄνευ μηδὲ ἐσθιέτωσαν μηδὲ καθευδέτωσαν
Soz. σὺν...ταῖς διφθέραις (=μηλωταῖς) καθεύδειν
G ἧς ἄνευ μὴ ἐσθιέτωσαν

11 B εἰσιόντες δὲ εἰς τὴν κοινωνίαν τῶν μυστηρίων τοῦ Χριστοῦ
Soz. ἐπὶ κοινωνίᾳ τῶν θείων μυστηρίων...προσιόντας
G ἀπιόντες δὲ εἰς τὴν κοινωνίαν

p. 90, 3

B	Soz.	G
ἐκέλευσε δὲ εἰκοσιτέσσαρα τάγματα εἶναι τῶν ἀδελφῶν, κατὰ τὸν ἀριθμὸν τῶν εἰκοσιτεσσάρων γραμμάτων· καὶ προσέταξεν ἑκάστῳ τάγματι τὸ ὄνομα τεθῆναι στοιχεῖον ἑλληνικόν	πᾶσαν δὲ τὴν συνοικίαν εἰς εἰκοσιτέσσαρα τάγματα διελεῖν καὶ ἐπονομάσαι ταῦτα τοῖς Ἑλλήνων στοιχείοις	ἐκέλευσε δὲ εἰκοσιτέσσαρα τάγματα εἶναι καὶ ἑκάστῳ τάγματι ἐπέθηκε στοιχεῖον ἑλληνικόν

p. 91, 9 B τὸν μέντοι εἰσελθόντα εἰσάπαξ συμμεῖναι αὐτοῖς
Soz. τὸν δὲ συνοικεῖν αὐτοῖς βουλόμενον
G τὸν μέντοι εἰσελθόντα συμμεῖναι αὐτοῖς

p. 92, 6 B ἑκάστῳ τάγματι καθ' ἑκάστην εὐχὴν
Soz. ἑκάστης εὐχῆς
G (ἐν) ἑκάστῃ εὐχῇ

p. 126, 15

B	Soz.	G
λέγει αὐτοῖς ὁ ἐνάρετος οὗτος· Τὰ περὶ ἐμοῦ πῶς ἔχετε; τί ὑμῖν δοκῶ ἐγώ; λέγουσιν αὐτῷ· Ἄνθρωπόν σε οἴδαμεν τοῦ θεοῦ. φίλη δὲ ἡ ἀλήθεια· μεγάλην ὑπόληψιν εἶχε παρὰ πᾶσιν οὐ ψευδῶς ἀλλ' ἀληθῶς.	ὑπολαβὼν δέ, Οἷος ὑμῖν δοκῶ; ἤρετο· τῶν δὲ ἀξιόχρεών τε καὶ μάλα καλὸν καὶ ἀγαθὸν εἶναι, καὶ τοιοῦτον οἷον ἡ περὶ αὐτοῦ δόξα ἐκράτει συνομολογούντων,	λέγει αὐτοῖς· Τί ὑμῖν δοκῶ ἐγώ; εἶχε δὲ μεγάλην ὑπόληψιν παρὰ πᾶσιν, οὐ ψευδῶς ἀλλ' ἀληθῶς. λέγουσιν αὐτῷ· Ἄνθρωπόν σε οἴδαμεν θεοῦ.
λέγει αὐτοῖς ὁ τοῦ Χριστοῦ δοῦλος· Εἰ οὕτως οἴεσθε τὰ κατ' ἐμέ, ἐμοὶ ἐμπιστεύσατε τὴν τῶν λιμωττόντων ἐπιμέλειαν.	Οὐκοῦν	Οὐκοῦν ἐμοί, φησίν, ἐμπιστεύσατε·
λέγουσιν αὐτῷ οἱ σοβαροί· Εἴθε καταξίοις. ἀποκρίνεται αὐτοῖς Ἐφραὶμ ὁ ἐκλεκτὸς τοῦ θεοῦ· Ἰδοὺ ἀπὸ σήμερον δι' ὑμᾶς χειροτονῶ ἐμαυτὸν ξενοδόχον τῶν δεομένων.	ἑκοντής, ἔφη, δι' ὑμᾶς ἐπὶ τοῦτο χειροτονήσω ἐμαυτόν.	ἰδοὺ δι' ὑμᾶς χειροτονῶ ἐμαυτὸν ξενοδόχον.

p. 127, 3 B καὶ λαβὼν παρ' αὐτῶν ἀργύρια
Soz. καὶ λαβὼν ἀργύριον παρ' αὐτῶν
G καὶ λαβὼν ἀργύρια

11 B κοιμᾶται Soz. ἐτελεύτησε G ἐτελεύτησε

p. 158, 3 B	φευκτὴ ἦν τοῖς ἐναρέτοις	διὰ τὸ κάλλος
Soz.	φευκτέαν τοῖς ἐπιείκειαν καὶ σωφροσύνην ἐπαγγελλομένοις	
G	φευκτὴ ἦν	διὰ τὸ κάλλος[1]

As to the general outcome of the comparison of Sozomen with B and G there cannot, I think, be a doubt. The positive agreements with G in actual readings, and still more the negative agreements in the omission of words and clauses found in B, are striking and cannot, as a whole, be due to chance coincidence. In these circumstances it is necessary to examine with special care the agreements of Sozomen with B.

The following may at once be set aside as negligible, the resemblances being too faint or too uncertain to afford any basis for an argument:—

	Soz. and B	G
p. 17, **9**	ἢ	οὐκ
14	ἐκ	ἀπὸ
p. 20, **16**	καθεζόμενος	καθήμενος
p. 88, **4**	κυρίου B; θεῖος Soz. (with ἄγγελος)	om
p. 89, **11**	τῶν μυστηρίων (after κοινωνία)	om

p. 90, **4** Sozomen's ἐπονομάσαι is so obviously suggested by the whole context that it cannot be taken as evidence of τὸ ὄνομα in his copy of the *Hist. Laus.*

These having been eliminated there remain for consideration the following:—

p. 20, **17** ἐν ἐκστάσει B Soz.; ἔκστασιν G.

p. 33, **9** the single word λοιπὸν in B and Soz.; (but the latter has wholly changed the context).

14 μόνον B Soz.; om G.

p. 35, **4** Sozomen's τοὺς κάμνοντας may represent B's ὁ ἐνοχλούμενος; (it is to be noted, however, that Sozomen, by turning the principal verb into the active, was compelled to supply an accusative, and as a fact uses a different word from that found in B).

p. 37, **7** τελευτᾶν μέλλων B Soz.; τελευτῶν G.

[1] Sozomen's story of Eutropius' visit to John of Lycopolis (VII. 22 fin.) is not based on *Hist. Laus.* p. 101, 2.

p. 43, **11** τῷ γένει B Soz.; τὸ γένος G.

p. 89, **10** B and Soz. stand alone in saying that the Tabennesiot monks slept in the μηλωτὴ (or διφθέρα).

p. 127, **3** παρ' αὐτῶν B Soz.; om G.

p. 158, **3** Sozomen's τοῖς ἐπιείκειαν καὶ σωφροσύνην ἐπαγγελλομένοις may be a paraphrase of B's τοῖς ἐναρέτοις; om G.

When these cases are considered it appears that the effective resemblances between Sozomen and B are reduced to some half dozen not very convincing agreements, which cannot weigh in the balance against the numerous and telling agreements between Sozomen and G,—agreements which stand out particularly clearly in the three longer pieces.

It may be taken as certain that Sozomen's copy of the *Hist. Laus.* contained substantially a G text and not a B text. Now Sozomen wrote his History about the years 439—450; therefore his copy of the *Hist. Laus.* must have been made within twenty or twenty-five years of the time when Palladius wrote the book.

The Apophthegmata Patrum.

From St Benedict's citation (see *Prol.* 209—11) it appears that the Latin version of the "Topical" redaction (no. ii.) of the *Apophthegmata*, found in Bks. v. and vi. of Rosweyd, existed in the early years of the sixth century, and the Greek collection itself must have been formed in the fifth. Now any apophthegma found in this Latin version of redaction ii., and also in the Greek Alphabetical redaction (no. i.), printed by Cotelier, must have belonged to the Greek original of ii., and therefore dates from the fifth century. Two apophthegmata, thus common to collections i. and ii., are taken from Palladius; and therefore in them we have fragments of a fifth century Greek text of the Lausiac History. The more considerable of these is no. 8 under Pambo's name (*P. G.* LXV. 369); for the Latin, see Rosweyd, Bk. v. i. 16; and for a second Latin version, *ibid.* Bk. III. 160.

I print the three Greek texts, using for the apophthegma the Brit. Mus. *Addit.* 22508 (saec. XII.), which contains a better text than Cotelier's of the Alphabetical collection.

B (*P. G.* xxxiv. 1033)

Οὗτος ὁ Παμβὼ τελευτᾶν μέλλων κατ' (αὐτὴν) τὴν ὥραν τοῦ ἐκλιμπάνειν αὐτὸν παρεστῶσιν [Ω. καὶ Α.] ἀνδράσι περιβοήτοις (σὺν) καὶ λοιποῖς ἀδελφοῖς τοῦτο λέγεται εἰρηκέναι, ὅτι Ἀφ' οὗ ἦλθον εἰς τὸν τόπον τοῦτον τῆς ἐρήμου καὶ ᾠκοδόμησά μου τὴν κέλλαν καὶ ᾤκησα ἐνθάδε, οὐκ ἐκτὸς ἔργου τῶν ἐμῶν χειρῶν πεποίηκα ἡμέραν μίαν· οὐδὲ μέμνημαι δωρεὰν ἄρτον φαγὼν ἀπό τινος· οὐ(δὲ) μεταμεμέλημαι ἕως τῆς ἄρτι ὥρας ἐπὶ (τῷ) λόγῳ ᾧ ἐλάλησα. καὶ οὕτως ἀπέρχομαι πρὸς τὸν θεὸν ὡς μηδὲ ἀρξάμενος τοῦ θεοσεβεῖν.

(See LP⁵ μδ (V¹V²) in Preuschen's apparatus, *Pall. u. Ruf.* 122.)

Apophth.

Διηγήσαντο περὶ τοῦ ἀββᾶ Π. ὅτι τελευτῶν κατ' αὐτὴν τὴν ὥραν τοῦ ἐκλιμπάνειν εἶπεν τοῖς παρεστῶσιν αὐτῷ ἁγίοις ἀνδράσιν, ὅτι Ἀφ' οὗ ἦλθον εἰς τὸν τόπον τοῦτον τῆς ἐρήμου καὶ ᾠκοδόμησά μου τὴν κέλλαν καὶ ᾤκησα ἐν αὐτῇ[1], ἐκτὸς[2] τῶν χειρῶν μου οὐ μέμνημαι ἄρτον φαγών· οὐδὲ μεταμεμέλημαι ἐπὶ λόγῳ ᾧ ἐλάλησα ἕως τῆς ἄρτι ὥρας. καὶ οὕτως ἀπέρχομαι πρὸς τὸν θεὸν ὡς μηδὲ ἀρξάμενος θεοσεβεῖν.

1 ἐν αὐτῇ Lat. doubtful

2 Lat. add *laborem*, or *opera*

G (p. 31, **10**)

Οὗτος ὁ Παμβὼ τελευτῶν κατ' αὐτὴν τὴν ὥραν τοῦ ἐκλιμπάνειν παρεστῶσι [Μ. καὶ Α.] ἀνδράσι περιβοήτοις καὶ λοιποῖς ἀδελφοῖς τοῦτο λέγεται εἰρηκέναι, ὅτι Ἀφ' οὗ ἦλθον εἰς τὸν τόπον τοῦτον τῆς[1] ἐρήμου[1] καὶ ᾠκοδόμησά μου τὴν κέλλαν καὶ ᾤκησα[2] ἐκτὸς τῶν χειρῶν μου οὐ μέμνημαι δωρεὰν ἄρτον φαγών·[3] οὐ μεταμεμέλημαι ἐπὶ λόγῳ ᾧ ἐλάλησα ἕως τῆς ἄρτι ὥρας. καὶ οὕτως ἀπέρχομαι πρὸς τὸν θεὸν ὡς μηδὲ ἀρξάμενος (τοῦ)[4] θεοσεβεῖν.

1 om P; stet WTverss.

2 +ἐν αὐτῇ verss.

3 ὅτι...ἔφαγον WP

4 τοῦ P; om WT

See List of Symbols, p. 2

Words in brackets are omitted by some of the authorities.

The second piece is the concluding sentence of the chapter on Or (p. 29, **12—14**). The apophthegma has already been printed (*Prol.* 284) and need not be repeated here. The only difference between B and G is that B has τί ποτε at the end, omitted by G; in this the apophthegma agrees with G.

Two other of Pambo's apophthegmata in Cotelier's Alphabetical collection are from the *Hist. Laus.*; but as they are not attested by the Latin of redaction ii., we cannot be sure that they date from the fifth century. It needs no comment to show that the two of which we can be sure side decisively with G against B, and support Sozomen's witness to the existence of the G text in the course of the fifth century.

Vita Melaniae Iunioris.

The younger Melania died about the year 440. Her Life,

written by one of her personal friends (the Bollandists surmise Gerontius †*c.* 485), was printed in Latin (*Anal. Boll.* VIII.) and then in Greek (*Anal. Boll.* XXII.). The *Vita*, c. 1, contains one citation from *Hist. Laus.*, c. 61 :—

B (*P. G.* xxxiv. 1228)	Vita Melaniae, Gr.	**G** (p. 155, **11**)
Εἰ μὲν αἱρῆσαι συνοικισθῆναί μοι κατὰ τὸν τῆς σωφροσύνης λόγον, καὶ δεσπότην σε οἶδα, καὶ κύριον τῆς ἐμῆς ζωῆς ὁμολογήσω σε· εἰ δὲ βαρύ σοι τοῦτο ὡς νεωτέρῳ φαίνεται,	*Εἰ μὲν βούλει, κύριέ μου, ἁγνεύειν σὺν ἐμοὶ καὶ κατὰ τὸν τῆς σωφροσύνης συνοικισθῆναί μοι νόμον, καὶ κύριόν σε καὶ δεσπότην τῆς οἰκείας ζωῆς ἐπιγράφομαι· εἰ δὲ τοῦτό σοι ἐπαχθὲς καταφαίνεται καὶ οὐκ ἰσχύεις ἐνέγκαι τὴν πύρωσιν τῆς νεότητος, ἰδοὺ πρόκεινταί*	*Εἰ μὲν αἱρῆσαι συνασκηθῆναι κἀμοὶ κατὰ τὸν τῆς σωφροσύνης λόγον, καὶ δεσπότην σε οἶδα καὶ κύριον τῆς ἐμῆς ζωῆς· εἰ δὲ βαρύ σοι τοῦτο καταφαίνεται ὡς νεωτέρῳ,*
πάντα μου λάβε τὰ πράγ-	*σοι ἅπαντά μου τὰ ὑπάρχοντα, ὧν ἐντεῦθεν ἤδη δεσπότης γενόμενος χρήσει*	*πάντα μου λαβὼν τὰ πράγ-*
ματα, καὶ μόνον τὸ σῶμά μου ἐλευθέρωσον, ἵνα	*καθὼς βούλει· μόνον τὸ σῶμά μου ἐλευθέρωσον, ἵνα τοῦτο σὺν τῇ ψυχῇ μου ἄσπιλον παραστήσω τῷ Χριστῷ κατὰ τὴν ἡμέραν ἐκείνην τὴν φοβεράν· οὕτω*	*ματα ἐλευθέρωσόν μου τὸ σῶμα, ἵνα*
πληροφορήσω μου τὴν κατὰ θεὸν ἐπιθυμίαν.	*γὰρ πληροφορήσω τὴν κατὰ θεόν μου ἐπιθυμίαν.*	*πληρώσω μου τὴν κατὰ θεὸν ἐπιθυμίαν.*

Vita Melaniae, Lat.

Si uolueris habitare mecum secundum legem castitatis et continentiae, dominum meum te cognoscam et dominatorem te uitae meae esse confitear; si autem graue tibi hoc quasi adolescenti uidetur, omnes meas facultates suscipe, et tantum corpus meum liberum effice, ut perficiam quod est secundum desiderium meum.

In this passage the differences between B and G which may be taken as critically certain and significant for the purpose in hand, are :—

B	G
συνοικισθῆναι	*συνασκηθῆναι*
ὁμολογήσω σε	om
μόνον	om
πληροφορήσω	*πληρώσω*

In all four readings the only two extant G authorities (hereafter called P and l) unequivocally support each other. The combined evidence of the Greek and Latin forms of the *Vita Melaniae* shows that in each case it presents the B reading: ***καταφαίνεται*** alone tells the other way, but it may well stand in some B MSS. It is conceivable, of course, that the passage was not in the *Vita* from the beginning, the earliest Latin MS. being only from the end of the eighth century, and the Greek MS. from the eleventh; but in the absence of any positive ground for suspecting it to be a later interpolation, it must be taken as probable evidence that the B text was in existence in the third quarter of the fifth century, fifty years after the *Hist. Laus.* was written[1].

DIONYSIUS EXIGUUS.

Dionysius made the old Latin translation (called *lat*[2] in *Prol.* 159—163) of the *Vita Pachomii* from a Greek redaction of the *Vita.* In the Latin occur two extracts from the *Hist. Laus.*: c. 22 = *H. L.* 32, and c. 28 (fin.) = *H. L.* 33 (init.). In the latter passage there is no difference between the B and G texts of the *Hist. Laus.*; but in the former occur the following cases wherein words and clauses found in B, but not in G, are represented in the Latin extract:—

Latin *Vita* 22 (Rosweyd, p. 120).	**B** (*P. G.* XXXIV. 1099—1100).
albam	λευκὴν
sacramentorum Christi	τῶν μυστηρίων τοῦ Χριστοῦ
iuxta numerum elementorum et graecarum litterarum	κατὰ τὸν ἀριθμὸν τῶν κδ′ (στοιχείων τῶν) γραμμάτων
nomina	τὸ ὄνομα
usque ad ω	ἕως τοῦ ω̄
archimandritam	ἀρχιμανδρίτην
semel	εἰσάπαξ
studiis	ἀγῶνα } (see *Prol.* 160—1)
stadium	στάδιον }

[1] The presence of this passage from *Hist. Laus.* in both forms of the *Vita* amounts to a demonstration that the Greek is the original—a translation from the Latin would not have reproduced the vocabulary of Palladius. But as the Latin is the closer to the *Hist. Laus.*, it follows that our Greek *Vita* has been revised and altered. The passage from *Hist. Laus.* exists in a still more altered form in the *Vita* that has gone under the name of Simeon Metaphrastes (*P.G.* CXVI. 753). In the shorter Latin form of the Life found in *Bibl. Casin.* III *Flor.* 308, instead of Melania's speech are the words: ut uirginitatis continentiam seruarent. I think that the Bollandists are correct in saying that this Life is an abridgment of the other Latin *Vita* (*Bibl. Hagiogr. Lat.*): at a later point it contains the passage in question, and more, from the *Hist. Laus.*, taken direct from the Latin version hereafter called l. Another Latin *Vita* was announced in 1900 by Card. Rampolla.

If the section from the *Hist. Laus.* already stood in the Greek *Vita* when Dionysius made his translation, it would be an irrefragable proof of the existence of the B text early in the sixth century (for Dionysius died before 544). But no Greek MS. of this redaction of the *Vita Pachomii* is known; nor have the numerous Latin MSS. been critically examined: so that we have no assurance that we are not here in the presence of a later Latin interpolation, like those from the *Hist. Mon.* found in the printed copies of the Second Latin version of the *Hist. Laus.*, but absent from one group of MSS. (*Prol.* 64—6).

I have found no other citations of the B text earlier than the middle of the seventh century; but at that date Anan-Isho beyond all doubt possessed a copy of the whole work in the B text (see p. lxxix). Accordingly I only append in a Note a brief list of the later citations that I have come across.

NOTE. *Later Citations of the Lausiac History.*

Considering how popular a book the Lausiac History evidently was, the citations from it by later writers are surprisingly few. Tillemont mentions only two: one is by Dorotheus Archimandrita (cent. VI.?), who quotes three lines from c. 38 (*P. G.* LXXXVIII. 1652)—the passage throws no light on the textual question; the other is in the Sermon on "the Faithful Departed," formerly attributed to St John Damascene, and is explicitly said to be from the *Hist. Laus.*, but is really from the *Apophthegmata* (see *Prol.* 142, note). I have myself made extensive searches in Migne among the Catenae and Scholia and other collections of extracts (such as St John Damascene's *Sacra Parallela*). My efforts have been rewarded only by a single citation: among the *Questions and Answers* of Anastasius Sinaita (end of cent. VII.) is an abridgment of c. 25, the text being of the B type (*P. G.* LXXXIX. 345). Several parts of Nicephorus are ultimately based on the *Hist. Laus.*, but only mediately through Sozomen: a passage, however, in Bk. VII. c. 13, may be based directly on c. 65 (see Note 114).

The so-called *Vita Athanasii ex Metaphrasto* embodies the bulk of c. 63 in a G text (see *infra*, p. 158); the Life of Olympias, compiled in the seventh century (*Anal. Boll.* XV.), makes use of c. 56

in a B text. A number of the notices in the "Synaxarion" and the "Menaeon" contain traces of the Lausiac History.

Finally, the extract given under Palladius' name in the Paris Catena MS. Gr. 174 (see Achelis, *Hippolytstudien*, 144) is not from *Hist. Laus.* or any work of Palladius of Helenopolis.

§ 5. HISTORY OF THE TEXT: THE VERSIONS.

The versions of the *Hist. Laus.* have been discussed at some length in *Prol.*, and further details concerning them, in so far as they bear on the criticism of the text, will be given later (§§ 8, 9): for present purposes it is sufficient to note that the chief versions at our disposal are:

Latin I (hereafter called l), containing the whole work.
Latin II (l_2), about half the work.
Syriac I (s), about half to two-thirds.
Syriac II (s_2), about one-third.

Of the two Syriac versions there exist MSS. written early in the sixth century, and the versions themselves probably both date from the fifth. Though no MSS. of the Latin versions are known older than the tenth or eleventh century, there are some grounds

---

B (*P. G.* XXXIV. 1084)

Πάχων τις ὀνόματι περὶ τὰ ἑβδομήκοντα ἐλάσας ἔτη, ἐκαθίζετο ἐν τῇ Σκήτει. συνέβη δέ με ὀχληθέντα ὑπὸ τοῦ δαίμονος, συνεχόμενον ἐπιθυμίᾳ γυναικείᾳ, δυσφορεῖν καὶ πρὸς τοὺς λογισμοὺς καὶ πρὸς τὰς φαντασίας τὰς νυκτερινάς. καὶ ἐγγὺς γενόμενος, ὑπὸ

1 *τὸ ἑβδομηκοστὸν ἐλ. ἔτος* A[B] **2** *ἐκάθητο* A[B] **2—4** *συνέβη δέ με ὑπὸ τοῦ πάθους τῆς γυναικικῆς ἐπιθυμίας ὀχληθέντα* A[B] **6, 7** om *ὑπὸ...πειρασμοῦ* A[B]

G (p. 74, 21)

Πάχων τις ὀνόματι ἀμφὶ τὸ ἑβδομηκοστὸν ἔτος ἐλάσας ἐκάθητο ἐν τῇ Σκήτει. συνέβη δὲ ὀχληθέντα με ἐπιθυμίᾳ γυναικὸς δυσφορεῖν καὶ πρὸς τοὺς λογισμοὺς καὶ πρὸς τὰς φαντασίας τὰς νυκτερινάς. καὶ ἐγγὺς γενόμενος

4 *γυναικικῇ* WVC

s (Tullberg, p. 29, MSS. AB: Brit. Mus. *Addit.* 17177 f. 75, 12173 f. 44).

There was also another man by name Pachom, seventy years of age: he resided on the mountain called Scetis. And I went to him once upon a time when the thoughts of the desire of women harassed me, when my mind was dark and obscured from the thoughts of lust and from the visions and troubles of the night.

for supposing that the versions themselves were made in the course of the fifth to the seventh centuries. In order to test the Greek texts represented by these four versions, I shall take the first half of the chapter on Pachon (c. 23), which has the advantage of being preserved in all four versions, and also in six good members of the G text; moreover s is in print and may be studied in Tullberg's MSS. A and B (*Paradisus Patrum* 29—33), so that the reader has not to rely on Anan-Isho's text. The passage is one which I should not have selected had there been any opportunity of choice; but as no other combines these textual advantages there is practically none.

I print a Table in four parallel columns:

Col. 1. The Greek B text } The resultant texts are given; only a few
Col. 2. The Greek G text } important variants are noticed.
Col. 3. l (from the *Cass.* and *Sess.* MSS., see p. lxxvi).
Col. 4. l_2 (based chiefly on *Barber.* MS. *lat.* 702, the only one (known to me) that gives Pachon's name correctly, the others all having Pasco).

A literal translation of s is given on the left-hand pages, under the Greek texts; and one of s_2 on the right-hand pages, under the Latin versions. I have to thank Prof. Guidi for the text of s_2, and Mr Norman McLean for revising my translations of both these pieces, and of others throughout the volume.

---

l

Pachon quidam nomine septuagesimum aetatis suae annum agens in ea quae Scithis dicitur regione degebat. cum interea

grandis cupiditas feminei coitus me coepit urguere, quod ego grauiter ac moleste ferebam aduersus sordidas cogitationes et contra insomnia nocturna confligens ut

l_2

Pacho quidam nomine erat septuagesimum agens aetatis annum in Scythi. itaque dum grauiter me

spiritus fornicationis temptaret super concupiscentia muliebri exagitantibus me cogitationibus, pene egressus sum de

1 quidam] om Barb

s_2 (Vat. *Syr.* 123 f. 286).

There was a certain Pachom of Memphis; he was in a cave (*or* cell) seventy years within in the desert of Scete. And it came about that I was harassed by the lust of woman, and I was troubled by the thoughts and the dreams of the phantasms of the night, and I was nearly withdrawing myself from the desert, because the

B

τούτου τοῦ πειρασμοῦ ἐξελθεῖν τῆς ἐρήμου, ἐλαύνοντός με σφοδροτάτως τοῦ πάθους, τοῖς μὲν γείτοσί μου οὐκ ἀνεθέμην τὸ πρᾶγμα, ἀλλ' οὔτε τῷ διδασκάλῳ μου Εὐαγρίῳ· λεληθότως δὲ παραβαλὼν εἰς τὴν πανέρημον συνετύγχανον ἐπὶ ἡμέρας δεκαπέντε τοῖς κατὰ τὴν Σκῆτιν πατράσι γηράσασιν ἐν τῇ ἐρήμῳ· ἐν οἷς δὴ περιέτυχον καὶ τῷ Πάχωνι. εὑρὼν οὖν αὐτὸν ἀκεραιότερον καὶ ἀσκητικώτερον ἐθάρρησα αὐτῷ ἀναθέσθαι μου τὰ τῆς διανοίας. καὶ λέγει μοι ὁ ἅγιος οὗτος· Μὴ ξενίσῃ σε τὸ πρᾶγμα· οὐ γὰρ αὐτὸ πάσχεις ἀπὸ ῥαθυμίας· μαρτυρεῖ γάρ σοι καὶ ὁ τόπος καὶ ἡ σπάνις τῶν χρειῶν, καὶ τὸ μὴ εἶναι συντυχίας θηλειῶν ἐνθάδε· ἀλλὰ μᾶλλον ἀπὸ σπουδῆς τῆς κατ' ἀρετὴν συμβαίνει σοι τοῦτο παρὰ τοῦ ἐναντίου. τριπλοῦς γάρ ἐστιν ὁ πόλεμος ὁ πορνικός. ποτὲ μὲν γὰρ ἡ σὰρξ ἡμῖν ἐπιτίθεται εὐπαθοῦσα· ποτὲ δὲ τὰ πάθη ἡμῖν ἐπανίστανται διὰ τῶν λογισμῶν· ποτὲ δὲ καὶ αὐτὸς ὁ δαίμων ἡμᾶς τυραννεῖ διὰ τῆς βασκανίας. ἐγὼ γὰρ πολλὰ παρατηρήσας εὕρηκα τοῦτο. ἰδοὺ ὡς ὁρᾷς με γέροντα ἄνθρωπον· τεσσαρακοστὸν ἔτος ἔχω ἐν τῇ κέλλῃ ταύτῃ φροντίζων τῆς

9 μου] τῶν πατέρων B 11 Εὐλογίῳ A^B 12 ἔρημον A^B

G

τοῦ ἐξελθεῖν τῆς ἐρήμου, ἐλαύνοντός με τοῦ πάθους, τοῖς μὲν γείτοσι τοῖς ἐμοῖς οὐκ ἀνεθέμην τὸ πρᾶγμα οὔτε τῷ διδασκάλῳ μου Εὐαγρίῳ· λεληθότως δὲ παραβαλὼν εἰς τὴν πανέρημον συνετύγχανον ἐπὶ ἡμέρας δεκαπέντε τοῖς κατὰ τὴν Σκῆτιν γηράσασι πατράσιν ἐν τῇ ἐρήμῳ· ἐν οἷς περιέτυχον καὶ τῷ Πάχωνι. εὑρὼν οὖν αὐτὸν ἀκεραιότερον καὶ ἀσκητικώτερον ἐθάρρησα ἀναθέσθαι μου αὐτῷ τὰ τῆς διανοίας. καὶ λέγει μοι οὗτος· Μὴ ξενίσῃ σε τὸ πρᾶγμα· οὐ γὰρ αὐτὸ πάσχεις ἀπὸ ῥαθυμίας· μαρτυρεῖ γάρ σοι καὶ ὁ τόπος καὶ ἡ σπάνις τῶν χρειῶν, καὶ τὸ μὴ εἶναι συντυχίας θηλειῶν· ἀλλὰ μᾶλλον ἀπὸ σπουδῆς.

τριπλοῦς γάρ ἐστιν ὁ πόλεμος ὁ πορνικός. ποτὲ μὲν γὰρ ἡ σὰρξ ἡμῖν ἐπιτίθεται εὐρωστοῦσα· ποτὲ δὲ τὰ πάθη διὰ τῶν λογισμῶν· ποτὲ δὲ καὶ αὐτὸς ὁ δαίμων τῇ βασκανίᾳ. ἐγὼ γὰρ πολλὰ παρατηρήσας εὕρηκα τοῦτο. ἰδοὺ ὡς ὁρᾷς με γέροντα ἄνθρωπον· τεσσαρακοστὸν ἔτος ἔχω ἐν ταύτῃ τῇ κέλλῃ φροντίζων τῆς

11 Εὐλογίῳ PW 36 12 ἔρημον P 26 εὐπαθοῦσα VC

S

And I was nearly withdrawing from the desert, as great lust assaulted me. And I did not disclose my affliction to my neighbours nor to the brethren that dwelt with me, nor even to my master Euagrius (AB 12173; 17177 Eurīgnus); but I set out and started wandering in the desert, and I saw some of the old men who ha grown old in the place, who were perfect fathers. And after this I saw that blessed Pachom, and I found that he surpassed them all in his way of life and in his thought. And I took heart that I should disclose to him the conflict of my mind And he said unto me thus: "Let not the matter be regarded by thee as something strange; for not because of thine own negligence hath it thus befallen thee; the very place that thou dwellest in beareth witness to thee, because it is straitened in all necessities, and because there is no woman there; but from zeal has this lust befallen thee. For the war of lust and of fornication is threefold. For at times our body opposes us, when it is healthy and well fed; and at times lust through passion; and at times the evil one because of his envy. And I have much observed and thus have I found as I have told thee." And he said to me: "I whom thou seest, an old man, have now for forty years been residing in this cell, and I have busied myself about my salvation and the saving of my soul; and in all this old

l

pene ab his ubi eram solitudinibus ui ipsius morbi perculsus exirem, uicinis quidem meis nihil de pestilentiae talis ardore dicebam, (sed) ne Euagrio quidem magistro meo tale aliquid confitebar: occulte tamen ad interiora ac uastiora deserta perrexi, ubi per quindecim dies in eo qui Scithis dicitur loco uenerabiles multos qui ibidem consenuerant patres uidi. inter quos et cum supradicto Pachone potui habere conloquium. et quia repperi eum inter ceteros monachos prope palmam tenere, confidenter ad eum detuli animi mei anxietatem. qui ita locutus est michi: Non sit tibi noua res ista quam pateris; nam quod non ex negligentia mentis atque desidia in id quo turbaris incurreris sufficienter tibi testimonium praebent et locorum natura et inopia omnium rerum, et ipsarum, quod nemini dubium est, absentia feminarum; sed magis temptatione ista laboras propter studium ac desiderium castitatis. triplex enim ex fornicationis nomine nascitur pugna: aliquando caro nostra in nobis si fuerit nimis sana lasciuit; saepe autem ex cogitationibus uanis morbus iste procedit; interdum contra nos daemon, dum nobis inuidet, facit. ego enim frequenter ista pertractans ista semper inueni. nam et ego ipse, ut uides, admodum senex per quadraginta annos in ista cellula degens maximamque salutis propriae gerens curam, etiam usque ad praesens tem-

10 sed] Sess; om Cass

l_2

eremo compellente me nimia passione. et uicinis michi quidem monachis non indicaui causam,

latenter autem perrexi in solitudinem et circuiui sanctos patres usque dies quindecim, eos qui in Scythi senuissent. in quibus repperi Pachum, quem omnes qui in illa eremo erant patres uenerabantur. itaque praesumpsi ego et cum lacrimis deprecans eum confessus sum (ei) passionem quae me nimis (et) incessanter impugnare non desinebat. et ipse ait mihi: Non conturbet te haec causa, non enim pateris haec a negligentia; attestantur enim tibi et locus et difficultas rerum, et quia non est in locis illis ulla uisitatio feminarum; sed magis

(*lacuna in all copies*)

ex inuidia diaboli qui semper insidiatur et decipere festinat animas hominum. ecce ut uides me iam senem hominem; quadragesimum annum habeo in cella hac et adiuuante gratia Christi sollicitus de salute animae meae; tamen usque nunc temptationem sustineo. nam cum

17 ei] om Barb et] om Barb

S_2

passion of lust pursued me. And to those who were my neighbours and near me I did not disclose the matter, nor even to my teacher Euagrius; I deluded them and did not inform them; and I came to the desert for fifteen days, and when I went I consorted with the fathers that were old men in Scete there in the desert, one of whom was Pachom. And finding that he was very perfect and pure and had passed his life in great asceticisms, I told him and showed to him what was in my thoughts. And he said to me: "Be not disturbed at thy case, for not from carelessness do these things befall thee; for the place also of thy asceticisms beareth witness to thee, both because thy needs are little, and because there is no association with women; but rather from solicitude. For in three ways occurs the war of fornication. For at times the flesh is disturbed and lustful; and from the passions it arises through the thoughts; and at times also Satan himself is disturbed. For I have for a long time been versed in these matters, and I have found this: as thou seest me (I am) an old man, and I have been seventy years in this cave (cell), and I have been solicitous for my salvation. And I am now ninety-three years old, and I am, reckoning from birth, in this advanced time of life; and to this day am

B

ἐμαυτοῦ σωτηρίας· καὶ ταύτην ἄγων τὴν ἡλικίαν μέχρις ἄρτι πειράζομαι. καὶ διώμνυτο λέγων ὅτι Δώδεκα ἔτη μετὰ τὸ πεντηκοστόν με ἄγειν ἔτος, οὐ νύκτα μοι συνεχώρησεν, οὐχ ἡμέραν, ἐπιτιθέμενός μοι. ὑπονοήσας οὖν ὅτι ἀπέστη μου ὁ θεός, διὸ καὶ καταδυναστεύομαι οὕτως, ἠρησάμην ἀποθανεῖν μᾶλλον ἀλόγως ἢ πάθει σώματος ἀσχημονῆσαι αἰσχρῶς. καὶ ἐξελθών μου τῆς κέλλης καὶ περιιὼν τὴν ἔρημον σπήλαιον εὗρον ὑαίνης· εἰς ὃ σπήλαιον ἔθηκα ἐμαυτὸν ἐν ἡμέρᾳ γυμνόν, ἵνα ἐξελθόντα φάγῃ με τὰ θηρία. ὡς οὖν ἐγένετο ἑσπέρα, κατὰ τὸ γεγραμμένον· Ὁ ἥλιος ἔγνω τὴν δύσιν αὐτοῦ· ἔθου σκότος καὶ ἐγένετο νύξ· ἐν αὐτῇ διελεύσονται πάντα τὰ θηρία τοῦ δρυμοῦ, σκύμνοι ὠρυόμενοι τοῦ ἁρπάσαι καὶ ζητῆσαι παρὰ τῷ θεῷ βρῶσιν αὐτοῖς. ἐξελθόντες οὖν οἱ θῆρες ἐν ἐκείνῃ τῇ ὥρᾳ, ὅ τε ἄρσην καὶ ἡ θήλεια, ὠσφράνθησάν με ἀπὸ ποδῶν μέχρι κεφαλῆς περιλείξαντές με· καὶ ὡς ἐδόκουν βρωθῆναι ἀνεχώρησαν ἀπ᾽ ἐμοῦ. πεσὼν οὖν ἐκεῖ διὰ πάσης νυκτὸς οὐκ ἐβρώθην· λογισάμενος ὅτι Πάντως ἐφείσατό μου ὁ θεός, αὖθις οὖν ὑπέστρεψα εἰς τὴν κέλλαν.

54 μου A^B **55** προσεδόκουν A^B

G

ἐμαυτοῦ σωτηρίας· καὶ ταύτην ἄγων τὴν ἡλικίαν μέχρι τούτου πειράζομαι. †καὶ ὡς† διώμνυτο ὅτι Ἐπὶ δώδεκα ἔτη μετὰ τὸ πεντηκοστὸν ἔτος οὐ νύκτα μοι συνεχώρησεν, οὐχ ἡμέραν, ἐπιτιθέμενος.

ὑπονοήσας οὖν ὅτι ἀπέστη μου ὁ θεός, διὸ καὶ καταδυναστεύομαι, ᾑρετισάμην ἀποθανεῖν ἀλόγως ἢ πάθει σώματος ἀσχημονῆσαι [αἰσχρῶς]. καὶ ἐξελθὼν καὶ περιελθὼν τὴν ἔρημον εὗρον σπήλαιον ὑαίνης· εἰς ὃ σπήλαιον ἔθηκα ἐμαυτὸν ἐν ἡμέρᾳ γυμνόν, ἵνα ἐξελθόντα φάγῃ με τὰ θηρία. ὡς οὖν ἐγένετο ἑσπέρα, κατὰ τὸ γεγραμμένον·

Ἔθου σκότος καὶ ἐγένετο νύξ· ἐν αὐτῇ διελεύσονται πάντα τὰ θηρία τοῦ δρυμοῦ,

ἐξελθόντες οἱ θῆρες, ὅ τε ἄρσην καὶ ἡ θήλεια, ὠσφράνθησάν μου ἀπὸ κεφαλῆς ἕως ποδῶν περιλείξαντες· καὶ ὡς προσεδόκων βρωθῆναι ἀνεχώρησαν ἀπ᾽ ἐμοῦ. πεσὼν οὖν διὰ πάσης νυκτὸς οὐκ ἐβρώθην· λογισάμενος δὲ ὅτι Ἐφείσατό μου ὁ θεός, αὖθις ὑποστρέφω εἰς τὴν κέλλαν.

34 καὶ ὡς] TVC; om καὶ PW; om ὡς 36 **39** ἠρησάμην PWT **41** αἰσχρῶς] PVC; om WT 36 **54** με VC ἀπὸ ποδ. ἕως κεφ. VC

S

age that thou seest in me I am greatly tempted by lust." And he swore thus to me: "After I was fifty years old, for twelve years did lust assault me never leaving me day or night. And I thought that God had abandoned me, and because of this it had thus obtained power over me. And I preferred in my heart to die like a brute beast, than that I should be a mockery and one worsted because of the lust of the body. And I went forth and wandered through the desert, and I found a den of hyenas. And I lay down at the entry, having stript, so that they might come out and devour me. And when it was evening, as it is written: *He made darkness and it was night wherein dwell* (sic) *all the beasts of the forest,* the hyenas came forth, the male and the female, and they smelt me, licking my body from my head to my feet; but when I thought that they would devour me they departed from me. And I remained there the whole night, and they did not devour me. And again I thought that God had pity on me, and forthwith I returned and went to my cell."

l

pus huiusmodi temptatione sollicitor. cum sacramento enim istud sanctus ipse dicebat: Per duodecim annos post quinquagesimum non nocte non die unquam hic a me morbus abscessit, usque adeo ut priuatum me iam dei auxilio suspicarer, ob quod merito me putarem daemonis uirtute superari; malui tamen eo tempore inrationabili quadam morte deficere quam tali corporis morbo cum tam obscaena deformitate succumbere. moxque progressus ac peragrans solitudines totas speluncam ferae alicuius inueni in qua me proieci per diem nudum, ut, quod sine dubio fore crederem, ab egredientibus ex ea bestiis deuorarer. cum autem ad uespertinas usque horas sic iacendo uenissem, iuxta id quod scriptum est:

Posuisti tenebras et facta est nox; in ipsa discurrent omnes siluarum ferae,

exeuntes bestiae

femina cum masculo, nidore ad me ducente uenerunt, a capite usque ad (ipsos) pedes lingua me blandiente lambentes: et dum me ab illis arbitror deuorandum, sic me intactum atque incolumem reliquerunt; iacensque illic per totam noctem nihil omnino perpessus sum. cogitans (igitur) et credens quod michi pepercisset deus, mox reuertor ad cellam.

53 ipsos] Cass; om Sess **57** igitur] Sess; om Cass **58** michi] + sic Cass

l_2

sacramento dicebat mihi quia Per duodecim annos post quinquagesimum annum non nocte mihi nec die pepercit, in tantum ut putarem quia dereliquit me fortasse deus, et ideo instanter sine cessatione huius passionis molestiam sustineo. elegi ergo magis mori irrationabiliter quam talem pati corporis confusionem. egressus igitur circuibam pene omnem solitudinem et inueni speluncam leaenae, et posui me iacere ibi nudum per totum diem, ut egredientes ferae comederent me. cum ergo facta esset uespera, secundum quod scriptum est:

Posuisti tenebras et facta est nox; in ipsa pertransibunt omnes bestiae siluarum,

egredientes bestiae,

masculus et femina, odorati sunt me a capite usque ad pedes, (et) lingentes me totum, recesserunt a me. ego autem putabam ut deuorarent me. iacui ergo ibi per totam noctem, sed non accesserunt ad me. cogitaui ergo quod deus pepercit mihi, et reuersus sum in cellam meam.

53 et] om Barb

s_2

I tempted by the demon of fornication." And he swore and said: "Thirteen years have passed without his ceasing by night or by day to agitate my heart; and I thought: 'Perhaps then God hath withdrawn himself from me'; and on account of this lust that pressed upon me I preferred to die without thought than that I should be contaminated by the passion of the flesh. And I went forth and wandered through the desert, and I found there a hyena's den, and I entered it and I lay down the whole day long stript, in order that the evil beast might come forth upon me and devour me. And when it was evening, as it is written: *Darkness was made and it was night, and in it passed every beast of the field*, and there came forth the male first and then the female, and they came and smelt me, and from the head to the toe nails they licked me. And according to what I did not expect they withdrew and went from me. And I lay there all the night. [And there came after them their cubs and they came and licked me, and laid themselves to sleep by my side; and they did not hurt me. And those beasts came, and there was in their mouths the flesh of a sheep, and they passed over me, and they led their cubs and went into the den.] And I thought that God had pity on me, and I arose in that hour and returned to my cell."

The following Table schedules the various words or phrases found in B in the preceding piece, but not in G, and indicates in each case which of the four versions retain them with B or omit them with G. Cases which are doubtful in any degree are enclosed in brackets.

	B	l	l_2	s	s_2
3	ὑπὸ τοῦ δαίμονος (πάθους A^B)	G	(B)	G	G
	συνεχόμενον (om A^B, but seems re-written)	G	G	G	G
[6	ὑπὸ τούτου τοῦ πειρασμοῦ (om A^B)	G	G	G	G]
8	σφοδροτάτως	G	(B)	(B)	G
18	ὁ ἅγιος	G	G	G	G
22	ἐνθάδε	G	B	B	G
	τῆς κατ' ἀρετῆς	(B)	vac	G	G
23	συμβαίνει σοι τοῦτο	(B)	vac	B	G
	παρὰ τοῦ ἐναντίου	G	vac	G	G
27	ἡμῖν ἐπίστανται	(G)	vac	G	(B)
28	ἡμᾶς τυραννεῖ	(G)	vac	G	(G)
36	με ἄγειν	G	G	(G)	vac
39	οὕτως	G	paraphr	B	paraphr
41	μοῦ τῆς κέλλης	G	G	G	G
46	ὁ ἥλιος ἔγνω τὴν δύσιν αὐτοῦ	G	G	G	G
49—52	οἱ σκύμνοι ...... βρῶσιν αὐτοῖς	G	G	G	G
52	οὖν	G	G	G	G
	ἐν ἐκείνῃ τῇ ὥρᾳ	G	G	G	G
55	με	B	B	(B)	B
56	ἐκεῖ	B	B	B	B
58	πάντως	G	G	G	G
59	οὖν	G	G	G	G

In this Table G largely predominates; and when the cases entered as B are more closely examined it will appear that most of them are very uncertain: all four versions are so loose that some of the resemblances to B may easily be due to mere paraphrase, while others (as *με* in 55 and *ἐκεῖ* in 56) are such natural additions that they cannot be taken as evidence that the words in question stood in the Greek MSS. from which the versions were made. In short, I think it is not too much to say that in this test passage the versions afford no clear evidence for any characteristic B reading. In any case, there can be no doubt that they one and all represent the G text.

It has been shown (*Prol.* 88—9) that the Life of Evagrius (c. 38) is not found in the extant copies of either Syriac version of the *Hist. Laus.*, but that three distinct Syriac translations exist of it as an independent life in MSS. dating from cent. VI. It is impossible to say whether any of them originally belonged to either S or S_2. Of these translations the first represents the G text; so perhaps does the third, of which, however, only a single fragment is known. These need not detain us. Of the other translation two copies are known to me: Brit. Mus. *Addit.* 14635, f. 5 (saec. VI.), contains only the commencement, down to **τὴν αἰτίαν οὐ λεγόντων** (p. 118, **6**); *Addit.* 14732, f. 166 (saec. XIII.), contains the entire life. One of the most decisive differences between the B text and the G text occurs in this chapter, the B text stating that the bishop who ordained Evagrius deacon was St Gregory of Nyssa, whilst the G text says that it was St Gregory of Nazianzus. The two Greek texts are as follows:—

B (*P. G.* XXXIV. 1188: Preuschen's C¹Lδ in app., 106—7)	**G** (pp. 116, **16**—117, **3**)
Μετὰ δὲ τὴν κοίμησιν τοῦ ἁγίου Βασιλείου τοῦ ἐπισκόπου, προσέχων αὐτοῦ τῇ ἐπιτηδειότητι ὁ σοφώτατος καὶ ἀπαθέστατος καὶ πάσῃ παιδείᾳ λάμπων Γρηγόριος ὁ Νυσσαεὺς ἐπίσκοπος, ἀδελφὸς τοῦ ἐν τιμῇ τῶν ἀποστόλων Βασιλείου τοῦ ἐπισκόπου, προχειρίζεται τοῦτον διάκονον.	**Μετὰ οὖν τὸν θάνατον τοῦ ἁγίου Βασιλείου προσχὼν αὐτοῦ τῇ ἐπιτηδειότητι ὁ σοφώτατος καὶ ἀπαθέστατος καὶ παιδείᾳ διαλάμπων Γρηγόριος ὁ Ναζιανζηνὸς ἐπίσκοπος, προχειρίζεται διάκονον.**

The second Syriac translation reads as follows (*Addit.* 14635, f. 5^b):

ܘܡܢ ܒܬܪ ܫܘܢܝܗ ܕܩܕܝܫܐ ܒܣܝܠܝܘܣ: ܚܟܝܡܐ ܘܡܥܠܝ ܡܢ
ܚ̈ܫܐ: ܘܡܕܪܫ ܒܟܠ ܝܘܠܦܢ: ܓܪܝܓܘܪܝܘܣ ܐܦܝܣܩܘܦܐ ܕܢܘܣܐ:
ܐܚܘܗܝ ܕܒܪܬܐ ܕܫ̈ܠܝܚܐ ܒܣܝܠܝܘܣ: ܕܚܙܝ ܠܬܫܡܫܬܗ: ܘܥܒܕܗ
ܠܗ ܠܗܢܐ ܡܫܡܫܢܐ.

And after the decease of holy Basil, the wise and the raised above passions and the skilled in **all** *doctrines Gregory, bishop of* **Nyssa, the brother of Basil fellow of the Apostles,** *beheld him that he was apt for his ministration, and he made him* (*namely*) **this one** *deacon.*

The Syriac reflects all the characteristic readings of B (except **τοῦ ἐπισκόπου** on the two occasions on which it is attached to St Basil's name), and in particular the decisive clause **ἀδελφὸς** κ.τ.λ. This stamps the Syriac unmistakably as a B text: besides this, other B readings occur in the portion preserved in *Addit.* 14635, *e.g.* the addition of v. 14 to Wisd. IV. 13 (p. 116, **13**), and ὑπερβολῇ τρόπων χρηστῶν for σφοδρῶς (p. 117, **8**); and in *Addit.* 14732 throughout. From the nature of the case we may argue safely from the single chapter that the whole work must have existed in the B form. Wright's judgment assigning the fragment in *Addit.* 14635 to the sixth century will not, I think, be challenged by any one accustomed to early Syriac MSS.; and it has been endorsed by three specialists who have examined the MS. at my request.

The sixth century fragment of the third Syriac translation of c. 38, designated s_o (see Note 71), seems to show influence of B (see apparatus to p. 122, **10** and **15**).

Here then we have indisputable evidence of the existence of the B text in the course of the sixth century; and it is quite possible, and even likely, that the Greek, if not the Syriac, existed in the fifth.

The outcome of this and the preceding section is, therefore, that the G text certainly dates from the middle of the fifth century; the B text most probably from the second half of the fifth century, certainly from the early part of the sixth.

§ 6. The History of the Text: Internal Evidence.

In §§ 2, 4, 5, 8 a number of pieces have been printed both in the B and in the G text, and from these it is possible to form an adequate notion of the respective characters of the rival texts. It will be seen that G is a shorter and simpler form of the text than B. This relative shortness is due to various causes:

(1) Dialogues (often with demons), formal prayers, and moralisings on the part of the author, are much less frequent in G than in B:—the passage from c. 21 printed p. xix illustrates this; also the story of the Girl who calumniated a Lector (c. 70), where a prayer of 18 lines, and 20 lines detailing the girl's repentance and confession, and another 20 lines of moralising at the end, are found in B but not in G.

(2) The adjectives perpetually attached in B to the names of the solitaries—such as ἅγιος, μακάριος, μέγας, θαυμαστός, πνευματικός, and the like—are comparatively rare in G.

(3) Adverbs and adverbial clauses not necessary to the sense are frequently absent in G.

(4) In B scriptural citations are often completed, and formal texts found instead of mere allusions.

(Cases of (3) and (4) occur in the passage from c. 23, printed out in § 5.)

(5) In B many of the lives end with a set finale: "This was the virtue of the true athlete of Christ" etc.: in G these finales are rare.

From the literary standpoint there can be no doubt at all of the superiority of G; as compared with it, B is rhetorical, turgid and overladen, and creates the impression of a text that has been rewritten. In short B has all the appearance of being a "metaphrastic" text, as Dr Preuschen happily styles it (*op. cit.* p. 213). It is in most places easy to see how B could have been rhetorically worked up out of G; but that G could have been formed out of B by any process of pruning and abbreviation is well nigh inconceivable (see the passage p. xix). I adduce one instance in which the B text has demonstrably been formed out of the G text. In the description of the personal appearance of Macarius of Alexandria (p. 58, 4) G says: ἦν δὲ τὸ εἶδος αὐτοῦ ὑποκόλοβον κ.τ.λ.

In B it stands thus: Ἦν δὲ τὸ εἶδος αὐτοῦ τοιοῦτον—δεῖ με γὰρ καὶ περὶ τούτου σημᾶναί σοι, δοῦλε τοῦ Χριστοῦ, ἀκριβῶς τοῦτο ἐμοῦ γινώσκοντος, ὡς ἅτε καὶ μετ' αὐτοῦ συγχρονίσασαν τὴν ἐμὴν βραχύτητα·—ἦν δὲ τὸ εἶδος τῆς ἡλικίας αὐτοῦ ὑποκόλοβον κ.τ.λ.

Here the traces of the process of insertion in B lie on the surface of the text.

There can, I think, be no doubt that the G text is the one that represents the Lausiac History as first written by Palladius. But the B enlargement in the piece just printed, being in the first person, claims to be by Palladius, and so raises the question whether it can have been Palladius himself who revised his own work and produced the metaphrastic text;—so that both forms of the text would be authentic. Although I do not think this hypothesis a likely one, it is proper to consider what can be said in its favour[1].

(1) Many of the additions contain what purport to be personal touches referring to the author, or direct addresses to Lausus: *e.g.* the piece just cited, and those at the end of cc. 23 and 28 (pp. 77 and 84). But such passages contain really nothing that could not have been written by a rhetorician dressing up Palladius' work. For instance, in regard to the piece printed above, Palladius had already stated several times that he had personally known Macarius and had lived with him.

(2) One of these passages, however, claims attention. We should naturally look for additional information in the expanded account of Olympias (c. 56), St John Chrysostom's friend and correspondent, whom Palladius must have known personally. The account in B is fully four times as long as that in G, indeed the maximum of difference throughout the entire book is here reached, for the whole of col. 1249 in Migne is represented by only three lines in G (p. 150). But the additional matter is the emptiest verbiage and contains no real information whatever,—except the passage cited in the note on p. 150, in which the writer says that he himself distributed much of Olympias' property according to her wish. This certainly has a genuine ring about it, and it is to be noted that nowhere in G does Palladius explicitly claim to have known Olympias; nor is the passage derived from the *Dial. de Vita Chrys.*

(3) One or two of the additions convey fresh historical information, in particular the piece at the end of c. 11 on the dedication of the basilica of Rufinus (p. 34). This piece, however, is encompassed by special textual difficulties, it being uncertain whether any, or how much, of it stood in G (see Note 22).

(4) Some linguistic arguments may be added. The following perhaps noteworthy expressions are found in the B enlargements and also in other places in G:

[1] It can hardly be necessary to point out that this question is quite different from that discussed in *Prol.* 50—viz. whether it was Palladius himself who made the fusion of the *Hist. Mon.* with his own *Hist. Laus.* The question of the Interpolated Redaction is distinct from that of the Metaphrastic Text.

B (references to *P. G.* XXXIV.)	Parallels in **G**
Proem[1]: *ἀκροθιγῶς* (995: *infra* p. 4, **7**) (a somewhat unusual adverb, but other authorities are cited in Hase's Stephanus)	p. 146, **1**
Proem: *τὴν τῶν ἐντυγχανόντων ὠφέλειαν* (995, *infra* p. 4, **12**); repeated	p. 11, **22**; p. 22, **4**; p. 64, **16**; p. 80, **17**;
c. 5 (fin.): *εἰς...ἀσφάλειαν καὶ παραφυλακὴν τῶν ἐντυγχανόντων* (1018 A) (but cf. Socr. IV. 23: *πρὸς ὠφέλειαν τῶν ἐντυγχανόντων*)	p. 116, **8**
Proem: *πεζῇ τῇ πορείᾳ* (995: *infra* p. 4, **24**)	p. 11, **7**
Proem: *τὴν μητέρα τῆς ὑπερηφανίας* (995: *infra* p. 5, **7**)	p. 12, **6**
c. 27 (fin.): *τημεληθεὶς* (1092 D)	p. 78, **4**
c. 32: *σύστημα* (for community) (1100 D) (but used by other writers)	p. 52, **16**
c. 40: *φίλη δὲ ἀλήθεια* (1204 D) (see Note 42)	p. 81, **11**
c. 54: *ἐὰν θέλω ἅπερ ἐπίσταμαι λέγειν ἐπιλείψει καὶ ὁ χρόνος* (1226 C)	p. 15, **19**

Such is the case, so far as I can see, in favour of the view that Palladius himself may have produced the metaphrastic recension of his own book. I do not think it comes to more than this, that the metaphrast had studied Palladius' text carefully, and now and then took pains to reproduce his environment and some of his expressions and vocabulary. On the other side, in addition to the rhetorical emptiness of the enlargements, lies the fact that the alteration of the bishop who ordained Evagrius deacon from Gregory Nazianzen to Gregory Nyssen is certainly an historical blunder (see Note 73). The change is no mere scribe's error, for the clause is added: *ἀδελφὸς τοῦ ἐν τιμῇ τῶν ἀποστόλων Βασιλείου.* And this clause is an integral part of the B text, being found in all the authorities for B, including the sixth century Syriac fragment (see p. xliii). It seems incredible that Palladius, who knew Evagrius so well, should, after having been right in his original draft, have gone wrong in his (supposed) revision. I cannot think that any one will be found to maintain this theory.

Even if it were maintained that the B text came from the pen of Palladius, there could be no reasonable doubt that G represents what he wrote in the first instance; and it is the only text of which the authenticity can be predicated with certainty, or even

[1] It is shown in Note 1 that the Proem is the handiwork of the metaphrastic redactor; it is a good sample of his style.

with likelihood. The investigations of the two preceding sections, if they failed to establish a clear priority on either side, did establish the fact that, no matter how far back we trace them, the two forms of the text stand as far asunder as they do now, and have not diverged from any intermediate form. We are in the presence of a double text. It would be an unhistorical method of editing to construct a text resulting from some conjectural combination of G and B. In these circumstances the course for an editor of Palladius is clear: he has to endeavour to produce the G text with such purity as the somewhat intractable materials at his disposal will allow. As to the B text, the inclusion of its readings in the apparatus would make the latter a veritable textual jungle. Moreover B is already in print, both in Meursius and in Du Duc (Migne): the latter edition, when the interpolations from the *Hist. Mon.* have been removed and the order of the later portion of the work has been restored (as can easily be done by means of the references in the head lines in the following Text), presents a very fair working edition of the metaphrastic text. For these reasons B has been left on one side in the present edition, attention being concentrated on G, which is now edited for the first time. There are, however, in B a few passages which do present additional facts, whether authentic or not; all such passages are printed beneath the text (pp. 34, 77, 84, 134, 150). Of course the metaphrast used a G MS as the basis of his revision, and it is often possible to discern from the B MSS. what was the reading of this archetype (called β in the rest of this Introduction): such readings of β supply valid and useful evidence for G, because β was a fifth century G MS. Thus a number of B readings find place in the ensuing discussions and in the apparatus.

§ 7. CONTENTS AND STRUCTURE OF THE LATER PORTION OF THE BOOK.

Up to the end of c. 39 (on Pior and Moses) there is substantial agreement among the authorities as to the contents and structure of the book; but from that point onwards two distinct sequences of the chapters are found, the one supported by the extant G MSS.

and by s, the other by the B MSS. and by l. In spite of aberrations in certain of the B MSS. there can be no doubt as to what was the sequence in B. This sequence is the same as that in l. Hence we conclude that the two Greek G MSS. β and λ, used respectively by the redactor of B and the translator of l, had the same sequence of matter as is now shown by the B MSS. and by l. Thus what will be called the βl order is a G order, and dates from the fifth century; and it is not in any degree compromised by the fact that its extant Greek representatives contain a secondary form of the text. The agreement of s with the extant G MSS. (PWT)[1] shows that the PWTs order can claim a like antiquity. Thus neither order can establish any advantage of priority over the other[2].

The rival orders are exhibited in the accompanying Table. The figures in both columns give the numbers which the chapters bear in this edition, so that, *e.g.*, the chapters which are 47 and 58 in βl occupy the 40th and 41st places in PWTs. The locality referred to in each chapter is indicated when it can be ascertained.

(*See Table on next page.*)

It is necessary to refer briefly to two other orders found in certain MSS.:

(1) The order found in the Long (interpolated) Recension (Hervet and the Greek editions, except Meursius) has been given on p. xx, along with the alternations of the G and B texts found in this redaction. It is easy to see that the order has been determined partly by the type of text (G or B) the redactor was using at the moment, and partly by the desire to secure a more geographical grouping (*e.g.* the group of Galatian monks, cc. 45, 66, 68). The order of such a tertiary text can have no significance.

(2) The group of MSS. 14—18 contains a B text which has been subjected to a free literary revision. Several violent transpositions have been made even in the earlier portion of the book. Towards the end the order is: cc. 47, 39, 40 (om. 41^b), 42, 43, 44, 45 (tr. 46, 47), 48, 49, 50, 51, 52 (om. 53; tr. 54, 55, 56; om. 57), 58, 70, 41^a, 46, 54, 61, 55, 56, 65, 63, 38, 71, 35 (om. 59, 60, 62, 64, 66, 67, 68, 69), *Hist. Mon.* (joined on as if part of same work). It will be apparent, in spite of all eccentricities, that this order is a corruption of that of βl, just as the whole text is a corrupt form of B (see Note 11). The agreement of 14—18 with the Long Recension in the sequence cc. 41^a, 46, 54, 61, must be attributed to coincidence: to bring together the chapters on the two Melanias (46, 54, 61) was natural to any one rearranging the book; it

[1] See p. xv or p. 2.

[2] Only fragments of l_2 and s_2 exist in this portion of the work, so that they do not help us in the present discussion.

TABLE.

	Locality	β1	**PWTs**
Pior and Moses	Egypt	39	39
Ephrem Syrus	Edessa	40	47
Introd. on holy women		41^{a} (ll. 1—5)	58
Paula, Eustochium and others	Palestine, Asia Minor and Rome	41^{b}	40 (om. 41^{b})
Julian	Edessa	42	(om. 42)
Adolius and Innocent	Jerusalem	43, 44	44, 43
Philoromus	Galatia	45	(om. 45)
Melania Elder and Rufinus	Egypt and Palestine	46	53
Chronius and Paphnutius	Egypt	47	50, 51
Elpidius	Jericho	48	48
Sisinnius	Jericho	49	(om. 49)
Gaddanas and Elias	Palestine	50, 51	(om. 52)
Sabas	Palestine	52	41^{a}
Abramius (an Egyptian)	?	53	63
Melania Elder	Rome and Jerusalem	54	59, 60
Silvania	Jerusalem to Egypt	55	46
Olympias and others	Constantinople	56, 57	69, 70
Monks at Antinoë	Egypt	58	54
Nuns at Antinoë	Egypt	59, 60	55
Melania Younger and others	Rome	61, 62	56, 57 61, 62
Story of Virgin and Athanasius	Alexandria	63	
Story of Juliana and Origen	Caesarea in Cappadocia	64	64
Story from Hippolytus		65	65
Verus, Magna and a monk	Ancyra in Galatia	66, 67, 68	66, 67, 68
Two stories of Virgins who fell	2nd at Caesarea in Palestine	69, 70	
The Brother		71	71

NOTE. The second column of figures represents the order of P throughout: W agrees down to c. 46, in the middle of which chapter it breaks off, the rest of the MS. being lost (see p. 176): T agrees down to c. 55 (incl.), then come cc. 65, 61, 62, 66, 67, 68, 71, so that cc. 56, 57, 64 are wanting. The only witness for this portion of s is the imperfect Brit. Mus. *Addit.* 12173 (see *Prol.* 84); its entire contents are: Ep. Μακαρίζω, cc. 35, 36, 47, 58, 40, 44, 50, 51, 48, 41^{a}, 63, 59 (half), 60, 46, 54, 55, 65, 71, 31, 25, 26, 27, 53, 28, 69, 70, 29, 30: in spite of all transpositions and omissions, it is quite clear that this VI.|VII. century MS. represents a Greek original which contained the same order as PWT.

(*From p.* xlix.)

has been done also in the Munich fragment (no. 7 in the List of MSS.), and in the Syriac *Paradise* of Anan Isho. The making c. 41^{a} introduce this Melania section, thus departing from βl and PWTs alike, will appear more remarkable; but, as a matter of fact, the junction is not effected in the same way: in 14—18 the preface stops at the word ἀσθενεστέρας, while in the Long Recension it goes on to the end, χήραις (p. 128). The motive of the alteration very possibly lies in the fact that the accounts of the Melanias, especially when brought together, are by far the most important of all the histories of women, so that it was natural to prefix to them the preface on holy women.

A reference to the note in *Prol.* 141 will show why it was necessary to deal at such length with the order of 14—18. But this order, and that of the Long Recension, may now be wholly neglected.

When we compare the two orders as exhibited in the Table opposite, we see that the difference between them lies partly in sequence and partly in the fact that certain sections found in βl (cc. 41^{b}, 42, 45, 49, 52) are not found in PWTs.

Let us begin by examining the differences of mere sequence.

The first difference which we notice on comparing the column PWTs with the column βl is that in PWTs c. 47 and c. 58 come between c. 39 and c. 40; but cc. 47, 58 are precisely the two chapters in the later part of the book that are concerned with monks in Egypt: thus, as the first thirty-nine have to do almost wholly with the Egyptian monks, it follows that in PWTs the body of matter concerning Egyptian monks stands all together before anything else. The next difference is the absence in PWTs of cc. 41^{b}, 42: now c. 41^{b} is a series of brief notes on a number of holy women whom Palladius had met; thus its absence, coupled with the facts that c. 46 comes later and c. 47 earlier than in βl, brings it about that in PWTs the accounts of Asiatic monks of Syria and Palestine stand all together (cc. 40, 44, 43, 53, 50, 51, 48), immediately after the Egyptian monks;—there are, however, in this section some differences of order and some lacunae in PWTs as compared with βl. After the Egyptian and Asiatic monks comes in PWTs the short preface on holy women, c. 41^{a}, introducing c. 63, a story about a virgin in Alexandria, followed by cc. 59, 60, which deal with nuns in Egypt. Then comes c. 46, the first of the chapters on Melania, followed by cc. 69, 70, stories of virgins who fell and repented. After them comes c. 54, the second of the Melania chapters; and from this point to the end the order in PWTs is identical with that of βl, allowance being made for the chapters that have already occurred in earlier positions.

The nett result is that in PWTs the subject-matter is grouped as follows:

(i) Egyptian monks (1—39, 47, 58)
(ii) Asiatic monks (40, 44, 43, (53,) 50, 51, 48)
(iii) Holy women (41[a])
  (*a*) in Egypt (63, 59, 60)
  (*b*) elsewhere (46, 69, 70, 54—57, 61, 62, 64, 65)
(iv) Three Galatian stories (66, 67, 68)
(v) The Brother (71)

On the hypothesis that βl give the original order, it is easy to see how the scribe of the archetype whence have come PWTs, set to work: he separated the women from the men, and brought together those of Egypt at the head of each category. Even the apparently motiveless insertion of cc. 69, 70 between c. 46 and c. 54 may be accounted for:—the opening words of c. 54 (ἄνω διηγησάμην) required that something should come between cc. 46 and 54; and of the remaining chapters, 69 and 70 are the most suitable, indeed the only available, ones for the purpose. On the other hand, it is impossible to discern any intelligible principles by which the order of βl may be supposed to have been derived from that of PWTs: the narrative alternates between accounts of men and women, and travels backwards and forwards between Egypt and Palestine and Asia Minor and Italy, without any apparent method; so that the alterations from PWTs to βl on the part of a redactor or scribe could be attributed only to mere caprice. The question may be raised whether it be more likely that disorder of such a kind should be due to the author or to a redactor: in the various cases of evident rearrangement of the subject-matter which have been before us (pp. xlix, li) the tendency has always been in the direction of attempts at a more logical grouping.

Yet in the order of βl there is one point that should not pass unnoticed: the accounts of the monks and nuns of Antinoë (cc. 58, 59, 60) stand together, and are separated from the great body of Egyptian reminiscences. Now Tillemont is probably right in placing Palladius' four years' stay at Antinoë during his second sojourn in Egypt, when he was banished to Syene (see Appendix V ii); and so it would seem that in this point βl reflects a fact in Palladius' life. It would be more striking still could we identify the voyage from Jerusalem to Egypt, mentioned in c. 55, with the journey into banishment in A.D. 406. At times I have been disposed to imagine that in the order of βl may be discerned a dim general correspondence with the outlines of Palladius' career:—a stay of twelve years in Egypt (cc. 1—39), ending with the death of Evagrius in 399 or 400 (c. 38); then four or five years as a bishop in different parts of the East, engaged in the struggle in behalf of St John Chrysostom (cc. 41—52, predominantly); next a journey to Rome on St John's business in 405, on which occasion he met the Melanias (c. 54); this was followed in 406 by his exile to Egypt (c. 55?), and his stay at Antinoë (cc. 58—60); finally we learn from Socrates (VII. 36) that, after his recall from banishment, Palladius was translated from his bishopric of Helenopolis in Bithynia to that of Aspuna in Galatia, and almost at the close of the book we have three stories (cc. 66—68) connected with Ancyra in Galatia.

The idea here suggested must not be pressed to the point of an argument, and obvious difficulties in detail can be urged against it[1]. Still when all allowances have been made, it can hardly, I think, be without significance that there has existed in the world just one man, and that man Palladius, to whom the order of βl would not have been mere disorder, but the perhaps unconscious reproduction of shadowy reminiscences of the course of events long past.

On the whole the result of the examination into the question of mere sequence is distinctly favourable to βl.

We must now consider the pieces found in βl, but not in PWTs.

c. 41[b] consists of a series of very brief notices on ten or eleven holy women whom Palladius had met in various places: he tells us that one of them whom he had seen at Antioch was the aunt of St John Chrysostom; he says that at Rome he met the new converts Avita and her husband Apronianus and daughter Eunomia, of whom he speaks again in c. 54 as living at Rome, Apronianus being a recent convert of Melania's, and in all this his statements are borne out by Paulinus of Nola and Rufinus (see Note 95); the "aged virgin" Asella, whom he saw at Rome, was

[1] In particular, the Asiatic experiences contained in cc. 41—52 cannot all have fallen within the years 399—405 (see Appendix V ii).

in all probability St Jerome's Roman friend (see Note 78); he states that he had never seen Eustochium. Throughout the information is precise and circumstantial, and where it can be tested it is accurate. The internal evidence is altogether in favour of the authenticity of the piece, and no reason, except its absence from PWTs, exists for suspecting it. Dr Preuschen accepts it as genuine (*Pall. u. Ruf.* 254). The fierce attack on St Jerome with which it opens is, like the similar passage in c. 36, an echo of the living controversies of the time, and is at once a proof of its authenticity and an explanation of its absence from various copies.

c. 42, on Julian of Edessa, is attested by Sozomen (III. 14, 29); for in this chapter Sozomen has made extensive use of the *Hist. Laus.*, and what he says of Julian is not to be found in the Greek Life to which he refers, nor anywhere else than in *Hist. Laus.* The account is so short that probably it was omitted by an oversight as part of c. 41—there was originally no division into chapters. Preuschen accepts it also as a genuine piece of the *Hist. Laus.* (*op. cit.* 228, 254).

c. 45, on Philoromus: Palladius says he lived with him. A stylistic argument of genuineness is given in Note 84.

c. 49, on Sisinnius: the chapter is quite naturally connected with c. 48, Sisinnius being introduced as a disciple of Elpidius.

c. 52, on Sabas, calls for no remark.

These three chapters (45, 49, 52) are quite in Palladius' manner, style and vocabulary, and no intrinsic ground exists for suspecting them; (see Preuschen, *loc. cit.*).

It will be in place here to refer to the passage concerning the swine in the description of the Pachomian Monastery at Panopolis (p. 94), dealt with in Note 55. It is found only in βl, being omitted in the other authorities; yet there can be little doubt that it was written by Palladius, and belongs to the context in which it stands in βl[1].

[1] One conceivable hypothesis in regard to the pieces just discussed should be stated in order to be definitely rejected; viz. that they did not properly belong to the Greek original of l, but had been introduced into it from B, so that their presence in l affords no ground for supposing that they stood in β; and that consequently they are to be regarded as the handiwork of the metaphrastic reviser. This hypothesis is excluded by what has just been said in favour of the authenticity of the individual pieces, notably c. 41[b]; and also by the general textual

It thus appears that there are strong reasons, external and internal, for accepting as genuine a number of pieces found in βl, but absent from PWTs.

Here once again the question naturally suggests itself: Can a revision of the book by Palladius himself be the explanation of the phenomena, PWTs representing the first draft, and βl a slightly enlarged second edition? This theory is very attractive, for it would help to solve not only the problems now engaging our attention, but also some of those that will arise in the sequel. Against it, however, stand two objections which seem peremptory.

(1) One of the chief points of difference lies in this, that in βl the short preface on holy women (c. 41[a]) introduces the series of notes on Paula, Eustochium and the rest (c. 41[b]); while in PWTs it introduces the story of the Virgin of Alexandria, who received St Athanasius into her house when he was fleeing from the Arians (c. 63). But the very grammar of the opening words of c. 41[b]—*ἐν αἷς καὶ Παύλῃ τῇ* Ῥωμαίᾳ, with no verb to govern the dative—shows that it must originally have been connected with the preface Ἀναγκαῖον (41[a]), which concludes: *πολλαῖς ἀστείαις συντετύχηκα παρθένοις τε καὶ χήραις* (see p. 128). Now supposing that PWTs contain the order first chosen by Palladius, and that he desired to introduce into his book an account of Paula and the other holy women, it is in the highest degree unlikely that he would, actually cutting a sentence in two, have moved from its original position the story of the Virgin and Athanasius, in order to put in its place the new material, instead of inserting an independent chapter somewhere else. Indeed, 41[a] and 41[b] fit together so naturally and so well, that no other hypothesis seems tolerable than that they formed integral parts of the same context from the beginning.

phenomena, as the reader may easily see for himself by examining the apparatus to the various passages. In particular let him turn to the close of c. 52 (p. 145), for which B and l are printed in full: it is quite clear that in β and the Greek original of l the passage stood substantially as in ll. 6—8 of the text, and that in B the metaphrastic reviser has expanded it six or sevenfold. His operations on these βl passages are precisely similar to his treatment of the rest of the text. It may be taken as certain that all these pieces stood in the G MSS. from which B and l were made.

(2) Moreover in βl the story of the Virgin of Caesarea, who received and sheltered Origen when fleeing from persecution (c. 64), follows immediately after the story of the Virgin of Alexandria, who did the like for Athanasius (c. 63). It will at once be felt that the two similar stories naturally fall together: nay, there is at the beginning of c. 64 a πάλιν referring to the analogous story that has just preceded. In PWTs the two stories are separated and the πάλιν becomes meaningless, referring to some men whom Palladius had met in Rome[1]. There can be little doubt that in PWTs c. 63 has been moved from its original position immediately in front of c. 64 in order to be substituted for c. 41[b], which someone desired to suppress, doubtless on account of the attack on St Jerome.

Thus the idea that PWTs represent the first draft and βl a revision by Palladius is excluded; and all the evidence considered in this section leads up to the conclusion that in contents and structure βl have preserved the original form of the *Hist. Laus.* Their order of chapters is accordingly adopted in this edition.

§ 8. Relations of the Textual Sources.

(I) The Greek MSS.

We have at our disposal for the construction of the G text the following Greek MSS.: **P**aris 1628 and **T**urin 141, for nearly the whole book; **W**ake 67, for about one-half; the twin MSS. **V**enice 346 and **C**oislin 282, for about one-fifth; the **A** MSS. for the portions of the G text which they contain, amounting to nearly one-half; and a few fragments. Moreover it is often possible to determine what was the reading of β, the MS. used by the metaphrast as the basis of his revision; in such cases we have an additional authority for the G text.

Now while presenting the same substantial text, the various

[1] The truth of this statement is not affected by the fact that WT and s are imperfect in various ways and do not contain c. 64; for in all of them c. 63 is followed by c. 59, as in P, which without any doubt has faithfully preserved the order of the archetype of PWTs in all this portion of the book.

authorities for G differ from one another frequently and considerably in matters of detail, so that the apparatus of variants is commonly very large. Our next step, therefore, must be to try to discover what laws underlie the relationships between these MSS. This must be by a process of induction; and in order to arrive at even approximately correct results, it will be necessary to experiment over a wide field. For this purpose those portions of the book are selected which are extant in all six of the chief G MSS., viz. cc. 25, 26, 27, 28, 31, 35, 36, 37, containing in all some 410 lines of the printed text. Two Schedules of readings will be constructed: the first will contain such readings as affect only the Greek text and would not be apparent in the versions; the second, those that can be discerned in the versions. Only those cases are included in which the authorities are divided between a single pair of readings, and in which there is no uncertainty or confusion as to the readings. Readings are omitted which are supported by only a single authority; and for the purposes of these Schedules the discussions of the succeeding sections are so far anticipated that the Venice and Coislin MSS. are treated as a single authority, and similarly the Paris and Wake MSS. when they agree: so that readings supported by VC alone or by PW alone are omitted.

(*The Schedules are printed in Appendix VII.*)

The first impression made by these Schedules is one of mere bewilderment; the authorities are found grouped in all possible combinations, and it would be easy by judicious selection to make out a plausible and even a telling case in support of any given relationship between the Greek MSS. We are evidently in the presence of a textual problem of unusual complexity. The first step must be to tabulate the results of the Schedules, by giving the number of times each combination of the Greek MSS. occurs. When this is done, it will be found that certain facts emerge from the chaos. The readings in Schedule II. marked with an asterisk are available for the purpose of the annexed Tabulation:

TABULATION OF COMBINATIONS OF GREEK MSS. IN SCHEDULES.

			Sched. I	Sched. II	Total
PWTA	versus	VCβ	34	43	77
PWT	v.	VCβA	6	5	11
PWA	v.	VCβT	7	4	11
PTA	v.	VCβW	2	—	2
PA	v.	VCβWT	2	2	4
PT	v.	VCβWA	2	2	4
PWVCβ	v.	TA	4	3	7
PTVCβ	v.	WA	—	1	1
PWTVC	v.	Aβ	6	5	11
PWAVC	v.	Tβ	3	4	7
PTAVC	v.	Wβ	2	—	2
PWVC	v.	TAβ	8	1	9
PTVC	v.	WAβ	1	1	2
PAVC	v.	WTβ	2	1	3
PVC	v.	WTAβ	2	1	3
PWTβ	v.	VCA	7	5	12
PWAβ	v.	VCT	9	1	10
PTAβ	v.	VCW	1	—	1
PWβ	v.	VCTA	4	7	11
PTβ	v.	VCWA	—	2	2
PAβ	v.	VCWT	1	—	1
Pβ	v.	VCWTA	3	—	3
	Total no. of readings		106	88	194

From this summary it appears that the combination

PWTA v. VCβ

stands in such marked excess above any other combination, that we may safely take as a working hypothesis that it represents a dominant and ultimate textual fact. And when we look further into the Table we shall discover that VCβ are found together 117 times in all out of the total of 194 cases; and also that, in addition to the 77 times that PWTA stand together, three members of this group stand together in various trios 73 times more. And these numerical considerations are strengthened materially by an examination of the nature of the readings in which PWTA stand over against VCβ: from Schedule II. it will appear that the difference often consists in the absence of a word or clause on one side or the other (oftenest on the side of PWTA); while from Schedule I. it will appear that equally often the difference lies only in the smallest minutiæ of grammar or order—and I venture to think that this latter class of differences is no less significant than the former.

For instance, the following series of minute differences occurs in c. 35:

PWTA	VCβ	PWTA	VCβ
ἐ(ι)ς ὕστερον	ὕστερον	εἶπον 2°	λέγω αὐτῷ
ὡς ἐτῶν κέ	om ὡς	μετὰ γὰρ	καὶ μετὰ
τὸ ὄρος τῆς Λυκῶ	τὸ ὄρος τὸ Λυκῶ	καὶ τοῦτο	om καὶ
τῇ συντυχίᾳ	συντυχίᾳ	om αὐτῷ	παραβαλούσῃ αὐτῷ
ἐν τῇ θυρίδι	τῇ θυρίδι	εἰς τὴν 'Αλεξ.	εἰς 'Αλεξ.
τὴν ἐμὴν	τὴν πρός με	ἔχεις	ἔχει
εἶπον	λέγω	om ἡ	ἡ παραλογισαμένη

To find the same groups of MSS. again and again consistently ranged against one another is a phenomenon that can be explained only on the hypothesis that there is a special affinity between P, W, T and A on the one hand, and a special affinity between VC and β on the other[1]. And the validity of the inference cannot be shaken by the numerous cross divisions, how perplexing soever they may be. The consideration, however, of the problems to which they give rise is reserved to the two succeeding sections. For the present, having ascertained that the principal extant Greek representatives of the G text fall into two clearly defined groups, we shall pass on to the determining of the relation in which each of the chief versions stands to these groups.

(II) The Versions.

Relation of l to the two groups of G MSS.

Schedule II. registers 120 readings of l, a few being in

[1] It is to be noticed that the Tabulation shows a specially close affinity between P and W, for they part company only 28 times; they are by far the most constant and characteristic members of the group PWTA.

brackets as somewhat doubtful—this distinction, however, will be disregarded in what follows. It is found that

l agrees with β 82 times,
with VC 60 times,
with PW 35 times (and, when P and W part company, with P once and with W 9 times),
with T 34 times,
with A 31 times.

Moreover, l is found without either VC or β only 17 times:—and it will appear later that in some of these cases VC have been contaminated by mixture with a B text:—but l is found 59 times without any one of the four, P, W, T, or A. The combination VCβl occurs 42 times, and 13 times these four stand alone, often in unmistakably significant readings; as the additions *τοῦ Νείλου* (p. 86, **13**); *πᾶσαν* (p. 87, **9**); *καὶ Ἀλβάνιον καὶ Ἀμμώνιον* (p. 101, **5**); *ἢ* (p. 106, **5**).

These figures indicate an affinity between l and the group VCβ.

The high number of agreements of l with β suggests a specially close affinity. They stand alone together in Schedule II., in opposition to the united witness of the other authorities, 16 (perhaps 23) times; and instances of this phenomenon occur throughout the whole book. An examination of these βl readings (see, for instance, those scheduled from c. 37), shows that usually they are of a kind that cannot be due to mere accident in the transmission of the text. A question at once arises: May their presence in l be due to the fact that λ (the Greek original of l) had suffered contamination by intermixture with a B text? In the following sections we shall meet many instances of such processes; but, after a careful consideration of the whole series of βl readings, I am satisfied that there is no sufficient reason for suspecting any such influence of B in λ or in l. The point is of such importance for forming a right judgment on the textual materials, that it is incumbent upon me to offer in justification of my conclusion some illustrations of the kind of reasons on which I rely. I take first a passage out of c. 37:

B (*P. G.* xxxiv. 1187 c)	G (*infra*, pp. 114, 15—115, 8)	l (*Bibl. Casin.* iii, *Flor.* 308)
Εἶτα λέγει αὐτῇ· Κάτελθε καὶ πρόελθε. ἀπεκρίνατο αὐτῷ ἐκείνη· Εἰκοστὸν πέμπτον ἔτος ἔχω μηδέποτε προελθοῦσα, καὶ ἵνα τί σήμερον προέλθω; λέγει αὐτῇ ἐκεῖνος· Οὐαί, οὐκ εἶπες ὅτι Ἐγὼ τῷ κόσμῳ τούτῳ ἀπέθανον;	Τότε λέγει αὐτῇ· Ἔξελθε (al. κάτελθε) καὶ πρόελθε. ἀπεκρίνατο αὐτῷ (ἐκείνη)· Εἰκοστὸν πέμπτον ἔτος ἔχω καὶ οὐ προῆλθον· καὶ (νῦν) ἵνα τί προέλθω; λέγει αὐτῇ·	.... et illa respondit: Vicesimum et quintum annum ago ex quo numquam ex hoc loco egredior; quam ob causam uis ergo procedam? ait ille:
δῆλον πάντως ὅτι καί σοι ὁ κόσμος οὐκ ἔστιν.	Εἰ ἀπέθανες τῷ κόσμῳ καί σοι ὁ κόσμος,	Tu saeculo mortua es et saeculum tibi;
εἰ οὖν τοῦτό ἐστι, νεκρὸς οὐδενὸς ἐπαισθάνεται· ταὐτὸν σοι οὖν ἐστι καὶ προελθεῖν καὶ μὴ προελθεῖν.	ταὐτόν σοί ἐστι καὶ προελθεῖν καὶ μὴ προελθεῖν· πρόελθε οὖν.	unum ergo est siue non procedas siue procedas: ergo progredere.
ἀκούσασα δὲ ταῦτα ἡ παρθένος προῆλθε· μετὰ δὲ τὸ προελθεῖν αὐτὴν ἔξω καὶ ἐλθεῖν ἕως ἐκκλησίας τινός, ἐλθὼν ὁ μακάριος εὗρεν αὐτὴν ἐν τῇ ἐκκλησίᾳ καὶ λέγει αὐτῇ·	(ἡ δὲ) προῆλθε· καὶ μετὰ τὸ προελθεῖν αὐτὴν ἔξω καὶ ἐλθεῖν ἕως ἐκκλησίας τινὸς λέγει αὐτῇ ἐν τῇ ἐκκλησίᾳ·	statimque tunc illa processit. posteaquam processit e cella sua (clause om in Sess and Cass 348, 143) et illic ad eam loquitur:
Εἰ ὄντως θέλεις (τελείως) πληροφορῆσαί με ὅτι ἀπέθανες καὶ οὐκέτι ζῇς ἀνθρώποις ἀρέσκουσα, ποίησον ὃ ἐγὼ δύναμαι ποιῆσαι καὶ τότε πληροφορήσεις με ὅτι **ἀληθῶς** τῷ κόσμῳ τούτῳ ἀπέθανες.	Οὐκοῦν εἰ θέλεις με πληροφορῆσαι ὅτι ἀπέθανες καὶ οὐκέτι ζῇς ἀνθρώποις ἀρέσκουσα, ποίησον ὃ ποιῶ, καὶ οἶδα (al. γνώσομαι) ὅτι ἀπέθανες·	Si ergo uis persuadere quod mortua sis nec iam hominibus placens uiuas fac et ipsa quod facio, et **uere** te mortuam scio:
καὶ ἡ παρθένος· Λοιπὸν τί θέλεις ποιήσω; (λέγει αὐτῇ ἐκεῖνος·) Ἐκδυσαμένη κ.τ.λ.	(λέγει αὐτῇ·) ἐκδυσαμένη κ.τ.λ.	exue te, inquit, etc.

It is most unlikely that the scribe of λ (or its progenitor), when copying out a G MS., should have taken from a B text just the single word *ἀληθῶς*, and have rejected all the other B enlargements and alterations; far more probable is it that λ and *β* both contained a G text which in this passage differed from the extant G MSS. only in having *ὅτι ἀληθῶς ἀπέθανες* instead of *ὅτι ἀπέθανες*.

Next I take a passage from c. 58, in which the argument is of quite a different character from the foregoing. Here, although a portion of B has been re-written after the manner of the metaphrastic reviser, it is possible to recover with security the Greek text underlying B and l.

B (*P. G.* xxxiv. 1203 D)	G (*infra*, p. 152, 10—12)	1
Οὗτος ἔλεγεν ἡμῖν ὅτι	PWTAs: Ἔλεγεν ἡμῖν ὅτι·	Nobis ista dicebat:
Ὁ νοῦς ἀποστὰς τῆς τοῦ	PW: Νοῦς ἀποστὰς	Sensus humanus cum a
θεοῦ θεωρίας κατ' ἔννοιαν	θεοῦ ἐννοίας	cognitione recesserit dei,
ἢ δαίμων γίνεται ἢ	ἢ κτῆνος γίνεται ἢ δαίμων·	aut quaecumque anima
κτῆνος. ἡμῶν δὲ φιλο-		laus daemonis incipiet
πευστούντων τὸν τρό-		fieri (*sic* l^{cass}; l^{sess} vac; dae-
πον ὃν εἶπεν, ἔλεγεν		moni efficitur similis l^{rev})
οὕτως ὅτι Νοῦς ἀνθρώπου	Ts: Νοῦς ἀποστὰς	aut mutis animalibus
θεοῦ θεωρίας ἀναχωρήσας	θεοῦ ἐννοίας	comparatur. cuius dicti
ἐξ ἀνάγκης ἢ τῷ τῆς ἐπι-		rationem cum ab eo cupe-
θυμίας δαίμονι περιπίπτει	περιπίπτει ἐπιθυμίᾳ·	remus accipere, ista di-
τῷ ἄγοντι εἰς ἀκολασίαν, ἢ	A: Νοῦς ἀποστὰς θεοῦ, ἐν-	cebat: Qui a deo recesserit
τῷ θυμικῷ πονηρῷ πνεύματι	νοίᾳ περιπίπτει ἐπιθυμίας·	necesse est ut aut in desi-
ὅθεν αἱ ἄλογοι τίκτονται		derium aliquod aut in ali-
ὁρμαί. καὶ τὴν μὲν ἀκό-	PWTAs: καὶ τὴν μὲν	quam iracundiam ruat:
λαστον ἐπιθυμίαν ἔλε-	ἐπιθυμίαν ἔλε-	desiderium quidem illud
γεν εἶναι κτηνώδη, τὸν	γε κτηνώδη, τὸν	insensatorum animalium,
δὲ θυμὸν κίνησιν δαιμο-	δὲ θυμὸν δαιμο-	iracundiam uero daemo-
νιώδη.	νιώδη.	num esse dicebat.

In spite of the corruption in l, it is possible to see that in λ the passage read substantially thus:—Ἔλεγεν ἡμῖν ὅτι Νοῦς ἀποστὰς θεοῦ ἐννοίας ἢ δαίμων γίνεται ἢ κτῆνος. ἡμῶν δὲ φιλοπευστούντων τὸν τρόπον ὃν εἶπεν, ἔλεγεν οὕτως ὅτι Νοῦς ἀποστὰς θεοῦ (ἐννοίας) ἐξ ἀνάγκης περιπίπτει ἐπιθυμίᾳ ἢ θυμῷ· καὶ τὴν μὲν ἐπιθυμίαν ἔλεγεν εἶναι κτηνώδη, τὸν δὲ θυμὸν δαιμονιώδη. It cannot be supposed that this is an abridgment of B made by the scribe of λ: the readings of Ts and of A in the middle column forbid such a notion. Rather did the passage stand substantially as restored above in λ and β and the type of G text they represented. The question whether the βλ text be the result of a conflation of the readings of PW and of TAs, or whether (as seems more likely) it be the original text, and the pair of readings be due to its breaking asunder into two parts owing to the repetition; is one which in no way affects the point here at issue, viz. that the series of agreements between B and l is due, not to any influence of B on λ or l, but to the fact that β and λ contained types of the G text closely akin.

I shall briefly indicate one further argument, still of a different character from both the preceding, in support of the same view. If the reader turns to Note 45 he will see that in a passage of c. 27, out of a mass of additional matter found in B, the clause *ἀλλὰ τὰ πάντα αὐτομάτως φέρεσθαι* is attested both by l and by s_2, there being no vestige of it in any other text. Here λ is supported by σ_2 (the Greek original of s_2), in which no trace is found of any B element, and which has no special affinity with l. That the scribes of λ and σ_2 should have independently picked out the same words, and no more, from the enlargements of B, is a supposition that cannot be entertained. We can only conclude that the clause stood in the three G MSS., β, λ and σ_2.

Thus the independence of λ from B, and consequently the reality of the relationship between the G texts β and l, is convincingly established. (But see p. lxxxi.)

Relation of s to the two groups of G MSS.

If the conclusions arrived at in § 7, as to βl having preserved the true order and structure of the concluding third of the book, be valid; nay, if the single point has been established that the series of notices of Paula and other holy women, contained in c. 41[b], is authentic, so that the junction in PWT and s of the story of Athanasius in c. 63 with c. 41[a] is erroneous; it follows that PWT and σ (the Greek original of s) were all descended from a single MS. in which this alteration had been made: for the substitution of c. 63 for c. 41[b] is a corruption of a kind that cannot have arisen by mere coincidence, but demonstrates descent from a common vitiated ancestor. Now about the authenticity of c. 41[b] and its primitive organic connection with c. 41[a], there cannot, I think, be any doubt at all. And so a close affinity of s with PWT (and A) is shown.

The phenomena of Schedule II. (App. VII) are in conformity with this result: the combination PWTAs occurs 38 times, and s is found with three of the Greek members of the group 12 times more. It has to be remembered that in the case of the Syriac versions it is difficult (much more frequently than in the case of the Latin versions), to determine whether the rendering really represents a given Greek reading, or is merely due to Aramaic idiom; *e.g.* whether a pronoun or pronominal suffix in s or s_2 is evidence of a pronoun in σ or σ_2: in this way a number of the minor readings of s and s_2 are by no means certain—far less certain than similar cases in the Syriac versions of the New Testament, where much closer fidelity in translation was naturally aimed at. In regard to the numerous readings in which s agrees with VCβl against PWTA, it has to be remembered that s is by far the oldest member of the group PWTAs, as it dates from the sixth or fifth century; when, therefore, s is ranged with VCβl, it is (commonly) evidence of a corruption in PWTA: this point will be reverted to in § 10. Throughout the book s often agrees in significant readings with PW, the best MSS. of the group; but its closest agreement is with T, with which it often stands alone in very remarkable readings. Instances will be found in the text at p. 108, **7**, **8**, **18**; p. 126, **9** and **11**; p. 138, **7**; p. 144, **14**; p. 149, **10** and **14**; p. 160, title of c. 65. These agreements, sometimes in manifest error, are so striking as to demonstrate a specially close affinity between T and σ. And thus, quite independently of the arguments from order and structure, and from the junction of c. 63 with c. 41[a], σ is shown to have belonged to the group PWTA.

Relation of s_2 to the two groups of G MSS.

The first four chapters in Schedule II. (App. VII) supply a sufficient number of readings of s_2 to enable us to form an adequate idea of the character of text that was presented by σ_2. The Schedule shows s_2 sometimes ranged with PWTA, sometimes with VCβ, and, as a matter of fact, throughout it thus fluctuates between the two main groups[1]. Attention has just been called to a place where s_2 supports βl against PWTAVCs (see Note 45); at p. 59, **19–21**, it similarly attests the curious piece of demonology found in B and l, but not in PTA[B] or l_2 (the only other extant authorities); at p. 40, **5**, **6**, it attests another βl reading; and at p. 34, **13–16**, in a passage where l is missing, it enables us to reconstruct β out of B. On the other hand, s_2 by no means always, or even usually, supports the βl readings. It thus appears that the Greek text underlying s_2 was intermediate between βl and PWTAs; when its readings can be ascertained with certainty

[1] I have not been able to verify the Schedule by the MS., so that I do not guarantee its accuracy or completeness in regard to s_2.

they are of great value, as representing Greek MSS. of the fifth century of a type not found among the MSS. I have examined.

Relations of l_2 and c to the two groups of G MSS.

In regard to these versions the Schedule does not help us. In § 5 it has been shown that l_2 represents a G text. So does c, the Coptic version, extant in only a few fragments. A comparison of the pieces translated from chap. 18 (*Prol.* 123–6 and 149) with the two Greek texts will show, in spite of all paraphrasings and additions, that c represents a G text. Moreover in the Table in *Prol.* 120–22, nearly all the pieces of Greek noted as omitted in c are proper to B, and do not occur in G; indeed, had the comparison of c been made with a G text, that Table would have been reduced to half its dimensions[1].

In *Prol.* 114 reasons were given for surmising that the Greek MSS. underlying l_2 and c were closely akin. An examination of the apparatus to the passages in which c is extant will bear out this view. It is true that most of the agreements between l_2 and c consist in the omission of words and short clauses found in the other authorities for G; and agreement in omission is more likely than other forms of corruption to be due to mere coincidence in error. But a time comes when persistent agreements in such omissions reach a point at which coincidence can no longer be a reasonable explanation of the phenomena; and so we are led to the conclusion that l_2 and c are derived from Greek MSS. containing a somewhat shortened type of text, whereof no Greek representative has yet been discovered. There are besides certain positive agreements that place the kinship between l_2 and c beyond doubt: *e.g.* the clause at p. 30, **23**, "nec tuam oblationem obliuioni tradit" (*al.* tradet) l_2; "will receive thy sacrifice also" c: also p. 120, **9**. The relationship between l_2 and c will be further illustrated in § 10. It seems that l_2c, like s_2, represent a Greek text that stood midway between βl and PWTAs, fluctuating between all known types of the text. Perhaps the most striking

[1] It is important to notice that these eliminations hardly affect the points taken as bases of arguments, *Prol.* 122; this remark applies to most of the similar arguments, *Prol.* 112—14, 118—19.

case of the agreement of the archetype of l_2c with a characteristic βl reading is at p. 116, **16**, where c adds to St Basil's episcopal city of Caesarea the description "among the Arkeans," the equivalent of *τῆς πρὸς τὸν Ἀργέα*, found only in B and l: there is a lacuna here in l_2, due to homoeoteleuton; but there can be no doubt that the clause stood in the Greek text whence l_2 and c are descended. (For l_2 see also pp. **44**, **7** and 48, **7**.)

The other versions, Ethiopic, Armenian and Arabic, are mere fragments, and will be sufficiently dealt with in the appropriate places.

We may sum up as follows the results of the investigations of this section:

(1) The chief extant Greek authorities for the G text fall into two distinct groups, one made up of PWTA, the other of VCβ.

(2) l is akin to VCβ, and in a specially close manner to β.

(3) s is akin to PWTA, and in a specially close manner to T.

(4) l_2 and c are derived from Greek MSS. closely related to one another: the case of chap. 38 in c is special (see Note 71).

(5) l_2c and s_2 represent Greek texts intermediate between PWTAs and βl, but neither type has yet been found in Greek.

The pedigree and relationship of the chief sources for the text are exhibited in the annexed Pedigree.

Fragments too small to be located in the Table are not included. Composite MSS. (A and VC) are included in respect only of the portions of the G text which they contain.

Capitals denote Greek MSS.

Greek letters denote lost Greek archetypes.

Small Roman letters denote versions.

§ 9. The Documents.

The purpose of the present section is to supply a sufficient description and characterisation of the actual MSS. used in this edition.

(I) The Greek MSS.

P—(Preuschen's P[2]) Paris, Bibl. Nat., *ancien fonds grec* 1628 (*Regius* 2623, later 3003).

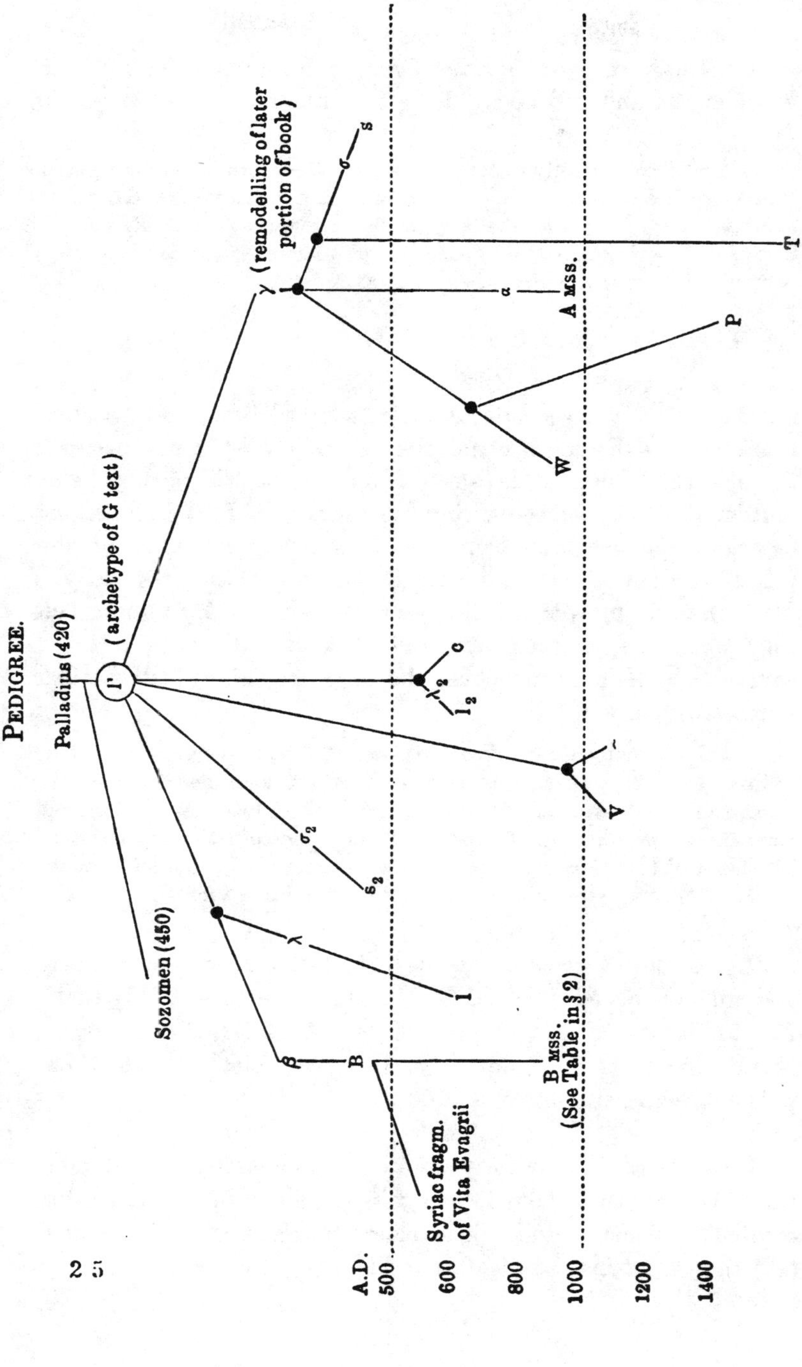
PEDIGREE.
Palladius (420)
Γ
(archetype of G text)
Sozomen (450)
γ
(remodelling of later portion of book)
σ
S
T
α
A MSS.
P
W
λ$_2$
c
l$_2$
V
σ$_2$
s$_2$
λ
l
β
B
B MSS.
(See Table in § 2)
Syriac fragm. of Vita Evagrii
A.D.
500
600
800
1000
1200
1400

Saec. XIV: paper: 14·5 × 20 cm.

Contents: ff. 1—144 *Hist. Laus.*, γ text (see § 7) complete except c. 38 and end of c. 36; rest of codex (ff. 144—244) *Hist. Mon.*

On the whole correctly written and accentuated, with breathings but no iotas subscr.: a certain number of itacisms, but not many considering date: also interchanges of ο and ω: a few absolute errors (not commonly recorded in this ed.): a few corrections, some by scribe himself (or contemporary), some by later hand: (see Preuschen, *Pall. u. Ruf.* 139.)

W—Oxford, Christ Church, *Wake* 67.

Saec. X: parchment: 16·5 × 25 cm.

Contents: a miscellaneous collection of Vitae, and ascetical tractates (see Kitchin's Catalogue p. 28). *Hist. Laus.* occupies ff. 193—251, where it breaks off incomplete, the codex being mutilated. Fol. 192, containing the beginning of *Hist. Laus.*, was detached and has been bound up in a wrong place, being now f. 150: it alone is mentioned in the Catalogue, the great body of *Hist. Laus.*, being without title, was overlooked. My finding this copy was a happy accident: having a half hour to spare, I amused myself in turning over the pages of the MS., till familiar words caught my eye.

No titles of chapters or marked divisions in the text: the page has usually 26 lines of writing, equivalent to 16 or 17 lines of this printed text: writing regular and good, with very few corrections: itacisms &c., misspellings and other errors somewhat more frequent than in P: accentuation fairly correct, but often omitted: thus W is less correctly written than P. Certain chapters (*e.g.* 32—34) never were in W; many others are wanting through the loss of several folios.

At present W contains about half of the γ text, viz. (in nos. and order of this ed.): Ep. ad Laus., Prol., cc. 1—6, 8—17, 18 (half) 23—31, 35—37, 40, 41[a], 43, 46 (half), 47, 48, 50, 51, 53, 58—60, 63.

(For readings of W, up to p. 100, see "List" p. 170; from p. 100 onwards, see note on p. 100.)

P and W are twin offspring of a common ancestor: throughout the whole text they stand alone again and again in readings often certainly erroneous: they alone place the chapter on Nathanael (16) after c. 12 instead of after c. 15; they alone insert the long apophthegma at p. 46, **17** (see note 28); at the end of c. 36 they break off with the words: "I knew this prophecy of this man" (p. 108, **6**), and omit the rest, though Ts no less than VCBl give the prophecy; they omit c. 38, on Evagrius, which is in T as well as VCBl (one sub-group of B, 1—6, omits it, and s is doubtful).

P is not a descendant of W, for it contains many portions of the text that never stood in W.

T—Turin, Università, *graec.* C. IV. 8, olim C. V. 33 (al. 141).

Saec. XVI: paper: 19 × 27 cm.

Contents: f. 1 homilies, apophth., Vitae (from Theodoret); f. 53 *Hist. Laus.*; f. 126 Hist. of the Brahmins; f. 138 *Hist. Mon.*; ff. 186—202 *Vita Pauli* and two apocalypses attributed to Jerome. At end: *τοῦτο τὸ σύγγραμμα εὑρόντες ἡμεῖς εἰς παλαιὸν βιβλίον ἀπεγραψάμεθα κ.τ.λ.* *Hist. Laus.* contains the whole γ text except cc. 56, 57, the latter half of 61, and 64, none of which were ever in the codex. Written with extraordinary incorrectness, abounding in grotesque errors of grammar and spelling, often not even Greek words at all: seems as if written down from dictation by a scribe imperfectly acquainted with Greek: a few samples are given, all from *Hist. Laus.*

p. 34, **1** ἡδονῆς αὐτῷ ἐπαναστὰς εἰς τῷ σαρκίῳ for ἡδονῆς αὐτῷ ἐπαναστάσης τοῦ σαρκίου.

p. 37, **14** ἐμαρτυρίσαντο τὰ ὑπάρχοντα αὐτοῦ ἐν ἐκείνῃ τῆς ἀς ἔχων for ἐμερίσαντο τὰ ὑπάρχοντα ἐν ἀκινήτοις ἃ ἔσχον.

p. 80, **13** τοῦ ἡμᾶς τοῦ καθελόντες for τὸ οἴημα αὐτοῦ καθελόντες.

Similarly κατακροντες ποιωμενος for κατ᾽ ἄκραν πεποιημένος: πισεὶ for τίς εἶ: μὲν for με ἐν: ἵνα for εἶναι: ἤκους ἔστινα for ἤκουσέν τινα.

Such errors occur on every page; there is throughout an interchange of β and κ: as καίνειν for βαίνεις, καὶ ἀς οὖν for βίας οὖν, παράβηται for παράκειται, βλεψιμαῖοι for κλεψιμαῖοι.

The text of T presents highly curious and interesting features. Its agreements with s in a number of striking readings found nowhere else, have been referred to on p. lxiv; they demonstrate a relationship so close that the facts can be accounted for only by the hypothesis that at a point in the pedigree lower than γ came a MS. of which the ancestors of T and σ were twin offspring. As MSS. of s exist dating from the sixth century, a higher antiquity is established for the peculiar type of text preserved in T than can be claimed by any other known Greek MS. Unfortunately T has suffered extensively from intermixture with a B text.

This intermixture reaches its acme in cc. 17, 18 and 66, 67, 68; in these chapters T has been so contaminated as to become practically a B text: in cc. 8, 14, 15, 16, 19, 21, 37, 61, 62, the same phenomenon is observable, but in a less degree. The large number of cases in the Schedules of § 8 (App. VII), in which T is found ranged with VCβ against PWA, and still more those in which Tβ stand alone, must be, for the most part, attributed to the working of the same process. The textual phenomena as a whole lead to the conclusion that throughout the entire book T has in varying degrees been subjected to this process of contamination by intermixture with a B text. For this reason the value of T as a source for the text is much impaired. The interrelations of T with PW and A will be examined in § 10.

ven—Rosweyd's Codex Venetus.

At the beginning of the "Notatio" to Bk. VIII. of the *Vitae Patrum* Rosweyd speaks of a MS. at that date (1615) at Venice, in the possession of Gabriel, Archbishop of Philadelphia[1]. It is no longer at Venice, and I have been unable to trace it. One MS. from the same collection is now at Milan in the Ambrosian Library[2], and I had hoped ven also might be there.

Excerpts were copied from ven for Rosweyd, as also from a Codex Augustanus (no. 7 in List, § 2): the copy of cod. Aug. is now in the Royal Library at Brussels, but not that of cod. Ven. I thought it might be among papers of Rosweyd in the Bollandist Library, but no trace of it could be found.

Rosweyd records a considerable number of readings of ven in the Notationes to Bk. VIII. and to the Appendices; all these are entered in the apparatus to this edition. They demonstrate a very close affinity between ven and T, which often stand alone in quite peculiar readings. But if Rosweyd's readings can be fully relied on, T is not itself the missing ven, but only a twin MS.; for there are a certain number of slight differences; indeed in Notatio 128 (ed. 1; = 191 ed. 2), Rosweyd records a reading of ven in one of the passages omitted in T (see p. 157, 8).

[1] On this personage and his anomalous ecclesiastical position—he was apparently in communion at once with the Pope and the Orthodox Patriarch of Constantinople—see an art. by Mgr Pisani in vol. I of *Rev. d'Hist. et de Lit. Rel.*

[2] Holl, *Sacra Parallela*, Texte u. Untersuch., N.F. I. i. 15.

A—(Nos 37—44^{c} in List § 2).

As has been explained in § 2, A includes the whole group of MSS. containing what was called in *Prol.* the "Long Recension." This form of the *Hist. Laus.*, besides being interpolated in regard to matter, is composite in regard to text, the *Hist. Laus.* it contains being partly a G text, which has been named A, and partly a B text, distinguished from other types of the B text as A^{B}. The MSS. used for this edition are no. 37, Paris *Gr.* 1626 (saec. XII., parchment), and no. 38, *Coislin* 295 (saec. XIV., paper) (see Preuschen, p. 147): no. 37 is the better MS. but it is not quite complete; no. 38 is therefore the MS. chiefly relied on for A and A^{B} readings: up to p. 126, however, most of the readings have been tested in no. 37 also: when necessary they are distinguished as A^{37} and A^{38}. Some of the Roman MSS. seem to contain slightly better texts, but I had not time to take their readings. A MSS. are extant dating from the tenth century. The archetype of the group will be called *a*.

The text is thus divided between A and A^{B} (the numbers and sequence of chapters are of this edition):

A: cc. 25—28, 30, 31, 35—37, 40, 43, 44, 46, 47, 53—55, 58—60, 71.

A^{B}: Proem, Ep., Prol., cc. 1—24, 29, 32—34, 38, 39, 41, 42, 45, 48—52, 56, 57, 61—70, Epil.

But six lines of c. 7, a considerable section in the middle of c. 18, and a piece in the middle of c. 39 are A; while the opening of c. 54 is A^{B}, and the conclusion nearly A^{B}. These insertions of small pieces of one text in the midst of great masses of the other seem curiously capricious. Nor is this all: throughout the G portions of the text (=A) is found every here and there a characteristic B reading; conversely, throughout the B portions (=A^{B}) is found every here and there a characteristic G reading. Instances of the first will be found in the Schedules in App. VII; the explanation must be that A (like T, but in a far less degree) has been contaminated by intermixture with a B text. Instances of the second will be found in the portions of A^{B} printed from c. 22 in *Prol.* 30—34; the most obvious explanation would be that A^{B} preserves a purer form of the B text than is found elsewhere. Against this theory, however, stands the fact that some of the agreements of A^{B} with PWT are in readings which are certainly erroneous (see Table on p. lxxxv). Moreover the B portions of MSS. 45-46, designated B^{45-6} (see p. xxi), similarly at times present PWT readings where the other B MSS. agree in a rival reading; and in those portions of the B text extant both in B^{45-6} and in A^{B}, sometimes B^{45-6} and sometimes A^{B} agrees with the G MSS., the other going with the great body of B MSS. The following instances from c. 22 will illustrate what I mean:

p. 71, 13	μοχθήσας	μόχθῳ πολλῷ
	PTOW^0	B MSS.
	B^{45-6}	A^B
15	om	τὸ πλέγμα
	PTOW^0	B MSS.
	A^B	B^{45-6}
20	οὔτε ἠγανάκτησεν	οὔτε κἂν πρὸς βραχὺ ἠγανάκτησεν
	PTOW^0	B MSS.
	B^{45-6}	A^B
p. 72, 3	ἐπιρρῖψαι	ἐπιτρέψαι
	POW^0	B MSS. (and T)
	A^B	B^{45-6}
p. 73, 23	κακόγηρε	φαγόγηρε λῆρε
	PTOW^0	B MSS.
		B^{45-6}

A^B combines κακόγηρε λῆρε

On a review of the phenomena throughout, I am disposed to think that it is B^{45-6} that approximates by nature to the G text, and so preserves a purer form of B; and that the G readings found every now and then in A^B were introduced by the scribe, just as he introduced occasional B readings into his G text.

From what has been said it appears that we must conceive the scribe of *α* (the archetype of the group) as having before him two MSS., the one a G MS. of the type PWT, the other a B MS., and as copying out the text now of one, now of the other, intertwining them in a manner that to us is quite unaccountable; and not only so, but often introducing into his transcript of one text individual readings from the other. so that A contains an admixture of A^B, and A^B of A

It has been explained in § 3 that none of Du Duc's Greek text is really A or A^B, and that Hervet's Latin was made from a contaminated copy, and cannot be trusted. This redaction of the *Hist. Laus.* contains two sections (c. 116 and the first paragraph of c. 150 in Du Duc and Hervet) not found in any other form of the work, and of unknown origin: they are not printed in this edition.

V—Venice, St Mark's, *Bessarion* 346.

Saec. XI: parchment: 21 × 28 cm.

Contents: f. 1 apophthegmata in the "topical" redaction (see

Prol. 209), the Greek of Rosweyd's Bks. v. and vi., but cc. 1 and 2 are missing; f. 127 *Hist. Laus.* (see below); f. 173 *Hist. Mon.* 1, 8, 16; ff. 189—208 more apophthegmata and sermons.

C—(Preuschen's C[2]) Paris, Bibl. Nat., *Coislin* 282.

Saec. xi: parchment: 23 × 27 cm.

Contents: f. 1 apophthegmata; f. 100 *Hist. Laus.* (see below); f. 137 *Hist. Mon.* 1, 8, 16; ff. 149—252 apophthegmata, sermons, and Vitae. (This ms. came from Mt. Athos.)

These two mss., in respect of the portions of *Hist. Laus.* and *Hist. Mon.* which they contain, are absolute twins, as is shown by their common peculiarities both of structure and of text. Their readings almost invariably agree, often in contradiction to all other authorities. When they diverge, sometimes V is correct, sometimes C; so that neither is a copy of the other.

These are the mss. numbered 45 and 46 in the List, § 2. It has been pointed out (p. xxi) that the portion of the *Hist. Laus.* contained in them is a composite text, having a section from an A^B ms., a section from a G ms., and a section from a B ms. (p. lxxi). The G section alone is considered here; it alone is designated by V and C: when the other sections are referred to they are cited as 45-46, or B^{45-6}. V occupies ff. 152—163; C ff. 120—130. The chapters of G text are 23—28, 31, 35—39: it appeared in § 8 that the text approximates to that of β, rather than to that of PWTA; and it was shown that the resemblances are not ordinarily due to intermixture with B. Individual cases, however, of such an element may be discerned in VC: a piece elsewhere found only in B is added at the end of c. 39; on p. 115 attention is called to the apparent influence of B in VC; and most of the cases in Schedule II., App. VII, where 1 stands with PWTAs against VCβ, may probably be attributed to intermixture of a B text with VC (see especially p. 105, 5). The apparatus shows that the G text preserved in VC has also been rewritten with considerable freedom. For the rest, the writing, spelling, itacisms, accentuation, &c. are those of fairly correct average mss. of the eleventh century. (On C see Preuschen, p. 148.)

O—Oxford, Bodleian, *Laud. Graec.* 84.

Saec. xi | xii: parchment.

Contains, in a miscellaneous collection of Vitae and Ascetica, on ff. 223—227 a fragment of *Hist. Laus.*: only cc. 32, half of 33, and 22: full of itacisms and absolute misspellings.

W°—ff. 61—70 of W (described above).

Contains cc. 22, 20, 21.

The fact that c. 22 is common to O and W° enables us to see that these two fragments preserve pieces of a single type of G text not found elsewhere: combining them we have cc. 20, 21, 22, 32, half 33. The collations of O are given in full, and those of W° in c. 21; but for W° in c. 20 and c. 22 see infra, p. 177. They show signs throughout of intermixture with B; in c. 32 especially O has been strongly assimilated to B (see Notes 55 and 57).

33—Paris, Bibl. Nat., *Gr.* 919 (Saec. XIV).

A miscellaneous collection of Ascetica: ff. 29—46 contain under the title Ἐκλογαὶ ἐκ τοῦ λαυσαϊκοῦ, *Hist. Mon.* c. 1, *Hist. Laus.* cc. 17, 11, *H. M.* c. 16, *H. L.* cc. 32, 33, 34, 37. The text of *Hist. Laus.* is fundamentally a G text, akin (apparently) to PW; but it has been rewritten and abridged with such freedom that it is only occasionally of service for textual purposes. Besides the rewriting, the text has been further vitiated by intermixture with a B text (see infra, p. 114, and Note 57). The curiously composite MS. no. 47 contains the same text in cc. 17 and 32—34. Full collations of MSS. 33 and 47 are given in c. 32; occasional readings in cc. 33, 34 (and elsewhere).

34—Paris, Bibl. Nat., *Gr.* 881 (Saec. X).

Contains among a collection of Acta and Vitae, on ff. 222—224, c. 32 only: a G text; but so altered as to be of little use for textual purposes: cited only in a few cases.

35—Brit. Mus., *Addit.* 14066 (saec. XII).

Contains in a miscellaneous collection on ff. 164—5, a single episode out of c. 17 (see infra, p. 44. 28—p. 46, 8): a G text, but extensively interpolated with the B enlargements. As PW are the only available authorities for the G text in cc. 17 and 18, the readings of the fragment no. 35 are given in full. When the obvious B interpolations have been removed, no. 35 substantially supports PW.

36—A fragment printed among the "Opera S. Nili" (Migne, *P. G.* LXXIX. 1312).

Contains c. 23 in a G text, akin to PW: free from all admixture of B. Its collations are given in full.

36^b^—Rome, Vatican, *Ottoboni* 436 (saec. XV).

Contains, at f. 186, c. 23 in a G text, but so altered as to be quite valueless: its readings are neglected.

ath—Fragments from c. 63 incorporated in one of the Lives of St Athanasius (see below p. 158): a G text.

This summary description of the Greek MSS. known to me which contain portions of the G text, shows that contamination in a higher or lower degree by mixture with the predominant B text, or else by literary revision, or by both processes, has been the fate of nearly every representative of the G text: PW and the fragments no. 36 and ath are the only ones in which the evidence of such deterioration does not lie on the surface.

B—It remains to speak of the great group of MSS. of the metaphrastic text. The Table on p. xxiii shows that the B MSS. coming under examination fall into seven sub-groups:—1—7, 8—11, 12-13, 14—18, 19—22, 37—44 (the A^B group), 45-46, (the last two groups only in respect of the portions of the B text which they contain). It is, I think, true to say that in some respect or other each one of these sub-groups has preserved more faithfully than any of the others the features of their common ancestor B; so that a critical edition of the metaphrastic text would be an undertaking of extreme difficulty. The sub-group 14—18 presents special features, indicated in Note 11. For the purposes of this edition the value of B lies almost exclusively in the possibility of recovering readings of *β*, the fifth century G MS. from which B was made (see p. xliv): *β* readings are to be identified, in varying degrees of probability, by observing attestations of B by one or more G authorities (often l): only in such cases are B readings regularly recorded, and no inference must ever be drawn from mere silence in regard to B.

(II) The Versions.

1—(*Prol.* 59—64).

It has been shown in § 5 that λ (the Greek MS. from which l was made) was a G MS., and in § 8 that it had a special affinity with *β*. Only three copies of l, and a few fragments, have hitherto been found:

Cod. Sessorianus 41, (l^{sess}), (Vittore Emanuele Library, Rome).
Cod. Casinensis 348, (l^{cass}) }
Cod. Casinensis 50 } (both at Monte Cassino).

Sess. 41 is assigned to the tenth century by Reifferscheid (Sitz. Wien. Akad. L. 772); but Signor Ambrosi, Custodian of MSS. in the Vit. Eman. Library, places it early in the eleventh: Dom Amelli places Cass. 348 late in the eleventh, and Cass. 50 in the twelfth. Cass. 348 was carelessly transcribed and then carefully corrected by the same, or a contemporary, hand: many of the corrections are restorations of the readings of the MS. copied, but many are clearly attempts at emendation that depart from the original. Cass. 50 is a clean copy of 348, adopting all the corrections; thus it is of no independent value as a textual source. Sess. is on the whole the most correct, but it has errors of its own, and also has lost several folios, from the beginning of c. 57 to near the end of c. 65. Sess. and both Cass. MSS. have a lacuna from p. 34, **3** to p. 37, **3**, and another from p. 164, **7** to p. 165, **12**: in each case the text runs on continuously, making complete nonsense, and thus showing that the MSS. are derived from a single exemplar which had lost a folio in each place. A third Cassinese MS., 143 (see *Prol.* 62), contains the text of l for cc. 6, 14, 29, 37, 58, and extracts from cc. 18 and 61 (see p. xxxiv, note), but in a corrupt form: these pieces are printed in *Bibl. Casin.* III. One piece of l is readily accessible in print—the version of c. 34 among the Latin *Apophthegmata* (Rosweyd, Bk V, xviii. 19). The Munich MS. *lat.* 3056 (f. 213) contains extracts from l, but abbreviated.

l^{rev}—l was revised on a Greek B MS. and a considerable number of the metaphrastic enlargements were incorporated from beginning to end. This debased form of l is found in the great majority of the MSS. and in the printed *Paradisus Heraclidis.* The pieces of l printed in the *Bibl. Casin.* and Rosweyd (*locc. citt.*), or in this *Introd.*, or else the apparatus to c. 45, will afford a sufficient idea of the character of l^{rev}. For an edition of l, the better MSS. of l^{rev} (*i.e.* nos. viii.—xi., *Prol.* 60) cannot be neglected; but the fact must be emphasised that for controlling the l readings in this volume only the Sess. and Cass. MSS. may be employed, all others as yet brought to light, as well as the printed text, being worthless for the purpose.

Mr Burkitt's investigation of the biblical citations in l leads him to the conclusion that there is no trace of any Vulgate reading, and to the surmise that l was translated not later than the sixth century, possibly in Africa. The reviser who produced l^{rev} was familiar with the Vulgate. (*Prol.* 70—75.)

l_2—(*Prol.* 64—69).

The MSS. fall into two groups:—

l_2^a—consisting of Brit. Mus. *Addit.* 33518 (f. 104), Barberini *lat.* 702 (f. 193), and Munich *lat.* 3056 (f. 213), 5823 (f. 100), 18553[a] (f. 114), 23757 (f. 129).

These MSS. range from saec. XI—XV.

l_2^b—consisting of the other MSS. known to me, and the printed texts: same date.

The main differences between l_2^a and l_2^b have been sufficiently explained in *Prol.*: l_2^a is on the whole a slightly more correct text.

But better than either are the fragments (cc. 18 (half), 19, 21) in Cod. Cass. 143, printed in *Bibl. Casin.* III.; two instances suffice to show the superiority: *fecit sensatam* instead of *mansuefecit*, p. 58, 2; and *ultima mala*, representing ἔσχατα (for σχάτα or σχάστα) instead of *multa mala*, p. 65, 8.

l_2 contains only fragments of the Ep. to Lausus and the Prologue, and cc. 1—6, 9—13, 16—19, 21, 23, 24, 38, 44, 70: all of this, except the fragment of Ep. (printed p. 6) and a few lines of the Prologue, appears in the printed editions. The date of the translation may be sixth, seventh, or eighth century.

s—(*Prol.* 84—86).

The chief MSS. are:—

Brit. Mus., *Addit.* 17177 (saec. VI).

Contents: cc. 1, 2, 6, 9, 10, 12—14, 16, (of 18, the few lines on Mark), 22, 23, 34, 37, 21.

Brit. Mus., *Addit.* 12173 (saec. VI | VII).

Contents already specified on p. 1, note.

Also in other places, among collections of apophthegmata, cc. 17, 18 (f. 111) and c. 23 (f. 44)—found similarly in other MSS. (see *Prol.* 90—94).

Tullberg's "MS. A" contained cc. 35, 40, 47, 22, 23, 41[a], 63, 57 (half), 60, 70, 29 (print breaks off imperfect): also apparently c. 21. His "MS. B" contained cc. 22, 23.

[The abridgment of c. 8 in *Addit.* 17262 is from a B text.]

Combining these, we find that s is extant, and in sixth century MSS., for Ep. to Lausus, and cc. 1, 2, 6, 9, 10, 12—14, 16—18, 21—23, 25—31, 34—37, 40, 44, 46—48, 50, 51, 53—55, 58, 59 (half), 60, 63, 65, 69—71.

Seeing that there are remains of three or four Syriac versions of the *Hist. Laus.*, the assumption that the above-mentioned MSS. all contain portions of the same version requires justification. It is reasonable to suppose that all the chapters found together in any given MS. containing a whole section of the book, really belong to each other, and are portions of one and the same version. Now Tullberg's A contains chapters in common both with 17177 and with 12173; and so it supplies the link that enables us to identify these two MSS. as containing portions of the same Syriac translation. In regard to cc. 17 and 18, the few lines on Mark (p. 56, 3—10) have been cut out of c. 18 in both 12173 and 14648; but they are found by themselves as one of the series of lives in 17177: this seems good reason for assigning the Syriac of cc. 17 and 18 to the same version as is found in 17177. Moreover we know that this version of c. 18 is not s_2.

In regard to Tullberg's MSS. some difficulty exists. The printing of his edition apparently was not completed; every copy I have seen breaks off at p. 42 in the middle of a sentence in c. 29; consequently no indication is given towards the identification of the MSS. employed. The title contains the general statement that they belong to the Vatican and the British Museum. There can be no doubt that Tullberg's V is the great Vatican copy of Anan-Isho's *Paradise* (Cod. Syr. 126); but neither in the Vatican nor in the British Museum did I find any MS. corresponding to his A; *Addit.* 12173 presents striking resemblances to A, but it does not contain cc. 22 or 23, for which chapters Tullberg cites readings from A. If Tullberg's readings are fairly inaccurate, his B may be *Addit.* 17177, for B is cited only for cc. 22 and 23, the only chapters printed by Tullberg which are found in 17177. He cites also an N and an O in one or two chapters: I can offer no conjecture concerning them. I was not able to search the Propaganda collection in Rome.

s_2—(*Prol.* 86—88).

The chief MSS. are:

Vat. *Syr.* 123, (s_2^{vat}) (saec. VI).

It contains: cc. 1—16, two episodes from 18 (*infra* pp. 49, 52), 19—21, beginning of 22, 23—29 (incomplete, the MS. being mutilated).

Assemani gives as the date century VIII.; but this is certainly an error arising from the fact that the codex is composed of two independent MSS. bound up together: century VIII. is a probable date for the first of them, but the second which contains the *Hist. Laus.* is much older. It is a Nitrian MS., and I at once perceived its likeness to the sixth century Nitrian MSS. at the British Museum. Professor Guidi and Mr Norman McLean independently passed the same judgment; so that I have no hesitation in assigning it to the sixth century.

(Vat. Syr. 371 is a modern transcript of 123.)

Brit. Mus. *Addit.* 12175, (s_2^{add}) (A.D. 534).

Contains: cc. 1—5, 15, 16, 20, 43, 24, 19, 39.

(Brit. Mus., *Addit.* 12172 (saec. IX) contains c. 16.)

Thus of s_2 we have cc. 1—29 (except 17, 18, 22), 39, 43.

The Vat. MS. contains the better text.

An idea of the general character of s and s_2 as translations may be gathered from the Table in § 5, where a literal rendering of half of c. 23 is supplied: see also Appendix V. ii.

s^{an}—(*Prol.* 77—84).

By s^{an} I designate Anan-Isho's Syriac redaction of the *Hist. Laus.* in Bk I. (and a few chapters of Bk II.) of his *Paradise*; it has been printed by Bedjan in his edition of the *Paradise* (*Acta Martyrum* VII). The relations of the text to s and s_2 are much more complex than I had imagined when writing *Prol.* Only after examining Vat. Syr. 123 was I in a position to give a full and precise account of s^{an}, as follows:

Anan-Isho (c. 650) had before him three Syriac MSS. almost identical in contents with *Addit.* 17177 and 12173 of s, and 12175 of s_2; also a copy of the two chapters (17, 18) found among the *Apophthegmata* in 12173 and 14648: he also had a Greek MS. of a B text. He then combined his Syriac MSS. so as to make them supply one another's deficiencies, building them up more or less on the model of his Greek MS., though often retaining the peculiar configuration of the Syriac MSS.: where the Syriac failed he commonly filled up the gap by a translation from his Greek B MS. And so the first portion of his Bk I. is made up thus:—

s		Ep.,			6,		9, 10		12—14,		16—18
s_2				1—5						15,	
fresh trans.	Proem,		Prol.			7, 8		11			

At c. 18 comes a break: c. 19 (s_2) occurs in Bk II.; c. 20 is omitted altogether (though in 12175); c. 21 comes later (after c. 37, as in 17177): thus cc. 22, 23, from s, follow c. 18. For the rest of Bk I. he used s when available, as in 12173, supplying the lacunae by translations from his Greek B MS.; and in Bk II. he used up the remaining pieces of 12175. But Anan-Isho also, especially in the early chapters, revised the Syriac G texts of s and s_2 by means of his Greek B MS., so that his Syriac contains a large admixture of B readings not found in the sixth century Syriac MSS. Fortunately he soon tired of this, and by the time he reached cc. 17 and 18 his Syriac commonly differs only now and then, and slightly, from s or s_2. Throughout the whole book, however, isolated B readings continue to occur, so that it is never safe to trust his text without reference to the MSS. of s and s_2 in their independent state. The more considerable enlargements of B, such as amount to several lines, are usually inserted by Anan-Isho; at the beginning of c. 17 he gives both forms of the short introduction on the Macarii, the G form from his

Syriac MS. and the B form translated from his Greek MS. In the later portion of the book the fact of translation from a B MS. is at once evident, since to find in the midst of a substantially G text, chapters of an absolutely B text, just where there are lacunae in s (as cc. 56, 57, 61, 62), immediately arrests attention; but in the early chapters, owing to the assimilation of the circumjacent G text to the B type, it is not equally obvious.

Anan-Isho's section on Pachomius (cc. 32—34) receives attention in Note 47; the Life of Evagrius (c. 38) in Note 71.

A word of warning to the textual critic is necessary in regard to Bedjan's edition of the *Hist. Laus.* in Anan-Isho. The primary purpose of his edition must always be kept in mind, viz. to supply Syriac literature to his own people. The readings of the earlier MSS. are of no value for this purpose. But as he has added an apparatus purporting to give the full collations of some of the old MSS., among others of *Addit.* 17177 and 12173, it is necessary to point out that this apparatus, owing to its incompleteness and capriciousness, is a snare and pitfall to the Occidental textual critic. Two or three instances will justify this statement. Under the symbol L he gives 3 variants of 12173 in the *Ep. ad Lausum* (Bedjan, pp. 1—4), not including the various Titles; but he omits 14 others, some fully as important as any he includes. Again, in c. 58, at the foot of p. 173 he records that L has ܠܒܒܕ instead of ܠܒܒܪ; but he neglects to state that it omits the first seven lines on the next page, one of the B enlargements inserted by Anan-Isho. Lastly (p. 137), at the beginning of c. 55, he does not notify that L omits the word ܒܐܒܡ, a point of some critical interest, on which, trusting to his text, I was misled when writing *Prol.* 296. These examples suffice to show that Bedjan's collations of L do not dispense us from recourse to the MSS.

c—(*Prol.* 110—128).

The only MSS. given in printed Catalogues are:

Vat. *Cop.* 64 (saec. X).

Contains: Ep. ad Lausum, Prologue, and parts of cc. 9, 10, 38.

Vat. *Cop.* 69 (A.D. 1153).

Contains c. 18 (incomplete).

(See Mai, *Script. vet. nov. Coll.* v, *159, *165: the MSS. mentioned by Zoega are copies of these.)

Bohairic dialect: a G text, akin to l_2.

eth—(*Prol.* 156).

Only cc. 32 and half 33.

A G text, translated with fair literalness (see Note 47).

arm—(*Prol.* 97—106).

The few fragments, so far as they adhere sufficiently closely to the Greek to allow of any judgment, are all B texts; except c. 38, which is beyond question a G text (see Note 71).

ar—(*Prol.* 164).

Only a few scraps of cc. 32, 33: though completely rewritten and paraphrased, features of the B text may be discerned.

One other point remains for brief discussion here. We have seen that in the case of the Greek G MSS. the question of intermixture with B always calls for careful consideration; and we have seen, too, that l has been subjected to extensive and systematic revision on a B text in l^{rev}, and s and s_2 in s^{an}: we have to ask now if there are grounds for suspecting the presence of any minor B element in l l_2 s s_2 c, in the states which have been recognised as substantially G.

l—It has been shown that the general series of agreements of l with B indicates not any adventitious influence of B on l, but an affinity between β and λ. There are, however, two readings of l to which attention may be directed, as conceivably indicating conflation:

p. 11, **17** G εἴδους	B προσώπου	l uultum ac figuram
p. 106, **10** G δάκτυλον ἦραν	B δ. ἀπέκοψαν	l abscidit ac rapuit

l_2—Only in c. 21 have I noticed any serious ground for suspecting B readings in l_2, see the apparatus to p. 67, **10, 11** and p. 68, **18**. See, however, pp. 11, **20**; 18, **22**; 21, **13**; 22, **9**; 44, **22**; 49, **19**; 53, **8**; 54, **15**; 64, **6**.

s—The question may arise as to p. 83, **6** ἐξεστηκὼς τῶν κατὰ φύσιν φρενῶν (see Note 45 fin.); p. 100, **3** λάθρα; p. 101, **1** (apparatus) ὅτι νικήσει αὐτόν; p. 103, **1** καὶ προγινώσκειν πάντα. See also: pp. 15, **7**; 30, **17**; 31, **8**; 36, **7**; 44, **24**; 73, **23**; 76, **3**; 86, **7**; 98, **23**; 99, **4**; 106, **13**; 114, **2**; 135, **2**; 139, **5**.

s_2—See pp. 16, **24**; 17, **7**; 27, **7**; 28, **9**; 38, **14**; 39, **2**: 61, **1**.

c—See pp. 30, **6**; 117, **9**; 118, **11**.

The cases cited are comparatively so few, and when examined are seen to be of a kind that might so easily have arisen independently, that they may safely be neglected.

§ 10. Method of Editing.

Now that all the materials are before us, the question remains: What is the editor to do?

It has already been settled (§ 6) that the proper course to pursue is to edit the G text without including the B enlargements in the apparatus. But of the G text there are two varieties: the βλ type, represented by B and l, with which VC and s_2 in some measure agree; and the γ type, represented by PWTA and s. We have now to make our choice between these two types of the G text.

The discussions of §§ 7 and 8 have shown that the distinctive Bl readings are of two kinds: (*a*) whole sections or considerable passages, found in Bl but omitted in γ; (*b*) minor variants consisting of the addition of a word or a phrase. Each class of reading is occasionally supported by s_2. The series of whole passages in Bl has already been discussed at some length in § 7, and in many cases distinct reason has been shown for accepting them as genuine. The case of the minor Bl readings must now be considered.

As Sozomen is the earliest witness to the text, we must examine the evidence he affords. In the following cases he may be supposed to support Bl:

p. 33, 4 B ἀπελθόντων οὖν αὐτῶν μετὰ βοηθείας πολλῆς **εἰς τὸ συλλαβέσθαι αὐτόν**
l cumque ad eum cum magna multitudine *quo facilius abstraheretur* intrassent
Soz μέλλων δέ ποτε πρὸς χειροτονίαν ἐπισκοπῆς **συλλαμβάνεσθαι**
PWTl_2s_2 ὡς οὖν ἀπῆλθον μετὰ βοηθείας
(s vac)

p. 60, 3 B ἐπειδὴ οὐκ**έτι** ἔξεστί μοι ἀδικεῖν οὐδένα
l quia nulli *ulterius iam* nocere possum
l_2 quia *iam* mihi non expedit nocere aliquem
Soz ὡς μὴ θεμιτὸν αὐτῷ **ἔτι** μηδένα κακῶς ποιεῖν
PTA$^B s_2$ ἐπειδὴ οὐκ ἔξεστί μοι ἀδικεῖν οὐδένα
(Ws vac)

p. 62, 20 B οὐκ ἔλαβέ **τι** παρά τινος
l non ab ullo *aliquid* accepit
Soz οὐδὲ ἐλάμβανέ **τι** παρά του
PTW° οὐκ ἔλαβε παρά τινος
(Wl_2s vac; s_2 om clause: B 14—18 om *τι*, see Note 11.)

p. 124, 8 B ὀρύξας **φρέαρ**
l fecisset sibi *puteum*
Soz **φρέαρ** ὀρύξας
PTVCs_2 ὀρύξας
(Wl_2s vac)

p. 125, 4 B ἐπιστὰς ἡμῖν ὁ μακάριος Πίωρ
l sanctus Pior......adstitit *nobis*
Soz ἐπιστάντα δὲ **αὐτοῖς**......τὸν Πίωρ
PTVCs_2 ἐπιστὰς ὁ Πίωρ
(Wl_2s vac)

p. 158, 4 B ἵνα μή τινα μῶμον δῷ ἐξ ὑπονοίας
l ne *qua*...ex suspicione quorundam uel macula notaretur
Soz ἵνα μή τινα ψόγον ἐξ ὑπονοίας αὐτοῖς προστρίψηται
PWTs ἵνα μή τινι μῶμον δῷ ἐξ ὑπονοίας
(l_2s_2 vac)

(To these without any doubt may be added the piece at p. 34, 6 in Table p. lxxxv.)

In the following cases Soz seems to support PWT against Bls_2

p. 39, 20 B τοιούτου χαρίσματος ἠξιώθη ὡς καταπτύειν δαιμόνων
l talem diuinam gratiam meruit *ut* contempneret daemones
s_2 has ὡς, but not τοιούτου
Soz ἐδόθη χάρις...ὑπερφρονεῖν τῶν δαιμόνων
PWT χαρίσματος ἠξιώθη καταπτύειν δαιμόνων
(l_2s vac)

p. 123, 13 B καὶ ἐσήμανε ὅτι Πίωρ παρεγένετο καὶ ἔξω ἕστηκεν. αἰσθόμενος δὲ τοῦ ψόφου τῆς θύρας κ.τ.λ.
l significauit dicens: Pior uenit et pro foribus assistit. datoque ianuae sono etc.
s_2 punctuates as Bl
Soz καὶ στὰς πρὸ τῆς πατρῴας οἰκίας ἐμήνυσεν ἐληλυθέναι. ἐπεὶ δὲ ψοφεῖν τὴν θύραν ᾔσθετο κ.τ.λ.

<table>
<tr><td>P</td><td rowspan="2">καὶ ἐσήμανεν ὅτι Π.</td><td>παραγέγονε.</td><td>στὰς οὖν ἔξω</td><td rowspan="2">καὶ τοῦ</td></tr>
<tr><td>TVC</td><td>παρεγένετο.</td><td>ἔξω οὖν (δὲ) στάς</td></tr>
</table>

ψόφου τῆς θύρας αἰσθόμενος κ.τ.λ.
(Wl_2s vac: a few unnecessary words are omitted.)

Thus Sozomen's testimony helps little towards a practical judgment as to the choice of text to be made, though he does seem to have had before him some out of the few Bl readings in question.

An examination of the whole series of minor Bl readings shows that they commonly are of the nature of single words or phrases or clauses which help to smoothen the construction, or to colour the narrative, or to suggest a reason for something said or done. In character they are not unlike the so-called Western readings in the Acts: and just as there are minds to whom the Western text of the Acts appeals as the more primitive, so it may be that to some literary critics the βl text of the *Hist. Laus.* will seem the better. For my own part, I do not think that these readings ordinarily improve the text, but rather weaken it by spoiling a terse rapidity of narrative often displayed in the γ text. But the Bl readings are very early; and some may be disposed to hold the view that they are due to a retouching of the text by Palladius himself. Certainly, though γ is the best on the whole, the βl text has some good qualities not shared by γ: in § 7 we have learned that βl almost certainly preserve the true sequence of the chapters in the last third of the book, and also a number of authentic pieces of the text not found in γ; in the next Table we shall see that B and l are consistently free from a number of "tendenziös" alterations in the Greek representatives of γ; and in Notes 45 and 69 will be found further points worthy of consideration.

Amidst these uncertainties the editor's course is clearly pointed out by the logic of facts. Not the very smallest fragment of a β Greek text has yet been brought to light: β is known only through B; even VC are forthcoming only for one-fifth of the book, and in that fifth they do not support nearly all the Bl readings. Under such circumstances any attempted reconstruction of β by inserting the Bl readings into γ, would be neither β nor γ, but a critical figment not representing any text that ever had a real existence: the morsels of B intruded into the text would often not be really β, but the metaphrast's revision; and the adjustments of grammar and construction necessary in order to make way for them would in all probability seldom faithfully reproduce β. The production of a Greek MS. of the β type would alter the situation; but with the materials at hand it is clear that the only historical method of editing the *Hist. Laus.* at the present time is to reproduce the γ text as faithfully as may be. Therefore the minor Bl readings are given only in the apparatus, and the text will present a critical edition of γ. In the case, however, of the whole sections not found in γ but only in Bl (viz. cc. 41^b, 42, 45, 49, 52, discussed in § 7), an approximate text is supplied between square brackets and printed closer; and a few lesser pieces attested by s_2 as well as Bl are inserted in the text between half brackets (⌜ ⌝): the removal of such pieces is easy, and will yield the γ text.

For the reasons developed in § 7 the order of Bl towards the end of the book is adopted.

The only problem that now remains is the investigation of the interrelations of the chief representatives of γ—of PWT and A with one another, and of all with s (see Pedigree, p. lxvii). As a starting point we shall examine the treatment of a number of heretical or suspected names that occur throughout the book. All the authorities, so far as they are in each case extant, are included in the following Table.

p. 29, 16	διδάσκαλος Διοσκόρου τοῦ ἐπισκόπου καὶ Ἀμμωνίου καὶ Εὐσεβίου καὶ Εὐθυμίου τῶν ἀδελφῶν PWBlss_2 (om τῶν ἀδ. ss_2)	διδάσκαλος Διοσκόρου τοῦ ἐπισκόπου καὶ Ἀμμῶνος T ven $A^{B}l_2c$ (Ammonius l_2)
p. 29, 17	καὶ Ὠριγένους PWBlss_2	καὶ Ἰωάννου T ven $A^{B}l_2c$
p. 30, 11	λέγει τῷ οἰκονόμῳ αὐτοῦ Ὠριγένει PWBlss_2	λέγει τῷ οἰκονόμῳ αὐτοῦ Θεοδώρῳ T$A^{B}l_2c$
p. 31, 11	Ὠριγένει τῷ πρεσβυτέρῳ καὶ οἰκονόμῳ καὶ Ἀμμωνίῳ Blss_2	Μακαρίῳ τῷ πρεσβυτέρῳ καὶ Ἀμμῶνι PWT ven $A^{B}l_2c$ (Ἀμμωνίῳ P$A^{B}l_2$: + Theodore c)
p. 31, 18	Ὠριγένης τε καὶ Ἀμμώνιος Bls_2	Θεόδωρός τε καὶ Ἀμμών PWTc (Ἀμμώνιος P: + Theodore and Jacob c)
	(οἱ πατέρες A^{B}: l_2s vac)	
p. 34, 6	ἀνδρῶν ἐλλογίμων Ὠριγένους καὶ Διδύμου καὶ Πιερίου καὶ Στεφάνου B Soz (l^{rev}) (Ὠ. καὶ Δ. καὶ τῶν ἄλλων Soz)	ἀνδρῶν ἐλλογίμων Ἀθανασίου καὶ Βασιλείου PWTA^{B}
	(lsc vac: s_2 om: l_2 paraphr)	
p. 35, 8	Διόσκορος ὁ ἐπίσκοπος PWB$A^{B}ss_2$ (l^{rev}) (om ὁ ἐπ. s)	ὁ Μακάριος Tl_2
	(lc vac)	
p. 35, 9	τὸν μακάριον Εὐάγριον PWB$A^{B}ss_2$ (l^{rev})	τὸν μακάριον Θεόδωρον Tl_2 (Theodorum et Macariolum)
	(lc vac)	
p. 75, 5	τῷ διδασκάλῳ μου Εὐαγρίῳ TVCBlss_2	τῷ διδασκάλῳ μου Εὐλογίῳ PW 35 36 A^{B}
	(l_2 om: c vac)	

p. 78, 1 καὶ Εὐάγριον		καὶ Εὐλόγιον
TVCBls_2		PWl_2
	(A^B om: sc vac)	
p. 81, 5 τὸν μακάριον Εὐάγριον		(τὸν) Μακάριον τὸν πρεσβύτερον
VCBlss_2		PWTA (om τὸν[1])
	(l_2c vac)	
p. 113, 18 μαθητῇ Ὠριγένους		om
VCBls		PWTA 33
	(l_2s_2c vac)	

In every one of these twelve pairs of readings, the reading in the left hand column is manifestly the true one, those on the right being all due to an orthodox "tendenz,"—the desire to get rid of objectionable names, even the very name of Origen when borne by one of the monks. Bl and s_2 (so far as they are extant) are entirely free from this taint; so are VC in the four cases for which they are extant. On the contrary, l_2 and c whenever their readings can be determined (7 and 5 times respectively) uniformly present the corruption. Turning to γ, we find that its Greek representatives pursue no consistent line, but that s when extant always supports Bl (VCs_2): whence it may be inferred that the taint was not in γ itself. When we remember that a close affinity between l_2 and c has already been proved (p. lxv); and when we observe that there is an evident unity about the series of falsifications in the Table (Theodore being substituted for other names three times, Macarius three times, Eulogius twice); we shall, in view of the various facts just recited, easily conclude that these corruptions in proper names arose in, and spread from, a Greek MS. of the type represented by l_2 and c.

The phenomena presented by PWTA (and A^B) in the Table are very curious, and very instructive for the present investigation into the character of these MSS. At the outset it must be again emphasised that the close textual affinity of the four MSS. PWT*a* (the archetype of the A MSS.), and their descent from a single ancestor γ, from which they inherited serious dislocations of the text, have been established in §§ 7 and 8. PW consistently go together in the Table; and in the two cases in which A (as distinguished from A^B) is extant, it goes with PWT. But the proceedings of T are very perplexing. It would seem that T and A^B have come more under the influence of the archetype of l_2c than have PW; this appears from the Table, and also from the passage p. 48, **25**—p. 49, **2**, where $TA^{B}l_2$ agree in a recasting of the text against the united witness of PBls (Ws_2 c vac.)[1]: see also Tl_2 at p. 49, **27**. The presence of T on the left hand in the passages in the Table taken from p. 75, **5** and p. 78, **1** may reasonably be attributed to the influence of B, which in varying degrees pervades T.

The most important result to be derived from the Table is that s in every case has preserved the original reading where the Greek representatives of γ have gone wrong, sometimes all of them together. This shows that corruptions from which s is free, have crept into the Greek γ MSS. at some time between the end of the fifth century (the date of s) and the tenth (the date of W and the earliest A MSS.). In such cases the agreement of s with Bl (VCs_2) shows that they, and not PWTA, have preserved the true γ reading. Similar instances occur throughout the book; there is a good one at p. 82, **6**, where s supports $VCBls_2$ in reading *τὸ δὴ λεγόμενον*, omitted by PWTA. Where s thus bears witness against the Greek representatives of γ, its evidence is to be followed. For this reason I have relegated to footnotes a series of passages in c. 18 (see p. 50, **5** and **9**, p. 51, **1**, p. 57, **12**) found in $PWTA^{B}l_2$ (and c when extant), but not in Bls (or s_2 when extant)[2]; their absence from s shows them to be interpolations, arising, probably, from Greek MSS. like the originals of l_2 and c. (The case of s is further discussed in Appendix V. ii.)

It is difficult to imagine how it can have come to pass that, though s has often thus kept right when PWTA have all gone wrong, at other times Ts agree in error, when PWA are right in company with Bl (see instances cited p. lxiv); while at p. 147, **3** TAs agree in the error *ἀδελφῆς* (see Note 95): moreover at p. 149, **3** P and s give *ἁπλότης* incorrectly for the *ἁπαλότης* of TABl (W vac); and at 137, **9** A and s alone read *ὁ μακάριος Εὐάγριος*.

And when we neglect s and consider only the Greek γ MSS., their interrelations are found to be no less perplexing. All the following combinations occur, most of them frequently:

[1] Such departures of A^{B} from B, where B is correct, form one of the grounds for surmising that A^{B} has been in some measure revised by a γ MS. (perhaps akin to T): (see p. lxxii).

[2] The addition at p. 50, 9 is not in W, and the context of p. 57 is completely lost.

PA	v.	WT(B)	WA	v.	PT(B)
PT	v.	WA(B)	WT	v.	PA(B)
TA	v.	PW(B)	WA	v.	PT(B)
PB	v.	WTA	WB	v.	PTA

Nor is this all: sometimes agreements in error are found, of a kind that indicate descent from a common ancestor: thus at p. 130, **17** TA have *πρὸς ἡμέρας* for *πρὸ ἡμέρας*, and p. 138, **19** they have *πᾶσιν* for *πρᾶξιν*; similarly at p. 147, **1** PA have *'Απριανόν* for *'Απρονιανόν* (see Note 95), and p. 168, **12** for the *μηδένα νύξαι* of TBls, we find in A *μηδὲν ἀνοῖξαι*, and in P *μηδαμῶς ἀνοῖξαι* with further alterations of the text. At other times, too, PT agree in such corruptions: at p. 79, **3** they read *φύσεως* for *φυσιώσεως*; and PT (but not A or s) append to the account of Silvania (c. 55, p. 149) a couple of lines which stand at the end of the story of Juliana (c. 64, p. 160) in Bl, and are repeated there word for word in P, (c. 64 is missing in T and in s).

Still more unaccountable are such cross divisions as the following:

p. 107, **6** *διεγενόμην*		*διεγενόμην*
WTA^{37}VB(l)	(om s)	PA^{38}C
p. 109, **5** *εὐγράμματος*		*ἀγράμματος*
WTA^{40}VBl		PA^{cet}33Cs

With the present materials it is futile to speculate on the hidden cross-currents that have given rise to results so inconsistent and seemingly defying all attempts at clear-cut classification. But whatever the explanations may be, the main textual facts acquired during the foregoing discussions stand out unmistakably, and cannot be obscured by the crowd of outstanding unexplained difficulties, which must be dealt with individually as they occur. The process known as "Intermixture of texts" has evidently been busily at work, and in a very subtle manner, among the ancestors of the MSS. with which we are occupied. We have seen (p. lxx) that T has been extensively contaminated throughout by mixture with a B text; and so the large number of TB readings seldom cause any embarrassment: and this is true also, and for the like reason, in regard to most of the AB readings. We have now to ask the question: Have P and W, the protagonists of the Greek members of the γ group, been subjected in any measure to similar deteriorating influences? We shall take first the case of P.

P. P has the Proem, found elsewhere only in B (see Note 1). Notes 4 and 31 contain further evidence of P having been corrupted by B. Sched. I in App. VII presents three cases in which PB stand together against WTA and VC; only one is sufficiently clear to be made the basis of an argument:

p. 113, 13 WTAVC ἐκεῖνοι δὲ οὔτε (οὐδὲ AVC) ἑκατὸν χρυσίνων ἡδέως (+οὐκ A) ἂν ἕλυον
P ἐκεῖνοι δὲ οὐδὲ εἰς ἑκατὸν χρυσίνους ἡδέως ἂν τοῦτο ἐποίουν
B λέγουσι·......οὔτε εἰ ἑκατὸν ἐδίδως χρύσινα τοῦτο ἐποιοῦμεν ἡδέως

Outside the Schedules we find:

p. 77, 3 οὐδὲ οὕτως ἐδήχθην PBl; οὐκ ἐδήχθην WT36VCss$_2$
p. 76, 4 the word αἰσχρῶς found in PVCBl, but not in WT36l$_2$ss$_2$

Of cases in which VC are not extant the following deserve consideration:

p. 48, 12 W ὀπῆς· ὡς τελώνης γάρ μοι οὐ συνεχώρει (see p. 173)
T ὀπῆς· ὁ τελώνης γάρ, φησί, οὐ συνεχώρει
P ὀπῆς· τὸ γὰρ παντελῶς μὴ ἐσθίειν ὁ τελώνης μοι οὐ συνεχώρει
B ὀπῆς· ὁ τελώνης γάρ μου οὐ συνεχώρει, φησί, τὸ παντελῶς μὴ ἐσθίειν

(Neither l nor s have any trace of the clause τὸ παντελῶς μὴ ἐσθίειν: Al$_2$s$_2$ vac)

p. 95, 11 the words ἀσθενέστεροι ὄντες found in PA^B and, with a slight difference, in B; but omitted in T and the other extant representatives of G (W vac)

p. 139, 5 WTs ἢ εἰς αἰσχρουργίαν ἢ εἰς αἰσχροπάθειαν καὶ αἰσχύνην ληφθέντες
P ἢ εἰς αἰσχρουργίαν ἢ αἰσχροπάθειαν περιπίπτουσι καὶ αἰσχύνῃ ληφθέντες
B(l) ἐμπίπτουσιν εἰς αἰσχρουργίαν ἢ αἰσχροπάθειαν καὶ αἰσχύνην
(A om)

p. 143, 9 WTls ὡς (+τὸν T) ἥλιον διαφαίνειν αὐτοῦ τῶν ὀστέων
P ὡς τὸν ἥλιον διαφαίνειν αὐτοῦ τῶν ὀστέων τὸ πῆγμα
B ὡς ἥλιον διαφαίνειν αὐτοῦ τῶν ὀστέων τὸ πῆγμα
(A vac)

It is not, I think, open to doubt that in all these cases the P reading is the result of assimilation to B; we shall therefore be prepared to find throughout the book a number of readings, less striking than these, also supported by PB, which are due to the same cause having been at work in P: (see Note 101).

W. Sched. I in App. VII contains two cases in which WB stand together against PTA and VC, but neither is significant. There is, however, at the beginning of the Prologue (p. 9, **12**) a long insertion in W, found in B, but not in any other authority for the text (see p. 170). The following appear to be cases of the same phenomenon:

p. 17, **15** PT *εἰ μή τι ἐργαζόμενος ἢ ἐσθίων*
Soz *πλὴν ὅσον ἐργαζόμενος ἢ ἐσθίων*
W *εἰ μή τι ἐν τῷ ἐργάζεσθαι αὐτὸν ἢ ἐσθίειν*
B *εἰ μή τι* (al. *που*) *ἐν τῷ ἐργάζεσθαι ἢ ἐσθίειν*
p. 27, **6** PT *σύμβιον* WBl *γνησίαν σύζυγον*
p. 41, **8** PT *κέλλαν* WB *σκέπην*
p. 48, **19** PT *τῇ δὲ νυκτὶ στυφόμενος τῇ ψυχρότητι*
WB *τῇ δὲ νυκτερινῇ στυφόμενος ψυχρότητι*

(In none of these cases is A extant, or do the versions help)

Except in the piece in the Prologue, and in that at p. 17, **15** (where Sozomen's witness seems very significant) the idea that B may have exercised a direct influence on W hardly rises above a suspicion, for the traces of B are few and slight—I have found no others sufficiently clear to be worthy of individual mention. Thus W is much freer than P from any taint of B. At the same time, the large number of minor readings on p. 170—5 in which WB stand against PT, and WT against PB, cannot but give rise to the suspicion that W and P have both suffered to an appreciable extent from intermixture with B.

PW. We have yet to consider whether P and W have inherited in common from their proximate ancestor any admixture of B readings. Here again the passages at the beginning of the Prologue, discussed in Note 4, compel us to return an affirmative answer. In the greater portion of the book, although the combination PWB v. TA frequently occurs, it is impossible to say whether PW have been corrupted by B, or TA have gone wrong together, as they certainly sometimes do. But in the portions of the text for which VC are available it may be possible to form a judgment on some such readings. The following passage is the chief instance:

p. 111, **4—7** (a few non-significant words are omitted):

TAVC (*καὶ* A) *προσδραμόντες δὲ* (om A) *ἄπαντες.............λέγουσιν αὐτῷ·*
PW *καὶ προσδραμόντες ὑφ' ἓν......λέγουσιν αὐτῷ·*
B *συνδραμόντες δὲ πάντες ὑφ' ἓν......λέγουσιν αὐτῷ·*
TAVC *Τί ἔχεις; καὶ πόθεν εἶ; καὶ τί πάσχεις; τότε* (om A) *λέγει*
PW *Τί ἔχεις, ἄνθρωπε; ἢ πόθεν εἶ; ἢ τί πάσχεις; λέγει*
B *Τί ἔχεις, ἄνθρωπε; ἢ πόθεν εἶ; ἢ τί πάσχεις; λέγει*
TAVC *αὐτοῖς·...τρίσι περιέπεσα* (-*σον* VC) *δανεισταῖς*
PW *αὐτοῖς·...τρίσι δανεισταῖς περιέπεσα*
B *αὐτοῖς·...τρίσι δανεισταῖς περιέπεσα*

When it is stated that s omits *ὑφ' ἓν* and *ἄνθρωπε*, and has *καὶ - - καὶ*, it will be difficult to resist the conclusion that the text of the common proximate ancestor of P and W had been assimilated to B in the foregoing passage, (or to *β*, for l is doubtful).

The following also may be noticed:

p. 106, **12** PWB *ἔβαψαν*	TAVC *ἔρριψαν*
p. 112, **2** PWB *ἕνα ἄρτον*	TAVC om *ἕνα*
p. 78, **4** PWB(A^B) *ἐπιμελούμενον*	TVC *τημελούμενον*
p. 144, **20** PWB *ἄρτους νεαρούς*	Tls om *νεαρούς*

From the foregoing investigations it follows that every single known Greek representative of the G text, with the possible exception of the fragments 36 and ath, has been to a greater or less extent contaminated by admixtures of B. In W, however, this element is sufficiently slight to be in practice negligible.

It is clear that P and W have to serve as the basis of the text, pre-eminently W where it is extant: but owing to the numerous and great gaps in W, P must still, even after the production of W, remain the principal MS. In those portions of the text for which a number of other G MSS. exist, it is possible to eliminate many, perhaps most, of the eccentricities of P and W, and to recover a text probably representing with fair accuracy that of *γ*. But where PWT are the only G MSS., and still more in the considerable sections where PT are the only G MSS., it is impossible to attain to any such security. An instructive example lies before us in the portion of the book, up to p. 54, printed off before the finding of W. Choice had to be made again and again between a reading supported by P and one supported by TB. On the one hand, I knew very well from later portions of the text that P has throughout a number of singular readings which are corruptions proper to itself; but on the other hand, still more frequent are the corruptions of T through assimilation to B, so that no confidence can be had in any reading supported merely by TB. Under these circumstances I elected to follow P in this whole class of readings, as it seemed that thus I should be less often in error than by following TB throughout:—and seldom are the readings of a kind in which intrinsic criteria of truth could be applied. The effect of W on the text may be seen by a glance at p. 170—5; W supports P much more frequently than it does TB; but often it does support TB, and often T: and in these cases its witness against P is decisive and final. Unfortunately W and P are very closely akin; and without any doubt the production of an independent G MS.,—*e.g.* one of the type of T, but free from the special corruptions of T,—would reveal the fact that several of the PW readings are false, and perhaps would call for greater alterations in the text than did W. In such cases as chapters 20, 21, 22, where W fails, but another G MS., viz. W°, is extant, a similar difficulty has to be faced. A large number of readings are supported by TW°B against P. We have seen that W° is tainted by B, though in a less degree than, and quite independently of, T: it is in each case possible that the agreement of T and W° with B may be due to accidental coincidence in assimilation to B. But a few lines of W are extant towards the end of c. 21, and in the single instance of TW°B that occurs in this piece (p. 68, 17 ἀφηγησάμενος), W goes with them against P, thus showing that many of the rejected TW°B readings are probably the true ones. Yet even in this series of readings I have thought it best to follow P, though with the full knowledge that often I must be leaning on a broken reed: the advantages of preserving a more homogeneous text seemed to outweigh the possible slightly greater accuracy that might have been obtained in the three chapters in question.

And so I have throughout endeavoured to adhere to the

principle of following PW (where W is extant), and P (where W is not extant), unless there be positive reasons for departing from them: where P and W differ I incline to W; but if T side with either of them I allow it to turn the balance. Thus I have throughout sought to construct the text by an objective method, choosing not that reading which seems in itself the best, but that one which seems best attested; and, except in a very small number of cases of evident corruption, I have excluded conjectural emendations, however attractive. Sometimes I have printed between † † words certainly corrupt (see p. 181)[1].

From all that has gone before, the practical conclusion follows that a text constructed out of materials of the kind at my disposal cannot pretend to finality: even under far more favourable conditions, the best critically constructed text can claim no more than to be an approximation to the original. I am painfully aware that on most pages there are readings in the apparatus just as likely to be the true ones as those in the text. In saying this, I do not for a moment doubt that the present edition is an immeasurably nearer approach than any of its forerunners to what Palladius wrote; nay more, I do not doubt that in substantials it reproduces the original with correctness. Beyond this it is not at present possible to go.

What may rightly be expected of an editor is that he should report fully and accurately the readings of the MSS. which he undertakes to record. I have taken exceeding pains to secure completeness and accuracy in collation and in the apparatus.

In the case of P, I constructed the text from Dr Preuschen's collations, which he kindly placed at my disposal; I then verified my text throughout,

[1] Friends in whose judgment I have much confidence have suggested various emendations: for instance at p. 71, 16 *σκῆψιν* for *σῆψιν* (O reads *σκέψιν*); p. 71, 18 *ἐρυσιβοῦσθαι* (suggested by B's *ἐρυσιδωμένους*) for *ἐρρυτιδῶσθαι*; p. 72, 6 *ψάλλει ψαλμόν* for *βάλλει ψαλμόν*. But in these, and in all cases in which the readings of the MSS. give any tolerable sense, I have followed their evidence. Thus *ἐπαγαγὼν τὴν σῆψιν* may mean "giving him a nausea, a disgust, a sickening (as we should say) of the monastic life": *ῥυτιδόω* ("wrinkled") suits the context far better than *ἐρυσιβόω* ("mildewed"): and as for *βάλλειν ψαλμόν*, I have found in the Apophthegmata (Macarius, no. 33, Romanus, no. 1) *βάλλειν τοὺς δώδεκα ψαλμούς*; also (Arsenius, no. 24, Theodora, no. 3) what seems to be an analogous expression, *βάλλειν* (al. *ποιεῖν*) *τὴν σύναξιν*: these cases suggest a technical use of *βάλλειν*.

first in manuscript, and again in proof, with P itself: I have to thank M. Léopold Delisle, Librarian at the Bibliothèque Nationale, for sending this MS., and also *Coislin* 295 (A), to the University Library, Cambridge, for my use.

At the time of my finding W the printing of the first portion of the text was in too advanced a stage to allow the evidence of W to be taken into account, so that up to p. 100 it was possible only to append a list of the differences of W from P (pp. 170—5); from p. 100 onwards the readings of W are incorporated in the manner explained in the note on that page. I collated W on my own proofs, but I have not had time to revise my collation on the MS. I have to thank the Wake Trustees for placing the MS. in the Bodleian to render it more easily accessible to me.

Through the courtesy of the Librarians of the University Library at Turin and the Vittore Emanuele Library at Rome, I was able to collate T in the latter library. My text and apparatus were compared, partly in proof and partly in manuscript, with T by Dom Rylance.

I collated V at Venice and constructed my text from these collations; I then compared the text in manuscript with C. All the readings wherein V and C differed were then checked for me by Dom Rylance, first with V, and then with C. The proofs of the long chapters 35 and 38 (John of Lycopolis and Evagrius) were compared with *Coislin* 282 itself by experienced eyes without the detection of a single omission or other error in the readings of C.

For A and O and W^o, and the other G fragments, all the readings have been revised in proof on the respective MSS. As explained on p. lxxi, *Coislin* 295 has been made the primary authority for A, so that A and A^B are to be taken as referring specifically to it.

As B is a large group of MSS. embracing a number of sub-groups, there must be a certain relativity about the B readings, dependent on the number and variety of B MSS. I have been able to consult in each individual case: to take any one MS. as spokesman for the whole class would have been altogether misleading. For cc. 19—42 a number of representative MSS. have been consulted for each B reading, and from c. 43 to the end four or five authorities have been employed; but for the first eighteen chapters most of the B readings depend on Meursius and Du Duc, for I unaccountably neglected to test them by the two Brit. Mus. MSS.: the defect has been remedied in part in the List of Readings of W (p. 170). Such rectifications would seldom or never affect the text, and would come to no more than that in the apparatus TB† should sometimes be read instead of TB or T. Only occasional B readings are included, in so far as they help to determine G; and the symbol *B* is used throughout the apparatus, to indicate that the readings are not those of any definite MS., but what appear to be the resultant readings of the group, so far as may be judged from the MSS. used in each case.

In regard to the versions, I took the readings of l from Cass. 348, often compared with Sess., and those of l_2 from *Addit.* 33518; many of the l readings have been checked by Dom Amelli and Dom Rylance. In the cases of s and s_2^{add} the readings have been carefully tested in proof: s_2^{vat} was examined by me at an early stage, and I have not had an opportunity of testing the accuracy or completeness of the s_2 readings that depend upon it. For c and arm I am indebted to the late Rev. Forbes Robinson and Dr Armitage Robinson respectively: but it is to be understood that they only answered my questions, and are not responsible for any omissions in the readings of these versions.

P being the principal MS., its spelling is followed; and this is the explanation of apparent inconsistencies, as in the employment of *σσ* and *ττ*, *οὕτως* and *οὕτω*; its practice has been adopted too in such points as the *ν* ephelk.: but adverbial expressions, as *καθυπερβολήν*, *ἐσύστερον*, are printed as two words. The itacisms and absolute mis-spellings and other errors, whether of P or any other MS., are not commonly recorded; though, indeed, it is quite possible that an expert in Byzantine Greek might recognise in some of the rejected forms examples of fourth century usage. But in the case of the Greek authorities named at the head of each portion of the apparatus, and not included in square brackets, all readings other than mere spellings are intended to be included, so that the argument from silence is to be rigidly applied. In the case of the versions, following Bishop Lightfoot's example in his edition of the Ignatian Epistles, I have as a rule recorded only those readings which may be supposed to represent Greek readings; I have, however, aimed at including readings apparently supported by two versions, even if there is no extant Greek attestation.

The various marks and abbreviations used are sufficiently explained in the "List of Symbols" (p. 2): it should have been there stated, however, that P* C* bear their recognised meaning of "original reading," P^{cor} C^{cor} signifying corrections, whether of "m. 1" (the first hand), or "m. 2" (a later one).

In W, l, B^{8-11}, and perhaps in s and s_2, the text is continuous; accordingly I believe there was originally no division into chapters. I therefore omit the titles in the text; but for convenience of reference, I number the chapters, following the authority which in each case seems to make the most reasonable division.

With this by way of introduction and explanation, I commit my edition of the Lausiac History to the judgment of the critics. One criticism there is which I feel the work will not deserve—the charge of failure on the part of the editor to take trouble, even in a measure which has at times caused a sense of oppression, as being perhaps disproportionate to the importance of the results achieved.

NOTE (to p. xvii).

The List of Greek MSS. in § 2 was made out before the appearance of Gardthausen's *Sammlungen u. Cataloge griechischer Handschriften* (Byzantinisches Archiv 3, Leipzig, 1903). This work has, however, guided me only to one additional MS.—that at Andros. Thus the claim made on p. xvii—viz. that I have dealt with all catalogued Greek MSS. of *Hist. Laus.* in Western Europe—still holds good, and indeed may be put forward with increased confidence. I have myself, by personal examination or by enquiry, made sure of the ground in England. Thanks to the various Lists due to MM. Omont, Graux, and Martin, the like security may be felt in regard to France, Switzerland, Holland, Belgium, Spain, Portugal, Sweden and Denmark. I have examined very nearly all the actual catalogues and lists mentioned by Gardthausen under Italy, Germany and Austria. It is not likely that there are any Greek MSS. of *Hist. Laus.* still lurking in German libraries; but in Italy, especially South Italy, there may well be some in the collections still uncatalogued. In regard to the Russian, Hellenic and Turkish dominions I do not pretend to any completeness, having examined only the more important catalogues.

The above statements are subject to two reservations:

(1) I have had to trust to the catalogues: but the case of the *Wdke* MS. (see p. lxviii) shows what surprises may be in store for anyone who turns over the pages even of MSS. described in competent catalogues.

(2) Most of the catalogues take count only of full copies or independent fragments of the various works, and do not mention mere extracts in *Catenae* and similar collections: since my last visit to Paris I have noticed that various *Coislin* MSS. (37, 117, 118, 122, 363) contain extracts from *Hist. Laus.* indicated in Montfaucon's *Bibl. Coisliniana*, but naturally omitted in Omont's *Inventaire Sommaire*; I regret that I have not had an opportunity of seeing if any of these extracts contain the G text.

MAP OF MONASTIC EGYPT (400 A.D.).

CHRONOLOGICAL TABLE.

The map illustrates the strictly monastic references in *Hist. Laus.*, *Hist. Mon.*, *Vita Antonii*, *Vita Pachomii*, *Apophthegmata*, *Cassian*, and other sources of the same date for the history of Egyptian monachism. An elaborate map, illustrating the whole course of Egyptian monastic history, is supplied in Evetts' ed. of Abu Salih's *Churches and Monasteries of Egypt* (Anecdota Oxon., Semitic Series VII).

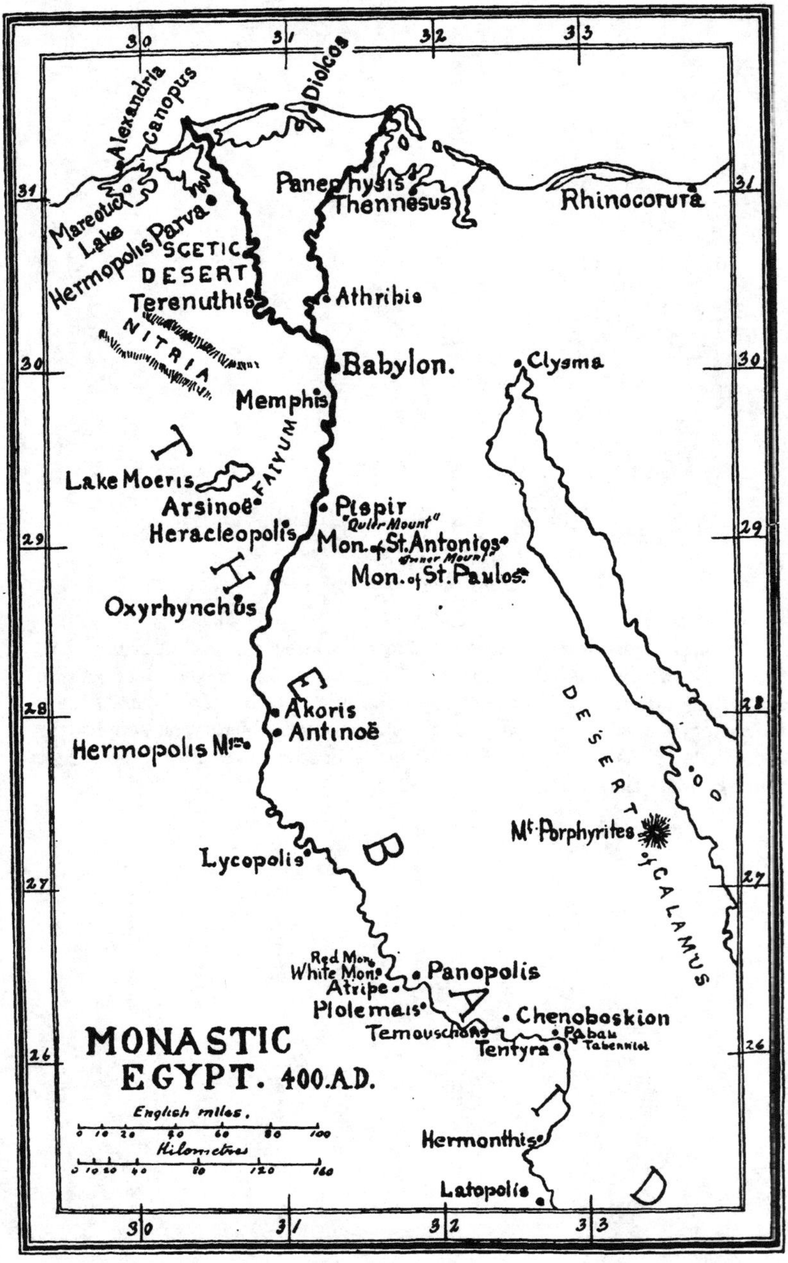
MONASTIC EGYPT. 400 A.D.
English miles
0 10 20 40 60 80 100
Kilometres
0 10 20 40 80 120 160
30
31
32
33
Alexandria
Canopus
Diolcos
Mareotic Lake
Hermopolis Parva
SCETIC DESERT
Terenuthis
NITRIA
Panephysis
Thennesus
Rhinocorura
Athribis
Babylon.
Clysma
Memphis
FAIYUM
Lake Moeris
Arsinoë
Heracleopolis
Pispir
"Outer Mount"
Mon. of St. Antonios
"Inner Mount"
Mon. of St. Paulos
Oxyrhynchus
THEBAID
Akoris
Antinoë
Hermopolis Ma.
DESERT of CALAMUS
Mt. Porphyrites
Lycopolis
Red Mon.
White Mon.
Atripe
Panopolis
Ptolemais
Chenoboskion
Temouschons
Pabau
Tabennisi
Tentyra
Hermonthis
Latopolis
29
28
27
26

Diolcos: *Hist. Mon.* 32, 33 (Soz. VI 29, Nicephorus, XI 35); Cassian, *Inst.* V 36, *Coll.* XVIII 1. I have been able to find no other references at all to Diolcos, so that its site is conjectural; it is placed in the position that seems to be indicated in *Hist. Mon.* and Cassian.

Canopus: Pachomian monastery, see Note 54.

Alexandria: monks in the neighbourhood, *Hist. Laus.* 1, 2, 5, 7 (*init.*).

Panephysis:
Thennesus (San): } Cassian (*Prol.* 204).

Rhinocorura: Sozomen VI 31 (*fin.*).

Hermopolis Parva (Damanhour): the bishop of Hermopolis was ordinary of Nitria and Scete.

Nitria, Cellia, and Scete: see Note 14.

Terenuthis: see Note 14.

Athribis: see Note 46.

Clysma (Suez): see *Prol.* 218.

Babylon (Fostal: close to Cairo)
Memphis (Tel Monf) } *Hist. Mon.* 20[1].

Arsinoë (Medinet el Faiyum): *Hist. Mon.* 20.

Heracleopolis (Ahnas el Medineh): *Hist. Mon.* 16.

Pispir (Der el Memun): the "Outer Mountain of Anthony"; see Note 37.

Mon. of St Anthony (Der Mar Antonios): the "Inner Mountain of Anthony"; see Note 37 and *Prol.* 231–2.

Mon. of St Paulos (Der Mar Boulos): the abode of Paul the Hermit; see Note 40 and *Prol.* 231–2.

Oxyrhynchus (Behneseh): *Hist. Mon.* 5.

Akoris (Tehneh): *Hist. Mon.* 14.

Antinoë (Sheikh Abadeh): *Hist. Laus.* 58–60, *Hist. Mon.* 7; see Note 69.

Hermopolis Magna (Eshmunen or Schmoun): *Hist. Mon.* 3, 8; Pachomian monasteries, see Note 54.

Lycopolis (Asyut or Siout): *Hist. Laus.* 35, *Hist. Mon.* 1; see Note 61.

Mount Porphyrites
Desert of Calamus } see Note 60.

Red Monastery of abbot Bishoi.

White Monastery of Bgoul and Schenoudi: see Note 46.

Atripè or Athribis: see Note 46.

Panopolis (Akhmim): *Hist. Laus.* 32; Pachomian monasteries, see Note 54.

Ptolemais (Absai el Menshiyeh)
Temouschons (Bahgoura ?)
Chenoboskion (Schenesit)
Pabau (Faou)
Tabennisi (Dechna ?)
Hermonthis (Erment)
Latopolis (Esneh) } Pachomian monasteries; see Note 54. (The sites of others cannot be determined.)

Tentyra (Denderah): the bishopric in which was situated the first group of Pachomian monasteries.

[1] For the Itinerary of *Hist. Mon.* see *Prol.* 201, with correction in Note 37.

Chronological Table

illustrating early monastic history, with special reference to the *Historia Lausiaca.* Few of the dates can be fixed with certainty within a year or two: those to which c. is prefixed are but approximations.

c. 250 During the Decian persecution many Christians in Egypt fled out of the cities and villages to the deserts and mountains; it is possible that one of these, named Paul, may have remained permanently in a mountain by the Red Sea (see *Prol.* 230–1).

St Anthony born.

250—270 Christian ascetics began to dwell in huts in the neighbourhood of the towns and villages of Egypt.

270[1] St Anthony adopts this mode of life.

285 St Anthony withdraws to Pispir.

292 St Pachomius born.

305 St Anthony comes out of his cave and organises the monastic life for the disciples that had gathered around him: **Inauguration of Christian Monachism**: St Anthony withdraws to the monastery by the Red Sea.

c. 310 St Hilarion visits St Anthony, and initiates monastic life in Palestine.

314 St Pachomius becomes a monk.

c. 318[2] He founds the first Christian monastery, at Tabennisi.

c. 325 Mar Awgin an Egyptian founds monastery at Nisibis,—beginnings of Mesopotamian and Syriac monachism (*Prol.* 218).

c. 320—330 Amoun inaugurates Nitrian monachism.

c. 330 Macarius of Egypt becomes a monk in Scete.

c. 333 St Athanasius' first visit to the Thebaid and Tabennisi.

[1] St Anthony's dates depend on the statements of the *Vita*, combined with St Jerome's entry in his *Chronicle*, that he died in the year equivalent to 356 or 357.

[2] The series of Tabennesiot dates are those of Ladeuze which appear on the whole to be the most carefully considered, and are accepted by Leipoldt: 340, 345, 348 have all been defended as the year of Pachomius' death; and 300, 305 for the foundation of Tabennisi (see Note 49).

c. 335 Macarius of Alexandria becomes a monk.
St Epiphanius, after spending some years in Egypt, founds monastery near Besanduke in Palestine (*Prol.* 219).

340 St Athanasius, Ammonius the Tall and Isidore in Rome, propagate monastic idea in Rome and Italy.

341 St Anthony visits Paul the hermit (?).

343 (?)[1] Schenoudi becomes monk at 9 years of age, under his uncle Bgoul at the White Monastery.

c. 345 John of Lycopolis encloses himself in his cave.

346[2] Death of Pachomius: Petronius succeeds as Superior General, but dies: Horsiesi succeeds.

350 Theodore becomes coadjutor to Horsiesi.

352 Ammon, writer of the *Ep. ad Theophilum*, goes to Tabennisi.

356—362 St Athanasius, driven from Alexandria, lies in concealment with the monks of Thebaid.

356-7 St Anthony dies.

c. 360 St Basil forms monastery at Neocaesarea in Pontus.
First Armenian monastery, under Nerses the Great.
St Martin inaugurates Gallic monachism at Ligugé, near Poitiers.
St Eusebius combines clerical and monastic life at Vercelli.

363 St Athanasius visits Tabennesiot monasteries.

365 (or 373) First Civil Edict concerning monks (Valens).

368 Death of Theodore of Tabennisi; Horsiesi resumes government of Tabennesiot order.

c. 372 St Martin founds Marmoutier at Tours.

373 Melania the Elder visits Egypt and Nitria: death of Pambo.

374 Banishment of Nitrian monks to Palestine.

c. 375 Rufinus in Egypt, at Nitria and Pispir.

376-7—398 Rufinus and Melania at Jerusalem.

c. 380 St Ambrose's monasteries at Milan.

380 C. of Saragossa forbids clerics to become monks—shows the spread of the institute in Spain[3].

382—399 Evagrius in Nitria and Cellia: he dies in 399.

c. 385 Monachism introduced into Babylonia and Arabia.

385 SS. Jerome and Paula in Egypt, in Nitria.

386—404 „ „ at Bethlehem: Paula dies 404.

386-8 Palladius at Bethlehem.

388—399 Palladius at Alexandria, Nitria and Cellia.

390—400 Cassian in Egypt and Scete.

[1] This date depends on statements of the *Lives* that Schenoudi was a monk during 109 years: see Leipoldt, 46.

[2] See Note 2 on preceding page.

[3] Dom Ferotin tells me there is no direct evidence of any monastery in Spain before the sixth century.

c. 390 St Augustine's monasteries of clerics at Thagaste and Hippo.
Macarius of Egypt dies.
394–5 Tour narrated in *Historia Monachorum*.
Macarius of Alexandria and John of Lycopolis die.
St Paulinus withdraws to Nola.
399 Palladius leaves Egypt.
c. 400 Organisation of Armenian monachism under Gind.
401–2 Postumianus in Egypt (*Dial.* I of Sulpitius Severus).
401 Tall Brothers driven out of Nitria and go to St John Chrys.
403 Conciliabulum of the Oak: death of Ammonius the Tall.
St Jerome (*Ep.* 107) speaks of monks in Persia, India and Ethiopia.
406–12 Palladius in banishment at Syene and Antinoë.
c. 410 Foundation of monastery of Lerins by Honoratus.
c. 415 Foundation of monastery of St Victor at Marseilles by Cassian.
419–20 Writing of *Historia Lausiaca.*
420–28 Cassian writes *Institutes* and *Collations.*
423 St Augustine's Letter (*Ep.* 211) to the Nuns of Hippo.
c. 425–50 Beginnings of Irish and Welsh monachism.
c. 440 Writing of Theodoret's *Historia Religiosa.*
440–70 Synods in various parts of Gaul legislate for monks.
451 C. of Chalcedon legislates for monks (canons 4, 8, 23, 24).
451–2 Schenoudi dies.
c. 490 Monachism in the Jura in Auvergne.
c. 500 St Benedict becomes a monk.
[By this date the monastic institute had spread to and taken firm root in every Christian country of both East and West.]

LIST OF CHAPTERS.

* Chapters 8, 9, 20, 28, 43 contain considerable interpolations from *Hist. Mon.* Chapters 44—46, 48—76, 116, 150 are interpolations.

THE
HISTORIA LAUSIACA
OF PALLADIUS.

LIST OF SYMBOLS.

(All necessary information may be found in *Introd.* §§ 9, 10.)

Greek Authorities.

P = Paris Gr. 1628 (xiv.).
T = Turin 141 (xvi.).
V = Venice Bess. 346 (xi.).
O = Oxford Laud. Gr. 84 (xi., xii.).
W = Oxford (Christ Church) Wake Gr. 67 (x.).
ven = Rosweyd's Cod. Venetus.
C = Paris Coislin 282 (xi.).
W^o = ff. 61—70 of W (cf. *Introd.* § 9).

A = those portions of the "Long Recension" (cf. *Introd.* § 1) which contain the pure text: where no other indication is given the ms. used is Coisl. 295 (xiv.); but Paris Gr. 1626 (xii.) has in nearly all cases been tested: they are distinguished, when necessary, as A^{38} A^{37} respectively. herv signifies Hervet's Latin trans. of A (Rosweyd *Vitae Patrum* Lib. viii.).

B = the Metaphrastic text: *B* indicates what, in spite of divergences among the mss., may be judged to be the true B reading: *B*† signifies "some B mss."

A^B = those portions of the "Long Recension" which contain a B text (Coisl. 295 and Paris Gr. 1626): when not mentioned A^B is included in *B*.

Other Greek mss. are cited by the number they bear in the List of mss. (*Introd.* § 2). Hyphens (1-2-3) indicate that the mss. so joined are closely akin: (1—6) signifies the whole group (1, 2, 3, 4, 5, 6).

Soz refers to Sozomen's citations, printed in full below the text (ed. Hussey).

Versions.

l = Latin Version I.
l^{rev} = the revision of l (the printed *Paradisus Heraclidis*, Rosweyd, App. I.).
l_2 = Latin Version II.
s s_2 = Syriac Versions I. and II. respectively.
s^{an} = s or s_2 as found (usually revised) in Anan Isho's *Paradise* (ed. Bedjan).
c ar arm eth = Coptic (bohairic), Arabic, Armenian, Ethiopic Versions (all fragmentary).

(The occasional symbols l^{cass} l^{sess} l_2^a l_2^b s_2^{vat} s_2^{add} are explained in *Introd.* § 9.)

It must be remembered that readings of l cannot be controlled at all by l^{rev}; nor ordinarily those of s or s_2 by s^{an}; nor always those of l_2^a by l_2^b (the printed text).

The following marks and abbreviations are also used:—

+ = add. tr = transfer.

vac signifies that the context is wanting: om that the context is there, but does not contain the word or words in question: paraphr that a version is a mere paraphrase: txt that the authority cited supports the text.

B or one of the versions is enclosed in ( ) as (s), when it is paraphrastic, or only doubtfully supports the reading to which it is attached.

Words in the apparatus enclosed in ( ) have reference only to the authority which has immediately preceded. In the case of the Greek authorities named as sources for the different portions of the text, full collations of all substantive readings (i.e. all other than spellings) are recorded. Sometimes one of the Greek sources is between [ ] as [T]; this indicates that its text in the passage in question is corrupt, and that only selected readings from it are given. As B is used in this manner throughout the book, it is not necessary to name it among the sources of each chapter. In the case of the versions, only those readings are ordinarily recorded which may be supposed to represent Greek readings.

Passages constructed out of B and one or more of the versions are enclosed in [ ]. Words which, in the editor's judgment, probably, but not certainly, belong to the text are enclosed in ⌜ ⌝.

† † indicate probable corruptions, or else the (very few) conjectural emendations.

Prol. signifies the previous volume of Prolegomena (*Texts and Stud.* vi. 1).

The references to Migne's reprint of Du Duc's text (*Patr. Gr.* xxxiv.) are given in the headlines; a | is placed in the text where a column ends in Migne.

INTRODUCTORY PIECES.

995] *ροοίμιον τοῦ βίου τῶν ἁγίων πατέρων*

Ἐν ταύτῃ τῇ βίβλῳ ἀναγέγραπται ἐνάρετος ἄσκησις καὶ θαυμαστὴ βίου διαγωγὴ τῶν μακαρίων καὶ ἁγίων πατέρων μοναχῶν καὶ ἀναχωρητῶν τῶν ἐν τῇ ἐρήμῳ, πρὸς ζῆλον καὶ μίμησιν τῶν τὴν οὐράνιον πολιτείαν ἐθελόντων κατορθοῦν καὶ τὴν εἰς βασιλείαν οὐρανῶν ἄγουσαν βουλομένων ὁδεύειν ὁδόν· καὶ γυναικῶν πρεσβυτίδων καὶ ἀοιδίμων θεοπνεύστων μητέρων μνῆμαι, τῶν ἀνδρείῳ καὶ τελείῳ φρονήματι τοὺς τῆς ἐναρέτου ἀσκήσεως ἄθλους ἐξανυσασῶν, πρὸς ὑπογραμμὸν καὶ ἔρωτα τῶν ἐθελουσῶν τὸν τῆς ἐγκρατείας καὶ ἁγνείας ἀναδήσασθαι στέφανον· διὰ τὸ † ἀνδρός τινος παγκρατίστου καὶ τῇ γνώμῃ πολυμαθοῦς καὶ τὸ ἦθος εἰρηνικοῦ καὶ τῇ καρδίᾳ εὐσεβοῦς καὶ τῇ διανοίᾳ θεοφιλοῦς, καὶ πρὸς τοὺς δεομένους τῶν χρειῶν κοινωνικοῦ, καὶ αὐτῇ κορυφῇ τῶν ἀξιωμάτων διὰ χρηστότητα τρόπων πολλῶν λογάδων ἀνδρῶν προτετιμημένου, καὶ τὸ ὅλον τῇ δυνάμει τοῦ θείου πνεύματος φρουρουμένου, ἐπιτάξαντος ἡμῖν, μᾶλλον δὲ, εἰ χρὴ τἀληθὲς εἰπεῖν, πρὸς τὴν τῶν κρειττόνων θεωρίαν τὸν νωθρὸν ἡμῶν νοῦν διεγείραντος πρὸς μίμησιν καὶ ἅμιλλαν τῶν ἀρετῶν τῆς

1 On this Prooemium see Note 1. Though all the texts are strictly speaking B texts, in the apparatus to this piece *B* may be taken as signifying readings of the group 1—5: 20 has not been collated, but it may be presumed to agree with 22: 45 agrees closely with 46.

In A 45-46 B (1—6, 13, 20, 22, 47) (P): om TB (8—11, 14—18, 19, 21) l (l_2css_2)
Title: Πρ. *τοῦ βίου τῶν ἁγίων πατέρων* 5, 6 (prefix Παλλαδίου *ἐπισκόπου* before Πρ.); + (*τοῦ* Χριστοῦ) *τοῦ λεγομένου* (al. *καλουμένου*) λαυσιακοῦ (al. λαυσαϊκοῦ) A 45-46, 47, 13
P 20, 22: Πρ. *τοῦ βίου τῶν ἐν τῇδε τῇ βίβλῳ ἀναγεγραμμένων θείων* (*ὁσίων* 20) *πατέρων*

A 46 P 22

1 *θαυμαστοῦ* A   5 *πατέρων* P   *τῶν*] *τῷ* A 46, 22   6 *ἐξανυσασῶν*] *B* 46; *ἐξανυσάντων* AP 22   7 *ἔρωτα*] + *θεῖον* *B*   8 *διὰ τὸ*] *B*; *δι' ὧν* A[37]; *διὸ* A[38], 46; *διὸ καὶ σὺ μακαριώτατε* P 22   *ἀνδρός τινος παγκρ.*] *B* (*ὑπὸ ἀνδ. τ. π.* *B*†); om A 46 P 22   *καὶ τῇ*] om 22   9 *πολυπαθοῦς* P   *τῷ ἤθει* *B*   10 *καὶ*[1]] + *τῇ* P; *τῆς* 22   11 *χρηστότητος* P   13 *τὸ νωθρὸν* (om *νοῦν*) P

ἀσκήσεως τῶν ὁσίων καὶ ἀθανάτων πνευματικῶν ἡμῶν πατέρων καὶ τῶν ἐν ἀρεσκείᾳ θεοῦ ἐν σκληραγωγίᾳ πολλῇ τοῦ σώματος βεβιωκότων· ὡς ἀναγραψαμένους ἡμᾶς τοὺς τῶν ἀνικήτων ἀθλητῶν βίους διαπέμψασθαι τούτῳ, ἀνακηρύττοντας ἑνὸς ἑκάστου τῶν μεγάλων τὰς ἐναργεῖς ἀρετάς. ἔστι δὲ ὁ τοῦ θείου τούτου καὶ πνευματικοῦ πόθου ἐραστὴς ὁ ἄριστος τῶν ἀνδρῶν Λαῦσος, ὁ μετὰ τὴν τοῦ θεοῦ ῥοπὴν φύλαξ τεταγμένος τῆς ἐνθέου καὶ εὐσεβοῦς βασιλείας.

Ἐγὼ τοίνυν ὁ καὶ τῇ γλώττῃ ἀπαίδευτος καὶ πνευματικῆς γνώσεως ἀκροθιγῶς πως γευσάμενος καὶ τοῦ καταλόγου τῶν ἁγίων πατέρων πνευματικοῦ βίου ἀνάξιος, δεδοικὼς τὸ ὑπὲρ ἐμὲ ἄμετρον τῆς ἐπιταγῆς μέγεθος, δυσανησχέτουν τῷ ἐπιτάγματι, πολλῆς δεομένῳ καὶ σοφίας τῆς ἔξωθεν [illegible] πνευματικῆς συνέσεως· ὅμως καταιδεσθεὶς πρῶτον τὸ σπουδαῖον τῆς ἀμ[illegible] εἰς ταύτην τὴν ἐπιταγὴν ἡμᾶς διεγείραντος, ἀναλογισάμενος δὲ καὶ τὴν τῶ[illegible] ἐντυγχανόντων ὠφελείαν, δεδιὼς δὲ καὶ τὸν ἐν τῇ εὐλόγῳ παρακοῇ κίνδυνον, τῇ προνοίᾳ πρῶτον ἀνατεθεικὼς τὸ γενναῖον ἐπίταγμα καὶ πολλῇ προσεχείᾳ χρησάμενος, τῇ τῶν ἁγίων πατέρων πρεσβείᾳ πτερούμενος, ἐνέβην εἰς τοὺς ἀγῶνας τοῦ σκάμματος, καὶ ὡς ἐν ἐπιτομῇ τῶν γενναίων ἀθλητῶν καὶ μεγάλων ἀνδρῶν τὰ ἔπακρα μόνον ἆθλά τε καὶ σημεῖα ἀναγραψάμενος, οὐ μόνον ἀνδρῶν ἀοιδίμων κατορθωκότων πολιτείαν ἀρίστην ἀλλὰ καὶ γυναικῶν μακαρίων καὶ εὐσχημόνων ἄκραν πολιτείαν ἐξασκησασῶν.

Καὶ τῶν μὲν τὰ ἱεροπρεπῆ πρόσωπα αὐτοπροσώπῳ θέᾳ ἰδεῖν κατηξιώθην, τῶν δὲ προτελειωθέντων ἐν τῷ σκάμματι τῆς εὐσεβείας παρὰ θεοφόρων ἀθλητῶν τοῦ Χριστοῦ τὴν οὐράνιον τούτων πολιτείαν μεμάθηκα. πολλὰς δὲ πόλεις καὶ πλείστας κώμας, σπήλαιόν τε ἅπαν καὶ πάσας σκηνὰς τῆς ἐρήμου τῶν μοναχῶν, πεζῇ τῇ πορείᾳ περινοστήσας θεοσεβείας σκοπῷ μετὰ πάσης ἀκριβείας, ἃ μὲν αὐτὸς ἱστορήσας ἀνεγραψάμην, ἃ δὲ παρὰ τῶν ἁγίων πατέρων ἀκήκοα, ἄθλους μεγάλων ἄνδρων καὶ ἀνδρειοτέρων τῆς φύσεως γυναικῶν διὰ τὴν εἰς Χριστὸν ἐλπίδα ἐνσημάνας ἐν τῷ βιβλίῳ τούτῳ, ἀπέσταλκα τῇ τῶν θείων λογίων φίλῃ ἀκοῇ σου, ἀνδρῶν ἀρίστων καὶ θεοφιλῶν ἐγκαλλώπισμα καὶ τῆς πιστοτάτης καὶ θεοφιλοῦς βασιλείας ἀγλάϊσμα, γνήσιε καὶ φιλόχριστε δοῦλε θεοῦ

A 46 P 22

1 ἀθανάτων] + καὶ 22   καὶ[2]] om *B*   **2** ὡς] *B*; ὧν A 46 P 22   **3** τοὺς] om 22   ἀνικήτων] *B*; νικητῶν A 46; νικητικῶν 22 P (βικ.)   τούτῳ] τούτων 46   **4** ἑνὸς ἑκάστου] *B* 46; ἑνὶ ἑκάστῳ P 22; ἑνὶ ἑκάστου A   δ' ὁ P 22   **6** θεοῦ] θείου AP 22   **8** ἁγίων] om 46   πν. βίου] om 46   **9** ἄμετρον] *B*; μέτρον A 46 P 22: + καὶ P 22   ἐπιταγῆς] + τὸ P 22   καὶ μ. καὶ A   δυσανησχέτουν] *B* 22; δυσανεσχέτουν P; καὶ δυσανασχετῶν 46; δυσανασχετούντος A: + ἐγχειρῆσαι τούτῳ *B*   **12** τὴν[2] after ἐντυγχ. *B*   ἐντευξομένων 46   **13** δεδιὼς] A 46; δεδειὼς *B*; δεδοιὼς P 22   ἐν] ἐπὶ *B*   τῇ[2]] A 46; θεοῦ *B*; ὅτι P 22   **14** χρησάμενος] + καὶ 22   **17** ἔπακρα] A*B*; ἐπ' ἄκρα P 22; om ἐπ' 46   **18** καὶ[2]] *B* 46; om AP 22   **19** ἐξασκησασῶν] *B*; ἀσκησάντων AP 22; ἠσκημένων 46   **21** δὲ] om P 22   τελειωθέντων 46   εὐσεβείας] + τῶν δὲ P 22   θεοφορήτων A 46   **22** πολ. τούτων 46   πολιτ.] ζωὴν *B*   ἐκμεμάθηκα *B*   **22–23** πολλὰς......κώμας] om 46   **23** σπήλαια *B*   ἅπαν] ἅμα *B*   **24** πεζῇ] πολλῇ *B*   σκόπου 22   εὐσεβ. A   **25** ἱστόρησα 46   ἆθλα A 22   **27** ἀπέσταλκα] om 46   **29** ἀγλάϊσμα] om 46   θεοῦ] Χριστοῦ 46

Λαῦσε, ἐγχαράξας κατὰ τὴν προσοῦσαν ἐμοὶ βραχύτητα ἑκάστου τῶν τοῦ Χριστοῦ ἀθλητῶν ἀρρένων τε καὶ θηλειῶν καὶ τὸ ἀοίδιμον ὄνομα, ἐξηγησάμενός τε ἀπὸ πολλῶν καὶ πάνυ μεγάλων ἄθλων ἑκάστου ὀλίγους καὶ σφόδρα βραχεῖς, προστεθεικὼς τῶν πλείστων καὶ τὸ γένος καὶ τὴν πόλιν καὶ τὸν τόπον τῆς μονῆς.

Ἐμνημονεύσαμεν δὲ ἀνδρῶν καὶ γυναικῶν κατορθωσάντων μὲν εἰς ἄκρον τὴν ἀρετὴν, διὰ δὲ τὴν μητέρα τῆς ὑπερηφανείας τὴν καλουμένην κενοδοξίαν εἰς ἔσχατον βάραθρον καὶ πυθμένα ᾅδου κατενεχθέντων, καὶ τὰ ἐκ μακρῶν χρόνων καὶ πολλῶν κόπων κτηθέντα αὐτοῖς ἐπέραστα καὶ περιμάχητα τῆς ἀσκήσεως κατορθώματα ἐν μιᾷ καιροῦ ῥοπῇ ὑπὸ τοῦ τύφου καὶ τῆς οἰήσεως διαρρυέντα· χάριτι δὲ τοῦ σωτῆρος ἡμῶν καὶ προνοίᾳ τῶν ἁγίων πατέρων καὶ συμπαθείᾳ σπλάγχνων πνευματικῶν ἐξαρπασθέντων τῶν τοῦ διαβόλου δικτύων καὶ ταῖς εὐχαῖς τῶν ἁγίων τὸν πρότερον ἀνακτησαμένων ἐνάρετον βίον.

A 46 P 22

1 ἐπιχαράξας P 22   3 ἑκάστου] om P   4 προστεθ.] A*B* 46; προτεθ. P 22: +τε P   6 κατωρθωκότων *B*   9 κτηθέντα] *B*A[38] 22, 46; κτισθέντα A[37]P   10 ἐν] om 22   13 τὸν] A 47; τῶν *B*P 22, 46   ἀνακτησαμένων] + τὸν P

Ἀντίγραφον ἐπιστολῆς γραφείσης Λαύσῳ πραιποσίτῳ παρὰ Παλλαδίου ἐπισκόπου

Μακαρίζω σου τὴν προαίρεσιν· ἄξιον γὰρ ἀπὸ μακαρισμοῦ ἄρξασθαι τῆς ἐπιστολῆς· ὅτι πάντων εἰς τὰ μάταια κεχηνότων καὶ λίθους οἰκοδομούντων ἐξ ὧν οὐκ ὠφεληθήσονται, αὐτὸς λόγους οἰκοδομῆς διδάσκεσθαι θέλεις. ἀδίδακτος

1 On this Letter see Note 2. In this piece the B MSS. are unusually divergent from one another: selections only are recorded from the readings of some of the more representative among them, but not the full collations of any single B MS.

In AB (except 1—5) l_2 cs (PT): om B (1—5) l (s_2)

Title: AB (12—18, 20, 22): ἀντίγραφον ἐπιστολῆς γραφείσης Λ. πραιποσίτῳ παρὰ Παλλαδίου ἐπισκόπου (A 22 παρὰ Ἡρακλειδοῦς ἐπισκόπου Καππαδοκίας: 20 om παρὰ to end)

21: ἐπιστολὴ Π. ἐπισκόπου Καπ.

10: Λ. πραιποσίτῳ ἐπιστολὴ γραφεῖσα

6: τοῦ αὐτοῦ (sc. Παλλ.) ἐπιστολὴ πρὸς Λ. πραιπόσιτον

P: ἐπιστολὴ Παλλαδίου ἐπισκόπου Ἑλληνουπολέως πρὸς Λαῦσον πραιπόσιτον

T: ἐπιστολὴ γραφεῖσα Λαύσῳ πρεποσίτῳ παρὰ Παλλαδίου ἐπισκόπου Ἐλεπόλεως (sic) τῆς Βηθυνίας

47: τοῦ ἐν ἁγίοις πατρὸς ἡμῶν Π. ἐπισκόπου Ἀσπώνωνος ἐπιστολὴ πρὸς Λ. τὸν φιλόχριστον πρεπόσιτον τοῦ εὐσεβεστάτου βασιλέως Θεοδωσίου περὶ τοῦ βίου τῶν ἁγίων καὶ σημειοφόρων πατέρων τῶν ἐν Αἰγύπτῳ καὶ πάσει πόλει καὶ χώρᾳ. (47 and 19) Π. ἐπίσκοπος Ἀσπώνωνος (Ἀσπώνων 19) Λ. τῷ φιλοχρίστῳ (+πρεποσίτῳ 19) χαίρειν. Μακαρίζω κ.τ.λ.

No title in s (add. 12173)

c: The letter written to Lausius the praepositus, the servant of Christ

l_2^a: (Munich MSS) Incipit Prologus Heraclidis uiri religiosissimi discipuli s̄cti Anthonii ad Lausum episcopum in librum de conuersatione sanctorum patrum.

(add. 33518) Incipit Prologus Heraclii episcopi De uita sanctorum patrum.

(As this fragment of l_2 has not yet been printed it is given here from add. 33518.)

Beatifico et admiror propositum tuum; dignum est enim a beatitudine incipere huius epistolae textum; quum omnes circa uana et inania praesentis saeculi studium suum impendunt et in edificatione lapidum ex quibus non ualde gaudebunt; ipse autem uerbum edificationis et sancte scripture doctrinam doceri desideras sanctorumque patrum conuersationem et instituta.........(erasure)

PTAl_2^a cs

2 μάταια]+τρεχόντων καίτοι 8—11, 6 (ἤτοι) καὶ λίθους οἰκοδομούντων] om 12—18, 20-21 3 ὠφεληθήσονται] A 12—18, 20—22, Ps; ὠφελήθησαν 8—11 c; ἐχάρησαν T 47, 19, 6 (l_2 gaudebunt) οἰκοδομῆς] οἰκοδομεῖς (itacism?) A[38] 22; οἰκοδομεῖς καὶ T (so too Du Duc; probably an emend.; for 13, his only MS. in this piece, reads οἰκοδομῆς, without καί); ψυχοφελεῖς P

γὰρ μόνος ἐστὶν ὁ τῶν ὅλων θεός, ἐπειδὴ καὶ αὐτοφυὴς καὶ πρὸ αὐτοῦ ἄλλον οὐκ ἔχων· τὰ δ' ἄλλα πάντα ἐστὶ διδακτά, ἐπειδὴ ποιητὰ καὶ κτιστά. καὶ τὰ μὲν πρῶτα τάγματα διδάσκαλον ἔχει τὴν ἀνωτάτω τριάδα· τὰ δὲ δεύτερα μανθάνει παρὰ τῶν πρώτων· τὰ δὲ τρίτα παρὰ τῶν δευτέρων· καὶ οὕτω καθεξῆς κατὰ τάξιν, μέχρι καὶ τῶν ἐσχάτων. οἱ γὰρ κρείττους ἐν γνώμῃ καὶ ἀρετῇ τοὺς ἐλαττουμένους ἐν γνώσει διδάσκουσιν. οἱ τοίνυν οἰόμενοι διδασκάλων μὴ χρῄζειν, ἢ μὴ πειθόμενοι τοῖς ἐν ἀγάπῃ διδάσκουσιν, ἄγνοιαν νοσοῦσι τὴν μητέρα τῆς ὑπερηφανίας· ὧν πρωτεύουσιν εἰς ἀπώλειαν οἱ τῷ αὐτῷ πάθει τῆς οὐρανίου διαγωγῆς ἐκπεσόντες, οἱ ἐν ἀέρι πετόμενοι δαίμονες τῶν ἐν τοῖς οὐρανοῖς ἀποδράσαντες διδασκάλων. οὐ γὰρ αἱ λέξεις ἢ αἱ συλλαβαί εἰσι διδασκαλία, ἃ ἔχουσιν ἐνίοτε καὶ οἱ ἐπὶ πλεῖστον φαῦλοι· ἀλλὰ τὰ τοῦ ἤθους κατορθώματα, ἥ τε ἀλυπία καὶ ἡ ἀπτοησία καὶ ἡ ἀδειλία καὶ τὸ ἀόργητον, καὶ ἡ ἐπὶ πάντων παρρησία, ἣ καὶ τοὺς λόγους ὡς πυρὸς φλόγα γεννῶσα. εἰ γὰρ μὴ ἦν τοῦτο, οὐκ ἂν ἔλεγεν ὁ μέγας διδάσκαλος τοῖς ἑαυτοῦ μαθηταῖς· ΜΑΘΕΤΕ ἀπ' ἐΜΟΥ̂ ὅτι ΠΡᾼόϹ ΕἰΜΙ ΚΑὶ ΤΑΠΕΙΝὸϹ Τῇ ΚΑΡΔίᾳ· οὐ τῇ εὐλεξίᾳ ῥυθμίζων τοὺς ἀποστόλους, ἀλλὰ τῇ εὐλαβείᾳ τοῦ ἤθους, μηδένα λυπῶν πλὴν τῶν μισολόγων καὶ διδασκάλους μισούντων. δεῖ γὰρ τὴν κατὰ θεὸν ἀσκουμένην ψυχὴν ἢ μανθάνειν πιστῶς ἃ οὐκ οἶδεν, ἢ διδάσκειν σαφῶς ἃ ἔγνω. εἰ δὲ ὁπότερον μὴ βούληται εἰ δύναται, μανίαν νοσεῖ. ἀρχὴ γὰρ ἀποστασίας διδασκαλίας κόρος καὶ ἀνορεξία λόγου, ὃν ἀεὶ πεινᾷ ἡ ψυχὴ τοῦ φιλοθέου. ἴσχυε οὖν καὶ ὑγίαινε καὶ ἀνδρίζου, καὶ χαρίσηταί σοι ὁ θεὸς τὸ μεταδιώκειν τὴν γνῶσιν τοῦ Χριστοῦ.

14 Mt. xi. 29.

PTAcs

1 *ἐστὶ μόνος* P 6, 10 *καὶ*[2]] om A 6, 10 **2** *πάντα*] + *τε* P *ἐπειδὴ*] + *καὶ* A **3** *μανθ.* after *πρώτων* *B*† **4** *δὲ*] om PT *καθεξῆς*] + *καὶ* A 6 *κατὰ τάξιν*] om 22 **5** *ἄχρι* A *κρείττονες* P *γνώμῃ*] *τιμῇ* A *ἀρετῇ*] + *ὄντες* A **6** *ἠλαττωμένους* P (*ἐλαττομ.* T 12, 22) *ἐν γνώσει*] om P **7** *ἢ*] TA 22; *οἱ* P*B* *πειθόμενος οἱ* (sic) T **9** *τοῖς*] om A 22 **10** *διδασκαλίαι* *B* *ἃ*] *αἳ* (sic) T: *ἃς* *B* **11** *τὰ*] om P: (' but this is education ' sc) **12** *ἡ*[3] om T (*καὶ* repeated) **16** *λοιπῶν* T **17** *θεὸν*] PTA*B*†s; *Χριστὸν* *B*†c **18** *σοφῶς* T 6 *ἃ ἔγνω*] *ἃ ἐπέγνω* A[38]; *ἅπερ ἐπίσταται* A[37] 47 *δὲ*] *γὰρ* *B*† *ὁπότερον*] + *τούτων* A 22 s **19** *εἰ δύναται*] T 47 A[37] (*δύνηται*) s; om A[38]*B*Pc *κόρος διδ.* T **20** *ὃν*] *ὧν* T: + *καὶ* P *καὶ ὑγίαινε*] om A *καὶ ἀνδρίζου*] om *B*† **21** *τὸ μεταδιώκειν*] *τὸ μέγα* *B* (before *χαρ.*)

NOTE ON THE TITLE.

Owing to the variety of titles for the book found in the MSS. the original title is irrecoverable. The evidence is here brought together from Titles, Explicits, Notes, Lists of Contents, &c.

(1) **Τὸ Λαυσιακόν** (or Λαυσαϊκόν): at a later period this was apparently the title most in popular use. Meursius cites from the Liturgical Books two instances of the rubric: Ἀνάγνωσις εἰς τὸ λαυσαϊκόν (p. 169). The extracts contained in MS. 33 are described as Ἐκλογαὶ ἐκ τοῦ λαυσαϊκοῦ: the colophon of 6 runs Τέλος τῆς πραγματείας τοῦ λαυσιακοῦ: that of 9 Ἐτελειώθη τὸ παρὸν βιβλίον τὸ λεγόμενον λαυσαϊκόν (similarly the title of the Προοίμιον in the A MSS. and 13, 45-46, 47, see p. 3). In 1_2^b the book bears the title *Palladii Lausiaca*, and in 6 and 13 Βιβλίον λαυσαϊκόν. Λαυσαϊκόν is the title in fifteen Athos MSS. (Lambros' *Catalogue*).

(2) **Παράδεισος**: this was another popular name, and is attested by l, in which the title is: "Liber qui appellatur Paradysus." In 13 and 20 the Explicit is Τοῦτο τὸ βιβλίον (αὕτη ἡ βίβλος 20) λέγεται παράδεισος: and again in 20–21 Τέλος ἐν θεῷ τοῦ πρὸς Λ. βιβλίου ἤτοι τοῦ νέου παραδείσου, and in 17 Ἡ ἐπιλεγομένη νέος παράδεισος. On the other hand T has Βίοι τῶν ἁγίων πατέρων τὸ λεγόμενον παράδεισος τὸ παλαιόν (see p. 9). But "Paradise" was a generic name for all works on the Egyptian monks—e.g. the *Historia Monachorum in Aegypto*, the *Apophthegmata*, Anan Isho's Syriac compilation, and others, were called "Paradise."

(3) **Βίος τῶν ἁγίων Πατέρων**: this stands, in one way or another, in the title of most of the B and A MSS., and in T (but βίοι). It is in P also, but in the Προοίμιον introduced from a B MS.: unfortunately the title-page is lost, so that P contains no other title or trace of title, except perhaps that the *Hist. Mon.*, which follows the *Hist. Laus.*, is said to be παράδεισος ἄλλος. Among the versions the title is found in 1_2^a, "Liber de conuersatione (al. uita) sanctorum Patrum"; c "The Life of holy men written for Lausius the praepositus"; s (add. 12173) "The book of the Egyptian Fathers of Palladius, bishop of Helenopolis, the disciple of holy Evagrius, which he wrote for Lauso the praepositus, who persuaded him to tell of the conversation of the holy Fathers." (The other MSS. of s, and of s_2, preserve no title.)

(4) Other titles:

Ἡ βίβλος ἡ πρὸς Λαῦσον and τὸ πρὸς Λ. βιβλίον 20-21.
Ἐκ τῶν πρὸς Λ. 50 (extracts).
Ἡ πρὸς Λαῦσον (Λαύσωνα 1) ἱστορία (τῶν ἁγίων πατέρων) 1, 5.
Ἡ πρὸς Λ. ἱστορικὴ βίβλος ps.-Damascene (see *Prol.* 142, note).
Λαυσιακὴ ἱστορία Athos MS. 2031 (Lambros).

This last is the only instance that has as yet appeared of the name by which the work has now commonly come to be known—*Historia Lausiaca*.

ΠΑΛΛΑΔΙΟΥ ΛΑΥΣΙΑΚΟΝ

1001]

Πολλῶν πολλὰ καὶ ποικίλα κατὰ διαφόρους καιροὺς συγγράμματα τῷ βίῳ καταλελοιπότων, τῶν μὲν ἐξ ἐπιπνοίας τῆς ἄνωθεν χάριτος θεοδότου εἰς οἰκοδομὴν καὶ ἀσφάλειαν τῶν πιστῇ προθέσει ἑπομένων τοῖς δόγμασι τοῦ σωτῆρος, τῶν δὲ ἐξ ἀνθρωπαρέσκου καὶ διεφθαρμένης προθέσεως ὑλομανησάντων εἰς παραμυθίαν τῶν κενοδοξίαν κισσώντων, ἑτέρων δὲ ἔκ τινος μανίας καὶ ἐνεργείας τοῦ μισοκάλου δαίμονος τύφῳ καὶ μηνίδι ἐπὶ λύμῃ τῶν κουφογνωμόνων ἀνθρώπων καὶ σπίλῳ τῆς ἀχράντου καὶ καθολικῆς ἐκκλησίας ἐπεισφρησάντων ταῖς διανοίαις τῶν ἀνοήτων ἐπὶ ἐγκότῳ τῆς σεμνῆς πολιτείας· ἔδοξε κἀμοὶ τῷ ταπεινῷ, αἰδεσθέντι τὴν ἐπιταγὴν τῆς σῆς μεγαλονοίας, φιλομαθέστατε, τὴν ἐπὶ προκοπῇ τῆς διανοίας, τριακοστὸν μὲν καὶ τρίτον ἔτος ἄγοντι ἐν τῇ τῶν ἀδελφῶν πολιτείᾳ δῆθεν

On the author of the work see Note 3. 1 On this Prologue see Note 4.

Title: *ἀντίγραφον ἐπιστολῆς γραφείσης Λαύσῳ πραιποσίτῳ παρὰ Παλλαδίου ἐπισκόπου Καππαδοκίας* P 20, 22, 42 marg 6 (om *Καπ.*, + *Διήγησις κ.τ.λ.* cf. below)

T: *βίοι τῶν ἁγίων πατέρων τὸ λεγόμενον παράδεισος τὸ παλαιόν*

AB (12—18) 47, 19: joined to preceding Letter without title or division (for Hervet cf. 42 marg. above)

B (1—6): *Διήγησις τοῦ βίου τῶν ἁγίων πατέρων*

10: *Λαύσῳ πραιποσίτῳ τῷ δούλῳ Χριστοῦ*

ll_2^b: Prologus (l_2^a apparently as A)

c: 'The Life of holy men written for Lausius the praepositus, the servant of Jesus Christ.'

PTll_2 (lines 1—4, 10—13) c

1 *καιροὺς*] om T 3 *ἄνωθεν*] + *καὶ* *B*l 4 *πίστει καὶ* T 4–10 *τῶν δὲ...... πολιτείας*] om l_2 6 *κισσόντων* PT*B*† *ἕτεροι* T 8 *μήνῃ* T *κουφογνώμων* (sic) TA^B*B*† *ἀνθρώπων*] om T 10 *πολιτείας*] + *διὰ τὴν εἰς Χρ. ἐλπίδα* P*B* (after *ταπεινῷ*)

καὶ τῷ μονήρει βίῳ, εἰκοστὸν δὲ τῆς ἐπισκοπῆς, πεντηκοστὸν δὲ καὶ ἕκτον ἐν τῇ πάσῃ ζωῇ, ποθοῦντί σοι τὰ τῶν πατέρων διηγήματα, ἀρρένων τε καὶ θηλειῶν, ὧν τε ἑώρακα καὶ περὶ ὧν ἀκήκοα, οἷς τε συνανεστράφην ἐν τῇ κατ' Αἴγυπτον ἐρήμῳ καὶ Λιβύῃ καὶ Θηβαΐδι καὶ Συήνῃ, ὑφ' ἣν καὶ οἱ λεγόμενοι Ταβεννησιῶται, ἔπειτα Μεσοποταμίᾳ Παλαιστίνῃ τε καὶ Συρίᾳ, καὶ τοῖς μέρεσι τῆς δύσεως Ῥώμῃ τε καὶ Καμπανίᾳ καὶ τῶν περὶ ταύτην, ἄνωθεν ἐκθέσθαι σοι ἐν διηγήματος εἴδει τὸ βιβλίον τοῦτο· ὅπως σεμνὸν καὶ ψυχωφελὲς ὑπομνηστικὸν ἔχων ἀδιάλειπτόν τε φάρμακον λήθης πάντα μὲν νυσταγμὸν τὸν ἐξ ἀλόγου ἐπιθυμίας, πᾶσαν δὲ διψυχίαν καὶ κιμβικίαν τὴν ἐν ταῖς χρείαις, πάντα τε ὄκνον καὶ μικροψυχίαν τῶν ἐν τῷ ἤθει, ὀξυθυμίαν τε καὶ τάραχον καὶ λύπην καὶ ἄλογον φόβον διὰ τούτου ἀποσκευαζόμενος καὶ τὸν μετεωρισμὸν τοῦ κόσμου, ἀδιαλείπτῳ πόθῳ προκόπτοις ἐν τῇ προθέσει τῆς εὐσεβείας, ὁδηγὸς καὶ σαυτοῦ καὶ τῶν μετὰ σοῦ καὶ τῶν ὑπὸ σὲ καὶ τῶν εὐσεβεστάτων γινόμενος βασιλέων· δι' ὧν κατορθωμάτων πάντες οἱ φιλόχριστοι ἑνωθῆναι θεῷ ἐπείγονται· συνεκδεχόμενος καὶ τὴν ἀνάλυσιν τῆς ψυχῆς καθ' ἡμέραν, κατὰ τὸ γεγραμμένον· Ἀγαθὸν τὸ ἀναλῦσαι καὶ σὺν Χριστῷ εἶναι· καὶ τὸ Ἑτοίμαζε εἰς τὴν ἔξοδον τὰ ἔργα σου, καὶ παρασκευάζου εἰς τὸν ἀγρόν· ὁ γὰρ μνημονεύων ἀεὶ τοῦ θανάτου ὡς ἐξ ἀνάγκης ἥξει καὶ οὐ μελλήσει, οὐ πταίσει μεγάλα· μήτε παραλογιζόμενος τὴν ὑποθήκην τῶν ὑφηγήσεων μήτε διαπτύων τὴν ἰδιωτείαν καὶ τὸ ἀκαλλὲς τῆς λέξεως. οὐ γὰρ δὴ τοῦτο τὸ ἔργον ἐστὶ θεϊκῆς διδασκαλίας σεσοφισμένως φράζειν, ἀλλὰ πείθειν τὴν γνώμην

20 Phil. i. 23. Prov. xxiv. 42 (al. 27).

PTll$_2$ (1—18) c

2 *ἕκτον*] PTls[an]; *τρία B*; (l$_2$c om *πεντηκοστὸν......ζωῇ*): (see App. v. ii) *ζωῇ*] + *ἀναγκαῖον ἡγησάμην B*P (see Note 4) *σοι*] + cognoscere l; enarrari l$_2$ **3** *διηγήματα*] + *ὠφελείας χάριν B*P **4** *οἷς τε*] *ὧν τε* T **6** *Ταβενησ.* T **7** *καὶ τῶν περὶ ταύτην*] PTl$_2$ (et eorum qui in his morantur); *καὶ τοῖς περὶ ταύτας μέρεσι B*; l et in ceteris circa ipsa loca; c paraphr. **9** *τὸ βιβλίον τοῦτο*] PTA[B]; *ἐν τῷ βιβλίῳ τούτῳ B*ll$_2$ **10** *τε*] om T*B*l *λήθης*] *ἀληθείας B*: (c paraphrases whole passage) *νυσταγμὸν*] + *λήθης B* **11–13** *καὶ......ἤθει*] om l$_2$ **12** *μικροτάραχον* (sic) T (om *τῶν...τάραχον*) **14** *τὸν*] + *μάταιον B*l **15** *προκόπτεις* P **18** *φιλόχριστοι*] T*B*ll$_2$c; *φιλόθεοι* P *συνεκδεχόμενος*] PTA[B]; *συνεκδεχόμενοι B*lc: + *δηλονότι* T*B* (after *ψυχῆς*) l **18–24** *συνεκδεχομ......ὑφηγήσεων*] om l$_2$ **19** *ψυχῆς*] + *ἀπὸ τοῦ σώματος B* (c) **22** *ὡς*] *ὃς* P *ἥξει*] + *πάντως B*l **23** *μήτε*] Pl; *μὴ* T*B* **24** *ἀφηγ.* T; *ἐξηγ. B* **25** *τῶν λέξεων B*(ll$_2$) *τὸ*] om T*B*

νοήμασιν ἀληθείας, κατὰ τὸ εἰρημένον· Ἄνοιγε σὸν στόμα λόγῳ θεοῦ· *καὶ πάλιν·* Μὴ ἀστοχήσῃς διηγήματος γερόντων, καὶ γὰρ καὶ αὐτοὶ παρὰ τῶν πατέρων ἔμαθον. |

Ἐγὼ τοίνυν, φιλομαθέστατε τοῦ θεοῦ ἄνθρωπε, ἐκ μέρους ἑπόμενος ταύτῃ τῇ ῥήσει πολλοῖς τῶν ἁγίων συντετύχηκα, οὐ περιέργῳ χρησάμενος λογισμῷ, ἀλλὰ καὶ τριάκοντα ἡμερῶν καὶ δὶς τοσούτων ὁδὸν ἐξανύσας, ὡς ἐπὶ θεοῦ πεζῇ τῇ πορείᾳ πατήσας πᾶσαν τὴν γῆν Ῥωμαίων, ἠσμένισα τὴν κακουχίαν τῆς ὁδοιπορίας ἐπὶ συντυχίᾳ ἀνδρὸς φιλοθέου, ἵνα κερδήσω ὅπερ οὐκ εἶχον. εἰ γὰρ ὁ πολλῷ κρείττων ἐμοῦ ὑπερβὰς πολιτείᾳ καὶ γνώσει καὶ συνειδήσει καὶ πίστει Παῦλος *τὴν ἀπὸ* Ταρσοῦ *εἰς τὴν* Ἰουδαίαν *ἐστείλατο ἀποδημίαν ἐπὶ συντυχίᾳ* Πέτρου *καὶ* Ἰακώβου *καὶ* Ἰωάννου, *καὶ ἐν εἴδει καυχήματος διηγεῖται, στηλιτεύων ἑαυτοῦ τοὺς πόνους εἰς παροξυσμὸν τῶν ὄκνῳ καὶ ἀργίᾳ συζώντων ἐν τῷ εἰπεῖν·* Ἀνέβην εἰς Ἱεροσόλυμα ἱστορῆσαι Κηφᾶν, *οὐκ ἀρκούμενος τῇ φήμῃ τῆς ἀρετῆς ἀλλ' ἐπιποθῶν καὶ τὴν τοῦ εἴδους αὐτοῦ συντυχίαν· πόσῳ μᾶλλον ἐγὼ ὁ μυρίων ταλάντων χρεωφειλέτης ὤφειλον τοῦτο ποιῆσαι, οὐκ ἐκείνους εὐεργετῶν ἀλλ' ἐμαυτὸν ὠφελῶν. καὶ γὰρ οἱ τοὺς τῶν πατέρων ἀναγραψάμενοι βίους,* Ἀβραάμ *τε καὶ τῶν καθεξῆς,* Μωσέως *καὶ* Ἡλίου *καὶ* Ἰωάννου, *οὐχ ἵνα ἐκείνους δοξάσωσιν ἐξηγήσαντο, ἀλλ' ἵνα καὶ τοὺς ἐντυγχάνοντας ὠφελήσωσιν.*

Ταῦτα *οὖν εἰδώς, πιστότατε δοῦλε* Χριστοῦ Λαῦσε, *καὶ σαυτὸν νουθετῶν, ἀνάσχου καὶ τῆς φλυαρίας τῆς ἡμετέρας ἐπὶ φυλακῇ τῆς εὐσεβοῦς γνώμης, ἣ διαφόροις κακίαις ὁραταῖς τε καὶ ἀοράτοις κυμαίνεσθαι πέφυκε, μόνῃ προσευχῇ συνεχεῖ καὶ ἰδιοπραγμοσύνῃ δυναμένη ἠρεμεῖν. πολλοὶ γὰρ τῶν ἀδελφῶν*

1 Prov. xxiv. 76 (al. xxxi. 8). **2** Sir. viii. 9. **15** Gal. i. 18.
23 On Lausus see Note 5.

PTlc

1 *νοήμασιν*] + *εὐσεβείας καὶ* P **3** *καὶ*] Pl; om TBl$_2$ **4–19** Ἐγὼ......*ὠφελῶν*] om l$_2$ **4** *τοῦ*] om T*B*: + *καὶ* T **5** *ἑπόμενος*] om T **6** *περιέργῳ*] PA^{B}c; *παρέργῳ* *B*T (*παρέργων* sic) l **9** *ἵνα*] + *τι* T*B*l **10** *ἐμοῦ*] + *καὶ* Tl **13** *καυχήματος*] + *αὐτὸ* *B*l **14** *ἑαυτοῦ τοὺς*] *αὐτοῖς* T*; *αὐτοῦ* T^{cor} *ἀργ. καὶ ὀκν.* T **16** Κηφᾶν] PTA^{B}c; Πέτρον *B*l *φήμῃ*] + *μόνον* *B*l **17** *τὴν*] om T *εἴδους*] PT; *προσώπου* *B*; uultum ac figuram l **19** *καὶ γὰρ*] l$_2$ recommences **20** Ἀβραὰμ] + Ἰσαὰκ *καὶ* Ἰακὼβ *B*l$_2$ **22** *ὠφελήσωσιν*] l$_2^a$ adds: Explicit Prologus, and the rest is wanting; in l$_2^b$ it breaks off at *εὐσεβείας* p. 10, l. 15 **23** *πιστότατε*] + *καὶ σεμνότατε* T*B*lc **24** *ἀνάσχου*] om P **26** *πεφύκαμεν* P *συν. προσευχ.* T(*B*) **27—6** (p. 12) *πολλοὶ*...... *ἰδιοπρ.*] c departs wholly from the Greek

καὶ πόνοις καὶ ἐλεημοσύναις κομῶντες, καὶ ἀγαμίαν ἢ παρθενίαν αὐχοῦντες, καὶ μελέτῃ θείων λογίων καὶ σπουδάσμασι θαρρήσαντες, ἠστόχησαν ἀπαθείας ἀδιακρίτῳ προσχήματι εὐσεβείας τὰς φιλοπραγμοσύνας νοσήσαντες, ἐξ ὧν τίκτονται πολυπραγμοσύναι ἢ κακοπραγμοσύναι ἀπελαύνουσαι καλοπραγμοσύνην, τὴν μητέρα τῆς ἰδιοπραγμοσύνης.

Ἀνδρίζου τοίνυν, παρακαλῶ, μὴ πιαίνων τὸν πλοῦτον· ὃ δὴ καὶ πεποίηκας, αὐτάρκως αὐτὸν σμικρύνας τῇ διαδόσει τῶν χρείαν ἐχόντων διὰ τὴν ἐκ τούτου τῆς ἀρετῆς ὑπηρεσίαν· μήτε ὁρμῇ τινι καὶ προλήψει ἀλόγῳ ἀνθρωπαρέσκως ὅρκῳ πεδήσας τὴν προαίρεσιν, καθὼς πεπόνθασί τινες φιλονείκως φιλοδοξίᾳ τοῦ μὴ φαγεῖν ἢ πιεῖν δουλώσαντες τὸ αὐτεξούσιον τῇ ἀνάγκῃ τοῦ ὅρκου, καὶ τούτῳ πάλιν ὑποπεσόντες οἰκτρῶς φιλοζωΐᾳ καὶ ἀκηδίᾳ καὶ ἡδονῇ τὴν ἐπιορκίαν ὠδίναντες. λόγῳ τοίνυν μεταλαμβάνων καὶ λόγῳ ἀπεχόμενος οὐχ ἁμαρτήσεις ποτέ. θεῖος γὰρ ὁ λόγος τῶν ἐν ἡμῖν κινημάτων, ἐξορίζων μὲν τὰ βλαβερὰ, προσλαμβανόμενος δὲ τὰ ἐπωφελῆ· ΔΙΚΑΙῼ γὰρ ΝΌΜΟϹ ΟΥ̓ ΚΕῖΤΑΙ. ἄμεινον γὰρ ἡ μετὰ λόγου οἰνοποσία τῆς μετὰ τύφου ὑδροποσίας. καὶ βλέπε μοι τοὺς μετὰ λόγου οἶνον πιόντας ἄνδρας ἁγίους, καὶ τοὺς ἄνευ λόγου πιόντας ὕδωρ ἀνθρώπους βεβήλους, καὶ μηκέτι ψέξῃς τὴν ὕλην ἢ ἐπαινέσῃς, ἀλλὰ μακάρισον ἢ ταλάνισον τὴν γνώμην τῶν καλῶς ἢ κακῶς χρωμένων τῇ ὕλῃ. ἔπιέ ποτε καὶ Ἰωσὴφ παρ' Αἰγυπτίοις οἶνον, ἀλλ' οὐκ ἐβλάβη τὴν φρένα, ἠσφαλίσατο γὰρ τὴν γνώμην. ὑδροπότησε δὲ Πυθαγόρας καὶ Διογένης καὶ Πλάτων, ἐν οἷς καὶ Μανιχαῖοι καὶ τὸ λοιπὸν σύνταγμα τῶν ἐθελοφιλοσόφων, οἳ καὶ ἐπὶ τοσοῦτον ἤλασαν κουφοδοξίας ἀκολασίᾳ ὡς καὶ τὸν θεὸν ἀγνοῆσαι καὶ προσκυνῆσαι εἰδώλοις. ἥψαντο δὲ καὶ οἱ περὶ τὸν ἀπόστολον Πέτρον τῆς χρήσεως τοῦ οἴνου, ὡς καὶ αὐτὸν ὀνειδίζεσθαι τὸν διδάσκαλον τούτων τὸν σωτῆρα ἐπὶ τῇ

3, 10 See Note 6. **17** 1 Tim. i. 9.

PTlc

3 *θαρσοῦντες* T*B* *ἀδιακρίτως* T **4** *τὰς*] P; *τινὰς* T; *τινὸς B*l **5** *ἢ*] P; *μεθ' ὧν* T; *μεθ' ἃς ἀλλοτριοπραγμοσύναι καὶ B*l; *ἀλλοτριοπρ.* (om. *ἢ κακοπρ.*) A[B] *καλοπρ.* and *ἰδιοπρ.* interchanged T **11** *τινες*] PTc; *πολλοὶ B*l *φιλονείκῳ* T*B* **12** *φιλοδοξίᾳ*] PT; *κενοδοξίᾳ B*l **16** *θεῖος*] PA[B]; *θεὸς* T*B*lc *κινημάτων*] *καὶ νοημάτων* (sic) T **19** *λόγου*] + *τὸν* T*B* *πίνοντας* T*B*† **20** *ὑδροποτήσαντας* T*B* **21** *καὶ*] + *διεφθαρμένους B*l *τὴν ὕλην* after *ἢ ἐπ.* T*B* *μακάρισον, ταλάνισον* P; *-σεις* T*B*†; *-σῃς B*† **23** *τῇ ὕλῃ*] *αὐτῇ* T *καὶ*] om T*B*l **26** *σύνταγμα*] P; *σύστημα* T*B* *οἳ*] Pc; om T*B*l **30** *τὸν*[2]] *καὶ* T

μεταλήψει, λεγόντων τῶν Ἰουδαίων· Ἵνα τί οἱ μαθηταί σου οὐ νηστεύουσιν ὡς καὶ οἱ τοῦ Ἰωάννου; καὶ πάλιν τοῖς μαθηταῖς ἐπεμβαίνοντες ὀνειδισμοῖς ἔλεγον· Ὁ διδάσκαλος ὑμῶν μετὰ τῶν τελωνῶν καὶ ἁμαρτωλῶν ἐσθίει καὶ πίνει. οὐκ ἂν δὲ ἐπὶ ἄρτου καὶ ὕδατος ἐπελαμβάνοντο ἀλλ' ἐπ' ὄψων καὶ οἴνου δηλονότι· οἷς πάλιν ἀλόγως θαυμάζουσιν ὑδροποσίαν καὶ ψέγουσιν οἰνοποσίαν ἔλεγεν ὁ σωτήρ· Ἦλθεν Ἰωάννης ἐν ὁδῷ δικαιοσύνης, μήτε ἐσθίων μήτε πίνων—δηλαδὴ κρέα καὶ οἶνον, δίχα γὰρ τῶν ἄλλων ζῆν οὐκ ἠδύνατο—καὶ λέγουσι· Δαιμόνιον ἔχει. ἦλθεν ὁ υἱὸς τοῦ ἀνθρώπου ἐσθίων καὶ πίνων, καὶ λέγουσιν· Ἰδοὺ ἄνθρωπος φάγος καὶ οἰνοπότης, τελωνῶν φίλος καὶ ἁμαρτωλῶν, διὰ τὸ ἐσθίειν καὶ πίνειν. τί οὖν ἡμεῖς ποιήσωμεν; μήτε τοῖς ψέγουσι μήτε τοῖς ἐπαινοῦσιν ἀκολουθήσωμεν, ἀλλ' ἢ μετὰ Ἰωάννου λόγῳ νηστεύσωμεν κἂν εἴπωσι· Δαιμόνιον ἔχουσιν· ἢ μετ' Ἰησοῦ ἐν σοφίᾳ οἰνοποτήσωμεν, εἰ χρῄζει τὸ σῶμα, κἂν εἴπωσιν· Ἰδοὺ ἄνθρωποι φάγοι καὶ οἰνοπόται. οὔτε γὰρ ἡ βρῶσίς ἐστί τι κατὰ ἀλήθειαν οὔτε ἡ ἀποχή, ἀλλὰ πίστις δι' ἀγάπης τοῖς ἔργοις παρεκτεινομένη. ὅταν γὰρ πάσῃ πράξει παρακολουθήσῃ ἡ πίστις, ἀκατάκριτος ὁ ἐσθίων καὶ πίνων διὰ τὴν πίστιν· πᾶν γὰρ ὃ οὐκ ἐκ πίστεως ἁμαρτία ἐστίν. ἀλλ' ἐπειδὴ πᾶς τις ἐρεῖ τῶν πλημμελούντων πίστει μεταλαμβάνειν ἢ ἕτερόν τι πράττειν ἀλόγῳ πληροφορίᾳ καὶ διεφθαρμένῳ τῷ συνειδότι, ὁ σωτὴρ διεστείλατο λέγων· Ἐκ τῶν καρπῶν αὐτῶν ἐπιγνώσεσθε αὐτούς. ὅτι δὲ ὁ καρπὸς τῶν λόγῳ πολιτευομένων καὶ συνέσει κατὰ τὸν θεῖον ἀπόστολον ἀγάπη ἐστὶ καὶ χαρὰ καὶ εἰρήνη καὶ μακροθυμία, χρηστότης, ἀγαθωσύνη, πίστις, πραΰτης, καὶ ἐγκράτεια, ὡμολόγηται. αὐτὸς γὰρ ἔλεγε Παῦλος· Ὁ γὰρ καρπὸς τοῦ πνεύματός ἐστι τὰ καὶ τά. ὅτι δὲ ὁ σπουδάζων τοιούτους ἔχειν καρποὺς ἀλόγως ἢ ἀσκόπως ἢ ἀκαίρως οὐ βρώσεται κρέα οὐδὲ πίεται οἶνον, | οὐδὲ συνοικήσει τινὶ κακῷ συνειδότι, πάλιν ἔλεγεν

1 Mc. ii. 18. **3** Mt. ix. 11 (Lc. v. 30). **7** Mt. xxi. 32 and xi. 18, 19. **19** Rom. xiv. 23. **23** Mt. vii. 16. **25** Gal. v. 22.

PTlc

1 ἵνα] P; εἰς T; διὰ *B* **2** τοῦ] om T*B* **3** τῶν] om T*B* **5** ἀλλ'] P; εἰ μὴ T*B* δῆλον T **6** ψέγ. μὲν οἰνοπ. θαυμ. δὲ ὑδροπ. *B*l **8** κρέας T*B*† **11** φιλ. τελ. T*B* **13** ἀλλ' ἢ] ἀλλὰ PA[B] λόγῳ] λέγω P **15** σοφίας (om ἐν) T χρῄζει] P*B*†; χρήζοι T*B*† **16** οὐδὲ T **17** ἀλλ' ἡ T*B*† **22** καὶ] P; ἢ *B*; om T **22, 23** συνειδότως ἦν (om ὁ σωτήρ) sic T **26** μακροθ.] + καὶ T πραΰτης] om T **27** ὁμολογεῖται T*B*† γὰρ[2]] δὲ T*B*

ὁ αὐτὸς Παῦλος ὅτι Πᾶς ὁ ἀγωνιζόμενος πάντα ἐγκρατεύεται, ὑγιαινούσης μὲν τῆς σαρκὸς ἀπεχόμενος τῶν πιαινόντων, ἀρρωστούσης δὲ ἢ ὀδυνωμένης ἢ καὶ λύπαις καὶ περιστάσεσι κοινωνούσης χρήσεται μὲν βρώμασιν ἢ πόμασιν ὡς φαρμάκοις εἰς ἴασιν τῶν λυπούντων, ἀφέξεται δὲ τῶν κατὰ ψυχὴν βλαβερῶν, ὀργῆς, φθόνου, κενοδοξίας, ἀκηδίας, καταλαλιᾶς καὶ ὑπονοίας ἀλόγου, εὐχαριστῶν ἐν κυρίῳ.

Αὐτάρκως τοίνυν περὶ τούτου διαλαβὼν πάλιν ἄλλην παράκλησιν προσάγω σου τῇ φιλομαθείᾳ. φεῦγε ὅση δύναμις συντυχίας ἀνδρῶν ὄφελος οὐδὲν ἐχόντων καὶ κοσμούντων τὸ δέρμα ἀκαταλλήλως, κἂν ὀρθόδοξοι εἶεν, μή τί γε αἱρετικῶν, βλαπτόντων τῇ ὑποκρίσει, κἂν δόξωσι πολιαῖς ἢ ῥυτίσιν ἐπισύρεσθαι μῆκος χρόνου. κἂν γὰρ μηδὲν βλαβῇς παρ' αὐτῶν δι' εὐγένειαν τρόπων, τὸ γοῦν ἔλαττον χαυνωθήσῃ ἢ ἐπαρθήσῃ καταγελῶν τούτων, ὅπερ ἐστί σοι βλάβη. ὑπὲρ δὲ θυρίδα φωτεινὴν μεταδίωκε ἀνδρῶν τε καὶ γυναικῶν ὁσίας συντυχίας, ἵνα διὰ τούτων, καθάπερ †λεπτόγραφον βιβλίον†, δυνηθῇς σαφῶς ἰδεῖν καὶ τὴν σὴν καρδίαν, διὰ τῆς παραθέσεως τὴν ῥᾳθυμίαν ἢ τὴν ἀμέλειαν δυνάμενος τὴν σὴν δοκιμάζειν. ἥ τε γὰρ χρόα τῶν προσώπων ἐπανθοῦσα τῇ πολιᾷ καὶ ὁ στολισμὸς τῆς ἐσθῆτος καὶ ἡ ἀτυφία τῶν λόγων καὶ ἡ εὐλάβεια τῶν λέξεων καὶ τὸ χαρίεν τῶν νοημάτων ἐνδυναμώσει σε, κἂν ἐν ἀκηδίᾳ τυγχάνῃς. Στολισμὸς γὰρ ἀνδρὸς καὶ βῆμα ποδὸς καὶ γέλως ὀδόντων ἀναγγελεῖ περὶ αὐτοῦ καθὼς ἡ σοφία λέγει.

1 1 Cor. ix. 25. **23** Sir. xix. 30.

PTlc

3 καὶ[1]] om T **6** καὶ φθ. T*B* καὶ κεν. T καὶ ἀκ. T*B*l καταλ.]+τε T **7** λόγου (sic) T ἐν] P; τῷ (om ἐν) T*B* κυρίῳ] θεῷ *B*†(herv)cs[an] **8** τούτου] τούτων *B*(c) **9** ὅση]+σοι *B* (T ὅσης ἡ sic) **11** ἀκαταλ.] om T **11, 12** μή τί γε......ὑποκρίσει] om T **12** δοξάσωσι T **16** μεταδοίω (sic) T **17** λεπτόγραφον βιβλίον] *B*l; λέγει τὸ γράφον βιβλίον P; λέγει τὸ γραφικὸν λόγιον T: (probably λεπτογράφων βιβλίων) **18** καὶ] om T **19** ἀμέλειαν] PA[B]; ἐμμέλειαν T*B*; (ἐπιμ. l) **20** προσώπων]+ἡ T*B* πολιᾷ] PTc; πολιτείᾳ *B*l **21** τῆς ἐσθῆτος] om T ἐσθῆτος]+καὶ τὸ ἀπέρπερον ἦθος *B*l (et inconfusa mens) **22** τῶν χαριέντων νοημ. (sic) T **23** ἀκηδίᾳ]+τε T **24** σημαίνει T*B*†: +τὰ T*B* σοφία] PT; παροιμία *B*l

Ἀρξάμενος τοίνυν τῶν διηγήσεων οὐ τοὺς ἐν ταῖς πόλεσιν οὔτε τοὺς ἐν ταῖς κώμαις ἢ ἐρημίαις σοι καταλείψω ἀγνώστους τῷ λόγῳ. οὐ γὰρ ὁ τόπος ἐστὶν ὁ ζητούμενος ἔνθα κατῴκησαν οὗτοι, ἀλλ' ὁ τρόπος τῆς προαιρέσεως.

(I) Πρώτως πατήσας τὴν Ἀλεξανδρέων πόλιν ⌜ἐν τῇ δευτέρᾳ ὑπατίᾳ Θεοδοσίου τοῦ μεγάλου βασιλέως, ὃς νῦν ἐν ἀγγέλοις ὑπάρχει διὰ τὴν αὐτοῦ πίστιν εἰς τὸν Χριστόν⌝, περιέτυχον ἐκεῖσε ἀνδρὶ θαυμασίῳ παντόθεν κεκοσμημένῳ ἔν τε ἤθει καὶ γνώσει, Ἰσιδώρῳ τῷ πρεσβυτέρῳ ξενοδόχῳ ὄντι τῆς Ἀλεξανδρέων ἐκκλησίας· ὃς τὰ μὲν πρῶτα τῆς νεότητος ἆθλα ἐλέγετο ἠνυκέναι ἐν τῇ ἐρήμῳ· οὗ καὶ τὴν κέλλαν ἐθεασάμην ἐν τῷ ὄρει τῆς Νιτρίας. κατέλαβον δὲ τοῦτον ἐτῶν ἑβδομήκοντα γέροντα, ὃς ἐπιζήσας πεντεκαίδεκα ἔτη ἄλλα τελευτᾷ ἐν εἰρήνῃ. οὗτος μέχρις αὐτῆς τελευτῆς οὐκ ὀθόνην ἐφόρεσεν ἐκτὸς φακιολίου, οὐ λουτροῦ ἥψατο, οὐ κρεῶν μετέλαβεν· ὃς ἔσχε τοιοῦτον τὸ σωμάτιον ὑπὸ τῆς χάριτος συγκροτούμενον, ὡς προσδοκῆσαι πάντας τοὺς ἀγνοοῦντας αὐτοῦ τὴν δίαιταν ὅτι ἐν τρυφῇ διάγει. τούτου τὰς ἀρετὰς τῆς ψυχῆς ἐὰν θέλω διηγήσασθαι κατὰ μέρος ἐπιλείψει μοι ὁ χρόνος· ὃς τοσοῦτον ἦν φιλάνθρωπος καὶ εἰρηνικός, ὡς καὶ αὐτοὺς τοὺς ἐχθροὺς αὐτοῦ τοὺς ἀπίστους αἰδεῖσθαι αὐτοῦ τὴν σκιὰν διὰ τὸ λίαν χρηστόν. τοσαύτην δὲ ἔσχε γνῶσιν τῶν ἁγίων γραφῶν καὶ τῶν θείων δογμάτων, ὡς καὶ | παρ' αὐτὰ τὰ συμπόσια τῶν ἀδελφῶν ἐξίστασθαι τὴν διάνοιαν καὶ ἐνεάζειν· καὶ παρακαλούμενος διηγήσασθαι τὰ τῆς ἐκστάσεως, ἔλεγεν ὅτι Ἀπεδή-

6 A.D. 388 (see App. v. II.) 9 On Isidore see Note 7.

PTlss_2c

1 οὐ......πόλεσιν] om T 2 ἢ ἐρημίαις] om P

I (Περὶ Ἰσιδώρου): PTll_2ss_2

5 Πρώτως] P (TA^B πρῶτος); πρῶτον *B*: + τοίνυν *B*(ss_2) πόλιν] om s_2^{add} (in s_2^{vat}) 5–7 ἐν τῇ δευτέρᾳ......Χριστόν] *B*A^Bls(s_2^{vat}); om PTl_2(s_2^{add}) (see App. v. II.) 6 τοῦ μεγ. βασ.] om $A^B s_2^{vat}$ (s om βασ.) 6, 7 τοῦ νῦν ἐν ἀγγ. ὑπάρχοντος A^B 7 τὴν] + ὀρθὴν A^B*B*s 8 ἐκεῖσε] Ps_2; ἐν τῇ πόλει T*B*l; om l_2; 'in the first place' s παντόθεν] P; πανταχόθεν T*B* 8, 9 ἔν τε] + λόγῳ καὶ *B*l_2 (after ἤθει) s_2^{add} (om ἤθει) 9 τῷ] om T*B* πρεσβυτέρῳ] om T 12 ὄρει] + τῷ T Νητρίας P 13 γέροντα] om ls_2 14 αὐτῆς τῆς *B*; τῆς αὐτοῦ T 15 ἐκτὸς φακ. om $l_2 s_2$ 16 σωμάτιον] Pl (corpusculum); σῶμα T*B* 19 διηγεῖσθαι T 20 καὶ[2]] om T 23 καὶ[2]] om T 24 τῇ διανοίᾳ T: + spiritualibus uisionibus l_2s ἐννεάζειν PT*B*† 24, 25 παρακαλούμενον and λέγειν T*B*

μησα τῇ διανοίᾳ, ἁρπαγεὶς ὑπὸ θεωρίας τινός. ἔγνων κἀγὼ τοῦτον πολλάκις δακρύσαντα ἐπὶ τραπέζης, καὶ τὴν αἰτίαν πυθόμενος τῶν δακρύων ἤκουσα αὐτοῦ λέγοντος ὅτι Αἰδοῦμαι μεταλαμβάνων ἀλόγου τροφῆς, λογικὸς ὑπάρχων καὶ ὀφείλων ἐν παραδείσῳ τρυφῆς διάγειν διὰ τὴν δοθεῖσαν ἡμῖν παρὰ Χριστοῦ ἐξουσίαν. οὗτος γνώριμος ὢν τῇ κατὰ Ῥώμην συγκλήτῳ πάσῃ καὶ ταῖς γυναιξὶ τῶν μεγιστάνων, ὁπηνίκα σὺν Ἀθανασίῳ τῷ ἐπισκόπῳ ἀπεληλύθει τὸ πρῶτον, ἔπειτα σὺν Δημητρίῳ τῷ ἐπισκόπῳ, καὶ περισσεύων πλούτῳ καὶ ἀφθονίᾳ χρειῶν, οὐ διαθήκην ἔγραψε τελευτῶν, οὐ νόμισμα καταλέλοιπεν, οὐ πρᾶγμα ταῖς ἰδίαις αὐτοῦ ἀδελφαῖς παρθένοις οὔσαις· ἀλλὰ παρέθετο αὐτὰς τῷ Χριστῷ λέγων· Ὁ κτίσας ὑμᾶς οἰκονομήσει ὑμῖν τὴν ζωὴν, ὡς κἀμέ. ἦν δὲ σὺν ταῖς ἀδελφαῖς αὐτοῦ σύστημα παρθένων ἑβδομήκοντα.

Οὗτος φοιτήσαντί μοι νέῳ ὄντι πρὸς αὐτὸν καὶ παρακαλοῦντι στοιχειωθῆναι ἐν τῷ μονήρει βίῳ, σφριγώσης ἔτι τῆς ἡλικίας καὶ λόγου μὴ δεομένης ἀλλὰ πόνων τῶν κατὰ σάρκα, ὡς καλὸς πωλοδάμνης ἐξήγαγέ με ἔξω τῆς πόλεως εἰς τὰ λεγόμενα ἐρημικὰ ἀπὸ σημείων πέντε· | (II) καὶ παραδοὺς Δωροθέῳ τινὶ ἀσκητῇ Θηβαίῳ ἑξηκοστὸν ἄγοντι ἔτος ἐν τῷ σπηλαίῳ, κελεύει μοι πληρῶσαι παρ' αὐτῷ τρία ἔτη πρὸς δαμασμὸν τῶν παθῶν· ἠπίστατο γὰρ τὸν γέροντα μεγάλῃ σκληραγωγίᾳ συζῶντα· πάλιν ἐπανακάμπτειν πρὸς αὐτὸν ἐντειλάμενος διδασκαλίας ἕνεκεν πνευματικῆς. μὴ δυνηθεὶς δὲ τρία ἔτη πληρῶσαι, ἀρρωστίᾳ περιπεσών, οὕτως πρὸ τῶν τριῶν ἤρθην ἀπ' αὐτοῦ· ἦν γὰρ αὐτοῦ ἡ δίαιτα αὐχμώδης καὶ ξηροτάτη. διὰ

9 On Demetrius see Note 8. 19, 26—4 (p. 17) Soz. VI. 29 (4) Ὑπερφυῶς δὲ ἐν τούτοις διέπρεπε Δωρόθεος, Θηβαῖος τὸ γένος· ᾧ βίος ἦν ἐν ἡμέρᾳ μὲν ἀπ τῆς πέλας θαλάσσης λίθους συλλέγειν, καὶ ἔτους ἑκάστου οἰκίδιον κατασκευάζειν, καὶ διδόναι τοῖς μὴ δυναμένοις ἑαυτοῖς οἰκοδομεῖν.

PTll$_2$ss$_2$

4 ὑπάρχων] factus a domino l; creatus a deo l$_2$ 5 παρὰ]+τοῦ T 6 Χριστοῦ] 'God' ss$_2$ 7 ταῖς τε TB (γε) 8, 9 Ἀθανασίῳ and Δημητρίῳ interchanged in P 8 ἀρχιεπισκόπῳ T 11 ἰδίαις~αὐτοῦ] P; ἑαυτοῦ TB 13 ὑμῶν TB (+καὶ τὰ πρὸς); uestram ll$_2$ κἀμέ] PA^{B}B†; κάμοὶ B†; κάμοῦ ^{T}B†; meam ll$_2$ 14 παρθένων]+ὡς Ts$_2$ 19 πέντε]+τῆς πόλεως P herv (see Note 9)

II (περὶ Δωροθέου): PTll$_2$ss$_2$

19 καὶ] om T παραδοὺς] PA^B (l$_2$); παραδίδωσι B; παρέδωκε δὲ T: +με TB 20 σπηλαίῳ]+καὶ TB 21 με TB 22 μεγάλη σκληραγωγίας (sic) T 24 πληρῶσαι]+κραταιᾷ Bs$_2$ 25 ἀπ'] παρ' T 26 αὐτοῦ ἡ δ.] TBll$_2$ss$_2$; ἡ τοῦ γέροντος δ. P

πάσης μὲν γὰρ τῆς ἡμέρας ἐν τῷ καύματι ἐν τῇ ἐρήμῳ τῇ παρὰ θάλασσαν συνῆγε λίθους, καὶ τούτους ἀεὶ οἰκοδομῶν καὶ κέλλας ποιῶν παρεχώρει τοῖς μὴ δυναμένοις οἰκοδομεῖν, κατ' ἔτος τελειῶν κέλλαν μίαν. ἐμοῦ δέ ποτε εἰρηκότος αὐτῷ· Τί ποιεῖς, πάτερ, ἐν γήρᾳ τοσούτῳ ἀποκτείνων σοῦ τὸ σωμάτιον ἐν τοῖς καύμασι τούτοις; ἀπεκρίνατο λέγων· Ἀποκτείνει με, ἀποκτείνω αὐτό. ἤσθιε μὲν γὰρ οὐγγίας ἓξ ἄρτου καὶ λεπτολαχάνων δέμα, ἔπινε δὲ ὕδατος τὸ ὅσον. ἐπὶ θεῷ μάρτυρι οὐκ ἔγνων αὐτὸν ἁπλώσαντα πόδας, οὐ καθευδήσαντα ἐπὶ ψιαθίου, οὐκ ἐπὶ κλίνης· ἀλλὰ διὰ πάσης νυκτὸς καθήμενος ἔπλεκε σειρὰν τὴν ἐκ θαλλῶν φοινίκων εἰς λόγον τροφῆς. προσδοκήσας δὲ ὅτι ἐπ' ἐμοῦ τοῦτο ἐποίει, ἐφιλοπεύστησα καὶ παρὰ ἄλλων τῶν τούτου μαθητῶν ἀκριβώσας, οἵτινες ἔμενον κατ' ἰδίαν, λέγοντες ὅτι ἀπὸ νεότητος ταύτην ἔσχε τὴν πολιτείαν, μηδέ ποτε κοιμηθεὶς ἐξεπίτηδες, εἰ μή τι ἐργαζόμενος ἢ ἐσθίων ἐκάμμυσε τὸν ὀφθαλμὸν κατενεχθεὶς ὕπνῳ, ὥστε πολλάκις καὶ τὸν ψωμὸν ἐκπίπτειν ἐκ τοῦ στόματος αὐτοῦ κατὰ τὸν καιρὸν τοῦ φαγεῖν ὑπερβολῇ νυσταγμοῦ. ἀναγκάζοντος δέ μου αὐτόν ποτε μικρὸν ἐπὶ τῆς ψιάθου ἀναπεσεῖν, ὑπολυπούμενος ἔλεγεν·

4—6 Soz. (6) Ὧδε δὲ αὐτῷ μοχθοῦντι προσελθών τις ἔφη· Τί τὸ σῶμα τὸ σὸν ἀποκτείνεις τοσοῦτον; Ὅτι με ἀποκτείνει, ἀπεκρίνατο. **7, 8** (5) Τροφὴ δὲ ἦν αὐτῷ ἄρτου οὐγγίαι ἓξ καὶ λεπτῶν λαχάνων δέμα, καὶ ὕδωρ ποτόν. **9, 10** (5) Οὐδέ ποτε ὠράθη ἐπὶ ῥιπὸς ἢ κλίνης καθευδήσας, ἢ τοὺς πόδας ἐκτείνας ἀνέσει. **10, 11** (4) Νύκτωρ δὲ εἰς αὐτοῦ διατροφὴν ἐκ φοινίκων φύλλων σειρὰς πλέκων σπυρίδας εἰργάζετο. **14** (5) Ἐκ νέου δὲ οὕτως ἀσκήσας, οὐ διέλιπε καὶ γέρων ὤν. **15—2** (p. 18) (5, 6) (Οὐδὲ) ἑκὼν ὕπνῳ ἑαυτὸν ἐκδούς, πλὴν ὅσον ἐργαζόμενος ἢ ἐσθίων, βιασθεὶς ὑπὸ τῆς φύσεως, ἔμυσε τοὺς ὀφθαλμούς· ὡς πολλάκις νυστάζοντος ἐν τῷ ἐσθίειν ἐκπεσεῖν τοῦ στόματος τὴν τροφήν· ποτὲ γοῦν εἰς ἄκρον κρατηθεὶς τῷ ὕπνῳ, ἔλαθεν ἐπὶ τοῦ ῥιπὸς πεσών· καὶ περίλυπος ἐπὶ τούτῳ γεγονὼς ἠρέμα ἔφη· Εἰ τοὺς ἀγγέλους πείσεις καθεύδειν, πείσεις καὶ τὸν σπουδαῖον· ὑπεδήλου δὲ ἑαυτὸν πρὸς τὸν ὕπνον ἴσως ἀποτεινόμενος ἢ τὸν δαίμονα τὸν ἐμποδὼν γενόμενον ταῖς σπουδαίαις πράξεσιν.

PTll_2ss_2

3 *ποιῶν*] om ss_2 *οἰκοδομεῖν*] P Soz; *οἰκοδομῆσαι* T*B* *κατ' ἔτος*] *καθ' ἕκαστον* (om *ἔτος*) T **4** *τελίσκων* T*B* *κέλλαν μίαν*] om T *αὐτῷ* before *ποτε* T **5** *ἀποκτένων* (sic) PA[B] (T *ἀπεκτένων*) **6** *ἀποκτένει* PTA[B] **7** *ἀποκτείνω*] ll_2ss_2; *ἀποκτενῶ* PT (but cf. *ἀποκτένων* and *ἀποκτένει* sup.) *B* *μὲν*] om T *οὐγγίας*] P (Soz); *οὐγκίας* T*B* *ἄρτου*] + *καθ' ἑκάστην ἡμέραν* *B*s_2 **8** *ἔπιε* T *ἐπὶ θεοῦ μάρτυρος* T*B* **11** *σειρὰν*] *σπυρίδας* l_2s_2 (cf. Soz) **12** *ποιεῖ* T **13** *τῶν τούτου*] *αὐτοῦ* T*B* **14** *λέγοντες*] om T **15** *ἐσθίων*] + *εἰ* T **17** *ἐκ*] PTA[B]: om *B* Soz *τοῦ*] om T **19** *πεσεῖν* T*B*

Ἐὰν πείσῃς τοὺς ἀγγέλους κοιμηθῆναι, πείσεις καὶ τὸν σπουδαῖον. ἐν τῷ φρέατι αὐτοῦ περὶ ὥραν ἐννάτην ἀπέστειλέ μέ ποτε πληρῶσαι τὸν κάδον εἰς λόγον μεταλήψεως. ἔτυχε δέ με ἀπελθόντα ἀσπίδα ⸢ἐν τῷ φρέατι⸣ κάτω ἰδεῖν, καὶ μηκέτι ἀντλῆσαι τὸ ὕδωρ, ἀλλ' ἀπελθόντα εἰπεῖν αὐτῷ· Ἀπεθάνομεν, ἀββᾶ· ἀσπίδα γὰρ εἶδον ἐν τῷ φρέατι. ὁ δὲ ὑπομειδιάσας σεμνὸν ἐπὶ πολύ μοι προσέσχε, καὶ σείσας τὴν κεφαλὴν ἔλεγεν· Ἐὰν δόξῃ τῷ διαβόλῳ κατὰ πᾶν φρέαρ γενέσθαι ὄφιν ἢ χελώνην καὶ ἐμπίπτειν εἰς τὰς πηγὰς τῶν ὑδάτων, σὺ μένεις μηδέποτε πίνων; καὶ ἐξελθὼν καὶ δι' ἑαυτοῦ ἀντλήσας, νῆστις πρῶτος | ἀπερρόφησεν εἰπών· Ὅπου σταυρὸς ἐπιφοιτᾷ οὐκ ἰσχύει κακία τινός.

(III) Ὁ μακάριος οὗτος Ἰσίδωρος συντετυχηκὼς Ἀντωνίῳ τῷ μακαρίτῃ γραφῆς ἄξιον διηγήσατό μοι πρᾶγμα, ἀκηκοὼς παρ' αὐτοῦ ὅτι Ποταμιαίνα τις οὕτω καλουμένη κατὰ τὸν καιρὸν Μαξιμιανοῦ τοῦ διώκτου ὡραιοτάτη κόρη ὑπῆρχε παιδίσκη τινός· ἣν πολλαῖς λιπαρήσας ὑποσχέσεσιν ὁ ταύτης δεσπότης ἀναπεῖσαι οὐκ ἠδυνήθη· τελευταῖον δὲ μανεὶς παραδίδωσιν αὐτὴν τῷ τότε ἐπάρχῳ τῆς Ἀλεξανδρείας, ἔκδοτον αὐτὴν δοὺς ὡς χριστιανὴν καὶ βλασφημοῦσαν τοὺς καιροὺς καὶ τοὺς βασιλεῖς ἐπὶ τοῖς διωγμοῖς, ὑποθέμενος αὐτῷ μετὰ χρημάτων ὅτι Ἐὰν συνθῆταί μου τῷ σκόπῳ, ἀτιμώρητον αὐτὴν φύλαξον· ἐὰν δὲ ἐπιμένῃ τῇ αὐστηρίᾳ, παρακαλῶ σε τιμωρηθῆναι

14 On Potamiaena see Note 10.

PTll$_2$ss$_2$

1 *τὸν σπουδαῖον*] *με* ss$_2$ **3** *ἀποπληρῶσαι* T *κάδδον* P *μεταλήψεως*] + *τῆς ἐνάτης ὥρας* T (l nonae ut solebat horae usibus profuturum) **4** *ἐν τῷ φρέατι*] *B*ll$_2$s; om PT: (s$_2$ 'there') *κάτω*] om ss$_2$ *μηκέτι*] + *φόβῳ* *B*s (l perhorruissem) **5** *τὸ*] om T *αὐτῷ*] + *ὅτι* T*B* **6** *ὁ δὲ*] om T: (*B* *ἐκεῖνος*) *ὑπομειδ.*] + *δὲ* T*P* **7** *σεμνὸν*] P*B*s; *μόνον* Tll$_2$; om s$_2$: (cf. *γελάσας σεμνόν* c. XXII. init.) **8** *πᾶν*⌟ *B*ll$_2$ss$_2$; om PT **9** *ἐμπεσεῖν* T **10** *καὶ* [2]] om T *νῆστις*] om ss$_2$ (*νήστης* T*B*†) **11** *τινός*] PTl (alterius sess, ulterius cass); *τοῦ Σατανᾶ* *B*s$_2$ (l$_2$ diaboli); om s

III (Περὶ Ποταμιαίνης): PTll$_2$s$_2$

12, 13 *τῷ μακαρίῳ Ἀντ.* T*B* **13** *μοι διηγ.* T **14** *Ποταμιαίνα*] P*B*l; om Tl$_2$s$_2$ *οὕτω καλουμένη*] Pl (nomine); om T*B*l$_2$s$_2$ *τὸν*] om T **15** *Μαξιμιανοῦ*] PTvenll$_2$; *Μαξιμίνου* *B*; (s$_2$ unpointed) **16** *τινός*] + *ἀκολάστου* *B* ('a worldling' s$_2$) *πολλὰ* T*B* *ὑποσχέσεσι*] + *διαφόροις* *B*l **17** *ἀπατῆσαι* T*B* *ἠδυνήθη*] + *καὶ τὸ* (om *δὲ*) T*B* **18** *αὐτὴν τῷ*] om T **19** *καὶ*] om T *βλασφ.*] + *καὶ* T*B*l$_2$ *καιρούς*] *B*ll$_2$s$_2$[vat] (om s$_2$[add]); *θεοὺς* PT: (see Note 11) **22** *διαφύλαξον* T *ἐμμείνῃ* T*B* *αὐστηρίᾳ*] + *τῶν νόμων* P *παρακαλῶ σε*] PA[B]; *παρεκάλεσε* T*B*; (ll$_2$s$_2$ altered) *τιμωρηθῆναι*] PTs$_2$ (+ 'with all tortures'); *τιμωρουμένην αὐτὴν ἀποθανεῖν* *B*; ut in tormentis deficeret l; ut torqueat usque ad mortem l$_2$.

αὐτήν, ἵνα μὴ ζῶσα καταγελάσῃ τῆς ἀσωτίας μου. ἀχθεῖσα δὲ πρὸ τοῦ βήματος διαφόροις ὀργάνοις τιμωρητικοῖς ἐπυργομαχεῖτο τὴν γνώμην. ἐν οἷς ὀργάνοις καὶ λέβητα μέγαν πλήσας πίσσης ἐκέλευσεν ὑποκαίεσθαι ὁ δικαστής. βραζούσης οὖν τῆς πίσσης καὶ σφοδρῶς ἐκκαιομένης, προέτεινεν αὐτῇ· Ἢ ἄπελθε, ὑποτάγηθι τοῖς θελήμασι τοῦ δεσπότου σου· ἢ ἵνα εἰδῇς ὅτι ἐν τῷ λέβητί σε καταβιβασθῆναι κελεύω. ἡ δὲ ἀπεκρίνατο λέγουσα· Μὴ γένοιτό ποτε τοιοῦτος δικαστὴς ὃς κελεύει ἀσωτίᾳ ὑποτάσσεσθαι. μανεὶς οὖν ἐκεῖνος κελεύει ἐκδυθεῖσαν αὐτὴν βληθῆναι ἐν τῷ λέβητι. ἡ δὲ φωνὴν ἀφίησιν εἰποῦσα· Τὴν κεφαλήν σοι τοῦ βασιλέως σου ὃν σὺ φοβῇ, εἰ κέκριταί σοι τιμωρήσασθαί με οὕτω, κατὰ μικρὸν κέλευσον χαλασθῆναί με ἐν τῷ λέβητι, ἵνα εἰδῇς πόσην μοι χαρίζεται ὑπομονὴν ὁ Χριστὸς ὃν σὺ ἀγνοεῖς. καὶ χαλωμένη κατὰ μικρὸν ἐπὶ παράτασιν ὥρας ἐξέψυξε, φθασάσης τῆς πίσσης περὶ τὸν τράχηλον αὐτῆς.

(IV) Πλεῖστοι μὲν οὖν ὅσοι καὶ ὅσαι ἐτελειώθησαν ἐν τῇ Ἀλεξανδρέων ἐκκλησίᾳ, ἄξιοι τῆς γῆς τῶν πραέων. ἐν οἷς καὶ Δίδυμος ὁ συγγραφεύς, ὁ ἀπὸ ὀμμάτων γενόμενος· οὗ καὶ συντυχίας ἔσχηκα τέσσαρας ἐκ διαλειμμάτων πρὸς αὐτὸν ἀπερχόμενος ἐπὶ δέκα ἔτη. τελειοῦται γὰρ ἐτῶν ὀγδοήκοντα πέντε. οὗτος ἀπὸ ὀμμάτων ὑπῆρχεν, ὡς αὐτός μοι διηγήσατο, τετραέτης τὰς ὄψεις ἀποβαλών, μήτε γράμματα μεμαθηκὼς μήτε διδασκάλοις φοιτήσας· εἶχε γὰρ τὸν κατὰ | φύσιν διδάσκαλον ἐρρωμένον, τὸ ἴδιον συνειδός· ὃς τοσαύτῃ χάριτι ἐκεκόσμητο γνώσεως ὡς καθ' ἱστορίαν πληροῦσθαι ἐπ' αὐτῷ

19 On Didymus see Note 12.

PTll$_2$s$_2$

1 ζῶσα] + λέγων *B* καταγέλασται T μου] αὐτοῦ T 3, 4 πισ. πλ. T*B* 4 ὑποκαίεσθαι] + λαμπροτάτῳ πυρὶ *B*ls$_2^{vat}$ οὖν] δὲ T 5 προέτεινεν] + ὁ ἄρχων *B*l(l$_2$s$_2^{vat}$) αὐτῇ] + ὅτι T*B* ἢ] om T 6 οἶδας T 7 καταγγίζεσθαι T*B* 8 πώποτε (after τοιοῦτος) T*B* ὁ κελεύων T*B* 8, 9 ὑπ. ἀσωτίᾳ T*B* 9 ἀπομανεὶς T*B* ἐκεῖνος] om T αὐτὴν ἐκδ. T*B* 10 εἰς τὸν λεβητα T ἀφ. φωνὴν T*B* εἰποῦσα] + ὅτι T 11 σοι[1]] om *B* σου] om PA^B φοβῇ] σέβῃ T 12 με after κ. μικρὸν T*B* 13 ἴδῃς T*B* ὑπομ. μοι ἐχαρίσατο T*B* 14 χαλασθεῖσα T*B*: (-μένης P) 15 ἐξέψυξε] om P 16 αὐτῆς] PA^{B}ll$_2$s$_2$; om T*B* : + παρέδωκε τὴν ψυχὴν τῷ θεῷ P

IV (Περὶ Διδύμου): PTll$_2$s$_2$

17 οὖν] om T 19 ὁ[2]] om T 20 πρὸς αὐτὸν] om T 21 τελευτᾷ T 26 γνώσεως] + πνευματικῆς *B*l ἐπ' αὐτῷ] om T*B*† (l$_2$ vac)

τὸ γεγραμμένον· Κύριος σοφοῖ τυφλούς. παλαιὰν γὰρ καὶ καινὴν διαθήκην ἡρμήνευσε κατὰ λέξιν· τῶν δὲ δογμάτων οὕτως ἐπεμελήθη, λεπτῶς καὶ ἰσχυρῶς ἐκθέμενος τὸν περὶ αὐτῶν λόγον, ὡς πάντας ὑπερβάλλειν τοὺς ἀρχαίους ἐν γνώσει. ἀναγκάζοντος δὲ αὐτοῦ ποτε ποιῆσαί με ἐν τῷ κελλίῳ αὐτοῦ εὐχήν, καὶ μὴ βουλομένου μου, ἔλεγε διηγούμενος ὅτι Εἰς τὴν κέλλαν ταύτην τρίτον εἰσῆλθεν ὁ μακάριος Ἀντώνιος ἐπισκεψάμενός με· καὶ παρακληθεὶς παρ' ἐμοῦ ⸢ποιῆσαι εὐχὴν εὐθὺς⸣ ἔκλινε γόνυ ἐν τῷ κελλίῳ, καὶ οὐ παρεσκεύασέ με δευτερῶσαι τὸν λόγον, ἔργῳ με παιδεύσας ἐν τῇ ὑπακοῇ. ὥστε εἰ κατ' ἴχνος βαίνεις τῆς αὐτοῦ πολιτείας, ἅτε μονάζων καὶ δι' ἀρετὴν ξενιτεύων, ἀπόθου τὴν φιλονεικίαν. διηγήσατο δέ μοι καὶ τοῦτο, ὅτι Φροντίζοντός μου περὶ τῆς ζωῆς Ἰουλιανοῦ τοῦ ἀθλίου βασιλέως ὡς διώκτου, καὶ ἀδημονοῦντος, μιᾷ τῶν ἡμερῶν ἤμην μέχρις ἑσπέρας βαθείας μὴ γευσάμενος ἄρτου ἕνεκεν τῆς φροντίδος ταύτης, ἔτυχεν ἐν τῷ θρόνῳ καθήμενόν με κατενεχθῆναι εἰς ὕπνον, καὶ ἰδεῖν ἔκστασιν ἵππους λευκοὺς διατρέχοντας μετὰ τῶν ἐπιβατῶν κηρυττόντων· Εἴπατε Διδύμῳ, σήμερον ἑβδόμην ὥραν ἐτελεύτησεν Ἰουλιανός· ἀναστὰς οὖν φάγε, καὶ ἐπίστειλον, φασί, τῷ ἐπισκόπῳ Ἀθανασίῳ, ἵνα κἀκεῖνος γνῷ.

1 Ps. cxlv. 8. 12—20 Soz. VI. 2 (6, 7) Κατ' ἐκείνην δὲ τὴν ἡμέραν καὶ Δίδυμος ὁ ἐκκλησιαστικὸς φιλόσοφος ἐν Ἀλεξανδρείᾳ διατρίβων, οἷά γε τοῦ βασιλέως εἰς τὴν θρησκείαν διασφαλέντος περίλυπος ὤν διά τε αὐτὸν ὡς πεπλανημένον καὶ διὰ τὴν καταφρόνησιν τῶν ἐκκλησιῶν, ἐνήστευέ τε καὶ τὸν θεὸν περὶ τούτου ἱκέτευεν. ὑπὸ δὲ τῆς μερίμνης οὐδὲ τῆς νυκτὸς ἐπιγενομένης μεταλαβὼν τροφῆς, ἐπὶ θρόνου καθεζόμενος εἰς ὕπνον ἠνέχθη· καὶ ὡς ἐν ἐκστάσει γεγονὼς ἔδοξεν ὁρᾶν ἵππους λευκοὺς ἐν τῷ ἀέρι διατρέχοντας· τοὺς δὲ ἐπ' αὐτῶν ὀχουμένους κηρύττειν· Ἀγγείλατε Διδύμῳ, σήμερον περὶ τήνδε τὴν ὥραν Ἰουλιανὸν ἀνῃρῆσθαι· καὶ Ἀθανασίῳ τῷ ἐπισκόπῳ τοῦτο μηνυσάτω· καὶ ἀναστὰς ἐσθιέτω.

$PTll_2s_2$

1 παλαιὰν]+μὲν T*B* 2 διαθ.] om T 3 , καὶ οὕτως ἰσχ. ἐξέθετο P ὀχυρῶς T 4 ὑπερβάλλει T 5 ποιῆσαι after εὐχὴν T κελλίῳ] $PA^B(ll_2)$; οἴκῳ T*B*; (om s_2) αὐτοῦ] om T 6 ἔλεγε]+μοι Bl_2 8 ποιῆσαι εὐχὴν εὐθὺς] Bll_2s_2; om PT: (s_2^{vat} om εὐθὺς) 9 παρεσκεύαζε T 10 ὥστε]+οὖν T*B* 11 βαίνειν T πολ.]+θέλεις T ὡς ἅτε TA^B; ὅσα τε *B* 12 τὴν om T 13 ὅτι]+Καθημένου καὶ P 14 ὡς διώκτου] om l_2s_2 ἤμην] P; καὶ (om ἤμην) T; (*B* alters) 15 γευσαμένου μου ἄρτον T 16 ταύτης] om T καθήμενον] PT; καθεζόμενον *B* Soz 17 εἰς ὕπνον] P Soz; ὕπνῳ T*B* ἔκστασιν PT(l); ἐν ἐκστάσει *B* Soz $l_2(s_2)$ 18 καὶ κηρύττοντας T*B* 19 φάγε]+καὶ T: +σὺ T*B* 20 ἀπόστειλον T*B* φασί· Ἀποστ. T Ἀθ.]+ἐν τῇ οἰκίᾳ *B*l γνῷ]+περὶ τούτου *B*l

καὶ ἐσημειωσάμην, φησί, καὶ τὴν ὥραν καὶ τὸν μῆνα καὶ τὴν ἑβδομάδα καὶ τὴν ἡμέραν, καὶ εὕρηται οὕτως.

(V) Διηγήσατο δέ μοι καὶ περὶ παιδίσκης τινὸς ὀνόματι Ἀλεξάνδρας, ἥτις καταλείψασα τὴν πόλιν καὶ ἐν μνήματι αὐτὴν καθείρξασα δι' ὀπῆς ἐλάμβανε τὰ πρὸς τὴν χρείαν, μήτε ·υναιξὶ μήτε ἀνδράσι συντυγχάνουσα κατ' ὄψιν ἐπὶ ἔτη δέκα. ῷ δὲ δεκάτῳ ἔτει ἐκοιμήθη σχηματίσασα ἑαυτήν, ὡς τὴν ἐν ·υνηθείᾳ ἀπελθοῦσαν καὶ μὴ τυχοῦσαν ἀποκρίσεως ἀπαγγεῖλαι ·μῖν. ἀποχρίσαντες οὖν τὴν θύραν καὶ εἰσελθόντες εὕραμεν ιὐτὴν κοιμηθεῖσαν. ἔλεγε δὲ περὶ αὐτῆς καὶ ἡ τρισμακαρία Μελανία, περὶ ἧς ὕστερον λέξω, ὅτι Κατ' ὄψιν μὲν αὐτὴν οὐκ εἶδον, περὶ δὲ τὴν ὀπὴν στᾶσα παρεκάλεσα εἰπεῖν τὴν αἰτίαν δι' ἣν ἔκλεισεν ἑαυτὴν εἰς τὸ μνῆμα. ἡ δὲ διὰ τῆς ὀπῆς ἐφθέγξατό μοι λέγουσα ὅτι Ἐβλάβη τις τὸν νοῦν εἰς ἐμέ· καὶ ἵνα μὴ δόξω λυπεῖν αὐτὸν ἢ διαβάλλειν, ᾑρησάμην ζῶσαν ἐμαυτὴν εἰς τὸ μνῆμα εἰσαγαγεῖν, ἢ σκανδαλίσαι ψυχὴν κατ' εἰκόνα θεοῦ γενομένην. ἐμοῦ δέ, φησίν, εἰπούσης· Πῶς οὖν καρτερεῖς μὴ συντυγχάνουσα μηδενί, ἀλλὰ πυκτεύουσα τῇ ἀκηδίᾳ; εἶπεν ὅτι Ἀπὸ πρωῒ μέχρις ἐννάτης ὥρας εὔχομαι καθ' ὥραν, νήθουσα τὸ λίνον· τὰς δὲ διαλοίπους ὥρας περιέρχομαι τῷ νῷ τοὺς ἁγίους πατριάρχας καὶ | προφήτας καὶ ἀποστόλους καὶ μάρτυρας· καὶ

2 For a similar story see Note 13.

PTll$_2$s$_2$

1 *καί*[2]] om P **1, 2** *τὴν ὥραν......τὴν ἡμέραν*] PTl$_2$s$_2$; interchange *μῆνα* and *ἡμέραν B*; *ὥραν* last l **2** *εὗρον* PA^B

V (Περὶ Ἀλεξάνδρας): PTll$_2$s$_2$

5 *τὰ τῆς χρείας* T*B* **6** *B*ll$_2$ interchange *ἀνδράσι* and *γυναιξί*; s$_2$ supports PT ('she saw neither woman nor man, and no human being saw her face, and she saw no one's face') *δέκα*] P*B*l; + *καὶ δύο* TA^{B}l$_2$s$_2$ **7** *δεκάτῳ*] P*B*l; *δωδεκάτῳ* TA^{B}l$_2$ (om s$_2$) *κοιμηθεῖσα ἐσχημάτισεν* T*B* **8** *ἀναγγεῖλαι* T*B* **9** *ἀποχρίσαντες*] PT*B*†A^B; *ἀποκρούσαντες B*†l$_2$; (l illisum (illitum l^{rev}) ostium clausumque patefecimus; s$_2$ 'opening') *εὗρον* P **10** *μακαρία* T **11** Μελανία] A^{B37}l$_2$s$_2$; Μελάνη P*B*A^{B38}; Μελάνιον T; Melanius l (cf. Note on c. XLVI.) *ἧς*] + *εἰς* T **12** *εἶδον*] *ἠδυνήθην θεάσασθαι B*l *εἰπεῖν*] + *μοι B*ll$_2$s$_2$ **13** *δι' ἣν*] + *ἀνεχώρησε μὲν τῆς πόλεως B*l$_2$ *ἔκλεισεν ἑαυτὴν*] *ἀνεχώρησεν* T *μνῆμα*] + *τοῦτο* Tl **14** *λέγουσά μοι* T **17** *ποιηθεῖσαν* T*B* *φησιν*] om T*B* *εἰρηκυίας* T*B* **18** *μηδενὶ συντ.* (om *μὴ*) T*B* *ἀλλὰ*] + *μόνη B*l **19, 20** *εὔχομαι ...ὥρας*] om P (homoeoteleuton): (s$_2$ 'I spin and recite psalms') **20** *διαλύπους* (sic) T; *ὑπολοίπους B* **21** *μάρτυρας*] + *τῆς δὲ ἑσπέρας καταλαβούσης B*l *καί*[4]] + *τὰς λοιπὰς ὥρας* Ts$_2$ (l$_2$ hora competenti)

φαγοῦσα τὸν ψωμὸν τὰς ἄλλας ὥρας περιμένω προσκαρτεροῦσα καὶ τὸ τέλος ἐκδεχομένη μετ' ἐλπίδος χρηστῆς.

(VI) Οὐ παραλείψω δὲ ἐν τῷ διηγήματι καὶ τοὺς ἐν καταφρονήσει βεβιωκότας, εἰς ἔπαινον τῶν κατωρθοκότων ἀσφάλειαν δὲ τῶν ἐντυγχανόντων. Παρθένος τις γέγονεν ἐν Ἀλεξανδρείᾳ τῷ μὲν σχήματι ταπεινὴ τῇ δὲ προαιρέσει σοβαρά, πλουσία ἐν χρήμασιν εἰς ἄγαν, μηδέποτε †προΐκασα† ξένῳ μηδὲ παρθένῳ, μὴ ἐκκλησίᾳ, μὴ πένητι ὀβολόν. αὕτη πολλαῖς νουθεσίαις τῶν πατέρων οὐκ ἀπεσκευάζετο τὴν ὕλην. ὑπῆρχε δὲ ταύτῃ καὶ γένος ἐν οἷς τεκνοποιεῖται θυγατέρα ἀδελφῆς ἰδίας, ᾗ νύκτωρ καὶ μεθ' ἡμέραν ἐπηγγέλλετο τὰ αὐτῆς, τοῦ οὐρανίου πόθου ἐκπεσοῦσα. εἶδος γὰρ καὶ τοῦτό ἐστι πλάνης τοῦ διαβόλου, ἐν προσχήματι φιλοσυγγενείας εἰς πλεονεξίαν ὠδίνειν παρασκευάζοντος· ὅτι γὰρ αὐτῷ οὐ μέλει περὶ γένους, ἀδελφοκτονεῖν καὶ μητροκτονεῖν καὶ πατροκτονεῖν ἐκδιδάσκοντος, ὡμολόγηται. ἀλλὰ κἂν δόξῃ συγγενῶν κηδεμονίαν ἐντιθέναι, οὐκ εἰς εὔνοιαν ἐκείνων τοῦτο ποιεῖ, ἀλλ' ὑπὲρ τοῦ τὴν ψυχὴν ἄδικον ἐξασκῆσαι, εἰδὼς τὴν ἀπόφασιν ὅτι Ἄδικοι βασιλείαν θεοῦ οὐ κληρονομήσουσι. δύναται δέ τις φρονήσει κινούμενος θεϊκῇ μήτε τῆς ἑαυτοῦ ψυχῆς καταφρονεῖν, καὶ τοῖς συγγενέσιν αὐτοῦ, εἴ γε λείπονται, διδόναι παραμυθίαν. ὅταν δέ τις ὅλην τὴν ψυχὴν ἑαυτοῦ καθυποτάξῃ κηδεμονίᾳ συγγενῶν, ὑποπίπτει τῷ νόμῳ, ἐπὶ ματαίῳ τὴν ἑαυτοῦ ψυχὴν λογιζόμενος. ᾄδει δὲ ὁ ἱεροψάλτης περὶ τῶν τῆς ψυχῆς

3 This cap. of l is printed in *Bibl. Casin. III. Florileg.* 314, from cod. Cass. 143 (cf. *Prol.* 62). It is cap. 13 in printed l_2. **18** 1 Cor. vi. 9.

PTll_2s_2

1 φαγοῦσα] + μου T*B*l_2s_2 περιμένω] ἔχω ἀναστὰς sic T (*B* quite altered)

VI (Περὶ τῆς πλουσίας Παρθένου): PTll_2s (5—12) s_2

4 κατωρθ.] + καὶ (om δὲ) T **7** †προΐκασα†] sic P; προήσασα T; προϊεμένη (παρασχομένη ἐκ A[B]) τῶν ἑαυτῆς τι *B*; 'she never gave' s_2; nusquam procedere solens l; numquam procedens l_2; 'she never helped' s. Probably we should read προικίσασα, which the metaphrast and the translators of ll_2s connected with the roots of ἧκα, ἥκω, or ἵκω **7, 8** μὴ ξ. μὴ π. T(*B*) **8** ὀβολὸν] + ἐπιδεδωκυῖα T(ll_2s) **9** τῶν] + ἁγίων *B*l(s) ὕλην] + τοῦ πλούτου *B*l_2 **10** αὐτῇ T **11** ἡ P ἐπήγγελτο T τὰ αὐτῆς] om T **12–6** (p. 23) εἶδος......συνδιαλύεσθαι] om s in add 17177 **12** ἐστι before καὶ T*B* **13** τοῦ] om T προσχήματι] + τῆς T εἰς] τὴν T*B* **14** ἐμέλησε T; μέλλει (sic) P περὶ γένους] οὗς (sic) T **15** πατρ. καὶ μητρ. P **17** ἐκτιθέναι T: + τισὶν *B*l τοῦτο] om T **20** θεϊκῇ κιν. T ψυχ. αὐτοῦ T **22** αὐτοῦ T καταπατήσῃ T*B* **24** ἱεροψάλτης] + Δαβὶδ *B*l_2s_2

φροντιζόντων ἐν φόβῳ, ὅτι Τίς ἀναβήσεται εἰς τὸ ὄρος κυρίου; ἀντὶ τοῦ, σπανίως· ἢ τίς στήσεται ἐν τόπῳ ἁγίῳ αὐτοῦ; ἀθῷος χερσὶ καὶ καθαρὸς τῇ καρδίᾳ, ὃς οὐκ ἔλαβεν ἐπὶ ματαίῳ τὴν ψυχὴν αὐτοῦ. οὗτοι γὰρ ἐπὶ ματαίῳ αὐτὴν λαμβάνουσιν ὅσοι τῶν ἀρετῶν ἀμελοῦσι, νομίζοντες αὐτὴν τῷ σαρκίῳ συνδιαλύεσθαι.

Ταύτην τὴν παρθένον, τὸ δὴ λεγόμενον, θελήσας ὁ ἁγιώτατος Μακάριος, ὁ πρεσβύτερος καὶ ἀφηγούμενος τοῦ πτωχείου τῶν λελωβημένων, φλεβοτομῆσαι εἰς κουφισμὸν τῆς πλεονεξίας, σοφίζεται πρᾶγμα τοιοῦτον· ἦν γὰρ ἐν νεότητι λιθουργὸς ὃν λέγουσι καβιδάριον. καὶ ἀπελθὼν λέγει αὐτῇ· Λίθοι ἀναγκαῖοι σμάραγδοι καὶ ὑάκινθοι ἐμπεπτώκασί μοι, καὶ εἴτε εὑρεσιμαῖοί εἰσιν εἴτε κλεψιμαῖοι οὐκ ἔχω εἰπεῖν. τιμῇ οὐχ ὑποβάλλονται, ὑπὲρ διατίμησιν ὄντες· πιπράσκει δὲ αὐτοὺς πεντακοσίων νομισμάτων ὁ ἔχων. | εἰ δοκεῖ σοι αὐτοὺς λαβεῖν, ἀπὸ ἑνὸς λίθου δύνασαι σῶσαι τὰ πεντεκόσια νομίσματα, τοῖς δὲ λοιποῖς εἰς κόσμον τῆς ἀδελφιδῆς σου συγχρήσασθαι. ἐκκρεμαμένη ἡ παρθένος δελεάζεται καὶ πίπτει αὐτοῦ εἰς τοὺς πόδας, Τῶν ποδῶν σου, λέγουσα, ἐφάπτομαι, μή τις ἄλλος αὐτοὺς λάβῃ. προτρέπεται οὖν αὐτὴν ὅτι Παραγένου ἕως τῆς οἰκίας μου καὶ βλέπε αὐτούς. ἡ δὲ οὐκ ἠνέσχετο, ἀλλὰ προσρίπτει αὐτῷ τὰ πεντακόσια νομίσματα λέγουσα· Ὡς θέλεις, λάβε αὐτούς· ἐγὼ γὰρ οὐ θέλω ἰδεῖν τὸν ἄνθρωπον τὸν πιπράσκοντα. ὁ δὲ λαβὼν τὰ πεντακόσια νομίσματα δίδωσιν εἰς τὰς χρείας τοῦ πτωχείου. χρόνου δὲ παριππεύσαντος, ἐπειδὴ μεγάλην ὑπόληψιν ἐδόκει ἔχειν ὁ ἀνὴρ ἐν Ἀλεξανδρείᾳ φιλόθεος ὢν καὶ

1—4 Ps. xxiii. 3, 4.   **8** On this Macarius see Note 26.

PTll$_2$s (7—26) s$_2$

1 *ὄρος*] + *τοῦ* T*B*   **2** *σπάνιος* P   **4, 5** *ὅσοι......ἀμελοῦσι* after *συνδιαλ.* T*B*l$_2$ (om l)   **5** *αὐτὴν*] om T   *σαρκικῷ* T   **7** *ταύτην*] s recommences: + *οὖν* T   *θελήσας* before *τὸ δὴ λεγ.* P   **9** *φλεβοτομῆσαι...πλεονεξίας* before *ὁ ἁγιώτατος* T*B*l$_2$s   **10** *δρᾶμα* T*B*   *νεότητι*] + *αὐτοῦ* *B*(ll$_2$s)   *ὃν*] *ὃς* P*   **12** *εὑρεμαῖοι* T   **16** *σῶσαι*] *λαβεῖν* T   **17** *χρήσασθαι* T   **17, 18** *ἐκκρεμ. ἡ παρθ.*] *ἡ δὲ ἡττημένη ὑπὸ φιλαργυρίας* P   **18** *πίπτει......πόδας*] om l   **19** *τῶν ποδῶν......ἐφάπτομαι*] PT (om *ἐφάπτομαι*) l (complexa pedes ipsius orat et petit) s ('I beg from your feet'); *B* om and reads: *καὶ λέγει αὐτῷ· Δέομαί σου*; so s$_2$: (l$_2$ per sanctitatem tuam)   **20, 21** P om *ὅτι* and reads: *παραγενέσθαι εἰς τὴν οἰκίαν αὐτοῦ καὶ ἰδεῖν αὐτούς* (others txt)   **21** *βλέπε*] *B*; *βλέπεις* T   **22** *λέγουσα*] om T, + *ὅτι*   *λάβε*] + *μοι* P   **23** *γὰρ*] om T   **24** *λαβὼν οὖν* (om *ὁ δὲ*) T*B*   **26** *ἐδόκει ἔχειν*] P; *εἶχεν* T (before *ὑπολ.*) *B*

ἐλεήμων, ἤκμασε γὰρ μέχρι τῶν ἑκατὸν ἐτῶν, ᾧ συνεχρονίσαμεν καὶ ἡμεῖς, εὐλαβεῖτο αὐτὸν ὑπομνῆσαι. τέλος εὑροῦσα αὐτὸν ἐν τῇ ἐκκλησίᾳ λέγει αὐτῷ· Δέομαί σου, τί κελεύεις περὶ τῶν λίθων ἐκείνων δι' οὓς δεδώκαμεν τὰ πεντακόσια νομίσματα; ὁ δὲ ἀπεκρίνατο λέγων· Ἔκτοτε ἀφ' οὗ δέδωκάς μοι τὸν χρυσόν, κατέβαλον αὐτὸν εἰς τὴν τιμὴν τῶν λίθων· καὶ εἰ βούλει ἐλθεῖν καὶ ἰδεῖν αὐτοὺς ἐν τῷ ὀσπιτίῳ, ἐκεῖ γὰρ κεῖνται, ἐλθὲ καὶ βλέπε, ἐάν σοι ἤρεσαν, ἐπεὶ λάβε σου τὸ χρυσίον. ἡ δὲ ἦλθεν ἀσμενέστατα. ἦν δὲ τὸ πτωχεῖον εἰς μὲν τὰ ἀνώγεα ἔχον γυναῖκας, εἰς δὲ τὰ κατώγεα ἄνδρας. καὶ ἀγαγὼν αὐτὴν εἰσάγει εἰς τὸν πυλῶνα καὶ λέγει αὐτῇ· Τί θέλεις πρῶτον ἰδεῖν; τοὺς ὑακίνθους, ἢ τοὺς σμαράγδους; λέγει αὐτῷ· Ὃ δοκεῖ σοι. ἀνάγει αὐτὴν εἰς τὰ ἀνώγεα καὶ δείκνυσιν αὐτῇ ἠκρωτηριασμένας γυναῖκας λελωβημένας ὄψεις ἐχούσας· καὶ λέγει αὐτῇ· Ἰδοὺ οἱ ὑάκινθοι. καὶ κατάγει αὐτὴν πάλιν κάτω καὶ λέγει αὐτῇ, δείξας αὐτῇ τοὺς ἄνδρας· Ἰδοὺ οἱ σμάραγδοι, ἐάν σοι ἀρέσκωσιν, ἐπεὶ λάβε σου τὸ χρυσίον. οὕτω διατραπεῖσα ἐκείνη ἐξῆλθε, καὶ ἀπελθοῦσα ἀπὸ πολλῆς λύπης, ὅτι οὐ κατὰ θεὸν πεποίηκε τὸ πρᾶγμα, ἐνόσησεν· ἐς ὕστερον εὐχαριστήσασα τῷ πρεσβυτέρῳ, τῆς κόρης ἧς ἐφρόντιζε μετὰ γάμον ἀτέκνου ἀποθανούσης.

(VII) Συντυχὼν οὖν καὶ συνδιατρίψας τοῖς περὶ Ἀλεξάνδρειαν μοναστηρίοις ἔτη τρία, καλλίστοις καὶ σπουδαιοτάτοις ἀνδράσιν ὡς δισχιλίοις, ἀναχωρήσας ἐκεῖθεν ἦλθον εἰς τὸ ὄρος τῆς Νιτρίας. μεταξὺ δὲ τοῦ ὄρους τούτου καὶ τῆς Ἀλεξανδρείας

21—23 Soz. VI. 29 (3) Ἐν δὲ τῷ τότε πολλοὶ καὶ ἀγαθοὶ σπουδαίως ἐφιλοσόφουν ἀνὰ τὴν Ἀλεξάνδρειαν, ἀμφὶ δισχίλιοι ὄντες. **24** On Nitria and Scete see Note 14 (compare *Hist. Mon.* cited *Prol.* 270–5).

$PTll_2ss_2$

2 αὐτὸν] αὐτὴν P* **3** λέγει αὐτῷ before εὑροῦσα T δέομαί σου] 'I beg from your feet' s_2 κελεύεις] λέγεις Bs_2 **4** δι' οὓς] P; ὧν T*B* δεδώκαμεν] $TBll_2s$; δέδωκά σοι Ps_2 **5** λέγων] + αὐτῇ *B* (ll_2s) ἀφ' οὗ] οὖν T κατεβαλόμην T **6** τὴν] om T **8** ἤρεσαν] P; ἀρέσουσι T*B* (-ωσι *B*†) ἐπεὶ] here and **16** the versions render ἐπεὶ as if εἰ δὲ μὴ λάβε] P (cf. **17**); αἴρεις T*B* (-ῃς *B*+) ἡ δὲ] om T ἦλθεν] + ad domum l; ad cellam l_2 **9, 13** ἀνώγεα] PA^B; ἀνέγεα (sic) T; ἀνάγαια *B*† **10** κατώγεα] PA^B; κατάγεα T; κατάγαια *B*† ἀπαγαγὼν δὲ T*B*; παραγενομένης δὲ αὐτῆς A^B **12** ὃ] ὡς T **14** λελωβισμένας T; the form λωβάζω exists **16** ἀρέσκουσιν T **17** ἐκείνη] om T **17, 18** ἀπῆλθεν ἐξελθοῦσα T **19** ἐς] om T πρεσβυτέρῳ] + δοῦσα δόξαν τῷ θεῷ P

VII (Περὶ τῶν ἐν τῇ Νιτρίᾳ): $PTls_2$

24 Νητρίας PA^B μεταξὺ......Ἀλεξανδρείας] om T

λίμνη κεῖται ἡ καλουμένη Μαρία, σημείων ἑβδομήκοντα· ἣν διαπλεύσας διὰ μιᾶς καὶ ἡμισείας ἡμέρας, ἦλθον εἰς τὸ ὄρος ἐπὶ τὸ μέρος τῆς μεσημβρίας· | ᾧ ὄρει παράκειται ἡ πανέρημος παρατείνουσα ἕως Αἰθιοπίας καὶ τῶν Μαζίκων καὶ τῆς Μαυριτανίας. ἐν ᾧ ὄρει οἰκοῦσιν ἄνδρες ὡς πεντακισχίλιοι διαφόρους ἔχοντες πολιτείας, ἕκαστος ὡς δύναται καὶ ὡς βούλεται· ὡς ἐξεῖναι καὶ μόνον μένειν, καὶ δεύτερον, καὶ πολλοστόν. ἐν τούτῳ τῷ ὄρει ἀρτοκοπεῖά εἰσιν ἑπτὰ ὑπηρετούμενα κἀκείνοις καὶ τοῖς εἰς τὴν πανέρημον ἀναχωρηταῖς, ἀνδράσιν ἑξακοσίοις. παροικήσας οὖν ἐν τούτῳ τῷ ὄρει ἐνιαυτὸν καὶ πολλὰ ὠφεληθεὶς ἀπὸ τῶν μακαρίων πατέρων Ἀρσισίου τοῦ μεγάλου καὶ Πουτουβαστοῦ καὶ Ἀσίωνος καὶ Κρονίου καὶ Σαραπίωνος, καὶ πολλοῖς διηγήμασι πατέρων παρ' αὐτῶν κεντρωθείς, εἰσῆλθον εἰς τὴν ἔρημον τὴν ἐνδοτάτω. ἐν τῷ ὄρει τούτῳ τῆς Νιτρίας ἐκκλησία ἐστὶ μεγάλη, ἐν ᾗ ἵστανται φοίνικες τρεῖς, ἕκαστος ἔχων μάστιγα κρεμαμένην. καὶ ὁ μέν ἐστιν εἰς λόγον μοναζόντων πταιόντων, ὁ δὲ λῃστῶν, ἐάν γε ἐμπέσωσιν, ὁ δὲ τῶν περιτυχόντων· ὡς πάντας πταίοντας καὶ διελεγχομένους ὡς ἀξίους πληγῶν περιλαμβάνειν τὸν φοίνικα, καὶ λαμβάνοντας ἐπὶ νώτου ῥητὰς οὕτως ἀπολύεσθαι. πρόσκειται δὲ τῇ ἐκκλησίᾳ ξενοδοχεῖον, εἰς ὃ τὸν ἀπελθόντα ξένον, μέχρις οὗ ἐξέλθῃ αὐθαιρέτως, δεξιοῦνται πάντα τὸν χρόνον, κἂν ἐπὶ διετίαν ἢ τριετίαν μείνῃ· συγχωρήσαντες δὲ αὐτῷ ἑβδομάδα μίαν ἐν ἀργίᾳ, τὰς λοιπὰς ἡμέρας περισπῶσιν ἐν ἔργοις, ἢ ἐν κήπῳ ἢ ἐν ἀρτο-

11, 12 On the monks here named see Note 15. **11—13** Soz. III. 14 (4) Ἐν τούτῳ δὲ περὶ τὸν αὐτὸν χῶρον ἐφιλοσόφουν Παμβώ τε καὶ Ἡρακλείδης καὶ Κρόνιος καὶ Παφνούτιος καὶ Πουτουβαστὴς καὶ Ἀρσίσιος καὶ Σεραπίων ὁ μέγας καὶ Πιτυρίων. VI. 30 (1) (Διέπρεπον) καὶ ὁ μέγας Ἀρσίσιος (al. Ὀρσ.) καὶ Πουτουβαστὴς καὶ Ἀρσίων καὶ Σεραπίων,

PTls_2

2 ἡμίσεως T **8** ὑπηρετοῦντα T **10** τούτῳ after τῷ ὄρει T*B* ἐνιαυτὸν] + ὅλον *B*l **11** Ἀρσισίου] Ἀρσασίου A[B] (here only); Arsenius s_2^{vat} **12** Ποτουβαστοῦ T (Qutifdustus s_2^{vat}) Ἀσίωνος] PT (Ἀσίονος) l; Ἀρσίων Soz; Ἁγίωνος *B* (Argenius s_2^{vat}) Κρονίου] PTA[B] Soz; Χρονίου *B*l Σαραπίωνος] PT*B*† (8–11) A[B37] Soz (title); Σεραπίωνος *B* (rest) A[B38] l Soz (text) **13** διηγήμασι] + ἀρχαιοτέρων *B*l (qui ante ipsos fuerant) **15** Νητρίας P ἐκκλ.] + μία *B*l μεγίστη T*B*l **18** πάντας] *B*l; πάντως P; πάντα T; om s_2 **19** ὡς] om T*B* περιλαμβάνει (sic) T καὶ] om T λαμβάνοντας] P (λαμβάνων τὰς) l; λαμβάνοντα T*B* **20** ἐπὶ] P; κατὰ *B*; om T (+ τοῦ) **22** δεξιῶνται P **23** μένῃ T; μεῖναι θελήσῃ *B*l **24** περισπ.] + αὐτὸν T*B*

κοπείῳ ἢ ἐν μαγειρείῳ. εἰ δὲ ἀξιόλογος εἴη, διδόασιν αὐτῷ βιβλίον, μὴ συγχωρήσαντες αὐτῷ ἕως ἕκτης ὥρας μηδενὶ συντυχεῖν. ἐν τούτῳ τῷ ὄρει καὶ ἰατροὶ διάγουσι καὶ πλακουντάριοι. κέχρηνται δὲ καὶ οἴνῳ, καὶ πιπράσκεται οἶνος. πάντες δὲ οὗτοι ὀθόνην ἐργάζονται ταῖς χερσίν, ὡς εἶναι πάντες ἀνενδεεῖς. καὶ δὴ καὶ περὶ ὥραν ἐννάτην ἔστι στάντα ἀκοῦσαι πῶς ἀφ' ἑκάστης μονῆς ψαλμῳδίαι ἐξέρχονται, ὡς προσδοκῆσαι μετάρσιον εἶναι ἐν τῷ παραδείσῳ. τὴν δὲ ἐκκλησίαν σαββάτῳ καταλαμβάνουσι μόνῳ καὶ κυριακῇ. ὀκτὼ δὲ ἀφηγούμενοι πρεσβύτεροι ταύτης τῆς ἐκκλησίας εἰσίν, ἐν ᾗ μέχρις οὗ ζῇ ὁ πρῶτος πρεσβύτερος ἄλλος οὐδεὶς προσφέρει, οὐχ ὁμιλεῖ, οὐ δικάζει, ἀλλ' ἡσύχως αὐτῷ προσκαθέζονται μόνον.

Οὗτος ὁ Ἀρσίσιος καὶ ἄλλοι πολλοὶ σὺν αὐτῷ γέροντες, οὓς ἡμεῖς ἑωράκαμεν, σύγχρονοι ἦσαν τοῦ μακαρίου Ἀντωνίου. ἐν οἷς διηγοῦντο καὶ τὸν Ἀμοῦν εἰδέναι τὸν Νιτριώτην, οὗ τὴν ψυχὴν εἶδεν ἀναλαμβανομένην ὁ Ἀντώνιος καὶ ὑπὸ ἀγγέλων ὁδηγουμένην. οὗτος ἔλεγε καὶ Παχώμιον εἰδέναι τὸν Ταβεννησιώτην, ἄνδρα προφήτην, ἀρχιμανδρίτην ἀνδρῶν τρισχιλίων, περὶ οὗ ἐς ὕστερον διηγήσομαι. |

(VIII) Ἔλεγε δὲ τὸν Ἀμοῦν βεβιωκέναι τοιούτῳ τρόπῳ· ὅτι ὀρφανὸς ὑπάρχων, νεανίσκος ὡς ἐτῶν εἴκοσι δύο βίᾳ παρὰ

13 (Soz.) οἳ καὶ αὐτοὶ σύγχρονοι Ἀντωνίου ἦσαν. **20** On Amoun see Note 16.

20—18 (p. 28) Soz. I. 14 (1–3) Περὶ τοῦτον τὸν χρόνον καὶ Ἀμοῦν ὁ Αἰγύπτιος ἐφιλοσόφει· ὃν δὴ λόγος βιασαμένων τῶν

Socr. IV. 23 (Ἀμμοῦν) νέος ὢν παρῃτεῖτο τὸν γάμον· ὡς δέ τινες τῶν προσηκόντων παρῄνουν μὴ καθυβρίζειν τὸν

PTls_2

1 ἀξιολ.] + τις *B*l **2** βιβλίον] + ἀναγινώσκειν *B*l συγχωροῦντες T ἕκτης] *B*ls_2; τῆς PT **3** πλακουντιάριοι P **6** καὶ δὴ] om T περὶ ὥραν ἐνν.] PTA^{B}; circa uespertinas horas ls_2; τῆς ἑσπέρας καταλαβούσης *B* ἔστι] altered to ἐπὶ in P: before περὶ T στάντα] T; πάντα P; ἑστάναι καὶ *B* **7** ὡς] καὶ T **9** μόνον T*B* **11, 12** οὐ δικ. before οὐχ ὁμ. T*B* **12** συγκαθέζονται *B*T (συγκα, om θεζονται μόνον)

PTAls_2

13 ὁ] om T: + μέγας A*B* Ὀρσίσιος P (here only) *B*† (cf. one Soz MS) πολλοὶ] om A γερ. σὺν αὐτῷ T*B* **14** ἁγίου A **15** διηγοῦντο] PA (+ μοι); διηγεῖτο T*B*l Ἀμοῦν] T*B*Al$^{sess}s_2$; Ἀμμοῦν P(*B*^{22})l^{cass} (see Note 16) Νητρ. P **16** ὁ] om T ὑπὸ ἀγγέλων] om s_2: + εἰς τοὺς οὐρανοὺς *B*ls_2 **17** οὗτοι (originally οὗτος) ἔλεγον P Ταβενησιώτην PA **18** προφήτην] PTA; προφητικὸν χάρισμα ἐσχηκότα *B*l; om s_2: + καὶ T τρισχιλίων] om T

VIII (Περὶ Ἀμοῦν τοῦ Νιτριώτου): PTls_2

20 Ἀμοῦν] T*B*A^{B}l$^{sJss}s_2$ Soz; Ἀμμοῦν Pl^{cass} (see Note 16) (P has Ἀμμοῦν throughout)

τοῦ ἰδίου θείου ἐζεύχθη γυναικί· καὶ μὴ δυνηθεὶς ἀντισχεῖν τῇ τοῦ θείου ἀνάγκῃ, ἔδοξε καὶ στεφανοῦσθαι καὶ καθέζεσθαι ἐν παστῷ, καὶ πάντα ὑπομεμενηκέναι τὰ κατὰ τὸν γάμον. μετὰ δὲ τὸ ἐξελθεῖν πάντας κοιμήσαντας αὐτοὺς ἐν τῷ παστῷ καὶ τῇ κλίνῃ, ἀναστὰς ὁ Ἀμοῦν ἀποκλείει τὴν θύραν, καὶ καθίσας προσκαλεῖται τὴν μακαρίαν αὐτοῦ σύμβιον καὶ λέγει αὐτῇ· Δεῦρο κυρία, λοιπὸν διηγήσομαί σοι τὸ πρᾶγμα· ὁ γάμος ὃν ἐγαμήσαμεν οὗτός ἐστι περισσὸν ἔχων οὐδέν. καλῶς οὖν ποιήσωμεν ἐὰν ἀπὸ τοῦ νῦν ἕκαστος ἡμῶν κατ' ἰδίαν καθευδήσῃ, ἵνα καὶ τῷ θεῷ ἀρέσωμεν φυλάξαντες ἄθικτον τὴν παρθενίαν. καὶ ἐξενεγκὼν ἐκ τοῦ κόλπου αὐτοῦ βιβλιδάριον ἐκ προσώπου τοῦ ἀποστόλου καὶ τοῦ σωτῆρος ἀνεγίνωσκε τῇ κόρῃ ἀπείρῳ οὔσῃ γραφῶν, καὶ τῷ πλείστῳ μέρει πάντα προστιθεὶς τῇ ἰδίᾳ διανοίᾳ τὸν περὶ παρθενίας καὶ ἁγνείας εἰσηγεῖτο λόγον· ὡς ἐκείνην τῇ χάριτι τοῦ θεοῦ πληροφορηθεῖσαν εἰπεῖν· Κἀγὼ πεπληροφόρημαι, κύριε· καὶ τί κελεύεις λοιπόν; Κελεύω, φησίν, ἵνα ἕκαστος ἡμῶν ἀπὸ τοῦ νῦν κατ' ἰδίαν μένῃ. ἡ δὲ οὐκ ἠνέσχετο, εἰποῦσα· Ἐν τῷ αὐτῷ οἴκῳ μένωμεν, ἐν διαφόροις δὲ κλίναις. ζήσας οὖν ἔτη δεκαοκτὼ μετ' αὐτῆς ἐν τῷ αὐτῷ οἴκῳ, διὰ πάσης ἡμέρας ἐσχόλαζε τῷ κήπῳ καὶ τῇ βαλσάμῳ· βαλσαμουργὸς γὰρ ἦν. ἥτις βάλσαμος ἀμπέλου δίκην φυτεύεται, γεωργουμένη

οἰκείων γυναῖκα ἀγαγέσθαι, μὴ πειραθῆναι δὲ αὐτῆς, ᾗ θέμις ἀνδράσι· ὡς γὰρ ἀρχὴν εἶχεν αὐτοῖς ὁ γάμος, καὶ νύμφην παροῦσαν οἷα νυμφίος εἰς τὸν θάλαμον λαβὼν ἐμονώθη· Ὁ μὲν δὴ γάμος ἡμῖν οὗτος, ἔφη, ὦ γύναι, μέχρι τούτων τετέλεσται· ἡλίκον δὲ ἀγαθόν ἐστι δυνηθῆναι παρθένον διαμεῖναι ἐκ τῶν ἱερῶν γραφῶν ὑφηγεῖτο, καὶ ἐπειρᾶτο καθ' ἑαυτὸν οἰκεῖν· ἀλλ' ἐπειδὴ τοὺς περὶ παρθενίας λόγους ἐπῄνει ἡ γυνή, χωρισθῆναι δὲ αὐτοῦ χαλεπῶς ἔφερεν, ἰδίᾳ καθεύδων ἐπὶ δέκα καὶ ὀκτὼ ἔτεσι συνῆν αὐτῇ,

γάμον, ἀλλὰ γυναῖκα ἄγεσθαι, πείθεται μὲν καὶ ἔρχεται ἐπὶ γάμον· εὐθὺς δὲ ἀπὸ τῆς παστάδος παραλαβὼν τὴν παρθένον, καὶ ἀγαγὼν ἐπὶ τὸν κοιτῶνα μετὰ τῆς εἰωθυίας πομπῆς, τέλος ἀναχωρησάντων τῶν ἐπιτηδείων, αὐτὸς βιβλίον λαβὼν ἀποστολικόν, τὴν πρὸς Κορινθίους Παύλου ἐπιστολὴν ἀνεγίνωσκε, κ.τ.λ.

[The rest of Socr.'s version of the story differs widely in the details from Pall. and Soz.]

PTls_2

2, 3 *ἐν παστῷ καθ.* T*B* **4** *κοιμήσαντες* P*TA^B **5** *ὁ*] + *μακάριος* *B*l(s_2) **6** *σύμβιον*] *καὶ γνησίαν σύζυγον* *B* (cf. Phil. iv. 3); et uere unanimem coniugem suam l **7** *κυρία*] + *μου* T: + *καὶ ἀδελφὴ* *B*s_2 **10** *θεῷ*] PTA^B; *Χριστῷ* *B*ls_2 *ἐκτελέσαντες* T*B* **11** *αὐτοῦ*] PA^B; om T*B*l **17** *μείνῃ* T **18** *μείνωμεν* T*B* **20** *τῃ*] P^{cor}; *τῷ* P*T*B* *βαλσάμῳ*] P; *βαλσαμῶνι* T*B*

καὶ κλαδευομένη, πολὺν ἔχουσα πόνον. ἑσπέρας οὖν εἰσερχόμενος εἰς τὸν οἶκον ἐποίει εὐχὰς καὶ ἤσθιε μετ' αὐτῆς· καὶ νυκτερινὴν πάλιν ποιῶν εὐχὴν ἐξήρχετο. τούτων οὕτως ἐπιτελουμένων, καὶ ἀμφοτέρων εἰς ἀπάθειαν ἐληλακότων, ἐνήργησαν αἱ εὐχαὶ τοῦ Ἀμοῦν, καὶ λέγει αὐτῷ τελευταῖον ἐκείνη· Ἔχω σοί τι εἰπεῖν, κύριέ μου· ἵνα, ἐάν μου ἀκούσῃς, πληροφορηθῶ ὅτι κατὰ θεόν με ἀγαπᾷς. λέγει αὐτῇ· Εἰπὲ ὃ βούλει. ἡ δὲ λέγει αὐτῷ· Δίκαιον πρᾶγμά ἐστι ἄνδρα σε ὄντα καὶ δικαιοσύνην ἀσκοῦντα, ὁμοίως κἀμὲ ἐζηλωκυῖαν τὴν αὐτήν σοι ὁδόν, κατ' ἰδίαν μένειν. ἄτοπον γάρ ἐστι κρύπτεσθαί σου τὴν τοιαύτην ἀρετὴν συνοικοῦντί μοι ἐν ἁγνείᾳ. ὁ δὲ εὐχαριστήσας τῷ θεῷ, λέγει αὐτῇ· Οὐκοῦν ἔχε σὺ τοῦτον τὸν οἶκον· ἐγὼ δὲ ποιήσω ἐμαυτῷ ἕτερον οἶκον. καὶ ἐξελθὼν κατέλαβε τὸ ἐνδότερον τοῦ τῆς Νιτρίας ὄρους· οὔπω γὰρ ἦν τότε μοναστήρια· καὶ ποιεῖ ἑαυτῷ δύο θόλους κελλίων. καὶ βιώσας ἄλλα εἴκοσι δύο ἔτη ἐν τῇ ἐρήμῳ ἐτελεύτησε, μᾶλλον δὲ ἐκοιμήθη, δὶς τοῦ ἔτους ὁρῶν τὴν μακαρίαν σύμβιον αὐτοῦ. |

Τούτου θαῦμα διηγήσατο ὁ μακάριος Ἀθανάσιος ὁ ἐπίσκοπος εἰς τὸν περὶ Ἀντωνίου βίον, ὅτι παρερχόμενος τὸν Λύκον

μηδὲ οὕτω μοναχικῆς ἀσκήσεως ἀμελῶν· ἐν τοσούτῳ δὲ χρόνῳ ζηλώσασα τὴν τοῦ ἀνδρὸς ἀρετὴν ἡ γυνή, ἐλογίσατο μὴ δίκαιον εἶναι τηλικοῦτον ὄντα οἴκοι κρύπτεσθαι δι' αὐτήν, καὶ χρῆναι ἑκάτερον κεχωρισμένως οἰκοῦντα φιλοσοφεῖν· καὶ περὶ τούτου ἐδεήθη τοῦ ἀνδρός. ὁ δὲ χάριν ὁμολογήσας τῷ θεῷ ὑπὲρ τῶν βεβουλευμένων τῇ γυναικί· Σὺ μὲν δή, ἔφη, τοῦτον τὸν οἶκον ἔχε· ἐγὼ δὲ ἕτερον ἐμαυτῷ ποιήσω. καὶ πρὸς μεσημβρίαν τῆς Μαρείας λίμνης καταλαβὼν ἔρημον τόπον, ἀμφὶ τὴν Σκῆτιν καὶ τὸ καλούμενον τῆς Νητρίας ὄρος, δύο καὶ εἴκοσι ἔτη ἐνθάδε ἐφιλοσόφησε, δὶς ἑκάστου ἔτους τὴν γυναῖκα θεώμενος. [The rest of Soz. account is based not on Pall. but on *Vita Ant.* and *Hist. Mon.*]

19—5 (p. 29) *Vita Ant.* § 60. Ποτὲ χρείας γενομένης παρελθεῖν αὐτὸν τὸν ποταμὸν τὸν λεγόμενον Λύκον· ἦν δὲ τότε πλήμμυρα τῶν ὑδάτων· ἠξίωσε τὸν σὺν αὐτῷ

PTls_2

2 ἐποίει] P καὶ ποιῶν T*B* ἤσθιε] P*B* (om καὶ[1]); ἠσθίων (sic) T καὶ[2]] om T **3** πάλιν νυκτ. T*B* ποιήσας T εὐχὴν] P; σύναξιν T; εὐχὰς καὶ συνάξεις *B*; nocturnis precibus ex more celebratis l; om s_2 ἐξήρχετο] PT; ὑπὸ βαθὺν ὄρθρον ἀπίει εἰς τὸν κῆπον *B*; ad opus solitum mane pergebat l; 'he went forth in the morning' s_2 **6** ἀκούσῃς μου T **8** αὐτῷ] οὐ inserted m. 2 in P πρᾶγμα] om T ἄνδρα] + γε T **9** ὄντα] + θεοσεβῆ *B*s_2 ('who fearest God') **11** συνοικοῦντα T*B* **12** κυρίῳ P ἔχε σὺ] ἔχες (sic) T τὸν] om T **13** ἐγὼ......οἶκον] om s_2 (homoeotel.) ποιῶ T κατέλαβε] P Soz; εἰσῆλθε *B*; om T **14** τὸ] om T Νητρ. P ἦν] + ἐκεῖ *B*ls_2 **15** καὶ[1]] Pl; om T*B* **17** αὐτοῦ σύμβ. T **18** τοῦτο τὸ θ. T (A^{B44}) **19** ὅτι περ T*B*

ποταμὸν ἅμα Θεοδώρῳ τῷ μαθητῇ αὐτοῦ, καὶ εὐλαβούμενος ἀποδύσασθαι ἵνα μὴ γυμνὸν αὐτὸν ἴδῃ, εἰς τὸ πέραν εὑρέθη δίχα πορθμείου μετενεχθεὶς ὑπὸ ἀγγέλου. οὗτος τοίνυν ὁ Ἀμοῦν οὕτως ἐβίωσε καὶ οὕτως ἐτελειώθη ὡς τὸν μακάριον Ἀντώνιον τὴν ψυχὴν αὐτοῦ ἰδεῖν ὑπὸ ἀγγέλων ἀναγομένην. τοῦτον τὸν ποταμὸν μετὰ δειλίας ἐγὼ πορθμείῳ παρῆλθον· διῶρυξ γάρ ἐστι τοῦ μεγάλου Νείλου.

(IX) Ἐν τῷ ὄρει τούτῳ τῆς Νιτρίας γέγονεν ἀνὴρ ἀσκητὴς Ὢρ ὀνόματι, | ᾧ πολλὴν προσεμαρτύρει ἀρετὴν καὶ πᾶσα μὲν ἡ ἀδελφότης ἐξαιρέτως δὲ ἡ ἄνθρωπος τοῦ θεοῦ Μελανία, πρὸ ἐμοῦ εἰσελθοῦσα εἰς ⌜τοῦτο⌝ τὸ ὄρος· ἐγὼ γὰρ αὐτὸν οὐ κατείληφα ζῶντα. καὶ τοῦτο ἔλεγον ἐν τοῖς διηγήμασιν ὅτι οὔτε ἐψεύσατό ποτε, οὔτε ὤμοσεν, οὔτε κατηρήσατό τινα, οὔτε ἐκτὸς τῆς χρείας ἐλάλησεν.

(X) Τούτου τοῦ ὄρους γέγονε καὶ ὁ μακάριος Παμβώ, διδάσκαλος Διοσκόρου τοῦ ἐπισκόπου καὶ Ἀμμωνίου καὶ Εὐσεβίου καὶ Εὐθυμίου τῶν ἀδελφῶν, καὶ Ὠριγένους τοῦ ἀδελ-

Θεόδωρον μακρὰν ἀπ' αὐτοῦ γενέσθαι, ἵνα μὴ ἀλλήλους ἴδωσι γυμνοὺς ἐν τῷ διανήχεσθαι τὸ ὕδωρ. εἶτα ἀπελθόντος τοῦ Θεοδώρου, ᾐσχύνετο πάλιν καὶ ἑαυτὸν ἰδεῖν γυμνόν. ἕως τοίνυν ᾐσχύνετο καὶ ἐφρόντιζεν, ἐξαίφνης ἀπηνέχθη εἰς τὸ πέραν κ.τ.λ. *Ibid.* Καὶ γάρ ποτε πάλιν καθήμενος ἐν τῷ ὄρει καὶ ἀναβλέψας, εἶδεν ἐν τῷ ἀέρι (al. ὄρει) ἀναγόμενόν τινα, πολλήν τε τῶν ἀπαντώντων γινομένην τὴν χαράν......ταύτην εἶναι τοῦ Ἀμοῦν τὴν ψυχὴν τοῦ ἐν τῇ Νιτρίου μοναχοῦ.

9 On Or see Note 17. 15 On Pambo see Note 18. (This is one of the caps. edited by Preuschen, *Pall. u. Ruf.* 119—123. On c see *Prol.* 128. On the variations in the proper names throughout the cap. see *Introd.* § 8.)

1 τῷ] om T*B* 2 ἴδῃ] + ποτέ *B*l εὑρέθη] ἀπηνέχθη T (l translatus est) 3, 4 οὗτος......ἐτελειώθη] Pl (iste igitur A. ita uixit atque ita obiit); οὗτός ἐστιν ὁ Ἀ. ὁ οὕτως βιώσας καὶ οὕτως τελευτήσας T*B*; om s_2 5 αὐτοῦ ψυχ. T ὑπὸ] ἐπ' T ὑπὸ ἀγγέλων] om s_2 ἀναγομένην] + εἰς τὸν οὐρανὸν *B*ls_2 6 τὸν] + Λύκον T*B*s_2

IX (Περὶ Ὢρ): PT apophth (12—14, cf. *Introd.* § 4) ll_2css_2

8 τούτῳ] om T Νητρίας P 9 Hor l_2s_2 ᾧ] c begins here καὶ] om T μὲν] om T 10, 11 ἐξαιρέτως......ὄρος] om Tl_2c 10 Μελάνη P 11 τοῦτο] om P; txt *B*ls αὐτὸν after κατ. T 12 καὶ] om *B*s(c) τοῦτο] + δὲ T*B*: apophth begins here ἔλεγον] ἔλεγεν *B*†l ἐν τοῖς διηγήμασιν] om apophth s_2 13 τινα] P*B*ls_2; ἄνθρωπον apophth (gr and lat); om T$l_2$cs 14 τῆς χρείας] ἀνάγκης apophth

X (Περὶ Παμβώ): PTll_2css_2

15 γέγονε] + πάροικος *B*l 16 Διοσκ. τοῦ ἐπ.] + 'he it was who made me a presbyter' s_2 Ἀμμωνίου] Ἀμμῶνος and om καὶ Εὐσεβ.......ἀδελφῶν TvenA[B]l_2 (Ammonius) c; txt P*B*lss_2 17 τῶν ἀδελφῶν] om ss_2 Ὠριγένους] P*B*lss_2; Ἰωάννου TvenA[B]l_2c ἀδελφοῦ Tven (l_2 fratres)

φιδοῦ Δρακοντίου ἀνδρὸς θαυμαστοῦ. ὃς Παμβὼ εἶχε μὲν ἀνδραγαθήματα καὶ προτερήματα πλεῖστα, ἐν οἷς δὲ καὶ τοῦτο· τοσοῦτον ἦν ὑπερόπτης χρυσοῦ καὶ ἀργύρου, ὡς ἀπαιτεῖ ὁ λόγος. διηγεῖτο γάρ μοι ἡ μακαρία Μελανία ὅτι Ἐν ἀρχαῖς παραγενομένη εἰς Ἀλεξάνδρειαν ἀπὸ τῆς Ῥώμης, καὶ ἀκούσασα περὶ τῆς τούτου ἀρετῆς, Ἰσιδώρου μοι τοῦ μακαρίου διηγησαμένου καὶ ὁδηγήσαντος πρὸς αὐτὸν εἰς τὴν ἔρημον, προσήνεγκα αὐτῷ ἀργενταρίαν τριακοσίων λιτρῶν ἀργυρίου, παρακαλοῦσα αὐτὸν ἐκ τῶν πραγμάτων μου μετασχεῖν. ὁ δὲ καθεζόμενος καὶ πλέκων θάλλους εὐλόγησέ με φωνῇ μόνῃ καὶ εἶπεν· Ὁ θεὸς δῴη σοι τὸν μισθόν. καὶ λέγει τῷ οἰκονόμῳ αὐτοῦ Ὠριγένει· Δέξαι καὶ οἰκονόμησον αὐτὸ πάσῃ τῇ κατὰ Λιβύην καὶ ταῖς νήσοις ἀδελφότητι· ταῦτα γὰρ τὰ μοναστήρια πένεται πλέον· παραγγείλας αὐτῷ μηδενὶ τῶν ἐν Αἰγύπτῳ δοῦναι, διὰ τὸ εὐπορωτέραν εἶναι τὴν χώραν. ἐγὼ δέ, φησίν, ἑστῶσα καὶ ἐκδεχομένη τιμηθῆναι ἢ δοξασθῆναι ὑπ᾽ αὐτοῦ ἐπὶ τῇ δόσει, μηδὲν παρ᾽ αὐτοῦ ἀκούσασα, εἶπον αὐτῷ· Ἵνα εἰδῇς κύριε πόσον ἐστί, τριακόσιαι λίτραι εἰσίν. ὁ δὲ μηδὲ ὅλως ἀνανεύσας ἀπεκρίνατό μοι· Ὦι ἤνεγκας αὐτά, τέκνον, σταθμοῦ χρείαν οὐκ ἔχει. ὁ γὰρ τὰ ὄρη σταθμίζων πολλῷ μᾶλλον ἐπίσταται τὴν ποσότητα τοῦ ἀργυρίου. εἰ μὲν γὰρ ἐμοὶ αὐτὸ ἐδίδως, καλῶς ἔλεγες· εἰ δὲ θεῷ, τῷ τοὺς δύο ὀβολοὺς μὴ παριδόντι, σιώπα. οὕτως ᾠκονόμησε, φησίν, ὁ

PTll$_2$css$_2$

1 ἀνδρὸς θαυμ.] 'bishop of Timenhor' (Hermopolis Parva) c (cf. *Prol.* 154) ὃς] οὗτος ὁ T*B* μὲν] om T 2 δὲ] om TB† 3 χρυσίου T*B* ἀργυρίου T*B* 4 Μελάνη P; Μελανίον T ἀρχῇ T 5 τῆς] om T 6 Ἰσιδώρου] + τοῦ πρεσβυτέρου *B*c (+ καὶ ξενοδόχου *B*) μοι] om ll$_2$ (obl. nar.) τοῦ μακαρίου] om ll$_2$c 7 ἔρημον] + ὅτι T*B* 8 παρακαλέσασα T*B* 10 φωνῇ μόνῃ] μόνον s; om l$_2$s$_2$; (c 'in a low voice') 12 Ὠριγένει] P*B*lss$_2$; Θεοδώρῳ TA^{B}l$_2$c αὐτὰ T*B* 12, 13 πάσῃ ...ἀδελφότητι] Ps; τῇ κατὰ Λ. πάσῃ καὶ τῇ ἐν ταῖς ν. ἀδελφότησι (sic) T; πάσαις ταῖς κατὰ Λ. καὶ ταῖς ἐν ταῖς ν. ἀδελφότησι A^B; πᾶσι τοῖς κ. Λ. καὶ τοῖς ἐν τ. ν. ἀδελφοῖς *B*ll$_2$cs$_2$ 14 πλέον] + παρὰ τὰ ἄλλα *B* (not A^B) lc 15–19 ἐγὼ δὲ...ἀπεκρίνατό μοι] 3rd pers. in l 17 ὑπ᾽ αὐτοῦ] om Tl$_2$s(lc) τῇ] + τοσαύτῃ *B*s δόσει] + καὶ T*B* 18 ὅτι Κύριε ἵνα οἶδας T*B* λίτραι] + ἀργύρου *B*†k(l) 19 ὁ δὲ] + πάλιν T*B* μήτε T ὅλως] om Tsl$_2$ νεύσασα (sic) T 21 πολλῷ μᾶλλον] om ss$_2$c πλέον T*B*† 22 καλῶς] + μοι καὶ T*B* (l$_2$s): + τὸν σταθμὸν *B*(l$_2$s) θεῷ] + αὐτὰ προσήνεγκας *B*(l$_2$c) 23 ὀβολοὺς] + τῆς χήρας sl$_2$c (l^{cass} interlined) παριδόντι] + nec tuam oblationem obliuioni tradit l$_2$; 'will receive thy sacrifice also' c σιώπα] om l$_2$; + ἡσύχαζε *B* (not A^B) ('do not boast' c) οὕτως] Ps$_2$; + οὖν T*B*ll$_2$cs: but in Tll$_2$s the clause οὕτως......ὅρος is connected with what follows

κύριος ἐν τῷ εἰσελθεῖν με εἰς τὸ ὄρος. μετ' ὀλίγον δὲ χρόνον κοιμᾶται ὁ ἄνθρωπος τοῦ θεοῦ ἀπύρεκτος, μὴ νοσήσας, ἀλλὰ τὴν σπυρίδα καταράπτων, ἐτῶν ὢν ἑβδομήκοντα· ὃς μεταστειλάμενός με, καὶ | τοῦ τελευταίου κεντήματος πρὸς ἀπαρτισμὸν ὄντος, μέλλων ἐκλείπειν λέγει μοι· Δέξαι ταύτην τὴν σπυρίδα ἐκ τῶν χειρῶν μου, ἵνα μέμνησαί μου· ἄλλο γάρ σοι οὐκ ἔχω τι καταλείψω. ὃν ἐνταφιάσασα καὶ ὀθονίοις τὸ σῶμα ἑλίξασα κατέθετο· καὶ οὕτως ἀνεχώρησε τῆς ἐρήμου, ἕως θανάτου ἔχουσα τὴν σπυρίδα μεθ' ἑαυτῆς.

Οὗτος ὁ Παμβὼ τελευτῶν, κατ' αὐτὴν τὴν ὥραν τοῦ ἐκλιμπάνειν παρεστῶσι Ὠριγένει τῷ πρεσβυτέρῳ καὶ οἰκονόμῳ καὶ Ἀμμωνίῳ, ἀνδράσι περιβοήτοις, καὶ λοιποῖς ἀδελφοῖς, τοῦτο λέγεται εἰρηκέναι, ὅτι Ἀφ' οὗ ἦλθον εἰς τὸν τόπον τοῦτον τῆς ἐρήμου καὶ ᾠκοδόμησά μου τὴν κέλλαν καὶ ᾤκησα, ἐκτὸς τῶν χειρῶν μου οὐ μέμνημαι δωρεὰν ἄρτον φαγών· οὐ μεταμεμέλημαι ἐπὶ λόγῳ ᾧ ἐλάλησα ἕως τῆς ἄρτι ὥρας· καὶ οὕτως ἀπέρχομαι πρὸς τὸν θεὸν ὡς μηδὲ ἀρξάμενος τοῦ θεοσεβεῖν. προσεμαρτύρουν δὲ ἀφηγούμενοι τοῦτο ἡμῖν Ὠριγένης τε καὶ

15 2 Thess. iii. 8.

PT apophth (10—18) lb_2css_2

1 δὲ] P; om T*B*: (18 days s_2) **2** κοιμᾶται] P; ἐκοιμήθη T; κεκοίμηται *B* ἀπύρεκτος] here $Plcs_2$; after καταράπτων Tl_2; ἀπυρ. μὴ νοσ. after ἑβδ. s; (*B* tr. to after καταλείψω) **3** καταράπτων] (+'he died' ll_2) ὢν] om T*B* μετεστείλατο (om ὃς) T*B* **4** με (and **5** μοι) third pers. in l **5** μέλλων ἐκλείπειν] Plc(s); ἐκλειμπάνει καὶ T; om Bs_2; (l_2 novissime) **6** ἐμῶν χειρῶν T*B* **7** καταλείψω] καταλεῖψαι T; (+in Bss_2c varying statements that he died) ὀθόνῃ T; ὀθόναις *B*† **8** κατέθετο καὶ] om T; (καὶ ἀποθεμένη *B*) ἀνεχώρησε]+ἐκ T: ἀνχώρησα (whole sentence in first pers.) *B*s ἔχουσα] after ἐκείνην T; after ἑαυτῆς *B* **9** σπυρίδα] +pro benedictione l_2s: +ἐκείνην T*B*s **10** οὗτος] apophthegma begins here (cf. *Introd.* § 4) **11–13** (apophth εἶπε τοῖς π. αὐτῷ ἁγίοις ἀνδράσιν ὅτι κ.τ.λ.) **11** Ὠριγένει] $Blss_2$; Μακαρίῳ and om καὶ οἰκονόμῳ PTA^Bl_2c **12** Ἀμμωνίῳ] Ἄμμωνι Tc (+Theodore) περιβοήτοις]+σὺν T*B*† καὶ λ. ἀδελφοῖς] om *B*† **13** τὸν τόπον] om ss_2c (montem l_2) **14** τῆς ἐρήμου] apophth (gr and both lat verss) $TBll_2css_2$; om P ᾤκησα]+ἐν αὐτῇ apophth (gr, lat doubtful) l_2css_2; ἐνθάδε *B* ἐκτὸς]+ἔργου *B* apophth (lat both verss) l_2css_2; txt PT apophth (gr); l paraphr **15** δωρεὰν] om apophth ἄρτον φαγών] apophth T*B*; ὅτι δ. ἔφαγον ἄρτον P οὐ] οὐδὲ apophth *B*† **17** μηδὲ] μὴ T τοῦ] P*B*; om T apophth θεοσεβεῖν] l_2 and s, add 17177, break off here to end of chapter; s^{an} presents a *B* text; c becomes a loose paraphrase, and apophth alters the text freely **18** δὲ]+αὐτῷ T*B* τοῦτο] om T*B* ἡμῖν]+οἱ δοῦλοι τοῦ Χρ. *B*l Ὠριγένης] Bls_2; Θεόδωρος PTc (Ammon, Theodore and Jacob) (apophth vac) Ὠρ. τε κ. Ἀμ.] οἱ πατέρες A^B

Ἀμμώνιος ὅτι Οὐδέποτε ἐρωτηθεὶς λόγον γραφικὸν ἢ ἄλλον τινὰ πραγματικὸν παραυτὰ ἀπεκρίνατο, ἀλλ' ἔλεγεν· Οὐδέπω εὕρηκα. πολλάκις δὲ παρῆλθε καὶ τρίμηνον καὶ ἀπόκρισιν οὐκ ἐδίδου, λέγων μὴ κατειληφέναι. οὕτω μέντοι τὰς ἀποφάσεις αὐτοῦ ἐδέχοντο, γινομένας περιεσκεμμένως κατὰ θεόν, ὡς ἀπὸ θεοῦ. ταύτην γὰρ τὴν ἀρετὴν ἐλέγετο ⌜καὶ ὑπὲρ τὸν μέγαν Ἀντώνιον⌝ καὶ ὑπὲρ πάντας ἐσχηκέναι, τὴν εἰς τὸ ἀκριβὲς τοῦ λόγου.

Φέρεται δὲ τοιαύτη πρᾶξις τοῦ Παμβώ, ὅτι Πίωρ ὁ ἀσκητὴς παραβαλὼν αὐτῷ ἴδιον ἀπήνεγκεν ἄρτον, καὶ ἐγκληθεὶς παρ' αὐτοῦ· Τίνος ἕνεκεν τοῦτο πεποίηκας; ἀπεκρίνατο· Ἵνα σε μὴ βαρήσω, φησίν. ὃν σιγῇ ῥητῶς ἐπαίδευσε· μετὰ χρόνον γὰρ παραβαλὼν αὐτῷ, βρέξας αὐτοῦ τὸν ἄρτον ἐβάσταζε, καὶ ἐπερωτηθείς· Τί πεποίηκας οὕτως; εἶπεν· Ἵνα μή σε βαρήσω καὶ ἔβρεξα.

(XI) Ἀμμώνιος οὗτος ὁ μαθητὴς αὐτοῦ ἅμα ⌜τρισὶν ἀδελφοῖς ἑτέροις καὶ⌝ δυσὶν ἀδελφαῖς αὐτοῦ εἰς ἄκρον φιλοθείας ἐλάσαντες, κατειλήφασι τὴν ἔρημον, κἀκεῖναι κατ' ἰδίαν ποιήσασαι μονὴν καὶ †οὗτοι† κατ' ἰδίαν, ὡς ἱκανὸν ἀπέχειν μεταξὺ ἀλλήλων. ἐπειδὴ δὲ καθ' ὑπερβολὴν φιλόλογος ἦν ὁ ἀνήρ, καὶ

9 On Pior see Note on c. XXXIX. **16** On Ammonius the Tall see Note 19. **17** Soz. VI. 30 (3) *Λέγεται δὲ τοῦτον τὸν Ἀμμώνιον εἰς ἄκρον φιλοσοφίας προελθεῖν,...* **20** (3) *καὶ φιλόλογον εἰς ἄγαν γενέσθαι.*

PT [apophth] l(c)s_2

1 *Ἄμμων* T(c) *λόγον*] + *ἢ* T*B*l **2** *παραυτὰ*] *εὐθὺς* apophth *B*†; *εὐθὺς ἢ παραυτὰ B*† **3** *οὐκ ἐδίδ. ἀποκρ.* apophth *B* **4** *μὴ*] *μήπω B*l **6–8** *ταύτην...... λόγου*] om c **6, 7** *καὶ ὑπὲρ......Ἀντώνιον*] *B*ls_2; om PT (homoeotel. ?) **7** *καὶ*] om P **8** *λόγου*] s_2 breaks off to end of chapter

PTl(c)

11 *πεποίηκεν*] T *μή σε* T*B*† **12** *φησίν*] om T*B* *ὃν*] *οὗ* T *μετὰ*] + *τινα B*l *γὰρ* after *βρέξας* T **13** *αὐτῷ*] om T *αὐτοῦ τὸν*] om T **14** *τί πεπ. οὕτως*] om T

XI (Περὶ Ἀμμωνίου): PTl$l_2$$s_2$

16 *Ἀμμὼν* PT **16, 17** *τρισὶν......καὶ*] *B*ls_2 (l_2 cf. *Prol.* 68); om PT (suppression of Tall Brothers probably due to Tendenz) **18–20** *κἀκεῖναι......ἀλλήλων*] P (but *οὗτος*) T (but *οὕτως*); l_2 sororibus suis sequestratim fecerunt monasterioli habitaculum et sibi ipsis separatim fecerunt, ut inter se et illas etc.; l separatas sibimet mansiones utrique fecerunt, ita ut etc.; s_2 'and they (masc.) allowed them (fem.) to dwell in the neighbourhood'; *B καὶ ἀμφοτέρας τὰς μονὰς κατ' ἰδίαν ἐποίησαν τῶν τε ἀνδρῶν καὶ τῶν γυναικῶν* **19** †*οὗτοι*† ex conject: *οὗτος* P, *οὕτως* T **20** *δὲ*] *περ* T

πόλις τις ἠράσθη αὐτοῦ εἰς λόγον ἐπισκόπου, προσῆλθον τῷ μακαρίῳ Τιμοθέῳ παρακαλέσαντες αὐτὸν χειροτονῆσαι αὐτὸν αὐτοῖς ἐπίσκοπον. καὶ λέγει αὐτοῖς· Ἀγάγετέ μοι αὐτὸν καὶ χειροτονῶ αὐτόν. ὡς οὖν ἀπῆλθον μετὰ βοηθείας καὶ εἶδεν ὅτι κατελήφθη, παρεκάλεσεν αὐτοὺς καὶ διωμόσατο μὴ καταδέχεσθαι | χειροτονίαν, μηδὲ ἐξέρχεσθαι τῆς ἐρήμου· καὶ οὐ συνεχώρησαν αὐτῷ. βλεπόντων οὖν αὐτῶν λαβὼν ψαλίδα τὸ οὖς αὐτοῦ τὸ ἀριστερὸν ἕως πυθμένος ἐψάλισε, λέγων αὐτοῖς· Κἂν ἀπὸ τοῦ νῦν πληροφορήθητε ὅτι ἀδύνατόν μοι γενέσθαι, τοῦ νόμου ἀπαγορεύοντος ὠτότμητον εἰς ἱερωσύνην μὴ ἀπάγεσθαι. οὕτως οὖν ἀφέντες αὐτὸν ἀνεχώρησαν, καὶ ἀπελθόντες εἶπον τῷ ἐπισκόπῳ. καὶ λέγει αὐτοῖς· Οὗτος ὁ νόμος παρὰ Ἰουδαίοις πολιτευέσθω· ἐμοὶ δὲ καὶ ῥινότμητον ἐὰν ἐνέγκητε, ἄξιον ὄντα τοῖς τρόποις, χειροτονῶ. ἀπελθόντες οὖν πάλιν παρεκάλουν αὐτόν· καὶ διώμνυτο αὐτοῖς ὅτι Ἐάν με ἀναγκάσητε, τὴν γλῶσσάν μου ἀποτέμνω. οὕτως οὖν ἀφέντες αὐτὸν ἀνεχώρησαν.

Τούτου τοῦ Ἀμμωνίου φέρεται τὸ θαῦμα τοῦτο, ὅτι οὐδέποτε

2 On Timotheus see Note 20. **4—17** Soz. (4) Μέλλων δέ ποτε πρὸς χειροτονίαν ἐπισκοπῆς συλλαμβάνεσθαι, ὡς ἀντιβολῶν οὐκ ἔπεισεν ἀπιέναι τοὺς ἐπ' αὐτὸν ἐληλυθότας, ἀποτεμὼν τὸ οὖς, Ἄπιτε, ἔφη· λοιπὸν γὰρ οὐδὲ ἑκόντα με ὁ ἱερατικὸς νόμος συγχωρεῖ χειροτονεῖσθαι, ἄρτιον γὰρ χρῆναι τὸν ἱερέα καθίστασθαι. (5) ἀναχωρήσαντες δὲ ἐπεὶ τάδε ἔγνωσαν Ἰουδαίοις φυλακτέα, τῇ δὲ ἐκκλησίᾳ σώματος μηδὲν μέλειν, ἢν μόνον ἄρτιος ᾖ τοῖς τρόποις ὁ ἱερεύς, αὖθις ἀνέστρεψαν ὡς συλληψόμενοι τὸν ἄνδρα. ὁ δὲ ἦ μὴν καὶ τὴν γλῶσσαν ἐκτεμεῖν διωμόσατο εἰ βιάσασθαι πειραθεῖεν. δείσαντες οὖν τὴν ἀπειλὴν ἀπεχώρουν. αὐτός τε ἐντεῦθεν Ἀμμώνιος ὁ Παρώτης ὠνομάζετο. (Cf. Socr. IV. 23: Οὗτος ὁ Ἀμμώνιος εἰς ἐπισκοπὴν ἑλκόμενος καὶ διαφυγὼν τὸ δεξιὸν οὖς αὐτοῦ ἐξέκοψεν, ὅπως ἂν τῷ ἀσχήμῳ τοῦ σώματος τὴν χειροτονίαν ἐκφύγῃ.) **18—3** (p. 34) (3) (Λέγεται)......ἡδονῆς τε καὶ ῥᾳστώνης ἀνδρείως κρατῆσαι.

PTll$_2$s$_2$

2 Τιμοθέῳ] + ἐπισκόπῳ *B*l$_2$ (om Τιμ. + Ἀλεξανδρείας l$_2$) παρακαλοῦντες T*B* αὐτὸν[1]] om T χειροτονηθῆναι T αὐτὸν[2]] Ἀμμώνιον *B*l$_2$ αὐτοῖς αὐτὸν T **3** ἐπίσκοπον καὶ] om T αὐτοῖς[2]] + ὅτι T **4** χειροτονῶ] + ὑμῖν *B*l αὐτὸν] om T: + ἐπίσκοπον ll$_2$ βοηθείας] + πολλῆς *B*l: + εἰς τὸ συλλαβέσθαι αὐτὸν *B*l (Soz) **6** χειροτονίαν] Pl$_2$ (*B* τὸ πρᾶγμα); om T(ls$_2$) καὶ] ὡς δὲ *B*(ll$_2$) **7** συνεχώρουν T*B* αὐτῶν] πάντων *B*l λαβὼν ψαλ.] T*B* (ἀφαρπάσας) ll$_2$s$_2$; om P **9** μοι] με *B*T (after γεν.) **10** γενέσθαι] + ὅπερ αὐτοὶ ἀναγκάζετε *B*l; episcopum l$_2$ ἀπαγορεύσαντος T **11** προάγεσθαι T*B* καὶ] om T ἀπελθόντες] + οὖν T **12** εἶπον] + ταῦτα *B*l ἀρχιεπ. T **14** ἐνέγκητε] + μόνον *B* Soz **16** ἀφέντες αὐτὸν after ἀνεχώρησαν T **18** Ἀμμὼν P; Ἀμμῶνος T (τοῦ Ἀμ. after τοῦτο) τὸ] om T

ἡδονῆς αὐτῷ ἐπαναστάσης τοῦ σαρκίου αὐτοῦ ἐφείσατο, ἀλλὰ σίδηρον ἐκπυρώσας προσετίθει τοῖς ἑαυτοῦ μέλεσιν, ὡς πάντοτε αὐτὸν ἡλκωμένον εἶναι. ἡ μέντοι τράπεζα αὐτοῦ γέγονεν ἐκ νεότητος ὠμοφαγία ἕως θανάτου· οὐδὲν γὰρ ὃ διὰ πυρὸς διήρχετο ἔφαγέ ποτε ἐκτὸς ἄρτου. παλαιὰν δὲ καὶ καινὴν γραφὴν ἀποστηθίσας καὶ ἐν συγγράμμασιν ἀνδρῶν ἐλλογίμων Ὠριγένους καὶ Διδύμου καὶ Πιερίου καὶ Στεφάνου διῆλθε μυριάδας ἑξακοσίας, ὡς μαρτυροῦσιν αὐτῷ οἱ τῆς ἐρήμου πατέρες. παρακλητικὸς δὲ ἦν τοῖς ἐν τῇ ἐρήμῳ ἀδελφοῖς εἴ τις καὶ ἄλλος. ⌜τούτῳ ψήφους ἐδίδου ὁ μακάριος Εὐάγριος ἀνὴρ πνευματοφόρος καὶ διακριτικός, λέγων ὅτι Οὐδέποτε αὐτοῦ ἀπαθέστερον ἑώρακα ἄνθρωπον⌝.

[Οὗτος ἐν Κωνσταντίνου πόλει ποτὲ παραγενόμενος διὰ χρείαν, - - - - - - μετ' ὀλίγον χρόνον κοιμᾶται, καὶ θάπτεται ἐν τῷ μαρτυρίῳ τῷ λεγομένῳ Ῥουφινιαναῖς. οὗ τὸ μνῆμα λέγεται θεραπεύειν πάντας τοὺς ῥιγιαζομένους.]

3—5 Soz. (3) *ἐκ νέου μέχρι τελευτῆς, πλὴν ἄρτου μηδενὸς γεύσασθαι ἐν πυρὶ γενομένου.* **6—8** (3) *...ὡς τοὺς Ὠριγένους καὶ Διδύμου καὶ τῶν ἄλλων ἐκκλησιαστικῶν λόγους διεξελθεῖν* (al. *διελθεῖν*). **7** On Pierius and Stephanus see Note 21. **10** On Evagrius see Note on c. XXXVIII.

13—16 *οὗτος......ῥιγιαζομένους*] The text is constructed from s_2 and B. The following is a translation of s_2 (the Syriac is given in Note 22): 'This man when there came a great need and necessity, had betaken himself to Constantinople, and slept in peace, and was buried in the house of the martyrs called the Rufinian; of whose sepulchre it is said that it cures those who are ailing from evil spirits, and it expels even fevers from men.'

The following is the text of B as found in Paris MS. 1627 (no. 47 in List) and attested by Anan Isho's Syriac (Bed. p. 47); it is a better text than that of the generality of B MSS. and l^{rev}: *Οὗτος ὁ μακάριος ἐν Κωνσταντίνου πόλει ποτὲ παραγενόμενος, διὰ χρείαν τῶν τῆς ἐρήμου πολιτῶν, πολλαῖς*

PTl_2 (1—9) s_2

1 *τῷ σαρκίῳ* T *ἐφείσατο*] + *τῆς σαρκὸς* T **2** *πυρώσας* T *ἑαυτοῦ*] om T *ὡς*] *ἀπὸ* (om *ὡς*) T **3** *εἶναι*] Here there is a lacuna in l in all three MSS., extending to *νόσους* p. 37, l. 3 **5** *διίει* *B*T (*διείη*) *δὲ*] om T **5–8** *παλαιὰν......ἑξακοσίας*] om s_2 **7** *Ὠριγ. καὶ Δ. καὶ Π. καὶ Σ.*] *B* Soz (l^{rev}); *Ἀθανασίου καὶ Βασιλείου* PTA^B; sanctorum antiquorum patrum orthodoxorum sacerdotum domini l_2: s_2 vac *διελθὼν* T **8** *μυριάδας*] $PTBl_2$ (myriadas); (cf. c. LV, and Soz. III. 16 (4): (*Ἐφραίμ*) *λέγεται τὰς πάσας ἀμφὶ τὰς τριακοσίας μυριάδας ἐπῶν συγγράψαι.*) **9** *πατέρες*] l_2 departs wholly from Greek to end of chapter *εἰ καί τις* T*B* **10–12** *τούτῳ... ἄνθρωπον*] $A^B B^\dagger s_2$(l^{rev}); om $PTB^\dagger$ (Tendenz?) **10** *ἀνὴρ πν.*] om A^B *καὶ*] *ὁ* A^B **11** *λέγων*] om A^B **13–16** *οὗτος...ῥιγιαζομένους*] s_2B ($l^{rev}s^{an}$); om PTA^B; ll_2s vac: (see above) **14** *χρείαν*] + *τῶν τῆς ἐρήμου πολιτῶν* *B*

(XII) Ἐν τούτῳ τῷ ὄρει τῆς Νιτρίας ἀνήρ τις Βενιαμὶν οὕτω καλούμενος, βιώσας ἐπὶ ὀγδοήκοντα ἔτη καὶ εἰς ἄκρον ἀσκήσας, κατηξιώθη χαρίσματος ἰαμάτων, ὡς πάντα ᾧ ἂν χεῖρα ἐπετίθει ἢ ἔλαιον εὐλογήσας ἐδίδου, πάσης ἀπαλλάττεσθαι ἀρρωστίας. οὗτος τοίνυν ὁ τοιούτου χαρίσματος ἀξιωθεὶς πρὸ ὀκτὼ μηνῶν τοῦ θανάτου αὐτοῦ ὑδρωπίασε, καὶ ἐπὶ τοσοῦτον ὠγκώθη αὐτοῦ τὸ σῶμα ὡς ἄλλον Ἰὼβ φαίνεσθαι. παραλαβὼν οὖν ἡμᾶς | Διόσκορος ὁ ἐπίσκοπος, ⸢τότε δὲ πρεσβύτερος ὢν τοῦ ὄρους τῆς Νιτρίας,⸣ ἐμέ τε καὶ τὸν μακάριον Εὐάγριον, λέγει ἡμῖν· Δεῦτε, ἴδετε νέον Ἰὼβ ἐν τοσούτῳ ὄγκῳ σώματος καὶ πάθει ἀνιάτῳ ἄμετρον κεκτημένον εὐχαριστίαν. ἀπελθόντες οὖν ἐθεασάμεθα τοσοῦτον ὄγκον σώματος ὡς μὴ δύνασθαι δάκτυλον χειρὸς αὐτοῦ περιλαμβάνειν ὅλοις δακτύλοις. μὴ δυνάμενοι δὲ ἀτενίζειν τῇ τοῦ πάθους δεινότητι τοὺς ὀφθαλμοὺς

ἱκεσίαις δυσωπηθεὶς παρὰ Ῥουφίνου τοῦ κατ' ἐκείνου καιροῦ ἐπάρχου τῶν πραιτωρίων· παρακληθεὶς δὲ καὶ παρὰ τῶν ἁγίων ἐπισκόπων τῶν ἐκ διαφόρων ἐπαρχιῶν συνεληλυθότων εἰς τὰ καταθέσια τῶν ἁγίων οὗπερ αὐτὸς ἔκτισε μαρτυρίου· ἐν αὐτοῖς τοῖς καταθεσίοις ἀποδέχεται τὸν Ῥουφῖνον ὁ ἅγιος ἀπὸ τοῦ ἁγίου καὶ ἀχράντου βαπτίσματος παρὰ τῶν ἐπισκόπων· ὃν ἐσεβάσθη ἀξίως τῆς αὐτοῦ πολιτείας εἰς πάντα ὑπακούων ὁ ἔπαρχος τῷ ὁσίῳ ἀνδρὶ Ἀμμωνίῳ. ὃς μετ' ὀλίγον χρόνον κοιμᾶται καὶ θάπτεται ἐν τῷ μαρτυρίῳ τῷ λεγομένῳ Ῥουφινιαναῖς. οὗ τὸ μνῆμα λέγεται θεραπεύειν παντοῖα νοσήματα (πάντας τοὺς ῥιγιαζομένους B (exc. 47) l^{rev}).

The other B MSS. and l^{rev} begin thus: Οὗτος ὁ μακάριος πολλαῖς ἱκεσίαις καταδυσωπηθεὶς παρὰ Ῥ. τοῦ κατ' ἐκεῖνο καιροῦ ἐπάρχου τῶν πραιτωρίων, εἰς τοὺς καιροὺς ἐκείνους ἐλθόντος τοῦ μεγάλου Ἀμμωνίου ἐν Κωνσταντίνου πόλει διὰ χρείας τῶν τῆς ἐρήμου πολιτῶν, ἱκανῶς παρακληθεὶς καὶ παρὰ τῶν ἁγίων ἐπισκόπων κ.τ.λ. (See Note 22.)

1—5 Soz. VI. 29 (9) Ἐν τούτῳ δὲ καὶ Βενιαμὶν γηραλέος εὖ μάλα λαμπρῶς ἀνὰ τὴν Σκῆτιν ἐφιλοσόφει, δῶρον ἔχων παρὰ θεοῦ δίχα φαρμάκων ἐπαφῇ μόνῃ χειρὸς ἢ ἐλαίῳ ᾧ ἐπηύχετο, πάσης ἀπαλλάττειν νόσου τοὺς κάμνοντας.

12 See Note 23.

XII (Περὶ Βενιαμίν): PTl$_2$s$_2$

1 Νητρίας P ἀνήρ τις] om T Βεν. καλ. τις οὕτω βιώσας T 2 ἔτη ὀγδ. T*B* 3 παντὶ T*B* ἐὰν T 4 χεῖρας T*B*l$_2$ ἀπηλλάττετο T*B* 5 τοίνυν] om T τοιούτου] τούτου τοῦ T καταξιωθ. T*B* 6 αὐτοῦ] om T*B* 7 ὤγκωσε T*B* γενέσθαι T 8 Διοσκ.] ὁ Μακάριος Tl$_2$ ὁ ἐπίσκοπος] om Tl$_2$s 8, 9 τότε...... Νιτρίας] T*B*l$_2$s$_2$ (l^{rev}); om Ps 8 τότε δὲ] ὁ (om ὢν) T 9 τὸν μακ. Εὐάγρ.] τὸν μακάριον Θεόδωρον Tl$_2$ (Theodorum et Macariolum) 10 βλέπετε T*B* 13 ἄλλους δακτύλους T

ἀπεστρέψαμεν. τότε λέγει ἡμῖν ὁ μακάριος ἐκεῖνος Βενιαμίν· Εὔξασθε, τέκνα, ἵνα μὴ ὁ ἔσωθέν μου ἄνθρωπος ὑδρωπιάσῃ· οὗτος γὰρ οὔτε με εὐπαθῶν ὤνησεν, οὔτε δυσπαθῶν ἔβλαψε. τοὺς οὖν ὀκτὼ μῆνας δίφρος αὐτῷ ἔκειτο πλατύτατος ἐν ᾧ ἀδιαλείπτως ἐκαθέζετο, μηκέτι ἐν κλίνῃ ἀναπεσεῖν δυνάμενος διὰ τὰς λοιπὰς χρείας τοῦ σώματος. ἐν τῷ πάθει δὲ τούτῳ ὢν ἄλλους ἰᾶτο. ἀναγκαίως οὖν ἐξηγησάμην τὸ πάθος τοῦτο, ἵνα μὴ ξενιζώμεθα ὅταν τι περιστατικὸν ἀνδράσι δικαίοις συμβαίνῃ. τελευτήσαντος δὲ αὐτοῦ, αἱ φλιαὶ τῆς θύρας ἐπήρθησαν καὶ αἱ παραστάδες, ἵνα δυνηθῇ τὸ σῶμα ἐξενεχθῆναι τοῦ οἴκου· τοσοῦτος ἦν ὁ ὄγκος.

(XIII) Ἀπολλώνιός τις ὀνόματι ἀπὸ πραγματευτῶν, ἀποταξάμενος καὶ οἰκήσας τὸ ὄρος τῆς Νιτρίας, μήτε τέχνην μαθεῖν δυνάμενος μήτε ἄσκησιν γραφικὴν διὰ τὸ ἠκμακέναι, ζήσας ἐν τῷ ὄρει εἴκοσι ἔτη ταύτην ἔσχε τὴν ἄσκησιν· ἐκ τῶν ἰδίων

1—3 Soz. (10) Μᾶλλον μὲν οὖν καὶ τοὺς ὁρῶντας παρεμυθεῖτο καὶ ἐλιπάρει τὸν θεὸν ἱκετεύειν ὑπὲρ τῆς αὐτοῦ ψυχῆς· σώματος δὲ αὐτῷ μηδὲν μέλειν· Ἐπεὶ καὶ εὐεκτοῦν οὐδέν με ὤνησεν, ἔφη, καὶ κακῶς πάσχον οὐκ ἔβλαψεν. **4—7** (10) Ἐν δὲ τῷ νοσεῖν ἐν κλίνῃ κεῖσθαι μὴ δυνάμενος, ἀμφὶ τοὺς ὀκτὼ μῆνας ἐπὶ δίφρου πλατυτάτου ἐκαθίζετο, συνήθως τοὺς κάμνοντας ἰώμενος, αὐτὸς μηδὲν δυσφορῶν ὅτι μὴ τῆς ἐχούσης αὐτὸν νόσου ἀπηλλάττετο. **9—11** (9) Τὸν δὴ τοιοῦτον λόγος ὑδέρῳ περιπεσόντα, τοσοῦτον οἰδῆσαι τὸ σῶμα ὡς μὴ δυνηθῆναι διὰ τῶν θυρῶν τοῦ οἰκήματος ἐν ᾧ διῆγεν ἐκκομισθῆναι εἰ μὴ σὺν ταῖς θύραις καὶ τὰς παραστάδας καθεῖλον. **12** The chapter on Nathanael (XVI.) comes here in P; but this is opposed to all the other authorities. **12—9** (p. 37) Soz. VI. 29 (14) Ἀπολλώνιος δὲ, τὸν ἄλλον χρόνον ἐμπορίαν μετιών, ἤδη πρὸς γῆρας ἐλαύνων ἐπὶ τὴν Σκῆτιν ἦλθε. λογισάμενος δὲ ὡς οὔτε γράφειν οὔτε ἄλλην τινὰ τέχνην μαθεῖν οἷός τέ ἐστι διὰ τὴν ἡλικίαν, παντοδαπῶν φαρμάκων εἴδη καὶ ἐδεσμάτων ἐπιτηδείων τοῖς κάμνουσιν ἐξ οἰκείων χρημάτων ὠνούμενος, ἀνὰ ἑκάστην θύραν μοναστικὴν περιῄει μέχρις ἐννάτης ὥρας, ἐφορῶν τοὺς νοσοῦντας. ἐπιτηδείαν δὲ ταύτην αὐτῷ ἄσκησιν εὑρὼν ὧδε ἐπολιτεύσατο. μέλλων δὲ τελευτᾶν ἄλλῳ παραδοὺς ἃ εἶχεν ἐνετείλατο τὰ αὐτὰ ποιεῖν. **14** See Note 24.

PTl$_2$ss$_2$

2 μου before ὁ ἔσ. T*B* ἔσω T **3** με] om T **4** ὀκτὼ οὖν T*B* ἐγένετο T*B* πλατύτερος T **6** τὰς χρείας τὰς λοιπὰς (om τοῦ σωμ.) T δὲ before τῷ T **7** οὖν] δὲ T τοῦτο] τούτου τοῦ ἁγίου *B*s **8** μὴ] μηδὲν T **9** δὲ] μέντοι T ἐπήρθη T*B*

XIII (Περὶ Ἀπολλωνίου): PTl$_2$ss$_2$

13 Νητρίας P **14** μήτε] + ἐπὶ T*B*† γραφικὴν] + ἐλθεῖν T διὰ τὸ ἠκμ.] τῷ ὑπερβεβηκέναι τὴν ἡλικίαν T*B* (παραβ.; προβ. A[B])

χρημάτων καὶ ἐκ τῶν οἰκείων πόνων παντοῖα ἰατρικὰ καὶ κελλαρικὰ ἀγοράζων εἰς τὴν Ἀλεξάνδρειαν, πάσῃ τῇ ἀδελφότητι ἐπήρκει εἰς τὰς νόσους. καὶ ἦν ἰδεῖν αὐτὸν ὄρθριον μέχρις ἐννάτης ὥρας κυκλεύοντα τὰ μοναστήρια, καὶ κατὰ θύραν εἰσερχόμενον καὶ ὁρῶντα τίς ἀνάκειται· ἐβάσταζε δὲ σταφίδας, ῥόας, ᾠά, σιλίγνια, ὧν ἐπιδέονται οἱ ἀσθενοῦντες. ταύτην αὐτῷ λυσιτελοῦσαν τὴν μέθοδον εὑρὼν εἶχεν ἕως γήρους. ὃς τελευτῶν ὁμοίῳ ἑαυτοῦ καταλιμπάνει τὰ γρυτάρια, παρακαλέσας αὐτὸν ταύτην ἐκτελεῖν τὴν διακονίαν. πεντακισχιλίων γὰρ μοναχῶν οἰκούντων τὸ ὄρος χρεία ἦν καὶ τῆς ἐπισκέψεως ταύτης διὰ τὸ ἔρημον εἶναι τὸν τόπον.

(XIV) Ἄλλος Παήσιος καὶ Ἡσαΐας οὕτω καλούμενοι, ἀδελφοὶ ὑπῆρχον πατρὸς ἐμπόρου Σπανοδρόμου· οἵτινες τοῦ πατρὸς τελευτήσαντος ἐμερίσαντο τὰ ὑπάρχοντα ἐν ἀκινήτοις ἃ ἔσχον, ἐν μὲν νομισματίοις πεντακισχιλίοις, ἐν ἱματίοις δὲ καὶ οἰκέταις τὰ εὑρεθέντα. οὗτοι μετ' ἀλλήλων ἐσκέψαντο καὶ συμβουλεύονται πρὸς ἑαυτοὺς λέγοντες· Ἐπὶ ποίαν ἔλθωμεν μέθοδον τοῦ βίου, ἀδελφέ; ἐὰν ἔλθωμεν ἐπὶ τὴν ἐμπορίαν ἣν ἐπῆλθεν ὁ πατὴρ ἡμῶν, καὶ ἡμεῖς ἑτέροις ἔχομεν καταλεῖψαι τοὺς πόνους· ἴσως δὲ καὶ κινδύνοις περιπεσούμεθα | λῃστρικοῖς ἢ θαλαττικοῖς. δεῦρο τοίνυν, ἐπὶ τὸν μονήρη βίον ἔλθωμεν, ἵνα καὶ τὰ τοῦ πατρὸς ἡμῶν κερδήσωμεν, καὶ τὰς ψυχὰς μὴ ἀπολέσωμεν. ἤρεσεν οὖν αὐτοῖς ὁ σκοπὸς τοῦ μονήρους βίου.

12 (XIV) In this chapter T contains manifest B interpolations. This phenomenon continues in varying degrees to the end of c. XXI. (cf. *Introd.* § 9). Such B readings in T will be indicated thus: (T)*B*. 1 of c. XIV. is printed in *Bibl. Casin. III. Florileg.* 299.

PTll_2ss_2

1 *οἰκείων*] *ἰδίων* TA[B] 3 *καὶ ἦν*] l recommences here 5 *καὶ ὁρῶντα*] om T: + *μὴ* T*B* 6 *ἀρρωστοῦντες* T*B* 7 *τὴν μέθοδον......γήρους*] *εὑρὼν πολιτείαν εἰς τὸ γῆρας* T*B* *τελευτᾶν μέλλων* *B* (Soz): (In p. 31 l. 10 *τελευτῶν* of PT is attested by apophth (cent. v.), but is turned into *τελευτᾶν μέλλων* in B) 10 *τῆς*] + *τοιαύτης* (om *ταύτης*) T*B* *διὰ τὸ*] *τῷ* T

XIV (Περὶ Πανσίου καὶ Ἡσαΐου): PTlss_2

13 *ὑπῆρχον*] + *υἱοὶ* T(s) *Πανοδρόμου* Tven 14 *ὑπάρχοντα*] + *αὐτοῦ* T(s) *ἀκινήτοις*] PT (*ἐκείνη τῆς* sic); *κινητοῖς* *B*l; 'outside and inside the house' s_2: s om 15 *νομίσμασι* T*B* 17 *συμβουλεύοντες ἑαυτοῖς λέγουσι* T(*B*) 18 *βίου μεθ.* (om *τοῦ*) T 19 *μετῆλθεν* T*B* 20 *πόνους*] + *ἡμῶν* (T)*B*s 21 *θαλαττικοῖς*] PA[B]; *θαλαττίοις* T*B* *τοίνυν*] *οὖν* + *ἀδελφὲ* (T)*B*

εὑρέθησαν οὖν ἄλλος κατ' ἄλλο διαφωνοῦντες. μερισάμενοι γὰρ τὰ χρήματα, τοῦ μὲν σκοποῦ εἴχοντο ἕκαστος τοῦ ἀρέσαι θεῷ, ἐνηλλαγμέναις δὲ πολιτείαις. ὁ μὲν γὰρ πάντα διασκορπίσας ἀσκητηρίοις καὶ ἐκκλησίαις καὶ φυλακαῖς, τεχνίδριον μαθὼν ὅθεν τὸν ἄρτον πορίσεται, τῇ ἀσκήσει καὶ εὐχῇ προσέσχεν. ὁ δ' ἄλλος μηδὲν διασκορπίσας, ἀλλὰ ποιήσας ἑαυτῷ μοναστήριον καὶ προσλαβόμενος ἀδελφοὺς ὀλίγους, πάντα ξένον ἐδεξιοῦτο, πάντα ἄρρωστον, πάντα γέροντα, πάντα πένητα, κατὰ κυριακὴν καὶ σάββατον τρεῖς τραπέζας ἱστῶν· οὕτως αὐτοῦ κατηνάλωσε τὰ χρήματα.

Ἀμφοτέρων δὲ τελευτησάντων, διάφοροι μακαρισμοὶ τούτων ἐγένοντο, ὡς ἀμφοτέρων τελειωθέντων· καὶ τοῖς μὲν ἤρεσκεν οὗτος, τοῖς δὲ ἐκεῖνος. φιλονεικίας οὖν ἐμπεσούσης τῇ ἀδελφότητι ἐπὶ τοῖς ἐπαίνοις, ἀπέρχονται πρὸς τὸν μακάριον Παμβὼ καὶ ἀνατίθενται αὐτῷ τὴν ἐπίκρισιν, ἀξιοῦντες μαθεῖν τὴν μείζονα πολιτείαν. ὁ δὲ λέγει αὐτοῖς· Ἀμφότεροί εἰσι τέλειοι· ὁ μὲν γὰρ Ἀβραμιαῖον ἐπεδείξατο ἔργον, ὁ δὲ τὰ τοῦ Ἠλία. τῶν μὲν οὖν λεγόντων· ⸢Τῶν ποδῶν σου,⸣ πῶς δυνατὸν αὐτοὺς εἶναι ἴσους; προτιμώντων τὸν ἀσκητὴν καὶ λεγόντων ὅτι Εὐαγγελικὸν πεποίηκε πρᾶγμα, πάντα πωλήσας καὶ δοὺς πτωχοῖς, καθ' ὥραν καθ' ἡμέραν τε καὶ κατὰ νύκτα τὸν σταυρὸν βαστάζων, καὶ ἀκολουθῶν τῷ σωτῆρι καὶ ταῖς προσευχαῖς· τῶν δὲ ἀντιφιλονεικούντων καὶ λεγόντων ὅτι Οὗτος τοσαῦτα ἐνεδείξατο τοῖς δεομένοις, ὡς καὶ εἰς τὰς λεωφόρους καθῆσθαι καὶ τοὺς θλιβομένους συνάγειν· καὶ οὐ μόνον τὴν ἰδίαν ψυχὴν ἀνέπαυσεν ἀλλὰ

$PTlss_2$

1 οὖν] δὲ T ἄλλο] ἄλλον βίον T γὰρ] δὲ T*B* **3** ἐνηλλαγμέναις δὲ πολιτείαις] $P^{cor}ss_2$; -νας δὲ -ας P*; -νῃ δὲ -ᾳ T*B*: (l neutral) διασκορπίσας] + ἔδωκεν *B*s **5** ἄρτον] + cotidianum ls; 'from day to day' s_2 πορίσεται P* (πορίζεται P^{cor}); πορίσηται T*B* καὶ] + τῇ T*B* **9** τρεῖς] + ἢ τέσσαρας Bls_2; txt PTs ἱστῶν] + omnibus l; τοὺς λειπομένους ἐδεξιοῦτο *B*; 'and he refreshed all who had chanced to come' s; 'he fed those in want' s_2 **11** δὲ] οὖν T*B* **12** ἐγίνοντο T τελείων ἐν τῇ ἀρετῇ εὑρεθέντων (T)*B* **13** ἀδελφότητι] + μάλιστα (T)*B* **14** τοῖς] + διαφόροις $(T)Bs_2$ **15** μαθεῖν] + παρ' αὐτοῦ (T)*B*†(l) ἀμείνω T*B* **17** τὰ] om T*B* Ἠλίου T*B* **18** τῶν ποδῶν σου] TA^BB† (+ ἀπτόμεθα A^BB†); om Pven*B*†s: (deprecantes l; 'we beg of thee' s_2) (cf. p. 23 l. 19) εἶναι αὐτοὺς T*B* **19** ἴσους] + καὶ T **20** πεποίηκε πρᾶγμα] PA^Bss_2; πεπλήρωκε πρόσταγμα T*B*l πωλήσας πάντα T **20, 21** καὶ καθ' ὥραν καὶ ἡμέραν καὶ νύκτα T; per omnes horas, omnes dies, omnesque noctes l (Bss_2 vary) **22** προσευχαῖς] + προσκαρτερῶν T(*B*) **23** ὅτι] + καὶ T*B*† τοσαῦτα] + σπλάγχνα $B(lss_2)$ **24** εἰς] + αὐτὰς (T)*B* **25** συνάγειν] + καὶ ἐπαρκεῖν (T)*B* ἀναπαύειν T

καὶ ἄλλων πολλῶν, καὶ νοσοκομῶν καὶ ἐπικουρῶν· λέγει αὐτοῖς ὁ μακάριος Παμβώ· Πάλιν ὑμῖν ἐρῶ ὅτι ἀμφότεροι ἴσοι εἰσίν· ἕκαστον δὲ ὑμῶν πληροφορῶ ὅτι οὗτος, εἰ μὴ ἤσκει τοσοῦτον, ἄξιος οὐκ ἐγένετο τῆς ἐκείνου ἀγαθότητος συγκριθῆναι· ἐκεῖνος πάλιν ἀναπαύων τοὺς ξένους καὶ συνανεπαύετο, καὶ εἰ καὶ ἐδόκει τὸ ἐκ κόπου ἔχειν φορτίον, ἀλλὰ καὶ τὴν παρ' αὐτὰ εἶχεν ἀνάπαυσιν. ἐκδέξασθε δὲ ἵνα καὶ παρὰ θεοῦ δέξωμαι τὴν ἀποκάλυψιν, καὶ μετὰ ταῦτα ἐλθόντες μαθήσεσθε. ἐλθόντες οὖν μετὰ ἡμέρας πάλιν παρεκάλεσαν αὐτόν, καὶ λέγει αὐτοῖς· Ὡς ἐπὶ θεοῦ ἀμφοτέρους ἅμα εἶδον ἑστῶτας ἐν τῷ παραδείσῳ. |

(XV) Νεώτερός τις ὀνόματι Μακάριος, ὡς ἐτῶν δεκαοκτώ, ἐν τῷ παίζειν μετὰ τῶν συνηλικιωτῶν παρὰ τὴν λίμνην τὴν λεγομένην Μαρίαν, τετράποδα νέμων, ἀκούσιον εἰργάσατο φόνον. καὶ μηδενὶ μηδὲν εἰρηκὼς καταλαμβάνει τὴν ἔρημον, καὶ εἰς τοσοῦτον ἤλασε φόβον θεῖόν τε καὶ ἀνθρώπινον, ὡς ἀναισθητῆσαι αὐτὸν ἐπὶ τριετίαν ἄστεγον μείναντα ἐν τῇ ἐρήμῳ. ἄβροχος δὲ ὑπάρχει ἡ γῆ τούτοις, καὶ τοῦτο ἴσασι πάντες, καὶ οἱ διὰ λόγων γενόμενοι καὶ οἱ διὰ πείρας. οὗτος ὕστερον ᾠκοδόμησε κέλλαν ἑαυτῷ· καὶ ζήσας ἄλλα εἰκοσιπέντε ἔτη ἐν τῷ κελλίῳ ἐκείνῳ χαρίσματος ἠξιώθη καταπτύειν δαιμόνων, ἐντρυφῶν τῇ μονότητι. τούτῳ πολλὰ συγχρονίσας ἠρώτων πῶς αὐτοῦ διά-

11—19 Soz. VI. 29 (12) Ἐγένετο δὲ αὐτῷ [Μ. τῷ νέῳ] τὴν ἀρχὴν πρόφασις τῆς φιλοσοφίας ἀκούσιος φόνος. ἔτι γὰρ βουπαις ὢν πρόβατα ἔνεμε περὶ τὴν Μαρείαν λίμνην, καὶ παίζων τινὰ τῶν ὁμηλίκων ἀνεῖλε· δείσας τε δοῦναι δίκην ἔφυγεν εἰς τὴν ἐρημίαν. (13) αἴθριος δὲ ἐπὶ τρία ἔτη μετὰ ταῦτα διάγων, αὐτόθι οἰκίδιον μικρὸν ἑαυτῷ κατεσκεύασεν, ἐν ᾧ εἴκοσι καὶ πέντε ἔτη διέτριψεν. **20** (12) Μ. ἐδόθη χάρις ὑπὸ θεοῦ ὑπερφρονεῖν τῶν δαιμόνων.

PTls$_2$.

1 *πολλῶν*] *πολλὰς* T *καὶ*^{2}] om T*B* **2** *ὅτι*] om T*B* *εἰσὶν ἴσοι πρὸς τὸν κύριον* *B* (T *θεὸν*) s$_2$ **4** *τῆς ἐκ. ἀγαθότητος*] P(*B*$^+$); *ἐκ. τῇ ἀγαθότητι* T(*B*$^+$); *ἐκ. τοῦ ἀγαθοῦ* A^B **5** *πάλιν*] om TA^B *ξένους*] + *εἰ* P *καὶ εἰ καὶ*] TA^{B}ls$_2$(*B*); om *καὶ εἰ* P **7** *δὲ*] + *μικρὸν* (T)*B*†s ('a few days') **8** *μάθητε* T *μετὰ*] + *ὀλίγας* *B*l **9** *αὐτὸν παρεκ.* T **10** *ἅμα*] om T

XV (Περὶ Μακαρίου τοῦ νεωτέρου (νέου Soz)): PTls$_2$

11 *ὡς ἐτῶν*] om T **12** *συνηλικιωτῶν*] PA^B; *συνηλίκων* T*B* (*ὁμηλίκων* Soz) **14** *καὶ*^{1}] Pl; *οὗτος* (T)*B*s$_2$ **16** *ἐπὶ*] P Soz; om T*B* *μεῖναι* T **17** *ἡ γῆ ἐκείνη ὑπ.* (om *τούτοις*) T*B* *τοῦτο*] T*B*ls$_2$^{vat} (s$_2$^{add} om clause); om P **18** *δι' αὐτῆς τῆς πορίας* (T) (*διὰ τῆς πείρας αὐτῆς* *B*) *ὁ αὐτὸς οὗτος* *B* (l iste ipse) **19** *κελλίον* T*B* *ἐν τῷ κελλίῳ ἐκείνῳ*] PT; *ἐν αὐτῷ* (before *ἄλλα*) *B*ls$_2$: + *τοιούτου* *B*l **20** *ἠξιώθη*] + *ὡς* *B*ls$_2$ **21** *συγχρ.*] + *ἐγὼ* T*B* *ἠρώτων*] Pl; *ἐμάνθανον* T*B*s$_2$: + *παρ' αὐτοῦ* (T)*B*

κειται ὁ λογισμὸς ἐπὶ τῇ τοῦ φόνου ἁμαρτίᾳ· ὃς τοσοῦτον ἔλεγεν ἀπέχειν λύπης ὡς καὶ προσευχαριστεῖν ἐπὶ τῷ φόνῳ· γεγένηται γὰρ αὐτῷ ὑπόθεσις σωτηρίας ὁ ἀκούσιος φόνος. ἔλεγε δὲ ἀπὸ γραφῶν φέρων τὴν μαρτυρίαν ὅτι οὐκ ἂν Μωσῆς ἠξιοῦτο τῆς θεϊκῆς ὀπτασίας ⌜καὶ τῆς τοσαύτης δωρεᾶς καὶ τῆς συγγραφῆς τῶν ἁγίων λόγων⌝, εἰ μὴ φόβῳ τοῦ Φαραὼ διὰ τὸν φόνον ὃν ἔδρασεν ἐν τῇ Αἰγύπτῳ κατειλήφει τὸ ὄρος τὸ Σινᾶ. ταῦτα δὲ λέγω οὐχ ὁδοποιῶν εἰς φόνον, δεικνύων δὲ ὅτι εἰσὶ καὶ περιστατικαὶ ἀρεταί, ὅταν μὴ ἑκουσίως τις τῷ ἀγαθῷ προσέλθῃ· τῶν γὰρ ἀρετῶν αἱ μέν εἰσι προαιρετικαί, αἱ δὲ περιστατικαί.

(XVI) Γέγονεν ἄλλος τις τῶν παλαιῶν ὀνόματι Ναθαναήλ. τοῦτον ἐγὼ ζῶντα μὲν οὐ κατείληφα· κεκοίμητο γὰρ πρὸ τῆς ἐμῆς εἰσόδου πρὸ ἐτῶν δεκαπέντε· τοῖς δὲ συνασκήσασιν αὐτῷ καὶ χρονίσασι περιτυχὼν ἐφιλοπραγμόνουν τοῦ ἀνδρὸς τὴν ἀρετήν· ἔδειξαν δέ μοι αὐτοῦ καὶ τὴν κέλλαν, εἰς ἣν ᾤκει οὐκέτι μὲν οὐδεὶς διὰ τὸ ἐγγυτέρω αὐτὴν εἶναι τῆς οἰκουμένης· ἐκεῖνος γὰρ τότε αὐτὴν ἔκτισεν ὅτε σπάνιοι ἦσαν οἱ ἀναχωρηταί. διηγοῦντο οὖν τοῦτο περὶ αὐτοῦ ἐξαιρέτως, ὅτι τοσαύτην ἔσχεν ὑπομονὴν ἐν τῷ κελλίῳ ὡς μὴ σαλευθῆναι τῆς προθέσεως. ἐν οἷς ἐμπαιχθεὶς κατ' ἀρχὰς παρὰ τοῦ πᾶσιν ἐμπαίζοντος καὶ ἀπατῶντος δαίμονος, ἔδοξεν ἀκηδιᾶν εἰς τὴν πρώτην κέλλαν· καὶ ἀπελθὼν ἄλλην ἔκτισε πλησιώτερον κώμης. μετὰ οὖν τὸ τελέσαι τὴν

1—3 Soz. (13) Ἔλεγον δὲ οἵ γε αὐτοῦ ἀκηκόεισαν ὡς πολλὴν ὡμολόγει χάριν τῇ συμφορᾷ καὶ σωτήριον ἀπεκάλει τὸν ἀκούσιον φόνον, φιλοσοφίας καὶ μακαρίου βίου αἴτιον αὐτῷ γεγενημένον. **12** In P XVI. comes between XII. and XIII.

PTls_2

2 καὶ] om Tl **3** αὐτῷ] Pl; μοι, φησίν, (T)*B* **4** Μωϋσῆς T*B* **5, 6** καὶ...... λόγων] *B*ls_2; om PT **6** τῷ δέει T*B* **7** διὰ τὸν φ.......Αἰγύπτῳ] Pls_2^{vat} (s_2^{add} slightly altered); διὸ ἔδρασεν ἐξ Αἰγ. καὶ *B*; ἀπέδρασε τῆς Αἰγ. καὶ T; ἀποδράσας γὰρ ἐξ Αἰγ. A[B] ἔδρασεν] + ἀκουσίως P **8** λέγων P* πρὸς T φόνον] + τινὰ *B*l: + ἀλλὰ T*B*: + μᾶλλον *B*l δὲ] P; om T*B* **11** περιστατικαί] s_2 adds a passage accounting for the Syriac name given to M. 'the Child of the Cross.' Anan-Isho inserted it in his *Paradise* (Bed. p. 55): it is printed also by Assemani and Budge (cf. *Prol.* 87).

XVI (Περὶ Ναθαναήλ): PTll_2ss_2

14 αὐτῷ after χρονίσασι T **15** χρονίσασι] Pl (per multum tempus) (s_2); συγχρ. (T)*B*; om l_2 **16** καὶ] T*B*ll_2ss_2; om P εἰς ἣν ᾤκει taken with each clause in ll_2 μὲν before οὐκέτι T*B* **17** ἐγγύτερον T αὐτὴν] + μὲν P ἐκεῖνος] ἐκεῖ P τότε] om P **18** ὅτε] ὅτι P **19** ἐξαιρέτως] Pl_2; ἐξαίρετον T*B*l **20** σαλευθ.] + ἀπὸ T*B* **21** πάντας T καὶ] + πάντας P

κέλλαν καὶ οἰκῆσαι, μετὰ μῆνας τρεῖς ἢ τέσσαρας παραγίνεται ὁ δαίμων ἐν νυκτί, ταυρέαν κατέχων καθάπερ οἱ δήμιοι, καὶ σχῆμα ἔχων στρατιώτου ῥακοδυτοῦντος, καὶ ψόφον εἰργάζετο ἐν τῇ ταυρέᾳ. πρὸς ὃν ἀπεκρίνατο ὁ μακάριος Ναθαναὴλ καὶ ἔλεγε· Τίς εἶ σὺ ὁ ταῦτα δρῶν ἐν τῇ ἐμῇ ξενίᾳ; ἀπεκρίνατο ὁ δαίμων· Ἐγώ εἰμι ὁ ἐξ ἐκείνης τῆς κέλλης ἐλάσας σε· ἦλθον οὖν καὶ ἐκ ταύτης φυγαδεῦσαί σε. γνοὺς οὖν ὅτι | ἐνεπαίχθη, ὑποστρέφει αὖθις εἰς τὴν πρώτην κέλλαν. καὶ πληρώσας τριάκοντα καὶ ἑπτὰ ἔτη, οὐχ ὑπερέβη τὴν θύραν, φιλονεικήσας τῷ δαίμονι· ὃς τοσαῦτα αὐτῷ ἐνεδείξατο καταναγκάζων αὐτὸν ἐξελθεῖν, ὅσα διηγήσασθαι οὐκ ἔστιν. ἐν οἷς καὶ τοῦτο· ἐπιτηρήσας ἑπτὰ ἐπισκόπων ἁγίων ἐπίσκεψιν, ἢ ἐκ θεοῦ προνοίας γενομένην ἢ ἐκ πειρασμοῦ ἐκείνου, παρ' ὀλίγον αὐτὸν ἐξώκειλε τῆς προθέσεως. τῶν γὰρ ἐπισκόπων μετὰ τὴν ἐπίσκεψιν ἐξερχομένων, οὐ προέπεμψεν αὐτοὺς οὐδὲ βῆμα ποδός. λέγουσιν αὐτῷ οἱ διάκονοι· Ὑπερήφανον πρᾶγμα ποιεῖς, ἀββᾶ, μὴ προπέμπων τοὺς ἐπισκόπους. ὁ δὲ λέγει αὐτοῖς· Ἐγὼ καὶ τοῖς κυρίοις μου τοῖς ἐπισκόποις καὶ τῷ κόσμῳ ὅλῳ ἀπέθανον· ἔχω γὰρ κεκρυμμένον

11—15 T*B*: Ἑπτὰ ἐπισκόπων ἁγίων ἐπισκεψαμένων αὐτὸν (τὸν ἅγιον *B*), ἢ ἐκ θεοῦ προνοίας ἢ ἐξ ὑποθέσεως τοῦ πειρασμοῦ (+ἐξ ἐκείνου *B*), παρ' ὀλίγον αὐτὸν ἐξώκειλε τῆς προθέσεως. τῶν γὰρ ἐπισκόπων μετὰ τὴν ἐπίσκεψιν εὐξαμένων καὶ μετὰ τὴν εὐχὴν ἐξιόντων, οὐ προέπεμψεν αὐτοὺς ὁ γενναῖος οὐδὲ βῆμα ποδός (+ἵνα μὴ δῷ χώραν τῷ μισοκάλῳ *B*). **17, 18** T*B*: Ἐγὼ καὶ τοὺς κυρίους μου τοὺς ἐπισκόπους σέβω καὶ πάντα τὸν κλῆρον τιμῶ, καὶ πάντων ἀνθρώπων (+ἐγὼ ὁ ἁμαρτωλὸς *B*) περίψημά εἰμι (*B* om εἰμι)· πᾶσι δὲ τούτοις καὶ ὅλῳ τῷ κόσμῳ (*B* ὅλῳ τῷ βίῳ ὅσον τὸ ἐπ' ἐμοὶ τῇ προθέσει) ἀπέθανον. s_2 begins: 'I worship my lords the bishops and all holy men; but know this, my brethren,'—and goes on quite differently.

P T l_2 s s_2

1 καὶ] + ἐν αὐτῇ *B*(l_2 s s_2) (cf. p. 31 l. 14) ἐνοικῆσαι T ὡς μετὰ μῆνας τέσσ. P; 'about 3 months' s_2 **2** ὥσπερ T*B* **3** ἐποίει δὲ ψόφους τῇ τ. T **4** ἀπεκρίνατο after Ναθ. T λέγων (om καὶ) T*B* **5** ὁ δὲ δ. ἀπεκρ. T*B* **6** ἐκείνης τῆς] PTl_2; τῆς πρώτης *B*l (priore) (s s_2) ἐξελάσας T σε] + καὶ T*B*: + νῦν *B*l οὖν] om T*B* **7** φυγαδεῦσαι] ἀπελάσαι T οὖν] + ὁ γέρων T **8** καὶ[2]] om T **9** ὑπερέβη] ἐξῆλθε T τὸν οὐδὸν *B*l(l_2) **10** ἵνα αὐτὸν ἀναγκάσῃ T*B* **11** παρατ. T **11–15** ἑπτὰ ἐπισκόπων......βῆμα ποδὸς] T here presents an interpolation from *B*: it is printed in full below the text **14** ἐπίσκεψιν] P; εὐχὴν l_2 s s_2; (T*B* see above) **15** διάκονοι] + τῶν ἐπισκόπων *B*l (s 'with them') **16** ποιεῖς] ἐργάζῃ T*B* ἀββᾶ] P*B*s_2; om Tl_2s **17** ὁ δὲ] om T **17, 18** ἐγὼ......ἀπέθανον] T presents the B text; see above **17** καὶ] l_2s(T*B*); om P(s_2) **18** γὰρ] δὲ T

σκοπόν, καὶ οἶδεν ὁ θεὸς τὴν καρδίαν μου, διὸ οὐ προπέμπω αὐτούς. ἀστοχήσας οὖν ὁ δαίμων τοῦ δράματος τούτου σχηματίζεται πρὸ ἐννέα μηνῶν τοῦ θανάτου αὐτοῦ, καὶ γίνεται παιδίον ὡσεὶ δέκα ἐτῶν, ἐλαῦνον ὄνον βαστάζοντα ἄρτους ἐν σαργάνῃ. καὶ γενόμενος ἐν ἑσπέρᾳ βαθείᾳ πλησίον τῆς κέλλης τούτου ἐσχηματίσατο πεπτωκέναι τὸν ὄνον καὶ κρᾶζον τὸ παιδίον· Ἀββᾶ Ναθαναήλ, ἐλέησόν με καὶ δός μοι χεῖρα. ὁ δὲ ἀκούσας τῆς φωνῆς τοῦ δῆθεν παιδίου καὶ παρανοίξας τὴν θύραν, ἑστὼς ἔνδοθεν ἐλάλει αὐτῷ· Τίς εἶ, καὶ τί θέλεις ἵνα ποιήσω σοι; λέγει αὐτῷ· Εἰμὶ τοῦδε τὸ μειράκιον, καὶ ἄρτους ἀποφέρω, ἐπειδὴ ἀγάπη ἐστὶ τοῦδε τοῦ ἀδελφοῦ, καὶ αὔριον σαββάτου διαφαίνοντος χρεία τῶν προσφορῶν· δέομαί σου, μὴ παρίδῃς με, μή ποτε καὶ ὑπὸ ὑαινῶν βρωθῶ. πολλαὶ γὰρ ὕαιναι γίνονται εἰς τοὺς τόπους ἐκείνους. στὰς οὖν ἐννεὸς ὁ μακάριος Ναθαναὴλ σφόδρα ἰλιγγίασε τὰ σπλάγχνα ταραττόμενος, καὶ ἐλογίζετο καθ' ἑαυτὸν λέγων· Ἢ τῆς ἐντολῆς ἔχω ἐκπεσεῖν, ἢ τῆς προθέσεως. ὕστερον μέντοι ἐπιλογισάμενος ὅτι ἄμεινόν ἐστι μὴ σαλεῦσαι τῶν τοσούτων ἐτῶν τὴν πρόθεσιν εἰς αἰσχύνην τοῦ διαβόλου, προσευξάμενος λέγει τῷ προσλαλοῦντι δῆθεν παιδίῳ· Ἄκουσον, παιδίον· πιστεύω εἰς τὸν θεὸν ᾧ λατρεύω, ὅτι, εἰ χρεία σοι ἐστί, πέμπει σοι ὁ θεὸς βοήθειαν, καὶ οὔτε ὕαιναί σε ἀδικήσουσιν οὔτε ἄλλο τι· εἰ δὲ πειρασμὸς εἶ, τὸ πρᾶγμα ἐντεῦθεν ἤδη ἀποκαλύψει ὁ

11, 12 See Note 25.

$PTll_2ss_2$

1 τὰ κρυπτὰ τῆς ἐμῆς καρδίας *B*l **2** αὐτοὺς] κυρίους μου T; sanctos uiros l δαίμων] + ἐκ T **3** γίνεται] + ὡς Tl_2 **4** ὡσεὶ] om Tl_2B (ὡς ἐλαῦνον *B*) ἐλαῦνον ὄνον] om T βαστάζων T **5** ἑσπέραν βαθεῖαν (om ἐν) T τούτου κελλ. T*B* **6** σχηματίζεται T καὶ κρᾶζον τὸ π.] + ἐβόα P (ll_2ss_2 inquit); καὶ κράζει φησὶ τὸ π.· Ἀβ. κ.τ.λ. T; txt *B* **7** ὁ δὲ ἀκούσας] Pll_2; ἤκουσεν ἐκεῖνος T*B* **8** δῆθεν] om T **9** ἔνδοθεν] ἔσω T*B* εἶ] + σὺ T **10** σοι ποιήσω T τοῦδέ εἰμι τοῦ μοναχοῦ μελλάκιον (T)Bs_2 **11** ἀδελφοῦ] μοναχοῦ P **12** χρεία] + ἐστὶ T **13** παρείδῃς T ὑαινῶν] $Bl_2s(ls_2)$; ὑαίνης PT **14** εὑρίσκονται T (l noscuntur) ἐνεὸς οὖν ἑστηκὼς T*B* **15** ταραττόμενος] om T **16** καθ' ἑαυτὸν] Pll_2; τί ποιήσει (T)*B* λέγων] + ὅτι T **17** προθέσεως] + ἐξολισθῆσαι *B*l μέντοι Pl_2; om T*B*l ἐπιλογ.] + τῷ εὐσεβεῖ λογισμῷ *B*l (rationabili ingenio) **18** ὅτι] εἶπεν ἐν αὐτῷ (T)*B* ἐστι] + τὸ T*B* σαλευθῆναι T τῶν] om T*B* **19** τὴν] om T*B* διαβόλου] + καὶ Tl_2 προσευξ.] + τοίνυν τῷ κυρίῳ *B*l (deum) **20** παιδίον] + ἢ ὃς τί ποτε εἶ (T)*B* (ἢ ὅστις δή ποτε εἶ) **21** τῷ θεῷ (om εἰς) T εἰ] om T **22** ἄλλος τις Tll_2 **23** πειρασμὸς] + τις T (πισει sic) *B* (txt A[B]) l καὶ τοῦτο (+ ὁ θεός μου *B*) ἐντεῦθεν ἤδη τὸ δρᾶμα ἀποκ. (om ὁ θεὸς) (T)*B*

θεός. καὶ κλείσας τὴν θύραν εἰσῆλθεν. αἰσχυνθεὶς δὲ ὁ δαίμων ἐπὶ τῇ ἥττῃ εἰς λαίλαπα ἀνελύθη καὶ εἰς ὀνάγρους σκιρτῶντας καὶ φεύγοντας καὶ ψόφους ἀποτελοῦντας. τοῦτο τὸ ἆθλον τοῦ μακαρίου Ναθαναήλ, καὶ αὕτη ἡ διαγωγή, καὶ τοῦτο τὸ τέλος. |

(XVII) Τὰ κατὰ τοὺς δύο Μακαρίους τοὺς ἀοιδίμους ἄνδρας, πολλὰ καὶ μεγάλα καὶ δύσπιστα ὄντα, ὀκνῶ καὶ λέγειν καὶ γράφειν, μήποτε καὶ ψεύστου ὑπόληψιν ἀπενέγκωμαι. ὅτι δὲ ἀπολλύει Κύριος πάντας τοὺς λαλοῦντας τὸ ψεῦδος ἀπεφήνατο τὸ πνεῦμα τὸ ἅγιον. ἐμοῦ τοίνυν μὴ ψευδομένου, πιστότατε, μὴ ἀπιστήσῃς. τούτων τῶν Μακαρίων ὁ μὲν εἷς Αἰγύπτιος τὸ γένος, ὁ δ' ἄλλος Ἀλεξανδρεύς, τραγήματα πιπράσκων.

Καὶ πρῶτον διηγήσομαι περὶ τοῦ Αἰγυπτίου, ὃς ἔζησε τὰ σύμπαντα ἔτη ἐννενήκοντα. ἐκ τούτων ἐν τῇ ἐρήμῳ πεποίηκεν ἑξήκοντα ἔτη, τριακονταετὴς ἀνελθὼν νέος· καὶ τοσαύτης ἠξιώθη διακρίσεως ὡς λέγεσθαι αὐτὸν παιδαριογέροντα· διὸ

5 (XVII) Throughout this and the next chapter, even more than in the preceding, T has been largely contaminated by revision on a B MS. Such B readings found in T are not recorded. As the texts here presented by T and 33 cannot be relied on, only occasional select readings are entered from them, and no conclusion must be drawn from silence in regard to these two MSS. Ordinarily only in cases where P and B differ from each other, and T differs from both, are the readings of T recorded. On 33 cf. *Introd.* § 9.

5 On the various Macarii see Note 26. 5, 6 Soz. III. 14 (1) Ἄρξομαι δὲ ἐξ Αἰγύπτου καὶ Μακαρίων τῶν δύο, τῶν ἀοιδιμωτάτων ἡγεμόνων τῆς Σκήτεως καὶ τοῦ τῇδε ὄρους. 10—12 (1) Τούτοιν δὲ ὁ μὲν Αἰγύπτιος, ὁ δὲ πολιτικὸς ὡς ἀστὸς ὠνομάζετο· ἦν γὰρ τῷ γένει Ἀλεξανδρεύς. 13—3 (p. 44) (2) Διεβίω δὲ ἀμφὶ τὰ ἐνενήκοντα ἔτη, ἑξήκοντα δὲ ἐκ τούτων ἐν ταῖς ἐρήμοις διέτριβεν. αὐτίκα τε φιλοσοφεῖν ἀρχόμενος ἔτι νέος ὢν διέπρεπεν, ὡς παιδαριογέροντα παρὰ τῶν μοναχῶν ὀνομάζεσθαι, καὶ τεσσαράκοντα ἔτη γεγονότα χειροτονηθῆναι πρεσβύτερον. 8 Ps. v. 7.

PTll$_2$ss$_2$

1 δὲ] οὖν T 3 ἀπολύοντας TB 4 τοῦτο] om TB

XVII (Περὶ Μακαρίου τοῦ Αἰγυπτίου): P[33]ll$_2$s[T]

5 δύο] om Bl$_2$ ἀοιδίμους] l de praedicabilibus ac beatis (sess. and rev), de beatis ac uenerabilibus (cass); de magnis et praecipuis et sanctis ac beatissimis l$_2$; 'the holy men whose name was one' s 6 μεγάλα καὶ δύσπ.] ἀξιάκουστα 33 (from hence to ἀπιστήσῃς (l. 10) is completely altered in 33) 10 τῶν Μ.] P33ll$_2$; om Ts (Soz); (B altered): + 'two' ll$_2$s εἷς] om 33 (Soz): + ἐστὶ 33; ἦν T 16 παιδαριογέροντα] PB† Soz; παιδιογέροντα TB†; neapoteponta (ΝΕΑΡΟΓΕΡΟΝΤΑ) l$_2$; (senis puer l, sim. s, [illegible])

καὶ θᾶττον προέκοψε· τεσσαρακονταετὴς γὰρ γενόμενος κατὰ πνευμάτων ἔλαβε χάριν ἰαμάτων τε καὶ προρρήσεων· κατηξιώθη δὲ καὶ ἱερωσύνης.

Τούτῳ συνῆσαν δύο μαθηταὶ εἰς τὴν ἔρημον τὴν ἐνδοτάτω, τὴν καλουμένην Σκῆτιν· ὧν ὁ μὲν εἷς ὑπηρέτης ἦν πλησίον αὐτοῦ διὰ τοὺς ἐρχομένους θεραπεύεσθαι, ὁ δ' ἄλλος ἐσχόλαζεν ἐν κελλίῳ ἐγγυτάτῳ. χρόνου δὲ προκόψαντος διορατικῷ ὄμματι προβλέψας λέγει τῷ ὑπηρετοῦντι αὐτῷ, καλουμένῳ Ἰωάννῃ, ἐς ὕστερον γενομένῳ πρεσβυτέρῳ εἰς τὸν τόπον αὐτοῦ τοῦ Μακαρίου· Ἄκουσόν μου, ἀδελφὲ Ἰωάννη, καὶ ἀνάσχου μου τῆς νουθεσίας· πειράζῃ γάρ, καὶ πειράζει σε τὸ πνεῦμα τῆς φιλαργυρίας. οὕτω γὰρ ἑώρακα· καὶ οἶδα ὅτι ἐάν μου ἀνάσχῃ τελειωθήσῃ ἐν τῷ τόπῳ τούτῳ καὶ δοξασθήσῃ, ΚΑῚ ΜΆΣΤΙΞ ΟΎΚ ἘΓΓΙΕῖ ἘΝ Τῷ ΣΚΗΝΏΜΑΤΊ ΣΟΥ· ἐὰν δέ μου παρακούσῃς, τοῦ Γιεζῆ ἥξει ἐπί σε τὰ τέλη, οὗ καὶ τὸ πάθος νοσεῖς. συνέβη δὲ αὐτὸν παρακοῦσαι μετὰ τὴν κοίμησιν τοῦ Μακαρίου μετὰ ἄλλα δεκαπέντε ἢ εἴκοσιν ἔτη, καὶ οὕτως ἠλεφαντίασε νοσφισάμενος τὰ τῶν πτωχῶν, ὡς μὴ εὑρεθῆναι εἰς τὸ σῶμα αὐτοῦ ἀκέραιον τόπον ἐν ᾧ τις δάκτυλον πήξει. αὕτη ἐστὶν ἡ προφητεία τοῦ ἁγίου Μακαρίου. περὶ μὲν οὖν βρώσεως καὶ πόσεως περιττὸν τὸ διηγήσασθαι, ὁπότε οὐδὲ παρὰ | τοῖς ῥᾳθύμοις ἔστιν εὑρεθῆναι ἀδδηφαγίαν ἢ ἀδιαφορίαν ἐν τοῖς τόποις ἐκείνοις, καὶ διὰ τὴν σπάνιν τῶν χρειῶν καὶ τὸν ζῆλον τῶν κατοικούντων. περὶ δὲ τῆς ἄλλης αὐτοῦ ἀσκήσεως λέγω· ἐλέγετο γὰρ ἀδιαλείπτως ἐξίστασθαι, καὶ μᾶλλον πλείονι χρόνῳ θεῷ προσδιατρίβειν ἢ τοῖς ὑπ' οὐρανὸν πράγμασιν. οὗ καὶ φέρονται θαύματα τοιάδε.

Ἀνήρ τις Αἰγύπτιος ἐρασθεὶς ἐλευθέρας γυναικὸς ὑπάνδρου, καὶ μὴ δυνάμενος αὐτὴν δελεάσαι, προσωμίλησε γόητι λέγων·

14 Ps. xc. 10.

P[33]ll_2s[T]

5 Σκίτην T **7** ἐσχόλαζεν ἐν κελλίῳ ἐγγυτάτῳ] P33 (πλησίον αὐτοῦ for ἐγγυτ.) s (‘that was near to him’); ἀνεχώρει κατ' ἰδίαν εἰς κέλλαν (T)Bll_2 **11** νουθεσίας] + καὶ συνενέγκαι σοι ἔχει *B*l **11, 12** πειράζῃ γὰρ καὶ πειράζει σε] *B*ls (ܢܣܐ ܘܡܢܣܝܐ ܠܟ ܪܘܚܐ ܗܝ); πειράζει γάρ σε (om πειράζῃ and καὶ) PT33l_2 **13** τῷ] om T **14** σκηνώματι] corpori l (cf. *Prol.* 72) **20** πήξει] + καὶ Bll_2 αὕτη] + τοίνυν T*B*l **22** ῥᾳθυμοτέροις Bl_2 **24** τὸν] + κατὰ θεὸν *B*s **25** γὰρ] αὐτὸν (om γὰρ) T; οὗτος ὁ ἅγιος *B* **28** 35 begins here (see *Introd.* § 9) Αἰγύπτιος] om P ἐλευθέρας] + τινὸς 35 **29** λέγων] + δέομαί σου P

Ἕλκυσον αὐτὴν εἰς τὸ ἀγαπῆσαί με, ἢ ἔργασαί τι ἵνα ῥίψῃ αὐτὴν ὁ ἀνὴρ αὐτῆς. καὶ λαβὼν ὁ γόης τὸ ἱκανὸν ἐχρήσατο ταῖς γοητικαῖς μαγγανείαις, καὶ παρασκευάζει φοράδα αὐτὴν φανῆναι. θεασάμενος οὖν ὁ ἀνὴρ ἔξωθεν ἐλθὼν ἐξενίζετο ὅτι εἰς τὸν κράββατον αὐτοῦ φορβὰς ἀνέκειτο. κλαίει, ὀδύρεται ὁ ἀνήρ· προσομιλεῖ τῷ ζῴῳ· ἀποκρίσεως οὐ τυγχάνει. παρακαλεῖ τοὺς πρεσβυτέρους τῆς κώμης· εἰσάγει, δεικνύει· οὐχ εὑρίσκει τὸ πρᾶγμα. ἐπὶ ἡμέρας τρεῖς οὔτε χόρτου μετελάβεν ὡς φορὰς οὔτε ἄρτου ὡς ἄνθρωπος, ἀμφοτέρων ἐστερημένη τῶν τροφῶν. τέλος, ἵνα δοξασθῇ ὁ θεὸς καὶ φανῇ ἡ ἀρετὴ τοῦ ἁγίου Μακαρίου, ἀνέβη ἐπὶ τὴν καρδίαν τοῦ ἀνδρὸς αὐτῆς ἀγαγεῖν αὐτὴν εἰς τὴν ἔρημον· καὶ φορβιάσας αὐτὴν ὡς ἵππον, οὕτως ἤγαγεν εἰς τὴν ἔρημον. ἐν δὲ τῷ πλησιάσαι αὐτοὺς εἱστήκεισαν οἱ ἀδελφοὶ πλησίον τῆς κέλλης τοῦ Μακαρίου, μαχόμενοι τῷ ἀνδρὶ αὐτῆς καὶ λέγοντες· Τί ἤγαγες ὧδε τὴν φορβάδα ταύτην; λέγει αὐτοῖς· Ἵνα ἐλεηθῇ. λέγουσιν αὐτῷ· Τί γὰρ ἔχει; ἀπεκρίνατο αὐτοῖς ὁ ἀνὴρ αὐτῆς ὅτι Γυνή μου ἦν, καὶ εἰς ἵππον μετεβλήθη, καὶ σήμερον τρίτην ἡμέραν ἔχει μὴ γευσαμένη τινός. ἀναφέρουσι τῷ ἁγίῳ ἔνδον προσευχομένῳ· ἀπεκαλύφθη γὰρ αὐτῷ, καὶ προσηύχετο περὶ αὐτῆς. ἀποκρίνεται οὖν τοῖς ἀδελφοῖς ὁ ἅγιος Μακάριος καὶ λέγει αὐτοῖς· Ἵπποι ὑμεῖς ἐστέ, οἱ τῶν ἵππων ἔχοντες τοὺς ὀφθαλμούς. ἐκείνη γὰρ γυνή ἐστι, μὴ μετασχηματισθεῖσα, ἀλλ' ἢ

P35[33]ll_2s[T]

1 ἢ ἕλον 35T*B* τι] + τῇ τέχνῃ σου 35*B*s ('by thy magic') **1, 2** ἵνα μισήσῃ αὐτὴν ὁ ἀν. καὶ ῥίψῃ 35 **2** λαβὼν δὲ 35; λ. οὖν T*B* **3** ταῖς αὐτοῦ γοητίαις καὶ μαγγ. 35*B* αὐτὴν φοράδα 35 (ὡς φ. T*B*) **4** οὖν] δὲ 35 ἔξωθεν] οἴκοι Tl **5** φορβὰς] P; φορὰς 35 33T*B* ἀνάκειται 35 **7** κώμης] + εἰς τὸν οἶκον (T)*B*l **8** εὑρίσκει] P35ls; συνῆκαν *B* (T -ον); ἔγνωσαν A^B; inuenerunt l_2 **10** τέλος] + οὖν 35 **12** φορβιάσας] P; φορβεώσας 35; *B* φορβαιάσας, φορβεάσας, φορτιάσας; T καπιστρώσας **13** ἀπήγαγεν 35 εἰς τ. ἔρημον] om 35T τῷ] τὸ P **14** τοῦ] + ἁγίου (T)*B*l(s) τοῦ Μ.] om 35 **15** ἦγες 35 ὧδε] om 35 **16** φοράδα 35 T*B* ἵνα ἰαθῇ τῇ πρεσβείᾳ τοῦ δικαίου Μ. 35 (τῇ προσευχῇ τοῦ δικ. *B*) οἱ δὲ πρὸς αὐτόν 35 *B* **17** ἔχει] + κακόν 35*B* ἀποκρ. καὶ λέγει (om ὁ ἀν. αὐτῆς) 35 **18** ἦν] + ἡ ἀθλία, καὶ οὐκ οἶδα τί γέγονεν αὐτῇ 35 (*B*) ἔχει τρ. ἡμ. 35T(*B*) **19** μηδενὸς γευσ. 35 T*B*: + οἱ δὲ ἀκούσαντες 35 T*B* ἁγίῳ] + Μακαρίῳ 35*B*ll_2 προσευχομένῳ] + περὶ αὐτῆς 35T*B* **20** αὐτῷ] + ἀπὸ θεοῦ *B*: ἦν γὰρ αὐτῷ κεκαλυμμένον παρὰ θεοῦ τὰ περὶ αὐτῆς T; ἀποκεκάλυφε γὰρ αὐτῷ ὁ θεὸς 35(ll_2s): txt PA^B: + καὶ λέγουσι· Φοράδα ἤγαγέ τις ἐνταῦθα 35(*B*) καὶ προσηύχ. π. αὐτῆς] om 35T*B* **21** οὖν] om 35 καὶ λέγει αὐτοῖς] om 35 **22** ἵπποι after ἐστὲ 35T

μόνον ἐν τοῖς ὀφθαλμοῖς τῶν ἠπατημένων. καὶ εὐλογήσας ὕδωρ καὶ ἀπὸ κορυφῆς ἐπιχέας αὐτῇ γυμνῇ ἐπηύξατο· καὶ παραχρῆμα ἐποίησεν αὐτὴν γυναῖκα φανῆναι πᾶσι. | δοὺς δὲ αὐτῇ τροφὴν ἐποίησεν αὐτὴν φαγεῖν, καὶ ἀπέλυσεν αὐτὴν μετὰ τοῦ ἰδίου ἀνδρὸς εὐχαριστοῦσαν τῷ κυρίῳ. καὶ ὑπέθετο αὐτῇ εἰπών· Μηδέποτε ἀπολειφθῇς τῆς ἐκκλησίας, ⌜μηδέποτε ἀπόσχῃ τῆς κοινωνίας⌝· ταῦτα γάρ σοι συνέβη τῷ ἐπὶ πέντε ἑβδομάδας μὴ προσεληλυθέναι τοῖς μυστηρίοις.

Ἄλλην αὐτοῦ πρᾶξιν τῆς ἀσκήσεως· τῷ μακρῷ χρόνῳ ὑπὸ τὴν γῆν ποιήσας σύριγγα ἀπὸ τῆς κέλλης αὐτοῦ μέχρις ἡμισταδίου σπήλαιον εἰς τὸ ἄκρον ἀπετέλεσε. καὶ εἴποτε πλείονες αὐτῷ ὤχλουν, κρυπτῶς ἐκ τῆς κέλλης αὐτοῦ ἐξιὼν ἀπίει εἰς τὸ σπήλαιον, καὶ οὐδεὶς αὐτὸν εὕρισκε. διηγεῖτο οὖν ἡμῖν τις τῶν σπουδαίων αὐτοῦ μαθητῶν καὶ ἔλεγεν ὅτι ἀπιὼν ἕως τοῦ σπηλαίου εἰκοσιτέσσαρας ἐποίει εὐχάς, καὶ ἐρχόμενος εἰκοσιτέσσαρας.

Περὶ τούτου ἐξῆλθε φήμη ὅτι νεκρὸν ἤγειρεν, ἵνα αἱρετικὸν πείσῃ μὴ ὁμολογοῦντα ἀνάστασιν εἶναι σωμάτων. καὶ αὕτη ἡ φήμη ἐκράτει ἐν τῇ ἐρήμῳ.

7 See Note 27. **17—19** Soz. III. 14 (2) Τὸν δὲ Αἰγύπτιον λόγος ὡς καὶ νεκρὸν ζῆν ἐποίησεν ἵν' ἑτερόδοξον πείσῃ νεκρῶν ἀνάστασιν ἔσεσθαι. P substitutes: Ἦλθε δὲ καὶ εἰς ἐμὲ ἄλλο αὐτοῦ διήγημα πάνυ μέγα καὶ θαυμαστόν· Παρὰ

P35(1—8)[33]ll$_2$s[T]

1 μόνον] + φαινομένη (om ἐν) (T)*B*l$_2$ **2** ἀπὸ κορ. after αὐτῇ 35 ἐπιχέας] 35 33T*B* (ἐκχέας *B*†) ls; ἐπιχρίσας Pl$_2$ (oleum for ὕδωρ) αὐτῇ γυμνῇ] 35T*B*ll$_2$; αὐτὴν ὅλην P (s 'her whole body'); om 33: + μέχρις ὀνύχων 35: (s 'he poured it (the water) on her head while it flowed down over her whole body') **3** ἐποίησεν ......πᾶσι] 35T*B*ll$_2$s; ἔδειξεν αὐτοῖς πᾶσιν ὅπερ ἦν τὸ πρότερον γυναῖκα P πᾶσι] + τοῖς ὁρῶσι 35(*B*) **4** καὶ] + ἰασάμενος *B*s ('in health') **5** ἀνδρὸς] + αὐτῆς (om ἰδίου) 35 εὐχαριστοῦντας *B*s κυρίῳ] P35s; θεῷ 33T*B*ll$_2$ **6** λέγων 35 μηδέποτε[1]...... ἐκκλησίας] om l$_2$ ἀπολειφθῇς] ἀπόσχῃ P (ὑστερεῖσθαι 33) **6, 7** μηδέποτε[2]...... κοινωνίας] om P35 33; txt T*B*ls ('do not withdraw thyself from the oblation and from the church') **6** μηδὲ T **7** κοινωνίας] + τῶν μυστηρίων *B*l διὰ τὸ 35 **8** τοῖς] + ἀχράντοις 35 33*B*; θείοις T; diuina ll$_2$ μυστηρίοις] 35 ceases **9** ἄλλην] + πάλιν *B* (txt A[B]) ll$_2$ **10** ποιήσας σύριγγα] 33T*B* (+ ὀρύγματος T*B*) ll$_2$s ('for a long time he made under the earth a cavity (ܫܘܟܐ) from his cell for half a mile'); ὑπενόησε καὶ ὀρύξας P: (s[an] appears to combine both readings) **10–12** αὐτοῦ...... κέλλης] om T (homœotel.) **13** σπήλαιον] + τοῦ ἀπερισπάστως τῷ θεῷ προσομιλεῖν T **17–19** περὶ......ἐρήμῳ] om P, but attested by all the other authorities, including Soz and s, (see Note above) **18** εἶναι] ἔσεσθαι Soz l; om T: + τῶν T **19** ἐκράτει] + περὶ αὐτοῦ *B*†

Τούτῳ προσηνέχθη ποτὲ δαιμονιῶν νεανίσκος παρὰ τῆς ἰδίας μητρὸς ὀλοφυρομένης, σὺν δυσὶ νεανίσκοις δεδεμένος. καὶ ταύτην εἶχε τὴν ἐνέργειαν ὁ δαίμων· μετὰ τὸ φαγεῖν τριῶν μοδίων ἄρτους καὶ πιεῖν κιλικίσιον ὕδατος, ἐρευγόμενος εἰς ἀτμὸν ἔλυε τὰ βρώματα· οὕτω γὰρ ἀνηλίσκετο τὰ βρωθέντα καὶ ποθέντα ὡς ὑπὸ πυρός. ἔστι γὰρ τάγμα τὸ λεγόμενον πύρινον. διαφοραὶ γάρ εἰσι δαιμόνων, ὥσπερ καὶ ἀνθρώπων, οὐκ οὐσίας ἀλλὰ γνώμης. οὗτος τοίνυν ὁ νεανίσκος μὴ ἐπαρκούμενος παρὰ τῆς ἰδίας μητρὸς τὴν οἰκείαν ἤσθιε κόπρον· πολλάκις καὶ τὸ ἴδιον ἔπινεν οὖρον. κλαιούσης οὖν τῆς μητρὸς καὶ παρακαλούσης τὸν ἅγιον, λαβὼν ἐπηύξατο αὐτῷ τὸν θεὸν ἱκετεύων. καὶ μετὰ μίαν ἢ δευτέραν ἡμέραν ὑπολωφήσαντος τοῦ πάθους λέγει αὐτῇ ὁ ἅγιος Μακάριος· Πόσον θέλεις ἵνα ἐσθίῃ; ἡ δὲ ἀπεκρίνατο λέγουσα· Δεκάλιτρον ἄρτου. ἐπιτιμήσας οὖν αὐτῇ ὅτι πολύ ἐστιν, ἐν ἑπτὰ ἡμέραις ἐπευξάμενος αὐτῷ μετὰ νηστείας, ἔστησεν αὐτὸν εἰς τρίλιτρον, ὡς ὀφείλοντα καὶ ἐργάζεσθαι· καὶ οὕτως ἀποθεραπεύσας ἀπέδωκεν αὐτὸν τῇ μητρί. καὶ τοῦτο τὸ θαῦμα πεποίηκεν ὁ θεὸς διὰ τοῦ θαυμασίου Μακαρίου. τούτῳ ἐγὼ οὐ συντετύχηκα· πρὸ ἐνιαυτοῦ γὰρ τῆς εἰσόδου μου τῆς εἰς τὴν ἔρημον ἐκεκοίμητο. |

(XVIII) Τῷ δὲ ἄλλῳ συντετύχηκα Μακαρίῳ τῷ Ἀλεξανδρεῖ, πρεσβυτέρῳ ὄντι τῶν λεγομένων Κελλίων. εἰς ἃ Κελλία παρῴκησα ἐγὼ ἐνναετίαν· ἐν οἷς τὴν τριετίαν τὴν ἐμὴν ἐπέζησε· καὶ τὰ μὲν εἶδον, τὰ δὲ παρ' αὐτοῦ ἀκήκοα, τὰ

γὰρ τὸν Ἀρσενοΐτην κ.τ.λ. (cf. Migne, *P. G.* xxxiv. 209, and for critical text, Preuschen *Pall. u. Ruf.* 124—130) (see Note 28).

22—2 (p. 48) Soz. III. 14 (3) Ὁ δὲ ἕτερος χρόνῳ μὲν ὕστερον πρεσβύτερος ἐγένετο, παντοδαπῆς δὲ σχεδὸν ἀσκήσεως ἐπειράθη, τὰ μὲν αὐτὸς περινοῶν, ἃ δὲ παρ' ἄλλοις ἤκουσεν ἐκ παντὸς τρόπου κατορθῶν.

P[33]ll_2s[T]

2 σὺν] P; om T; *συνδεδ.* *B* δυσὶ δεδεμένος αὐτῷ νεανίσκοις ἑκατέρωθεν T
5 ἀτμὸν] ἑαυτὸν P (33 as text) γὰρ] om P **6** τάγμα] + δαιμόνων T*B*ls; txt Pl_2
8 γνώμης] + ἀλλοιουμένης *B* (txt A[B]) l **11** τῆς μητρὸς] ἐκείνης P **13** αὐτῇ] Ps; τῇ μητρὶ αὐτοῦ 33ll_2 (*B* τοῦ νεανίσκου); (T καὶ προσκαλεσάμενος τὴν μ. τοῦ ν. λέγει αὐτῇ) ὁ ἅγιος M.] om ll_2s (om M. T) **14** ἐσθίῃ] + ὁ υἱός σου (T)*B*l δέκα λιτρῶν P*B*†
15 ἄρτους P πολλή P **16** τριλιτρ.] + ἄρτου *B*l

XVIII (Περὶ Μακαρίου τοῦ Ἀλεξανδρέως): P[33]ll_2s[T cf. Note p. 43]
25 μὲν] + σημεῖα ls(*B*) παρ' αὐτοῦ] om l_2s(*B*)

δὲ καὶ παρ᾽ ἑτέρων μεμάθηκα. | ἡ τοίνυν ἄσκησις αὐτοῦ ἦν αὕτη· εἴ τι ἀκήκοε πώποτε, πάντως τοῦτο κατώρθωσεν. ἀκούσας γὰρ παρά τινων ὅτι οἱ Ταβεννησιῶται διὰ πάσης τῆς τεσσαρακοστῆς ἐσθίουσιν ἄπυρον, ἔκρινεν ἑπταετίαν τὸ διὰ πυρὸς διαβαῖνον μὴ φαγεῖν, καὶ πλὴν λαχάνων ὠμῶν εἴ ποτε παρευρέθησαν καὶ ὀσπρίων βρεκτῶν οὐδενὸς ἄλλου ἐγεύσατο. κατορθώσας οὖν ταύτην τὴν ἀρετήν, ἤκουσε περί τινος πάλιν ἄλλου ὅτι λίτραν ἐσθίει ἄρτου· καὶ κλάσας ἑαυτοῦ τὸν βουκέλλατον καὶ καταγγίσας εἰς †σαΐτας τὰ κεράμια†, ἔκρινε τοσοῦτον ἐσθίειν ὅσον ἂν ἡ χεὶρ ἀνενέγκῃ. καὶ ὡς διηγεῖτο χαριεντιζόμενος ὅτιπερ Ἐδρασσόμην μὲν πλειόνων κλασμάτων, οὐκ ἠδυνάμην δὲ ὅλους ἐξενεγκεῖν ὑπὸ τοῦ στένου τῆς ὀπῆς· τὸ γὰρ παντελῶς μὴ ἐσθίειν ὁ τελώνης μοι οὐ συνεχώρει. ἐπὶ τρία οὖν ἔτη ταύτην ἔσχηκε τὴν ἄσκησιν, τέσσαρας ἢ πέντε οὐγγίας ἄρτου ἐσθίων καὶ τοσοῦτον πίνων ὕδωρ, ξέστην δὲ ἐλαίου τὸν ἐνιαυτόν.

Ἄλλη αὐτοῦ ἄσκησις· ἔκρινεν ὕπνου περιγενέσθαι, καὶ διηγήσατο ὅτι οὐκ εἰσῆλθεν ὑπὸ στέγην ἐπὶ εἴκοσι ἡμέρας ἵνα νικήσῃ ὕπνον, τοῖς μὲν καύμασι φλεγόμενος, τῇ δὲ νυκτὶ στυφόμενος τῇ ψυχρότητι. καὶ ὡς ἔλεγεν ὅτι Εἰ μὴ τάχιον εἰσῆλθον ὑπὸ στέγην καὶ ἐχρησάμην ὕπνῳ, οὕτω μου ἐξηράνθη ὁ ἐγκέφαλος, ὡς εἰς ἔκστασίν με ἐλάσαι λοιπόν. καὶ τὸ μὲν ὅσον ἐπ᾽ ἐμοὶ ἐνίκησα· τὸ δὲ ὅσον ἐπὶ τῇ φύσει τὴν χρείαν ἐχούσῃ τοῦ ὕπνου παρεχώρησα.

Τούτου καθεζομένου πρωὶ ἐν τῷ κελλίῳ κώνωψ στὰς ἐπὶ τοῦ ποδὸς ἐκέντησεν αὐτόν· καὶ ἀλγήσας κατέαξεν αὐτὸν τῇ

25—2 (p. 49) Τούτου......ἐκδικήσαντος ἑαυτὸν] P*B*ls ; TA^{B}l$_2$ read : Οὗτός ποτε ὠχλήθη ὑπὸ τοῦ πάθους (Tl$_2$; πνεύματος A^{B}) τῆς πορνείας· καὶ κατεδίκασεν κ.τ.λ.

P[33]ll$_2$s[T]

2 πώποτε]+τινα πεποιηκότα (T)*B*l **3** Ταβεννησ. PT*B*† **5** καὶ] om T*B*l$_2$ πλὴν λ. ὠμ.] ἤσθιε δὲ ὠμὰ λάχανα T **6** παρευρέθη T ; παρεῦρε *B* ἐγεύσατο] P ; γευσάμενος (T)*B*l$_2$; (l alters ; s om οὐδενὸς ἀλ. ἐγεύσ.) **7** ταύτην τὴν ἀρετὴν] Ps; τοῦτο 33*B*ll$_2$; om T : + κατέπτυσε ταύτης τῆς πολιτείας (T)*B*ll$_2$ **9** καταγγίσας] T (-σαι); καταλύσας P; κατήγαγε *B*† ; ἔβαλε A^{B}*B*† ; (ll$_2$s misit) εἰς σαΐτας τὰ κεράμια] P ; the others om σαΐτας τὰ κεράμιον Tl$_2$s **10** διηγεῖτο]+ἡμῖν *B*l (mihi) **11** ὅτι Περιεδρασσ. (T)*B* **12, 13** τὸ γὰρ......συνεχώρει] om l$_2$; (l and s alter text independently, yet somewhat similarly) **15** οὐγγίας P ; οὐγκίας T*B*† ; ὀγκίας *B*† ἄρτου] Pls ; om T*B*l$_2$ **17** αὐτοῦ]+πάλιν Tll$_2$ **19** ὕπνον] αὐτὸν P φλεγόμενος] +τὴν ἡμέραν *B*ll$_2$; (s 'at midday')

χειρὶ μετὰ κόρον τοῦ αἵματος. καταγνοὺς οὖν ἑαυτοῦ ὡς ἐκδικήσαντος ἑαυτόν, κατεδίκασεν ἑαυτὸν εἰς τὸ ἕλος τῆς Σκήτεως, ὅ ἐστιν ἐν τῇ πανερήμῳ, καθίσαι γυμνὸν ἐπὶ μῆνας ἕξ, ἔνθα οἱ κώνωπες καὶ συάγρων δέρματα τιτρώσκουσιν, ὡς σφῆκες ὄντες. οὕτως οὖν κατετρώθη ὅλος καὶ σπονδύλους ἐξέβαλεν ὡς νομίσαι τινὰς ὅτι ἠλεφαντίασεν. ἐλθὼν οὖν μετὰ μῆνας ἓξ εἰς τὸ κελλίον αὐτοῦ, ἀπὸ τῆς φωνῆς ἐγνώσθη ὅτι αὐτός ἐστιν ὁ Μακάριος.

Ἐπεθύμησέ ποτε οὗτος εἰς τὸ κηποτάφιον εἰσελθεῖν Ἰαννῇ καὶ Ἰαμβρῇ, ὡς αὐτὸς ἡμῖν διηγήσατο. | τοῦτο δὲ τὸ κηποτάφιον ἐγένετο παρὰ τῶν τότε μάγων παραδυναστευόντων τῷ Φαραῷ. ὡς οὖν κεκτημένοι τὴν δυναστείαν ἐκ μακρῶν τῶν χρόνων, ἐν τετραποδικοῖς λίθοις ἔκτισαν τὸ ἔργον, καὶ τὸ μνῆμα δὲ αὐτῶν ἐκεῖ ἐποίησαν, καὶ χρυσὸν ἀπέθεντο πολύν· ἐφύτευσαν δὲ καὶ δένδρα, ὕπικμος γάρ ἐστιν ὁ τόπος, ἐν οἷς καὶ φρέαρ ὤρυξαν. ἐπεὶ οὖν τὴν ὁδὸν ἠγνόει ὁ ἅγιος, στοχασμῷ δέ τινι ἠκολούθει τοῖς ἄστροις καθάπερ ἐν πελάγει τὴν ἔρημον διοδεύων, λαβὼν καλάμων δέμα κατὰ μίλιον ἓν ἵστα σημειούμενος ἵνα εὕρῃ τὴν ὁδὸν ὑποστρέφων. διοδεύσας οὖν ἐντὸς ἐννέα ἡμερῶν τῷ τόπῳ ἐπλησίασεν. ὁ τοίνυν δαίμων ὁ ἀεὶ τοῖς ἀθληταῖς τοῦ Χριστοῦ ἀντιπράττων, συναγαγὼν ὅλους τοὺς καλάμους, καθεύδοντος ὡς ἀπὸ σημείου τοῦ κηποταφίου πρὸς τῇ κεφαλῇ αὐτοῦ τέθεικεν. ἀναστὰς οὖν εὗρε τοὺς καλάμους, τάχα καὶ τοῦτο τοῦ θεοῦ συγχωρήσαντος εἰς πλείονα αὐτοῦ γυμνασίαν, ἵνα μὴ καλάμοις ἐπελπίζῃ, ἀλλὰ τῷ στύλῳ τῆς νεφέλης τῷ ὁδηγήσαντι τὸν Ἰσραὴλ τεσσαράκοντα ἔτη ἐν τῇ ἐρήμῳ. ἔλεγεν ὅτι Ἑβδομήκοντα

9 On this episode see Note 29.

P[33]ll_2s[T]

2 ἑαυτὸν[2]] + ὥστε *B*l **3** μῆνας] T*B*ll_2s; ἡμέρας P **4** δέρμα ll_2T (συάγρου δέρμα) **5** ἐξέβαλεν] + καθ' ὅλου τοῦ σώματος (T)*B*l (per omnia ipsius membra) **6** μῆνας] ἡμέρας P **7** ἐγνώσθη] + μόνον *B*l (T μόνης)

P[33]ll_2ss_2[T]

9 ἐπεθύμησε] s_2 begins **10** Ἰαμβρῇ] PT*B*ss_2; Mambre ll_2 herv. (from the Latin Bibles) **16** ὁδὸν] + ἄγουσαν ἐπὶ τοῦτον τὸν τόπον *B*l (κῆπον *B*†) **17** τινι] + μόνον *B*l καθάπερ] + οἱ ναυτικοὶ *B*l$l_2$$s_2$ **19** σημειούμενος] Pl; χάριν σημείου *B*l_2; (om ss_2) τὴν ὁδὸν] om *B*l ὑποστρέφων] Ps_2; ὑποστρέψαι *B*ll_2s **21** ὁ] ὡς P **22** καθεύδοντος] + τοῦ ἁγίου P; τοῦ Μ. *B* **27, 1** (p. 50) ἑβδ. δαίμονες ἐξῆλθον] P*B*lss_2; παρατάξεις δαιμόνων ὑπήντων ἐξερχόμενοι Tl_2

δαίμονες ἐξῆλθον εἰς συνάντησίν μου ἀπὸ τοῦ κηποταφίου, βοῶντες καὶ πτερυσσόμενοι ὡς κόρακες κατὰ τῆς ὄψεώς μου, καὶ λέγοντες· Τί θέλεις, Μακάριε; τί θέλεις, μοναχέ; τί ἦλθες ἡμῶν εἰς τὸν τόπον; οὐ δύνασαι μεῖναι ὧδε. εἶπον οὖν αὐτοῖς, φησίν, ὅτι Εἰσέλθω μόνον καὶ ἱστορήσω καὶ ἀπέρχομαι. εἰσελθὼν οὖν, φησίν, εὗρον κάδιον χαλκοῦν κρεμάμενον καὶ ἅλυσιν σιδηρᾶν κατὰ τοῦ φρέατος, λοιπὸν τῷ χρόνῳ ἀναλωθέντα, καὶ | καρπὸν ῥοῶν οὐκ ἐχουσῶν ἔνδον οὐδὲν τῷ ἐξηράνθαι ὑπὸ τοῦ ἡλίου. οὕτως οὖν ὑποστρέψας ἦλθε διὰ εἴκοσι ἡμερῶν. ἐκλείψαντος δὲ τοῦ ὕδατος οὗ ἐβάσταζε καὶ τῶν ἄρτων, ἐν πολλῇ περιστάσει ἐγένετο. καὶ ὡς ἐγγὺς ἐγένετο τοῦ ὀκλάσαι ὤφθη αὐτῷ κόρη τις, ὡς διηγήσατο, καθαρὰν ὀθόνην φοροῦσα καὶ κατέχουσα βαυκάλιον ὕδατος στάζον· ἣν ἔλεγεν ἄποθεν αὐτοῦ εἶναι, ὡς ἀπὸ σταδίου, καὶ ἐπὶ ἡμέρας τρεῖς ὁδεύειν, βλέπων μὲν αὐτὴν μετὰ τοῦ βαυκαλίου ὡς ἑστῶσαν καταλαβεῖν δὲ μὴ δυνάμενος, †ὡς ἐπὶ τῶν ἱερέων,† τῇ δὲ ἐλπίδι τοῦ πιεῖν ὑπομείνας ηὐτόνει. μεθ' ἣν ἐφάνη πλῆθος βουβάλων, ἐξ ὧν ἡ μία ἔστη ἔχουσα μόσχον· εἰσὶ γὰρ πολλαὶ ἐν τοῖς τόποις ἐκείνοις·

5 *ἀπέρχομαι*] Here and infra, pp. 51, 57, occur passages in PTAl_2(c) which are not found in *B*lss_2: on this series of interpolations cf. *Introd.* § 10.

PTAl_2 (c vac): + *εἰσερχομένου δὲ αὐτοῦ ἐν τῷ κηποταφίῳ ὑπήντησεν αὐτῷ ὁ σατανᾶς μετὰ ῥομφαίας ἐσπασμένης ἀπειλῶν αὐτῷ. πρὸς ὃν ταύτην ἀπεκρίνατο τὴν ῥῆσιν ὁ ἅγιος Μακάριος·* Σὺ ἔρχῃ πρός με ἐν ῥο[μ]φαίᾳ ἐσπασμένῃ, κἀγὼ ἔρχομαι πρός σε ἐν ὀνόματι Κυρίου σαβαὼθ θεοῦ παρατάξεως Ἰσραήλ (om *B*lss_2).

[**1** *ἐν τῷ κ.*] *εἰς τὸν παράδεισον* TA(l_2) **2** *διάβολος* A *ἐπαπειλῶν* TA *ταύτην*] + *τὴν φωνὴν* (om *τὴν ῥῆσιν*) A **3** 1 Regn. xvii 45 **4** *πορεύομαι* A; *πορεύσομαι* T **4, 5** *ἐν παρατάξει θεοῦ Ἰσ.* TA]

9 *ἡλίου*] PTAl_2 (c vac): + *καὶ ἀναθήματα δὲ* (+ *ἦν ἐκεῖ* A) *πλεῖστα χρυσᾶ* (om *B*lss_2).

PA[33]ll_2ss_2[T]

1 *εἰς συνάντ. μου*] *B*ls (ܠܦܘܓܥܐ ܕܝܠܝ); om P (Tl_2 cf. p. 49) **6** *κάδδιον* P *ἁλύσει σιδηρᾷ* (om *καὶ*) T*B*l **13** *καυκάλιον* *B* *ἄποθεν*] TA[B] (*ἄπωθεν*); *μακρόθεν* *B*†; *ἀπὸ μήκοθεν* *B*†; a se separatam l; longe esse a se l_2; ‘distant from him’ ss_2; *ἔμπροσθεν* P*B*† **14** *εἶναι*] *ἰέναι* P *ὡς*] om Tl *καὶ*] om P *ὥδευσε* T*B*s(ll_2) s_2 ‘she came after him and she was distant from him about a stade, and for three days he saw her coming after him’ (om *μετὰ τοῦ......ἱερέων*) **15** *δὲ*] + *αὐτὴν* T*B* (*ταύτην*) l **16** *ὡς ἐπὶ τῶν ἱερέων*] PT*B* (+ *καὶ τῶν μυστηρίων ἔστιν ἰδεῖν* T*B*); sicut somnians l_2; quod in curuatura celi fieri (ras.) uideri ambulantibus solet l[cass] (erasures in l[sess]); om A[B]s_2l[rev]; s quite altered: l_2 suggests ωсєπιгєонєιρωɴ **17–2** (p. 51) *ἐξ ὧν......ἠρκέσθη*] om s_2

καὶ ὡς ἔλεγεν ὅτι ἔρρει αὐτῆς τὸ οὖθαρ τοῦ γάλακτος. ὑπεισελθὼν οὖν τῇ βουβάλῳ καὶ θηλάσας ἠρκέσθη. καὶ ἕως τοῦ κελλίου αὐτοῦ ἦλθεν ἡ βούβαλος θηλάζουσα αὐτόν, τὸ δὲ μοσχάριον αὐτῆς μὴ δεχομένη.

Ἄλλοτε πάλιν ὀρύσσων φρέαρ πλησίον βλαστῶν φρυγάνων ὑπὸ ἀσπίδος ἐδήχθη· ἀναιρετικὸν δέ ἐστι τὸ ζῷον· λαβὼν οὖν αὐτὴν ταῖς δύο χερσὶν ἀπὸ τῶν χελυνίων κρατήσας διέσχισεν, εἰπὼν αὐτῇ· Μὴ ἀποστείλαντός σε τοῦ θεοῦ, πῶς ἐπελθεῖν μοι ἐτόλμησας; |

Εἶχε δὲ κέλλας διαφόρους ἐν τῇ ἐρήμῳ· μίαν ἐν τῇ Σκήτει τῇ ἐνδοτέρᾳ πανερήμῳ, καὶ μίαν εἰς Λίβα, καὶ μίαν εἰς τὰ λεγόμενα Κελλία, καὶ μίαν εἰς τὸ ὄρος τῆς Νιτρίας. ὧν ἔνιαί εἰσιν ἀθυρίδωτοι, εἰς ἃς ἔλεγετο καθέζεσθαι τῇ τεσσαρακοστῇ ἐν σκοτίᾳ· ἡ δὲ ἄλλη στενωτέρα, εἰς ἣν ἐκτεῖναι πόδας οὐκ ἴσχυεν· ἄλλη δὲ πλατυτέρα, ἐν ᾗ συνετύγχανε τοῖς φοιτῶσι πρὸς αὐτόν.

Οὗτος τοσοῦτον πλῆθος δαιμονιζομένων ἐθεράπευσεν ὡς ἀριθμῷ μὴ ὑποπεσεῖν. ὄντων δὲ ἡμῶν ἐκεῖ παρθένος ἠνέχθη αὐτῷ ἀπὸ Θεσσαλονίκης εὐγενής, πολυετίαν ἔχουσα ἐν παραλύσει. ταύτην ἐν εἴκοσι ἡμέραις ἐλαίῳ ἁγίῳ ἀλείφων ταῖς ἑαυτοῦ χερσὶ καὶ προσευχόμενος, ὑγιῆ ἀπέστειλεν εἰς τὴν ἰδίαν πόλιν. ἥτις ἀπελθοῦσα πολλὴν καρποφορίαν αὐτῷ ἀπέστειλεν. |

1 *γάλακτος*] $PTAl_2c$: + *καὶ φωνὴ ἐγένετο ἄνωθεν λέγουσα· Μακάριε, πρόσελθε τῇ βουβάλῳ καὶ θήλασον* (om *B*ls) (s_2 vac).

[**1** *ἐγένετο*] *γέγονεν αὐτῷ* TA(c) *ἄνωθεν*] om Tc **2** *θηλάσθητι* A]

10—23 In A, this section, which presents a pure text, is transferred to p. 54, l. 21. **10—12** See Note 14.

$P[33]ll_2cs s_2$ (1—4) [T]

1 *ἔρρει*] c begins here **4** *δεχομένη*] s_2 ceases **5** *βλαστῶν φρυγάνων*] Pl_2(l) ; *θρύων καὶ φ.* (T)*B* ; 'reeds' c ; (s om)

$PA[33]ll_2cs$[T]

10 *οὗτος ὁ ἅγιος εἶχε διαφ. κελ.* (om *ἐν τῇ ἐρ.*) A *μίαν*] + *μὲν* A *τῇ*[2]] om A **11** *τῇ ἐνδοτέρᾳ παν.*] $ATBll_2c$ (om *τῇ Σκήτει*) s; *τῆς πανερήμου* (om *τῇ ἐνδοτέρᾳ*) P *Λίβα*] PA ; *Λιβύην* TBlc (s Aulbia); (l_2 om clause) *καὶ μίαν*[2]] om (T)*B* **12** *λεγόμενα*] om A *Νητρίας* PA *ὧν ἔνιαι*] Ps ; *καὶ αἱ μὲν* AT*B* **13** *καθ.*] + *ἐν* A **17–23** For trans. of c see *Prol.* 149 **17** *δαιμονιώντων* A **18** *ἡμῶν*] 'I and holy Evagrius' s^{an} **19** *αὐτῷ*] $A(B)l_2cs$; illuc l ; om PT *εὐγενὴς*] om l_2cs *ἐν*] + *τῇ* A **20** *ἐν*] om A **21** *ἐξαπέστ.* A **22** *αὐτῷ*] PA (after *ἀπ.*) s(c) ; *τῷ ἁγίῳ* 33 ; *τοῖς ἁγίοις B* ; *τοῖς ἐν τῇ ἐρήμῳ ἁγίοις* T ; ad solitudines l ; per diuersa sancta monasteria l_2

Οὗτος ἀκούσας ὅτι μεγάλην ἔχουσι πολιτείαν οἱ Ταβεννησιῶται, μεταμφιασάμενος καὶ λαβὼν κοσμικὸν σχῆμα ἐργάτου, δι' ἡμερῶν δεκαπέντε ἀνῆλθεν εἰς τὴν Θηβαΐδα διὰ τῆς ἐρήμου ὁδεύσας. καὶ ἐλθὼν ἐν τῷ ἀσκητηρίῳ τῶν Ταβεννησιωτῶν ἐπεζήτει τὸν ἀρχιμανδρίτην τούτων, Παχώμιον ὀνόματι, ἄνδρα δοκιμώτατον καὶ χάρισμα ἔχοντα προφητείας· ᾧ ἀπεκρύβη τὰ κατὰ τὸν Μακάριον. περιτυχὼν οὖν αὐτῷ λέγει· Δέομαί σου δέξαι με εἰς τὴν μονήν σου ἵνα γένωμαι μοναχός. λέγει αὐτῷ ὁ Παχώμιος· Λοιπὸν εἰς γῆρας ἤλασας, καὶ ἀσκεῖν οὐ δύνασαι· οἱ ἀδελφοί εἰσιν ἀσκηταί, καὶ οὐ φέρεις αὐτῶν τοὺς πόνους· καὶ σκανδαλίζῃ καὶ ἐκβαίνεις κακολογῶν αὐτούς. καὶ οὐκ ἐδέξατο αὐτὸν οὔτε τὴν πρώτην οὔτε τὴν δευτέραν, μέχρις ἡμερῶν ἑπτά. ὡς δὲ ηὐτόνησε παραμένων νῆστις, ὕστερον λέγει αὐτῷ· Δέξαι με, ἀββᾶ, καὶ ἐὰν μὴ νηστεύσω κατ' αὐτοὺς καὶ ἐργάσωμαι, κέλευσον ἐκριφῆναί με. πείθει τοὺς ἀδελφοὺς εἰσδέξασθαι αὐτόν· ἔστι δὲ τὸ σύστημα τῆς μιᾶς μονῆς χίλιοι τετρακόσιοι ἄνδρες μέχρι τῆς σήμερον. εἰσῆλθεν οὖν· παρελθόντος δὲ χρόνου ὀλίγου | ἐπέστη ἡ τεσσαρακοστή, καὶ εἶδεν ἕκαστον διαφόρους πολιτείας ἀσκοῦντας· τὸν μὲν ἐσθίοντα ἑσπέρας, τὸν δὲ διὰ δύο, τὸν δὲ διὰ πέντε· ἄλλον δὲ πάλιν ἑστῶτα διὰ πάσης νυκτός, ἐν ἡμέρᾳ δὲ καθήμενον. βρέξας οὖν θαλλοὺς τοὺς ἐκ φοινίκων εἰς πλῆθος ἔστη ἐν γωνίᾳ μιᾷ, καὶ μέχρις οὗ αἱ τεσσαράκοντα ἐπληρώθησαν ἡμέραι καὶ τὸ πάσχα παραγέγονεν οὐκ ἄρτου ἥψατο, οὐχ ὕδατος· οὐ γόνυ ἔκαμψεν, οὐκ ἀνέπεσε· παρεκτὸς φύλλων κράμβης ὀλίγων οὐκ ἐλάμβανε, καὶ τοῦτο κατὰ κυριακήν, ἵνα δόξῃ ἐσθίων. καὶ εἴ ποτε ἐξέβαινεν εἰς τὴν χρείαν ἑαυτοῦ, θᾶττον πάλιν εἰσιὼν ἵστατο, μὴ λαλήσας μηδενί, μὴ ἀνοίξας τὸ στόμα, ἀλλὰ σιωπῇ ἑστώς· ἐκτὸς δὲ προσευχῆς τῆς ἐν τῇ καρδίᾳ καὶ τῶν θαλλῶν τῶν

1 For l_2 see *Bibl. Casin. III. Florileg.* 294. **9** See Note 30.

P[33]ll_2css_2[T]

1 s_2 recommences: for c see *Prol.* 120—22 αὐτὸς οὗτος *B*l (hic ipse) ἀκούσας] + ὁ Μακάριος *B*l_2c **5** τούτων] + θεάσασθαι T(l_2) **6** ἀπεκρύβη] + nutu dei l_2 (c 'God did not tell him') **7** σου] + κύριε T*B*s_2; ἀββᾶ sc; domine pater l_2 **8** σου] om P (l_2^a) **10** πόνους] κόπους 33 **13** ηὐτόνησε] c as if ἠτόνησε cf. *Prol.* 122, and ὑπομείνας ηὐτόνει p. 50, l. 17 where s translates as if ἠτόνει **15** ἐργάσωμαι] + sicut et illi l_2c(*B*) με] + τῆς μονῆς (T)*B*c; foras l_2s: + (ἀκούσας) ll_2 **19** ἀναλαβόντα[s] *B*; ποιοῦντα T **26** τοῦτο] τούτων T καὶ[2]] From this point to the end of the chapter l_2 becomes rather loose

ἐν ταῖς χερσὶν οὐδὲν ἐποίει. θεασάμενοι οὖν πάντες οἱ ἀσκηταὶ ἐστασίασαν κατὰ τοῦ ἡγουμένου λέγοντες· Τοῦτον ἡμῖν πόθεν ἤγαγες τὸν ἄσαρκον, εἰς κατάκρισιν ἡμῶν; ἢ ἔκβαλε αὐτόν, ἢ ἵνα εἰδῇς ὅτι πάντες ἡμεῖς ἀναχωροῦμέν σου. ἀκούσας οὖν αὐτοῦ τὰ τῆς πολιτείας, προσηύξατο τῷ θεῷ, ἵνα αὐτῷ ἀποκαλυφθῇ τίς ἐστίν. ἀπεκαλύφθη οὖν αὐτῷ· καὶ κρατήσας αὐτοῦ τῆς χειρὸς ἐξάγει αὐτὸν εἰς τὸν εὐκτήριον οἶκον, ἔνθα τὸ θυσιαστήριον ἦν, καὶ λέγει αὐτῷ· Δεῦρο, καλόγηρε· σὺ εἶ Μακάριος, καὶ ἀπέκρυψας σεαυτὸν ἀπ' ἐμοῦ. διὰ πολλῶν σε ἐτῶν ἐπεπόθουν ἰδεῖν. χάριν σοι ἔχω ὅτι ἐκονδύλισας τὰ παιδία μου, ἵνα μὴ μέγα φρονῶσιν ἐπὶ ταῖς ἑαυτῶν ἀσκήσεσιν. ἄπελθε οὖν εἰς τὸν τόπον σου· αὐτάρκως γὰρ ᾠκοδόμησας ἡμᾶς· καὶ εὔχου ὑπὲρ ἡμῶν. τότε ἀξιωθεὶς ἀνεχώρησεν.

Ἄλλοτε πάλιν διηγήσατο ὅτι Πᾶσαν πολιτείαν ἣν ἐπεθύμησα κατορθώσας, τότε εἰς ἄλλην ἦλθον ἐπιθυμίαν ὅθεν ἠθέλησά ποτε πέντε ἡμέρας μόνον τὸν νοῦν μου ἀπερίσπαστον ἀπὸ τοῦ θεοῦ ποιῆσαι. καὶ κρίνας τοῦτο ἀπέκλεισα τὴν κέλλαν καὶ τὴν αὐλήν, ὥστε μὴ δοῦναι ἀνθρώπῳ ἀπόκρισιν, καὶ ἔστην ἀρξάμενος ἀπὸ τῆς δευτέρας. παραγγέλλω οὖν μου τῷ νῷ εἰπών· Μὴ κατέλθῃς τῶν οὐρανῶν· ἔχεις ἐκεῖ ἀγγέλους, ἀρχαγγέλους, τὰς ἄνω δυνάμεις, τὸν θεὸν τῶν ὅλων· μὴ κατέλθῃς ὑποκάτω τοῦ οὐρανοῦ. καὶ διαρκέσας ἡμέρας δύο καὶ νύκτας δύο, οὕτω παρώξυνα τὸν δαίμονα ὡς φλόγα πυρὸς γενέσθαι καὶ κατακαῦσαί μου πάντα τὰ ἐν τῷ κελλίῳ, ὡς καὶ τὸν ψιάθιον ἐν ᾧ εἱστήκειν πυρὶ καταφλεχθῆναι καὶ νομίσαι με ὅτι ὅλως ἐμπέπρησμαι. τέλος πληγεὶς φόβῳ ἀπέστην τῇ τρίτῃ

P[33]ll_2css_2[T]

2 *ἡγουμένου*] + *αὐτῶν* *B*l(s); monasterii l_2c **3** *αὐτὸν*] + *ἐντεῦθεν* *B*(c); *ἔξω* T; a nobis l **4** *οὖν*] + *ὁ Παχώμιος* (T)*B*c; praepositus monasterii l_2s **6** *ἐστιν*] + *οὗτος* *B*l *αὐτῷ*] + *ὅτι οὗτός ἐστι Μακάριος* (T)*B*l_2 (+ *ὁ μοναχὸς* *B*; 'the Alexandrian, he who dwelt in Scete,' c) (s_2 'then God said to him: "This is M." for he had changed his name') **8** *καὶ*[1]] + *ἀσπασάμενος αὐτὸν* *B*l_2 **10** *ἰδεῖν*] om P

P[33]lcs[T]

14 *διηγήσατο*] + *ἡμῖν* *B*lc **17** *ποιῆσαι*] + *καὶ μηδὲν ἄλλο τι ὅλως* (om T) *ἐννοῆσαι* (T)*B*; 'being above all anxiety and thought of creatures' s; 'taking no trouble in any work (way) of this world' c *τοῦτο*] + *ἐν ἐμαυτῷ* *B*lc **20** *εἰπὼν*] om P: + *βλέπε* (T)*B*c(l) **21** *δυνάμεις*] + *τὰ Χερουβίμ, τὰ Σεραφίμ* *B*c (which, however, has long list—patriarchs, prophets, apostles &c.) **26** *ἀπέστην*] + *τῆς προθέσεως ταύτης* *B*l

ἡμέρᾳ, μὴ δυνηθεὶς ἀπερίσπαστόν μου τὸν νοῦν ποιῆσαι, ἀλλὰ κατῆλθον εἰς θεωρίαν τοῦ κόσμου, | ἵνα μή μοι λογισθῇ τῦφος.

Τούτῳ ποτὲ τῷ ἁγίῳ Μακαρίῳ παρέβαλον ἐγώ, καὶ εὗρον ἔξω τῆς κέλλης αὐτοῦ πρεσβύτερον κώμης κατακείμενον, οὗ ἡ κεφαλὴ πᾶσα ἐβέβρωτο ὑπὸ τοῦ πάθους τοῦ λεγομένου καρκίνου, καὶ αὐτὸ τὸ ὀστέον ἀπὸ τῆς κορυφῆς ἐφαίνετο. παρεγένετο οὖν ἰαθῆναι, καὶ οὐκ ἐδέχετο αὐτὸν εἰς συντυχίαν. παρεκάλεσα οὖν αὐτὸν ὅτι Δέομαί σου, κατοικτείρησον αὐτόν, καὶ δὸς αὐτῷ τὴν ἀπόκρισιν. καὶ λέγει μοι· Ἀνάξιός ἐστι τοῦ ἰαθῆναι· παιδεία γὰρ αὐτῷ ἀπεστάλη. εἰ δὲ θέλεις αὐτὸν ἰαθῆναι, πεῖσον αὐτὸν ἀποστῆναι τῆς λειτουργίας· πορνεύων γὰρ ἐλειτούργει, καὶ διὰ τοῦτο παιδεύεται· καὶ ὁ θεὸς αὐτὸν ἰᾶται. ὡς οὖν εἶπον τῷ κακουμένῳ συνέθετο, ὀμόσας μηκέτι ἱερατεύειν. τότε ἐδέξατο αὐτὸν καὶ λέγει αὐτῷ· Πιστεύεις ὅτι ἔστι θεός; λέγει αὐτῷ· Ναί. Μὴ ἠδυνήθης διαπαῖξαι τὸν θεόν; ἀπεκρίνατο ὅτι Οὔ. ⌜λέγει αὐτῷ·⌝ Εἰ γνωρίζεις σου τὴν ἁμαρτίαν καὶ τὴν τοῦ θεοῦ παιδείαν δι' ἣν τοῦτο ὑπέστης, διορθώθητι εἰς τὸ ἑξῆς. ἐξωμολογήσατο οὖν τὴν αἰτίαν, καὶ ἔδωκε λόγον μηκέτι ἁμαρτῆσαι μήτε λειτουργῆσαι, ἀλλὰ τὸν λαικὸν ἀσπάσασθαι κλῆρον. καὶ οὕτως ἐπέθηκεν αὐτῷ χεῖρα, καὶ ἐν ὀλίγαις ἡμέραις ἰάθη καὶ ἐτρίχωσε καὶ ἀπῆλθεν ὑγιής.

Ἐπ' ὄψεσιν ἐμαῖς προσηνέχθη αὐτῷ παιδαρίσκος ἐνεργούμενος ὑπὸ πονηροῦ πνεύματος. ἐπιθεὶς οὖν αὐτῷ χεῖρα ἐπὶ τῆς κεφαλῆς καὶ τὴν ἄλλην ἐπὶ τῆς καρδίας, ἐπὶ τοσοῦτον

P[33]lcs[T]

2 *τῦφος*] + 'he said also: "I have spent fifty years in ascetical practices; I have not suffered as on that day"' c

P[33]ll$_2$cs[T]

3 *ἐγὼ*] + 'with the holy Albinus' c (cf. *Prol.* 151) **4** *κώμης*] om l$_2$s **6** *καρκίνου*] + *ὡς* (T)*B*l **7–11** *εἰς συντυχίαν...πεῖσον αὐτὸν*] om T **8** *σου*] om P **10, 11** *παιδεία......ἰαθῆναι*] om l$_2$c (c om *πεῖσον......λειτουργίας*) **10** *γὰρ*] + *κυρίου* *B*†l (ex praecepto diuinitatis) s ('from God') *αὐτῷ*] + *αὕτη* *B*†l **12** *παιδεύεται*] (*B*ll$_2$s each inserts a clause here, but the clauses are different) **13** *κακουμένῳ*] + *ταῦτα* T*B*(ll$_2$s); txt PA[B] **15** *θεός*] + *ὃν οὐδὲν λανθάνει* (T)*B*l$_2$ *Ναί*] + *εἶτα* (om l$_2$) *λέγει αὐτῷ* (+ *ὁ* M. *B*) *B*l$_2$s **16** Οὐ] PT (*οὐχὶ κύριέ μου*) l$_2$s; *οὐκ ἠδυνήθην* *B*l *λέγει αὐτῷ*] *B*l$_2$s(l); om PT **21** *ὑγιής*] + *εἰς τὸν οἶκον αὐτοῦ* *B* (l ad propria)

PA[33]ll$_2$cs[T]

22–10 (p. 56) A presents a pure text **22** *ἐπ' ὄψ. ἐμ.*] In ls attached to preceding section; in l$_2$ it occurs in both places *ἐπ'*] P*B*†; *ὑπ'* AT*B*† *ὄψεσιν*] + *δὲ* AT *παῖς* A **23** *πονηροῦ*] om Alcs *οὖν*] *δὲ* A*B*

ηὔξατο ἕως οὗ αὐτὸν ἀπὸ ἀέρος ἐποίησε κρεμασθῆναι. οἰδήσας οὖν ὡς ἀσκὸς ὁ παῖς τοσοῦτον ἐφλέγμανεν ὡς γενέσθαι †πᾶς ρυσιπέλαντος†. καὶ αἰφνίδιον ἀνακράξας, διὰ πασῶν τῶν αἰσθήσεων ὕδωρ ἐνήνοχε, καὶ λωφήσας πάλιν γέγονεν εἰς τὸ μέτρον ὃ ἦν. παραδίδωσιν οὖν τῷ πατρὶ αὐτόν, ἀλείψας ἐλαίῳ ἁγίῳ, καὶ ἐπιχέας ὕδωρ, | παρήγγειλεν ἐπὶ τεσσαράκοντα ἡμέρας μὴ κρεῶν ἅψασθαι, μὴ οἴνου. καὶ οὕτως αὐτὸν ἰάσατο.

Ὤχλησαν τούτῳ ποτὲ λογισμοὶ κενοδοξίας ἐκβάλλοντες αὐτὸν τῆς κέλλης, καὶ ὑποτιθέμενοι οἰκονομίας χάριν καταλαμβάνειν τὴν Ῥωμαίων πρὸς θεραπείαν τῶν ἀρρωστούντων· μεγάλως γὰρ ἐνήργει ἡ χάρις εἰς αὐτὸν κατὰ πνευμάτων. καὶ ὡς ἐπὶ πολὺ οὐχ ὑπήκουσε, σφοδρῶς δὲ ἠλαύνετο, πεσὼν ἐπὶ τῆς φλιᾶς τῆς κέλλης τοὺς πόδας ἀφῆκεν ἐπὶ τὰ ἔξω καὶ λέγει· Ἕλκετε, δαίμονες, καὶ σύρετε· ἐγὼ γὰρ τοῖς ποσὶ τοῖς ἐμοῖς οὐκ ἀπέρχομαι· εἰ δύνασθέ με οὕτως ἀπενεγκεῖν ἀπελεύσομαι· διομνὺς αὐτοῖς ὅτι Κεῖμαι ἕως ἑσπέρας· ἐὰν μή με σαλεύσετε, οὐ μὴ ὑμῶν ἀκούσω. ἐπὶ πολὺ οὖν πεσὼν ἀνέστη. ἐπιγενομένης δὲ νυκτὸς πάλιν αὐτῷ ἐπέθεντο· καὶ σπυρίδα μοδίων δύο ψάμμου πληρώσας καὶ θεὶς ἐπὶ τῶν ὤμων, διεκίνει ἀνὰ τὴν ἔρημον. συνήντησεν οὖν αὐτῷ Θεοσέβιος ὁ κοσμήτωρ, Ἀντιοχεὺς τῷ γένει, καὶ λέγει αὐτῷ· Τί βαστάζεις, ἀββᾶ; παραχώρησον ἐμοὶ τὸ φορτίον, καὶ μὴ σκύλλου. ὁ δὲ λέγει αὐτῷ· Σκύλλω τὸν σκύλλοντά με· ἄνετος γὰρ ὢν

PA[33]ll_2(1—18)cs[T]

1 ἐπηύξατο A*B* οὗ] om A*B*† αὐτὸν] τὸ πνεῦμα 33 sc(cf. *Prol.* 151) (l_2 suspendit eum ille immundus spiritus) ἐποίησε before αὐτὸν A 2 παῖς] + ὅλῳ τῳ σώματι *B*; totus ll_2: + ἐπὶ A 2, 3 τοσοῦτον......ρυσιπέλαντος] om s πᾶς ρυσιπέλαντος] (sic) P; πολυτάλαντον A33T*B* (+ τῷ σηκώματι (T)*B*); supra quam aestimare quis possit l; ($l_2$cs om clause): (perhaps ἐρυσιπέλατος?) 4 πάλιν] PA; om T*B*ll_2cs 5 καὶ παραδίδ. αὐτὸν A 6 καὶ ἐπ. ὕδωρ] om l_2s ὕδωρ] + ηὐλογημένον *B*l 7 καὶ] om A ἰάσατο] A folio of P has here been displaced in binding: f. 57 should come before f. 56 8 ποτε τούτῳ AT*B* πειρώμενοι ἐκβάλλειν (T)*B*l (uolentes ..abstrahere) 10 Ῥωμαίων] P; Ῥώμην AT*B*; ἐν Ῥώμῃ 33 θεραπ.] Pll_2cs; εὐεργεσίαν AT*B* 11 εἰς αὐτὸν before ἐνήργει A*B* πνευμάτων] + immundi ll_2 12 σφόδρα (om δὲ) A ἠλαύνετο] + καὶ A 13 τῆς[2]] + ἑαυτοῦ T*B*(ll_2cs) 14 δαίμονες] + ἐὰν δύνασθε 33 (+ βαστάζετε καὶ ἀπαγάγετε) *B*lc τοῖς ἐμοῖς π. A*B* 15 εἰ δύνασθε......ἀπελεύσομαι] om A 16, 17 ἐὰν......ἀκούσω] om l_2c 17 σαλεύσητε A*B* οὖν] δὲ AT 18–2 (p. 56) ἐπιγενομένης......σῶμα] om l_2 18 ὤχλησαν AT*B* 20 ἀνὰ] ὅλην A ἔρημον] + τούτῳ (om οὖν αὐτῷ) AT*B*(l) 23 αὐτῷ] Plcs; om AT*B*

ἀποδημίας μοι ὑποβάλλει. ἐπὶ πολὺ οὖν διακινήσας εἰσῆλθεν εἰς τὴν κέλλαν, συντρίψας τὸ σῶμα. |

Οὗτος ἡμῖν ὁ ἅγιος Μακάριος διηγήσατο, ἦν γὰρ πρεσβύτερος, ὅτι Ἐπεσημηνάμην κατὰ τὸν καιρὸν τῆς διαδόσεως τῶν μυστηρίων ὅτι Μάρκῳ τῷ ἀσκητῇ οὐδέποτε ἔδωκα ἐγὼ προσφοράν, ἀλλὰ ἄγγελος αὐτῷ ἐπεδίδου ἐκ τοῦ θυσιαστηρίου· μόνον δὲ τὸν ἀστράγαλον ἐθεώρουν τῆς χειρὸς τοῦ διδόντος. Μάρκος δὲ οὗτος νεώτερος ἦν, παλαιὰν καὶ καινὴν γραφὴν ἀποστηθίζων, πραῢς καθ' ὑπερβολήν, σώφρων εἴ καί τις ἄλλος.

Μιᾶς οὖν τῶν ἡμερῶν εὐκαιρηθεὶς ἐγώ, εἰς τὸ ἔσχατον αὐτοῦ γῆρας, ἀπέρχομαι καὶ παρακαθέζομαι αὐτοῦ τῇ θύρᾳ νομίσας αὐτὸν ὑπὲρ ἄνθρωπον, ὡς ἅτε ἀρχαῖον, ἀκροώμενος τί λέγει ἢ τί διαπράττεται. καὶ μονώτατος ὢν ἔνδον, περὶ τὰ ἑκατὸν ἐλάσας ἔτη ἤδη καὶ τοὺς ὀδόντας ἀπολέσας, ἑαυτῷ διεμάχετο καὶ τῷ διαβόλῳ, καὶ ἔλεγε· Τί θέλεις, κακόγηρε; ἰδοὺ καὶ ἐλαίου ἥψω καὶ οἴνου μετέλαβες· λοιπὸν τί θέλεις, πολιόφαγε; ἑαυτὸν ὑβρίζων. εἶτα καὶ τῷ διαβόλῳ· Μὴ ἀκμήν

3—10 Soz. VI. 29 (11) *Φασὶ δὲ Μάρκον μὲν καὶ ἐν τῷ νέῳ τῆς ἡλικίας εἰς ἄγαν πρᾷον καὶ σώφρονα καὶ μνήμονα ἱερῶν γραφῶν γενέσθαι· θεοφιλῆ δὲ ἐπὶ τοσοῦτον ὡς ἰσχυρίζεσθαι Μακάριον τὸν αὐτόν, πρεσβύτερον ὄντα τῶν Κελλίων, μηδὲ πώποτε παρ' αὐτοῦ λαβεῖν ἃ θέμις ἱερεῦσι διδόναι τοῖς μεμυημένοις περὶ τὴν ἱερὰν τράπεζαν· ἄγγελος δὲ αὐτῷ ἐδίδου οὗ τὴν χεῖρα μέχρι τοῦ καρποῦ μόνου ἔλεγε θεωρεῖν.*

PA[33]ll$_2$cs[T]

1 *οὖν*] PT; *δὲ* A; *καὶ B* **3–10** For s in this paragr. cf. *Introd.* § 9 **3–3** (p. 57) This section is transferred to end of cap. in A **3** *ἦν γὰρ πρεσβ.*] AT*B* Soz ll$_2$cs (om *ἦν γάρ*); om P **5** *τῶν*] + *θείων* Tll$_2$ (sacrosancta communio) *ἐγὼ ἐδ.* A **6** *ἐπεδ. αὐτῷ* A **8** *Μάρκος*] On confusions in the Greek MSS. between Marcus and Macarius, from this point to the end of the chapter, see Note 30: at this point a new cap. begins in P (and several B MSS.), *περὶ Μάρκου τοῦ νεωτέρου* *γραφὴν*] om P **9** *καὶ σ. εἰς ἄκρον*] A: here A ceases and A^B recommences

P[33]ll$_2$cs[T]

11 *εὐκαιρηθεὶς*] P*B*† (*εὐκαιρούμενος*) l; *ἀκαιρούμενος* T*B*†A^B; om l$_2$c; (s 'when a feverish chill held me') **12** *αὐτοῦ* viz. Macarius, named in l$_2$c; but the Greek MSS. understand it of Marcus *ἀπέρχομαι*] + *πρὸς αὐτὸν B*ll$_2$c *θύρᾳ*] + *ἡσυχῇ* P **13** *νομίσας......ἄνθρωπον*] om l$_2$c *ὑπὲρ ἄνθ.*] om s *ὡς ἅτε ἀρχαῖον*] Ps; *ὡς ἅτε ἐγὼ ἀρχάριος ὢν B*l (quasi inperitus ac nouus) before *νομίσας*; om Tl$_2$c **17** *καὶ ἐλαίου ἥψω*] om P; (*B*c transfer clauses) **18** *πολιόφαγε*] T*B*†A^{B}lsc (l in extremis aetatis tuae canis: sc 'thou that eatest white hairs'); *πολύφαγε* P*B*†; decrepite senex l$_2$ (so l for *κακόγηρε* l. 16) **18–3** (p. 57) *μὴ ἀκμὴν......μετὰ σοῦ*] om l$_2$

τί σοι χρεωστῶ; οὐδὲν εὑρίσκεις· ἄπελθε ἀπ' ἐμοῦ. καὶ ὡς τερετίζων ἑαυτῷ διελέγετο· Δεῦρο, πολιόφαγε· ἕως πότε ἔσομαι μετὰ σοῦ; |

Διηγεῖτο δὲ ἡμῖν Παφνύτιος ὁ μαθητὴς αὐτοῦ, ὅτι μιᾷ τῶν ἡμερῶν ὕαινα λαβοῦσα τὸν ἑαυτῆς σκύμνον, τυφλὸν ὄντα, ἤνεγκε τῷ Μακαρίῳ· καὶ τῇ κεφαλῇ κρούσασα τῆς αὐλῆς τὴν θύραν εἰσῆλθεν ἔξω αὐτοῦ καθημένου, καὶ ἔρριψεν ὑπὸ τοὺς πόδας αὐτοῦ τὸν σκύμνον. λαβὼν δὲ ὁ ἅγιος καὶ ἐπιπτύσας τοῖς ὀφθαλμοῖς αὐτοῦ ἐπηύξατο, καὶ παραχρῆμα ἀνέβλεψε. καὶ θηλάσασα αὐτὸν ἡ μήτηρ αὐτοῦ λαβοῦσα αὐτὸν ἀπῆλθε. καὶ τῇ ἄλλῃ ἡμέρᾳ κώδιον μεγάλου προβάτου ἐνήνοχε τῷ ἁγίῳ. ὡς δὲ ἡ μακαρία Μελανία μοι εἶπεν ὅτι Παρὰ τοῦ Μακαρίου ἐγὼ ἔλαβον τὸ κώδιον ἐκεῖνο ξένιον.

12 *τῷ ἁγίῳ*] PTAl_2c: + *καὶ θεασάμενος ὁ ἅγιος τὸ κώδιον ταῦτ' ἔλεγε τῇ ὑαίνῃ· Πόθεν σοι τοῦτο, εἰ μὴ βεβρώκεις πρόβατόν τινος; τὸ οὖν ἐξ ἀδικίας ὃν ἐγὼ οὐ λαμβάνω παρὰ σοῦ. ἡ δὲ ὕαινα κλίνασα τὴν κεφαλὴν ἑαυτῆς εἰς τὸ ἔδαφος ἐγονυπέτει αὐτῷ, καὶ πρὸς τοῖς ποσὶ τοῦ ἁγίου ἐτίθει τὸ κώδιον. αὐτὸς δὲ ἔλεγεν αὐτῇ· Εἴρηκά σοι ὅτι οὐ λαμβάνω αὐτό, ἐὰν μή μοι ἀπὸ τοῦ νῦν συνθῇ τοῦ μηκέτι λυπεῖν πένητας κατεσθίουσα αὐτῶν τὰ πρόβατα. ἡ δὲ καὶ ἐπὶ τούτῳ ἐπένευσε τῇ κεφαλῇ αὐτῆς, ὡς συντιθεμένη τῷ ἁγίῳ. τότε ἐδέξατο τὸ κώδιον παρὰ τῆς ὑαίνης* (om Bls) (s_2 vac).

[**1** *ἅγιος*] + *Μάρκος* P; *Μακάριος* T *ταῦτ'*] om T *λέγει* T **2** *βεβρώκεις* (sic) PTA *τινος*] + *πτωχοῦ* Tl_2 **3** *ὃν ἐγὼ*] om T *δέχομαι* A *ἑαυτῆς*] om TA **4** *αὐτῷ καὶ*] om TA *ἁγίου*] + *Μακαρίου* T: + *καὶ* A **5** *ἔφη* T *αὐτὸ*] om A *μοῦ* (sic) P **5, 6** *ἀπὸ......τοῦ*] *ὀμόσεις* A **5** *συνθῇ*] *σωθῇ* (sic) T **6** *μηκέτι*] *μὴ* T **7** *τοῦτο* A *διένευσε* A *ἁγίῳ*] + *Μακαρίῳ* TA *τότε*] + *οὖν* A **8** *παρὰ τῆς ὑαίνης*] om T]

12, 13 *ὡς δὲ......ξένιον*] The text has been reconstructed in the following manner: the B MSS present a progressive series of corruptions, and the group A[B] preserves in this place the purest extant form of the B text. It reads: *Ὡς δὲ ἡ μακαρία δούλη τοῦ Χριστοῦ Μελάνη μοι εἶπεν ὅτι Παρὰ τοῦ μακαρίου ἐκείνου ἐγὼ ἔλαβον τὸ κώδιον ἐκεῖνο ξένιον [ξένην] τῆς*

P[33]l$l_2$cs[T]

1 *εὑρίσκεις*] + *ἐν* (or *παρ'*) *ἐμοὶ* (T)*B*sc: (+ *ὃ θέλεις συλῆσαι* (T)*B*; 'that belongeth to thee' c) **2** *πολιόφαγε*] T*B*† (*λῆρε, πολ., φαγόγηρε B*); *πολύφαγε* P*B*†; pessime senex l; 'traitorous horse' c; om s **4** *διηγεῖτο κ.τ.λ.*] c of this episode is translated *Prol.* 123—6 **6** *Μακαρίῳ*] P (*Μάρκῳ* interlined m. 2) TA[B]l_2; *Μάρκῳ B*; om lsc **7** *εἰσῆλθεν*] added in margin of P; attested by T*B*ll_2 (s 'she came and knocked'; c altered) **8** *ὁ ἅγιος*] PT*B* (+ *Μακάριος* or *Μάρκος*); om l$l_2$cs **10** *θηλάσαντα* T*B*l; txt PA[B]l_2s **12** *τῷ ἁγίῳ*] *αὐτῷ* Pl_2: + *Μακαρίῳ* TA[B]*B*†l; *Μάρκῳ B*† **12, 13** *ὡς δὲ......ξένιον*] *B*lsc; om Pl_2: T influenced by B: (for text see above)

καὶ τί θαυμαστὸν εἰ ὁ τοὺς λέοντας τῷ Δανιὴλ ἡμερώσας, καὶ τὴν ὕαιναν ἐσυνέτισεν;

Ἔλεγε δὲ ὅτι ἀφ' οὗ ἐβαπτίσθη οὐκ ἔπτυσε χαμαί, ἑξηκοστὸν | ἔχων ἔτος ἀφ' οὗ ἐβαπτίσθη. ἦν δὲ τὸ εἶδος αὐτοῦ ὑποκόλοβον, σπανόν, ἐπὶ τοῦ χείλους μόνον ἔχων τρίχας, καὶ εἰς τὸ ἄκρον τοῦ πώγωνος· ὑπερβολῇ γὰρ ἀσκήσεως οὐδὲ αἱ τρίχες τῆς γενειάδος αὐτοῦ ἐφύησαν.

Τούτῳ ἐγὼ προσῆλθόν ποτε ἀκηδιάσας, καὶ λέγω αὐτῷ· Ἀββᾶ, τί ποιήσω; ὅτι θλίβουσί με οἱ λογισμοὶ λέγοντες ὅτι Οὐδὲν ποιεῖς, ἄπελθε ἔνθεν. καὶ λέγει μοι ὅτι Εἰπὲ αὐτοῖς· Ἐγὼ διὰ τὸν Χριστὸν τοὺς τοίχους τηρῶ.

Ταῦτα ἐκ τῶν πολλῶν ὀλίγα σοι ἐσήμηνα τοῦ ἁγίου Μακαρίου.

(XIX) Μωσῆς οὕτω τις καλούμενος, Αἰθίοψ τῷ γένει, μέλας, οἰκέτης ὑπῆρχε πολιτευομένου τινός· ὃν διὰ πολλὴν δυστροπίαν καὶ λῃστείαν ἔρριψεν ὁ ἴδιος δεσπότης· ἐλέγετο γὰρ καὶ μέχρι φόνων φθάνειν· ἀναγκάζομαι γὰρ λέγειν αὐτοῦ τὰ τῆς πονηρίας, ἵνα δείξω αὐτοῦ τὴν ἀρετὴν τῆς μετανοίας.

ὑαίνης ἐπιλεγόμενον. The words in spaced type represent the text of s: 'As also the holy Melanou said to me that: "That fleece I received from the hands of Macarius as a blessing"': l quam mihi et sancta Melania [Melanius l^{sess}, sanctae Melaniae (sic) l^{cass}] postea accepisse se dixit: c 'he (Macarius) gave her (Melania) as an inheritance that skin' (cf. *Prol.* 126). On the corruptions in BT, and the introduction of St Athanasius' name, see Note 31. **6, 7** Soz. III. 14 (3) Ὡς ὑπὸ τοῦ ἄγαν κατεσκληκέναι μὴ φύειν τοῦ γενείου τὰς τρίχας. **14** On Moses see Note 33. For l_2 see *Bibl. Casin. III. Florileg.* 296. **14—2** (p. 59) Soz. VI. 29 (15) Μωσῆς δὲ δοῦλος ὢν διὰ μοχθηρίαν ἐξηλάθη τῆς οἰκίας τοῦ κεκτημένου· καὶ εἰς λῃστείας τραπεὶς λῃστρικοῦ τάγματος ἡγεῖτο.

P[33]l$l_2$cs[T]

1, 2 *καὶ τί......ἐσυν.*] om s **1** *τῷ*] + *προφήτῃ* *B*l_2 **2** *τὴν ὕαιναν ἐσυνέτισεν*] Tl_2 (hienam fecit sensatam, *Bibl. Casin.*) *B* (*ταύτῃ τῇ ὑαίνῃ σύνεσιν ἐχαρίσατο*) l (huic beluae talem sapientiam dedit) c ('who giveth understanding to beasts also,' altered, cf. *Prol.* 125); *τὴν ὕαιναν τεταπείνωκεν* P; (s om, 33 vac): + *εἰς τὴν τιμὴν τοῦ δούλου αὐτοῦ* T **3** *ἐλέγετο* T*B*l *ἀφ' οὗ ἐβαπτ.*] 'it is seven years to-day' c *οὐκ ἔπτυσε χαμαί*] om T; (l_2 non est locutus otiosum sermonem) *ἔπτυσε*] *ἤπλωσε* P **3, 4** *ἑξηκοστὸν......ἐβαπτ.*] om c **4** *ἀφ' οὗ ἐβαπτ.*] om P **6** *πώγωνος*] PA^B; *γενείου* T*B*s: + *εἶχεν ὀλίγας* *B*l(s) **7** c ceases here **13** *Μάρκου* P*B*† (cf. Note 30)

XIX (Περὶ Μωσέως τοῦ Αἰθίοπος): Pll_2s_2[T]

14 *Μωσῆς*] P*B*†$l^{cass}l_2^a$ Soz; *Μωϋσῆς* T*B*†$l^{sess}l_2^b$ **18** *τὴν ἀρετὴν τῆς μετανοίας*] T*B*ll_2s_2; *τῆς ἀρετῆς τὴν μεγαλόνοιαν* P

διηγοῦντο γοῦν ὅτι καὶ ἀφηγούμενος ἦν λῃστηρίου ἑνός· οὗ καὶ τὸ ἔργον φαίνεται ἐν τοῖς λῃστρικοῖς, ὅτι ποιμένι τινὶ ἐμνησικάκησέ ποτε παρεμποδίσαντι αὐτῷ εἰς πρᾶγμά τι | μετὰ τῶν κυνῶν ἐν νυκτί· ὃν ἀποκτεῖναι θελήσας περινοστεῖ τὸν τόπον ἔνθα τὴν στάσιν εἶχε τὴν τῶν προβάτων· καὶ ἐμηνύθη αὐτῷ πέραν τοῦ Νείλου· καὶ πλημμυροῦντος τοῦ ποταμοῦ καὶ κρατοῦντος ὡσεὶ σημεῖον ἕν, δακὼν τὴν μάχαιραν ἐν τῷ στόματι καὶ τὸν χιτωνίσκον θεὶς τῇ κεφαλῇ διεπέρασεν οὕτω κολυμβήσας τὸν ποταμόν. ἐν τῷ τοῦτον οὖν διακολυμβᾶν ἠδυνήθη ὁ ποιμὴν διαλαθεῖν αὐτόν, ἑαυτὸν καταχώσας εἰς τὴν ἄμμον. τοὺς οὖν ἐξ ἐπιλογῆς τέσσαρας κριοὺς σφάξας καὶ δήσας σειρᾷ, διεκολύμβησεν αὖθις· καὶ ἐλθὼν εἰς μικρὸν προαύλιον ἀπέδειρε, καὶ φαγὼν τὰ κάλλιστα τῶν κρεῶν καὶ εἰς οἶνον διαπωλήσας τὰ κώδια καὶ σαΐτην πιὼν ὡς ἰταλικῶν δεκαοκτὼ ξεστῶν, πεντήκοντα σημεῖα ἀπῆλθεν ὅπου τὸ κολλήγιον εἶχεν.

Οὗτος ὁ τοσοῦτος ὀψέ ποτε κατανυγεὶς ἔκ περιστάσεώς τινος, ἐπέδωκεν ἑαυτὸν μοναστηρίῳ καὶ οὕτως τῷ πράγματι τῆς μετανοίας ὡς ⌜καὶ αὐτὸν τὸν συμπράκτην αὐτοῦ τῶν κακῶν ἐκ νεότητος δαίμονα τὸν αὐτῷ συναμαρτόντα ἄντικρυς εἰς ἐπίγνωσιν ἀγαγεῖν τοῦ Χριστοῦ⌝. ἐν οἷς λέγεταί ποτε ὅτι λῃσταὶ τούτῳ ἐπέπεσον ἐν τῷ κελλίῳ καθημένῳ ἀγνοήσαντες

17—4 (p. 60) Soz. (15) Πολλοὺς δὲ κακουργήσας καὶ πολλοὺς φόνους τολμήσας, ἐκ περιπετείας τινὸς τὸν μοναδικὸν μετῆλθε βίον, καὶ ἀθρόον εἰς ἀρετὴν φιλοσοφίας ἐπέδωκεν. (18) Λέγεται γοῦν ποτὲ λῃστὰς καταδραμόντας τὸν τόπον ἐν ᾧ μόνος ἐφιλοσόφει συλλαβέσθαι πάντας καὶ δῆσαι, καὶ τέσσαρας ὄντας τοῖς ὤμοις ἐπιθεῖναι καὶ εἰς τὴν ἐκκλησίαν ἀγαγεῖν, καὶ συμμονάζουσιν ἐπιτρέψαι τὰ περὶ αὐτῶν, ὡς μὴ θεμιτὸν αὐτῷ ἔτι μηδένα κακῶς ποιεῖν.

19 See Note 34.

Pll$_2$s$_2$[T]

1 γοῦν] οὖν TA^B **2** καὶ] + τοῦτο T*B*ls$_2$ φαίνεται] Pl$_2$ (ostenditur); φέρεται T*B*ls$_2$ **3** ποτε] P; om T*B*(ll$_2$s$_2$) **6** πέραν] + εἶναι T; ὅτι...ἐστί *B* **7** ἐν] + ἐν πλάτει *B*l$_2$ μάχαιραν] + αὐτοῦ *B*l **10** διαβρᾶσαι (sic) T εἰς τὴν ἄμμον] Pls$_2$; om Tl$_2$; (εἰς κρύφιον *B*; που A^B) **12** σειρᾷ] Pll$_2$; σειρὰν TA^B; σειράδην *B*; om s$_2$ προαύλιον] P*B*†; ἐπαύλιον TA^B; ἐναύλιον *B*† **13** ἀπέδειρε] + τοὺς κριοὺς *B*(l)s$_2$ **18** οὕτως] + προσῆλθε (T)*B* (Soz ll$_2$s$_2$) **19–21** ὡς καὶ αὐτὸν...τοῦ Χρ.] *B*ls$_2$; ὡς ἔδει P; ὡς τὰ πράγματα ἔδειξαν A^B; om T; (l$_2$ enlarges and alters): (l^{rev} clemonem is for demonem) **19** αὐτοῦ] + καὶ ὑποβολέα *B*† **20** τὸν] + εἰς πάντα *B* **22** καθημένῳ] P*B* (καθεζομένῳ); om Tll$_2$s$_2$: + εἰς τὴν ρημον (sic) P

τὸ τίς ἐστιν. ἦσαν δὲ τέσσαρες· οὓς δήσας πάντας καὶ καθάπερ ζαβέρναν ἐπιθεὶς ἀχύρου τῷ νώτῳ ἤνεγκεν εἰς τὴν ἐκκλησίαν τῶν ἀδελφῶν εἰπών· Ἐπειδὴ οὐκ ἔξεστί μοι ἀδικεῖν οὐδένα, τί κελεύετε περὶ τούτων; οὕτως ἐκεῖνοι ἐξομολογησάμενοι, καὶ γνόντες ὅτι Μωσῆς ἐστὶν ἐκεῖνος, ὅ ποτε ὀνομαστὸς καὶ περιβόητος ἐν τοῖς λῃσταῖς, δοξάσαντες τὸν θεὸν κἀκεῖνοι ἀπετάξαντο διὰ τὴν τούτου μεταβολήν, λογισάμενοι ὅτι Εἰ οὗτος ὁ οὕτως ἱκανὸς καὶ δυνάμενος ἐν τοῖς λῃστρικοῖς τὸν θεὸν ἐφοβήθη, ἡμεῖς τί ἀναβαλλόμεθα τὴν σωτηρίαν;

Τούτῳ τῷ Μωσεῖ ἐπέθεντο δαίμονες εἰς τὴν συνήθειαν τῆς ἀκολασίας τῆς πορνικῆς κατελαύνοντες· ὃς ἐπὶ τοσοῦτον ἐπειράσθη, ὡς αὐτὸς διηγεῖτο, ὡς μικροῦ δεῖν τῆς προθέσεως ἐξοκεῖλαι. παραγενόμενος οὖν πρὸς τὸν μέγαν Ἰσίδωρον τὸν ἐν τῇ Σκήτει, ἀνήνεγκε τὰ τοῦ πολέμου. καὶ λέγει αὐτῷ· Μὴ λυπηθῇς· ἀρχαί εἰσι, καὶ διὰ τοῦτο σφοδρότερόν σοι ἐπέθεντο ζητοῦντες τὴν συνήθειαν. ὥσπερ γὰρ κύων ἐν μακέλλῳ τῇ συνηθείᾳ οὐκ ἀφίσταται, ἂν δὲ κλεισθῇ τὸ μάκελλον καὶ μηδεὶς αὐτῷ μηδὲν δῷ, οὐκέτι ἐγγίζει· οὕτω καὶ σὺ ἐὰν ἐπιμείνῃς, ἀκηδιάσας ὁ δαίμων ἔχει σου ἀποστῆναι. ἀναχωρήσας οὖν ἀπὸ τῆς ὥρας ἐκείνης σφοδρότερον ᾐσκεῖτο, καὶ μάλιστα | ἀπὸ βρωμάτων, οὐδενὸς μεταλαμβάνων πλὴν ἄρτου ξηροῦ ἐν δώδεκα οὐγγίαις, ἐργαζόμενος ἔργον πλεῖστον, καὶ πεντήκοντα προσευχὰς ἐκτελῶν. κατατήξας οὖν αὐτοῦ τὸ σωμάτιον, ἔμεινε πυρούμενος ἔτι καὶ ἐνυπνιαζόμενος. πάλιν παρέβαλεν ἄλλῳ τινὶ τῶν ἁγίων καὶ λέγει αὐτῷ· Τί ποιήσω ὅτι σκοτίζουσί

20—23 Soz. (16) Ἐπεὶ γοῦν ἐκ τῆς προτέρας διαίτης εὐεξίᾳ ζέων καὶ πρὸς φαντασίας ἡδονῶν κινούμενος, μυρίαις ἀσκήσεσι τὸ σῶμα κατέτηξε· πῇ μὲν δίχα ὄψου ὀλίγῳ ἄρτῳ ἀρκούμενος· πῇ δὲ πλεῖστον ἔργον ἀνύων καὶ πεντηκοστὸν εὐχόμενος.

Pl_2 (1—13) s_2[T]

1 *πάντας*] om TA^B **2** *ζαβέρναν*] PT ven (*-νον*) l_2 (see Du Cange); *σάκκον* *B*l marsupium = [illegible] s_2 **3** *οὐκ*] PT$A^B s_2$; *οὐκέτι* *B*l(Soz) **4–7** *οὕτως..... λογισάμενοι*] T adds to and alters the B text in a manner not found in any othe authority **9** *σωτηρίαν*] + *ἑαυτῶν* A^Bl (nostram); *τῶν ἡμετέρων ψυχῶν* *B*(T *τῶ ψ. ἡμῶν*); ($l_2 s_2$ altered) **10** *εἰς*] *οἱ* P *τὴν*] + *ἀρχαίαν* *B*l$l_2 s_2$ **13–9** (p. 61) *παραγενόμενος* . . *ἠδυνήθη*] l_2 omits nearly all **13** *οὖν*] *δὲ* TA^B **14** *ἀνήνεγκε*] + *αὐτ* T*B* (*τούτῳ*) ls_2 **15** *ἀρχαί*] + *γὰρ* T*B*ls_2 *ἐπέθεντο*] + *οἱ δαίμονες* P huiusmodi cogitationes l; txt T*B*s_2 **16** *τὴν*] + *προτέραν* *B*l **23** *ἐκτελῶν*] + *τὴ ἡμέραν* T*B*s_2

μου τὸν λογισμὸν τὰ ἐνύπνια τῆς ψυχῆς κατὰ συνήθειαν ἡδονῆς; λέγει αὐτῷ· Ἐπειδὴ τὸν νοῦν σου οὐκ ἀπέστησας τῶν περὶ ταῦτα φαντασιῶν, τούτου χάριν ὑφίστασαι τοῦτο· ⸢δὸς ἑαυτὸν εἰς ἀγρυπνίαν καὶ προσεύχου νηφόντως καὶ ἐλευθεροῦσαι ἀπὸ τούτων ταχέως⸣. ὃς ἀκούσας καὶ ταύτης τῆς ὑποθέσεως ἀπελθὼν ἐν τῇ κέλλῃ ἔδωκε λόγον μὴ κοιμηθῆναι διὰ πάσης νυκτός, μὴ κλῖναι γόνυ. μείνας οὖν ἐν τῷ κελλίῳ ἐπὶ ἔτη ἕξ, τὰς νύκτας πάσας εἰς τὸ μέσον τοῦ κελλίου ἵστατο προσευχόμενος, ὀφθαλμὸν μὴ καμμύων· καὶ τοῦ πράγματος περιγενέσθαι οὐκ ἠδυνήθη. ὑπέθετο οὖν ἑαυτῷ πάλιν ἄλλην πολιτείαν, καὶ ἐξερχόμενος τὰς νύκτας ἀπῄει εἰς τὰς κέλλας τῶν γερόντων καὶ ἀσκητικωτέρων, καὶ λαμβάνων τὰς ὑδρίας αὐτῶν λεληθότως ἐπλήρου ὕδατος. ἀπὸ μήκους γὰρ ἔχουσι τὸ ὕδωρ, οἱ μὲν ἀπὸ δύο, οἱ δὲ ἀπὸ πέντε σημείων, ἄλλοι ἀπὸ ἡμίσεος. μιᾶς οὖν τῶν νυκτῶν ἐπιτηρήσας ὁ δαίμων καὶ μὴ καρτερήσας, ἐγκύψαντι αὐτῷ εἰς τὸ φρέαρ δέδωκε κατὰ τῶν ψοῶν ῥοπάλῳ τινὶ καὶ ἀφῆκεν αὐτὸν νεκρόν, μὴ αἰσθανόμενον μήτε ὃ πέπονθε μήτε παρὰ τίνος. τὴν ἄλλην οὖν ἡμέραν ἐλθών τις ἀντλῆσαι ὕδωρ εὗρεν αὐτὸν ἐκεῖ κείμενον, καὶ ἀνήγγειλε τῷ μεγάλῳ Ἰσιδώρῳ τῷ πρεσβυτέρῳ τῆς Σκήτεως. λαβὼν οὖν αὐτὸν ἀνήνεγκεν εἰς τὴν ἐκκλησίαν· καὶ ἐπὶ ἔτος ἓν ἐνόσησεν ὡς μόλις γενέσθαι τὸ σῶμα αὐτοῦ καὶ τὴν ψυχὴν ἐν ἰσχύϊ. λέγει οὖν αὐτῷ ὁ

5—14 Soz. (16) *πῆ δὲ ἐπὶ ἓξ ἔτεσιν ὁλόκληρον ἑκάστην νύκτα ἑστὼς προσηύχετο, μήτε γόνυ κλίνων, μήτε τοὺς ὀφθαλμοὺς μύων εἰς ὕπνον.* (17) *ἄλλοτε δὲ νύκτωρ περιϊὼν τὰς οἰκήσεις τῶν μοναχῶν, λάθρα τὴν ἑκάστου ὑδρίαν ἐπλήρου ὕδατος· ἦν δὲ τοῦτο λίαν ἐργῶδες· τῶν μὲν γὰρ σταδίους δέκα, τῶν δὲ εἴκοσι, τῶν δὲ καὶ τριάκοντα καὶ πλέον διειστήκει ὁ τόπος ὅθεν ὑδρεύοντο. διέμεινε δὲ ἐπὶ πολὺ τὴν προτέραν ἰσχὺν ἔχων καίπερ ταῖς πολλαῖς ἀσκήσεσι καθελεῖν ταύτην σπουδάζων καὶ τὸ σῶμα ταῖς ταλαιπωρίαις πιέζων.*

Pll_2 (10—22) s_2[T]

1 *κατὰ*] + *τὴν ἀρχαίαν* (T)*B*s_2 **3–5** *δὸς......ταχέως*] T*B*ls_2; om P: (l_2 vac) **4** *ἀγρυπνίαν*] + *κατὰ μικρὸν B*l *ἐλευθεροῦσαι*] T*B*†A^B; *ἐλευθερωθήσῃ B*† *ἀπὸ τούτων*] om T **7** *κλῖναι*] T*B* Soz; *κάμψαι* P **9** *καὶ*] + *ταῦτα ποιῶν B*† (l nec sic quidem) **10** *ὑπέθετο*] l_2 recommences *καὶ*] Pl; om T*B*l_2s_2 *ἐξερχόμενος*] + *γὰρ* Ts_2 **11** *καὶ ἀσκητικωτέρων*] om l_2s_2 **12** *λεληθότως*] P(Soz); *ἀγνοούντων ἐκείνων* (T)*B*; nullo sentiente l; om l_2s_2 **14** *ἄλλοι ἀπὸ ἡμίσεος*] om ll_2 **16** *φρέαρ*] + dum aquam tollit ll_2 (hauriret) **19** *ἐκεῖ*] P*B*; om Tll_2s_2 **20** *Σκήτεως*] + qui misit l_2s_2 **21** *ἓν*] PT; *πλήρη B*; *ὅλον* A^B; totum l **22** l_2 much paraphrased to end

μέγας Ἰσίδωρος· Παῦσαι φιλονεικῶν, Μωσεῖ, τοῖς δαίμοσι· μέτρα γάρ εἰσι καὶ τῆς ἀνδρείας τῆς ἐν τῇ ἀσκήσει. ὁ δὲ λέγει αὐτῷ· Οὐ μὴ παύσωμαι μέχρις οὗ παύσηταί μου ἡ φαντασία τῶν δαιμόνων. λέγει οὖν αὐτῷ· Ἐν τῷ ὀνόματι Ἰησοῦ Χριστοῦ πέπαυταί σου τὰ ἐνύπνια· κοινώνησον οὖν μετὰ παρρησίας· ἵνα γὰρ μὴ καυχήσῃ ὡς περιγενόμενος | πάθους, τούτου χάριν κατεδυναστεύθης πρὸς τὸ συμφέρον. καὶ ἀπῆλθε πάλιν ἐπὶ τὴν κέλλαν αὐτοῦ. μετὰ ταῦτα ἐρωτηθεὶς παρὰ Ἰσιδώρου ὡς μετὰ μῆνας δύο, ἔλεγε μηκέτι μηδὲν πεπονθέναι. κατηξιώθη δὲ οὗτος χαρίσματος κατὰ δαιμόνων οὕτως ὡς τὰς μυίας ταύτας ἡμᾶς φοβεῖσθαι μᾶλλον ἢ ἐκεῖνον τοὺς δαίμονας. αὕτη ἡ πολιτεία Μωσέως τοῦ Αἰθίοπος, ὃς καὶ αὐτὸς ἦν ἐν τοῖς μεγάλοις τῶν πατέρων συναριθμούμενος. τελευτᾷ οὖν ἐτῶν ἑβδομήκοντα πέντε ἐν τῇ Σκήτει γενόμενος πρεσβύτερος, καταλιπὼν καὶ μαθητὰς ἑβδομήκοντα.

(XX) Ὄρος ἐστὶν ἐν τῇ Αἰγύπτῳ ἀπάγον ἐπὶ τὴν Σκῆτιν τὴν πανέρημον ὃ καλεῖται Φέρμη. ἐν τούτῳ τῷ ὄρει καθέζονται ὡς πεντακόσιοι ἄνδρες ἀσκούμενοι· ἐν οἷς καὶ Παῦλός τις, οὕτω καλούμενος, ταύτην ἔσχε τὴν πολιτείαν· οὐκ ἔργου ἥψατο, οὐ πράγματος, οὐκ ἔλαβε παρά τινος παρεκτὸς οὗ ἤσθιεν. ἔργον

10—15 Soz. (19) *Φασὶ γὰρ ἀπὸ κακίας εἰς ἀρετὴν μηδενὶ τοσαύτην ὑπάρξαι μεταβολήν, ὥστε ἄκρου μὲν ἐπιψαῦσαι μοναστικῆς φιλοσοφί..., ἐξαίσιον δὲ φόβον τοῖς δαίμοσιν ἐμποιῆσαι καὶ πρεσβύτερον γενέσθαι τῶν ἐν Σκήτει μοναχῶν. ὁ μὲν οὖν τοιοῦτος ὢν πολλοὺς ἀρίστους μαθητὰς καταλιπὼν ἀμφὶ τὰ ἑβδομήκοντα καὶ πέντε ἔτη γεγονὼς ἐτελεύτησεν.*

16 See Note 35.

16—4 (p. 63) Soz. VI. 29 (20) *Ὤικουν δέ, Παῦλος μὲν ἐν Φέρμῃ· ὄρος δὲ τοῦτο ἐν Σκήτει οὐ μείους πεντακοσίων ἀσκητὰς ἔχον* (al. *ἔχων*). *εἰργάζετο δὲ οὐδέν, οὐδ'* †*ἐλάμβανέ τι παρά του*† *πλὴν ὅσον ἤσθιεν.* (21) *ηὔχετο δὲ μόνον ὥσπερ φόρον τινὰ τριακοσίας εὐχὰς ἑκάστης ἡμέρας ἀποδιδοὺς τῷ θεῷ· ἵνα δὲ μὴ λαθὼν διαμάρτῃ τοῦ ἀριθμοῦ, τριακοσίας ψηφίδας τῷ κόλπῳ ἐμβάλλων καθ' ἑκάστην εὐχὴν ψηφίδα ἐκρίπτει· ἀναλωθέντων δὲ τῶν λίθων δῆλον ἐγένετο τὰς ἰσαρίθμους τοῖς λίθοις εὐχὰς πεπληρῶσθαι.*

Pll_2s_2[T]

1 *δαίμοσι*] + *καὶ μὴ αὐτοῖς* (+ *οὕτως* *B*†l) *ἐπέμβαινε* (T)*B*ls_2('and do not wish to attack them') **4** *δαιμόνων*] *ἐνυπνίων* (T)*B*l **5** *οὖν*] + *τοῖς μυστηρίοις* *B*ls_2
14 *Σκήτει*] T*B*ll_2s_2 Soz; *ἀσκήσει* P

XX (Περὶ Παύλου): PTls_2

17 *Φέρμη*] T*B*ls_2 Soz; *Φερμᾶν* P **19** *καλούμενος*] + *ὅς* T*B*l *ἥψατο*] + *ποτε* *B*l
20 *πραγματείας* T*B* *ἔλαβε*] + *τι* *B*†l (Soz) *ἐκτὸς* T

δὲ αὐτῷ καὶ ἄσκησις γέγονε τὸ ἀδιαλείπτως προσεύχεσθαι. τετυπωμένας οὖν εἶχεν εὐχὰς τριακοσίας, τοσαῦτα οὖν ψηφία συνάγων καὶ ἐν τῷ κόλπῳ κατέχων, καὶ ῥίπτων καθ' ἑκάστην εὐχὴν ἔξω τοῦ κόλπου μίαν ψῆφον. οὗτος παραβαλὼν συντυχίας ἕνεκεν τῷ ἁγίῳ Μακαρίῳ τῷ λεγομένῳ πολιτικῷ, λέγει αὐτῷ· Ἀββᾶ θλίβομαι. ἠνάγκασεν οὖν αὐτὸν εἰπεῖν διὰ ποίαν αἰτίαν. ὁ δὲ λέγει αὐτῷ· Ἐν κώμῃ τινὶ παρθένος κατοικεῖ τις τριακοστὸν ἔτος ἔχουσα ἀσκουμένη· περὶ ἧς μοι διηγήσαντο ὅτι παρεκτὸς σαββάτου ἢ κυριακῆς οὐδέποτε γεύεται· ἀλλὰ τὸν χρόνον ὅλον ἕλκουσα τὰς ἑβδομάδας διὰ πέντε ἐσθίουσα ἡμερῶν ποιεῖ εὐχὰς ἑπτακοσίας. καὶ ἀπευδόκησα ἐμαυτοῦ ὅτι ὑπὲρ τὰς τριακοσίας οὐκ ἠδυνήθην ποιῆσαι. ἀποκρίνεται αὐτῷ ὁ ἅγιος Μακάριος· Ἐγὼ ἑξηκοστὸν ἔτος ἔχω τεταγμένας ἑκατὸν εὐχὰς ποιῶν καὶ τὰ πρὸς τροφὴν ἐργαζόμενος καὶ τοῖς ἀδελφοῖς τὴν ὀφειλὴν τῆς συντυχίας ἀποδιδούς, καὶ οὐ κρίνει με ὁ λογισμὸς ὡς ἀμελήσαντα. εἰ δὲ σὺ τριακοσίας ποιῶν ὑπὸ τοῦ συνειδότος κρίνῃ, δῆλος εἶ καθαρῶς αὐτὰς μὴ εὐχόμενος, ἢ δυνάμενος πλείονας εὔχεσθαι καὶ μὴ εὐχόμενος.

(XXI) Κρόνιός μοι διηγήσατο ὁ πρεσβύτερος τῆς Νιτρίας ὅτι Νεώτερος ὢν καὶ ἀκηδίας χάριν φυγὼν ἐκ τῆς μονῆς τοῦ ἀρχιμανδρίτου μου, ἀλώμενος ἔφθασα ἕως τοῦ ὄρους τοῦ ἁγίου Ἀντωνίου. | ἐκάθητο δὲ μεταξὺ Βαβυλῶνος καὶ Ἡρακλέους εἰς τὴν πανέρημον τὴν φέρουσαν κατὰ θάλασσαν τὴν ἐρυθρὰν ὡς ἀπὸ τριάκοντα σημείων τοῦ ποταμοῦ. ἐλθὼν οὖν αὐτοῦ εἰς τὸ μοναστήριον τὸ παρὰ τὸν ποταμόν, ἔνθα οἱ τούτου μαθηταὶ ἐκαθέζοντο εἰς τὸ λεγόμενον Πίσπιρ Μακάριος καὶ

9 See Note 36. **19** For l_2 see *Bibl. Cusin. III. Florileg.* 297. **21, 26** See Note 37. **26, 1** (p. 64) On Macarius and Amatas see Note 26.

$PTls_2$

2 *τριακοσίας*] + *καὶ* T *οὖν*] om *B* **4** *ψ. μίαν* T*B* *οὗτος*] + *ποτε* Tl **6** *ἀββᾶ*] + *Μακάριε* T*B*ls_2 *θλίβομαι*] + *σφόδρα* *B*ls_2^{add} (om s_2^{vat}) *τὴν αἰτίαν διὰ ποίαν* T **7** *τις κατ.* T*B* **8** *τις διηγήσατο* Ts_2 ('abba Pior') **10** *σύμπαντα χρ.* T*B* *ἑβδομ.*] + *καὶ* T*B* *ἡμερῶν*] om T **11** *ποιεῖ*] + quotidie ls_2 *ἐμαυτοῦ*] + *τοῦτο μαθὼν* *B*ls_2 **12** *ποιῆσαι*] om T *ἀποκρ.*] + *οὖν* T **17** *εἶ*] + *ἢ* T*B*†l *ταύτας* T

XXI (Περὶ Εὐλογίου καὶ τοῦ λελωβημένου): $PTW^o ll_2 ss_2$

19 Chronius ll_2^a *Νητρίας* PW^o **20** *ἐξελθὼν* W^o **21** *ὄρους*] 'monastery' ss_2 **22** *Ἡρακλίου* W^o; *-κλείας* *B*† **23** *κατὰ τὴν ἐρ. θαλ.* T*B*; *ἐπὶ* (om *θαλ.*) W^o **24** *αὐτοῦ*] om Tl_2 **25** *ἔνθα*] + *αὐτοῦ* (om *τούτου*) W^o **26** *Πίσπιρ*] TW^o*B*†l Rufinus (Pispiri *Hist. Eccl.* II. 8); *Πίσπηρ* *B*†l_2; *Πίσπις* P; Isper s; Pester s_2

Ἀμάτας οἳ καὶ ἔθαψαν αὐτὸν κοιμηθέντα, ἐξεδεξάμην ἡμέρας πέντε ἵνα συντύχω τῷ ἁγίῳ Ἀντωνίῳ. ἐλέγετο γὰρ παραβάλλειν τῷ μοναστηρίῳ τούτῳ, ποτὲ μὲν διὰ δέκα, ποτὲ δὲ διὰ εἴκοσι, ποτὲ δὲ διὰ πέντε ἡμερῶν, καθὼς ἂν αὐτὸν ὁ θεὸς ἦγεν ἐπ' εὐεργεσίᾳ τῶν παρατυγχανόντων ἐν τῷ μοναστηρίῳ. διάφοροι οὖν συνήχθησαν ἀδελφοί, διαφόρους ἔχοντες χρείας· ἐν οἷς καὶ Εὐλόγιός τις Ἀλεξανδρεὺς μονάζων καὶ ἄλλος λελωβημένος, οἳ παρεγένοντο δι' αἰτίαν τοιάνδε·

Οὗτος ὁ Εὐλόγιος σχολαστικὸς ὑπῆρχεν ἐκ τῶν ἐγκυκλίων παιδευμάτων, ὃς ἔρωτι πληγεὶς ἀθανασίας ἀπετάξατο τοῖς θορύβοις, καὶ πάντα διασκορπίσας τὰ ὑπάρχοντα κατέλιπεν ἑαυτῷ βραχέα νομίσματα, ἐργάσασθαι μὴ δυνάμενος. ἀκηδιῶν οὖν καθ' ἑαυτὸν καὶ μήτε εἰς συνοδίαν βουλόμενος εἰσελθεῖν μήτε μόνος πληροφορούμενος, εὗρέ τινα κατὰ τὴν ἀγορὰν ἐρριμμένον λελωβημένον ὃς οὔτε χεῖρας εἶχεν οὔτε πόδας. τούτῳ μόνη ἡ γλῶττα ἀκατάτριπτος ὑπῆρχε πρὸς συμφορὰν τῶν ἐντυγχανόντων. ὁ οὖν Εὐλόγιος στὰς ἐνατενίζει αὐτῷ καὶ προσεύχεται τῷ θεῷ, καὶ διατίθεται διαθήκην μετὰ τοῦ θεοῦ ὅτι Κύριε, ἐπὶ τῷ ὀνόματί σου λαμβάνω τοῦτον τὸν λελωβημένον καὶ διαναπαύω αὐτὸν μέχρι θανάτου, ἵνα διὰ τούτου κἀγὼ σωθῶ. χάρισαί μοι ὑπομονὴν τῆς τούτου ὑπηρεσίας. καὶ προσελθὼν τῷ λελωβημένῳ λέγει αὐτῷ· Θέλεις, ὁ μέγας, λαμβάνω σε εἰς τὴν οἰκίαν καὶ διαναπαύω σε; λέγει αὐτῷ· Καὶ πάνυ. Οὐκοῦν, φησί,

PTW°ll_2ss_2

1 Ἀμάτας *B*†l_2[a] Hieron. (Amathas et Mac. *Vita Pauli*); Ἀμμάτος PA[B] (-τᾶς); Ἀμάτος W°ll_2[b]; Ματώιος *B*†; Σαρματὰς T (cf. Hieron. *Chron.* 'Sarmata Amathas et Macarius discipuli Antonii'); s ܐܡܬܐܣ ἐξεδεχόμην T; ἐξεδεξάμεθα W° 2 συντύχωμεν W° μακαρίῳ T παραβαλεῖν W° 3 δέκα] + πέντε W° 4 ποτὲ δὲ διὰ πέντε ἡμ.] om ll_2s_2 5 εὐεργεσίας T; (εὐεργετεσίᾳ P) 6 συνήχθημεν *B*l_2 7 μονάζων] om l_2s 8 λελωβημένος] elephantiosus l; leprosus l_2; 'a leper mutilated in his body' s; (s_2 sim.) 9 ὁ] om T ἐκ] om W° 10 τοῖς θορύβοις] P*B*[45–6]; τοῖς βιωτικοῖς θορ. W°; τῶν θορύβων T*B*† 11 ὑπάρχοντα διασκορπ. (om τὰ) W° κατέλειπεν T 12 βραχέα] ὀλίγα T ἐργάζεσθαι T*B* μὴ] οὐ TW° 12, 13 ἀκηδιῶν......ἑαυτὸν] om l_2s 13 οὖν] om T 13, 14 μήτε μόνος πλ. before μήτε......εἰσελθεῖν W° 15 λελωβ.] om T οὔτε χ. ἔχοντα (om ὃς) W°*B*[45–6] 16 μόνον W° ἀκατάτρ. ἡ γλ. W° συμπάθειαν T 17 ἐντυγχ.] P*B*[45–6]; παρατυγχ. TW°*B*† στὰς οὖν ὁ Εὐλ. W° 18 τίθεται T*B* θεοῦ] + εἰπὼν *B*l_2($ls s_2$) 19 ἐπὶ] ἐν W° τὸν λελ. τ. W° 20 ἀναπαύω W° μέχρι] + ἡμέρας *B*l τούτου] PA[B]*B*†; αὐτοῦ TW°*B*[45–6] κἀγὼ before διὰ T*B*† (not A[B]*B*[45–6]) 21 χάρισαι] + οὖν T*B*ll_2 μοι] + Χριστὲ *B*ll_2: + τὴν TW°*B* 23 οἰκίαν] + μοῦ TW°*B*[45–6]ll_2(s) ἀναπαύω TW°*B* σε] om T*B*l: + ὁ δὲ W° φησί] om TW°

φέρω ὄνον καὶ λαμβάνω σε; συνέθετο. ἐνέγκας οὖν ὄνον ἦρεν αὐτόν, καὶ ἀπήνεγκεν εἰς τὸ ἴδιον ξένιον, καὶ ἦν αὐτοῦ ἐπιμελούμενος. διακαρτερήσας οὖν ὁ λελωβημένος ἐπὶ ἔτη δεκαπέντε ἐνοσοκομεῖτο παρ' αὐτοῦ, λουόμενος καὶ θεραπευόμενος ταῖς χερσὶ τοῦ Εὐλογίου καὶ ἀξίως τρεφόμενος τῆς νόσου. μετὰ δὲ τὰ δεκαπέντε ἔτη δαίμων ἐνέσκηψεν εἰς αὐτὸν καὶ ἀποστασιάζει πρὸς τὸν Εὐλόγιον· καὶ ἤρξατο τοσαύταις δυσφημίαις καὶ λοιδορίαις πλύνειν τὸν ἄνδρα, ἐπιλέγων· Σχάστα, φυγοκύρι, ἀλλότρια χρήματα ἔκλεψας, καὶ δι' ἐμοῦ θέλεις σωθῆναι. | ῥῖψόν με εἰς τὴν ἀγοράν· κρέα θέλω. ἤνεγκεν αὐτῷ κρέα. πάλιν οὖν ἀνέκραξεν· Οὐ πληροφοροῦμαι· ὄχλους θέλω· εἰς τὴν ἀγορὰν θέλω. ὦ βία· ῥῖψόν με ὅπου με εὗρες. ὡς εἰ εἶχε χεῖρας τάχα ἂν καὶ ἀπήγξατο, τοῦ δαίμονος αὐτὸν οὕτως ἀγριώσαντος. ἀπέρχεται τοίνυν πρὸς τοὺς ἐκ γειτόνων ἀσκητὰς ὁ Εὐλόγιος καὶ λέγει αὐτοῖς· Τί ποιήσω, ὅτι εἰς ἀπελπισμόν με ἤγαγεν ὁ λελωβημένος οὗτος; ῥίψω αὐτόν; θεῷ δεξιὰς ἔδωκα καὶ φοβοῦμαι. ἀλλὰ μὴ ῥίψω αὐτόν; κακάς μοι ἡμέρας καὶ νύκτας δίδωσι. τί οὖν αὐτῷ ποιήσω οὐκ οἶδα. οἱ δὲ λέγουσιν αὐτῷ· Ὡς ἔτι ζῇ ὁ μέγας, οὕτω γὰρ ἐκάλουν τὸν Ἀντώνιον, ἄνελθε πρὸς αὐτὸν βαλὼν τὸν λελωβημένον εἰς πλοῖον, καὶ ἀνένεγκε

19—1 (p. 66) s (add. 17177) 'Go to him, taking him with thee in a boat and going up to him, and convey him to his monastery, and wait there till he come from the desert.'

PTW°ll_2ss_2

1 *ζῷον* T   *λαμβάνω*] *ἀπενέγκω* W°   *σε*] + *ὁ δὲ* TW°*B*   *ἐνεγκὼν* T*B*   *ἤνεγκεν οὖν ὄν. καὶ* W°   *ἐπῆρεν* TW°*B*   **2** *ξενίδιον* TW°*B*   *ἐπιμελούμενος*] + diligenter l_2s; 'in everything' s_2 (cf. *B κατὰ πᾶσαν αὐτοῦ χρείαν*)   **4, 5** *αὐτοῦ* and *τοῦ Εὐλ.* tr P   **5** *καὶ* before *ταῖς χ.* W°   *δὲ*] om T   **6** *τὰ*] PW°*B*$^{45-6}$; om T*B*†   *στασιάζει* TW°: + *ὁ λελ.* W°   **7** *τοιαύταις* TW°   **8** *λέγων* T: + *αὐτῷ* W°*B*   *σχάστα*] PTW°*B*†; *σχάτα B*†; *ἔσχατα* l_2 (ultima mala); fugitive l; om ss_2: + *γλούττων B*   *φυγοκύρι*] PTW°*B*†l_2s; *φαγοκύρι B*†ls_2 **10** *θέλω*] + *ἐσθίειν* *B*ll_2ss_2 *αὐτῷ*] *αὐτὸν* W°: + *καὶ* W°*B*$^{45-6}$ *οὖν*] om TW°   **11** *ἀνέκραξεν*] P; *ἀνέκραζεν* TW° (*ἐκρ.*); *ἀνακράζει B*   *θέλω*] + *θεωρεῖν* W°; *βλέπειν B*†; (ll_2ss_2)   **12** *θέλω*] on insertion in T cf. *Introd.* § 2   **13** *οὕτως*] om W°   *ἐξαγρ.* W°*B*   **14** *τοίνυν*] *οὖν* TW°; om *B*   *ἐκ γείτ.*] *ἔγγιστα* W°   **16** *αὐτὸν*] + *ἀλλὰ B*l: + *τῷ* T*B*   **17** *ἀλλὰ* after *αὐτὸν* B†l   **18** *οὖν*] om W°   *οὐκ οἶδα*] om TW°   *οἱ δὲ*] om TW°   **19** *μέγας*] + *Ἀντώνιος* l_2 *οὕτω......Ἀντ.*] om. l_2s   *ἄνελθε*] *B*(P)l; *ἄπελθε* TW°   **20** *καὶ ἄνελθε π. αὐτὸν* after *πλοῖον* P(s)   *πρὸς αὐτὸν*] om TW°   *βαλὼν*] W°*B*(ls); *λαβὼν* T; *βάλε* P   *καὶ ἀνένεγκε αὐτὸν*] om P   *ἀπένεγκαι* W° (*ἀν.* corr. m. 1); *ἀπένεγκον* A^B

αὐτὸν εἰς τὸ μοναστήριον καὶ ἔκδεξαι ἕως ἐξέλθῃ ἐκ τῆς ἐρήμου, καὶ ἀνένεγκε αὐτῷ τὸ κρῖμα· καὶ ὃ ἐάν σοι εἴπῃ, στοίχησον αὐτοῦ τῇ ἐπικρίσει, ὁ θεὸς γάρ σοι λαλεῖ δι' αὐτοῦ. καὶ ἠνέσχετο αὐτῶν, καὶ βαλὼν τὸν λελωβημένον εἰς σκαφίδιον βουκολικόν, ἐξῆλθεν ἐν νυκτὶ τῆς πόλεως, καὶ ἀνήνεγκεν αὐτὸν εἰς τὸ μοναστήριον τῶν μαθητῶν τοῦ ἁγίου Ἀντωνίου. συνέβη δὲ τὴν ἄλλην ἡμέραν ἐλθεῖν τὸν μέγαν ἑσπέραν βαθεῖαν, ὡς διηγήσατο ὁ Κρόνιος, ἐμπεφιβλωμένος χλανίδα δερματίνην. ἐρχόμενος οὖν εἰς τὸ μοναστήριον αὐτῶν ταύτην εἶχε τὴν συνήθειαν καλεῖν τὸν Μακάριον καὶ ἐρωτᾶν αὐτόν· Ἀδελφὲ Μακάριε, ἦλθόν τινες ἀδελφοὶ ὧδε; ἀπεκρίνατο· Ναί. Αἰγύπτιοί εἰσιν ἢ Ἱεροσολυμῖται; σημεῖον δὲ αὐτῷ δεδώκει ὡς Ἐὰν ἀπραγοτέρους ἴδῃς, λέγε ὅτι Αἰγύπτιοί εἰσιν· ὅταν δὲ εὐλαβεστέρους καὶ λογιωτέρους, λέγε Ἱεροσολυμῖται. ἠρώτησεν οὖν αὐτῷ κατὰ τὸ εἰωθός· Αἰγύπτιοί εἰσιν οἱ ἀδελφοί, ἢ Ἱεροσολυμῖται; ἀπεκρίνατο ὁ Μακάριος καὶ λέγει αὐτῷ· Μίγμα εἰσίν. ὅτε μὲν ἔλεγεν αὐτῷ· Αἰγύπτιοί εἰσιν, ἔλεγε πρὸς αὐτὸν ὁ ἅγιος Ἀντώνιος· Ποίησον φακὸν καὶ δὸς αὐτοῖς φαγεῖν· καὶ ἐποίει αὐτοῖς εὐχὴν μίαν, καὶ ἀπέλυεν αὐτούς. ὅτε δὲ ἔλεγεν ὅτι Ἱεροσολυμῖταί εἰσιν, ἐκάθητο διὰ πάσης νυκτός, λαλῶν αὐτοῖς τὰ πρὸς σωτηρίαν. ἐν ἐκείνῃ οὖν τῇ ἑσπέρᾳ καθεσθείς, φησί, προσκαλεῖται | πάντας, καὶ μηδενὸς μηδὲν αὐτῷ εἰρηκότος ὁποῖον ὄνομα

PTW°ll$_2$ss$_2$

1 *εἰς τὸ μον.* after *ἔκδεξαι* P *ἀσκητήριον* W° *ἔκδεξαι*] + ibi ll$_2$s *ἕως*] + *οὗ* T*B*; *ὅτε* W° *ἔλθῃ* TW°A^B *τῆς ἐρήμου*] Ps; *τοῦ σπηλαίου* TW°*B*ll$_2$ **2** *ἀνένεγκαι* P; *-κον* A^B *ὡς ἂν* (om *σοι*) T; *εἴ τι ἐὰν* W° **3** *ὁ γὰρ θ.* TW°*B* *λαλεῖ*] Ps; *λέγει* TW° (after *αὐτοῦ*) *B*l$_2$: (l paraphr.) *δι' αὐτοῦ*] *ὁ δ' ἄν σοι εἴπῃ* T(l) *ἠνέσχ. οὖν αὐτῶν* W°; om Tl$_2$ **4** *τὸν λελ.*] *αὐτὸν* TW° *σκαφίδιον*] PW°*B*$^{45-6}$; *σκάφος* *B*†; *σκάφην* (*βουκολικὴν*) T **4, 5** *βουκολικὸν......πόλεως*] om l$_2$s **6** *δὲ*] *οὖν* W **7** *διηγεῖτο* TW° **8** *ὁ*] om T*B* *ἐμπεφληβομένος* W° *χλανίδα*] PTA^B; *χλαμύδα* *B*W°(ls) **9** *αὐτῶν*] Pl; *ἑαυτοῦ* W°*B*T (*αὐτοῦ*) s; om l$_2$ *τὴν*] om T **11** *ἦλθαν* W° *ἀδ. τινες* T *ὧδε*] + *ὁ δὲ* T*B* *εἰσὶν*] om W° **12** *ὡς*] P; *ἵνα* T; *ὅτι* *B*$^{45-6}$; om W°*B*† *ἐὰν*] P; *ὅταν* TW°*B* **13** *ἴδῃ λέγει* T *εἰσὶν*] om W° **14** *λογικοτέρους* W°; *ὀλιγωτέρους* T *λέγει* T: + *ὅτι* TW°*B* *αὐτῷ*] (sic) P; *αὐτὸν* T; om W° **16** *ἀποκρίνεται* TW° *αὐτῷ*] PTW°*B*s; om A^{B}ll$_2$s$_2$ *μὲν*] P; *δὲ* TW°; *οὖν* *B* **17** *αὐτῷ*] P; *ὅτι* TW°*B* *εἰσὶν*] om W° *ἔλεγε*[2]] *φησὶ* T *πρὸς......Ἀντ.*] om W° *Ἀντώνιος*] om T*B*s **18** *ποίησον*] + *αὐτοῖς* TW°*B* **18, 19** *καὶ ἐποίει......αὐτοὺς*] TW° (om *μίαν*) *B*ll$_2$ss$_2$; om P **19** *ὅτι*] om T **20** *εἰσὶν*] om W°*B* **21** *οὖν*] om W° *νυκτὶ* W° *παρακαθ.* W° *φησὶ*] om T*B*$^{45-6}$ **22** *μηδὲν*] om TW°*B* *εἰρηκότος*] + *ὅτι* T: + *τίς* Tl(s): + *τὸ* *B* *ποῖον* T*B*

ἔχει, σκοτίας οὔσης φωνεῖ καὶ λέγει· Εὐλόγιε, Εὐλόγιε, Εὐλόγιε, ἐκ τρίτου. ἐκεῖνος οὐκ ἀπεκρίνατο ὁ σχολαστικός, οἰόμενος ἄλλον Εὐλόγιον καλεῖσθαι. λέγει αὐτῷ ἔπειτα πάλιν· Σοὶ λέγω, Εὐλόγιε, τῷ ἀπὸ Ἀλεξανδρείας ἐλθόντι. λέγει αὐτῷ ὁ Εὐλόγιος· Τί κελεύεις, δέομαί σου; Τί ἧκες; ἀποκρίνεται ὁ Εὐλόγιος καὶ λέγει αὐτῷ· Ὁ ἀποκαλύψας σοι τὸ ὄνομά μου, καὶ τὸ πρᾶγμά σοι ἀπεκάλυψε. λέγει αὐτῷ ὁ Ἀντώνιος· Οἶδα διὸ ἦλθες· ἀλλ' ἐπὶ πάντων τῶν ἀδελφῶν εἰπέ, ἵνα καὶ αὐτοὶ ἀκούσωσι. λέγει αὐτῷ ὁ Εὐλόγιος· Τοῦτον τὸν λελωβημένον εὗρον ἐν τῇ ἀγορᾷ· καὶ δεξιὰς ἔδωκα τῷ θεῷ ἵνα αὐτὸν νοσοκομήσω, κἀγὼ σωθῶ δι' αὐτοῦ, καὶ αὐτὸς δι' ἐμοῦ. ἐπεὶ οὖν μετὰ τοσαῦτα ἔτη εἰς ἄκρον με χειμάζει καὶ ἐνεθυμήθην αὐτὸν ῥῖψαι, τούτου χάριν ἦλθον πρὸς τὴν σὴν ἁγιωσύνην, ἵνα μοι συμβουλεύσῃς τί ὀφείλω ποιῆσαι, καὶ προσεύξῃ περὶ ἐμοῦ· δεινῶς γὰρ χειμάζομαι. λέγει αὐτῷ ὁ Ἀντώνιος ἐμβριθεῖ καὶ αὐστηρᾷ τῇ φωνῇ· Ῥίπτεις αὐτόν; ἀλλ' ὁ ποιήσας αὐτὸν οὐ ῥίπτει αὐτόν. ῥίπτεις αὐτὸν σύ; ἐγείρει ὁ θεὸς τὸν καλλίονά σου καὶ συνάγει αὐτόν. ἐφησυχάσας οὖν ὁ Εὐλόγιος κατέπτηξε. καὶ καταλείψας πάλιν τὸν Εὐλόγιον ἄρχεται τῇ γλώττῃ μαστίζειν τὸν λελωβημένον καὶ ἀποβοᾶν· Λελωβημένε πεπηρωμένε, ἀνάξιε τῆς γῆς καὶ τοῦ οὐρανοῦ, οὐ παύῃ θεομαχῶν; οὐκ οἶδας ὅτι ὁ Χριστός ἐστιν ὁ ὑπηρετῶν σοι; πῶς τολμᾷς κατὰ τοῦ Χριστοῦ τοιαῦτα φθέγγεσθαι; οὐ διὰ τὸν Χριστὸν ἑαυτὸν ἐδούλωσεν εἰς

PTW°ll_2ss_2

1 οὔσης] + subito l_2s　Εὐλογ. Εὐ. Εὐ.] twice only in TA[B]l_2; suo illum nomine ter uocauit ls_2　**2** ἐκ τρίτου] om Ts　ἐκεῖνος] + δὲ TW°　ὁ ἀπὸ σχολαστικῶν W°　σχολ.] + Εὐλόγιος *B*sl_2 (om σχολ.)　**3** Εὐλόγιον] om *B*s　εἶπε (om αὐτῷ) W°　ἔπειτα] Pl_2; ἐκ δευτέρου *B*; om TW°A[B]ss_2; l vac　πάλιν] om A[B]l_2　**4** ἐξ W°　**5** σου] + λέγει ὁ μέγας T*B*; ἔφη ὁ Ἀντ. W° (various similar clauses in $ss_2l_2l^{rev}$(l vac))　ἧκας TW°　ἀπεκρίθη TW°　**6** ὁ Εὐ. κ. λεγ. αὐτῷ] om T　**7** ἀποκαλύψει *B*ss_2: + δι' οὗ ἦλθον *B*s_2(ls)　**8** διὸ] πῶς W°　καὶ αὐτοὶ] om TW°s　**9** ὁ δὲ ἔφη (om ὁ Εὐλ.) W°　αὐτῷ] PTW°s; ἐπὶ πάντων *B*; om ll_2s_2　**10** ἀγορᾷ] + ἐρριμμένον ... ἀνέλαβον αὐτὸν *B*l_2 (iacentem in platea et leuaui eum)　**11** αὐτὸς] + ἀναπαυθῇ *B* (ἀναπαῇ B^{45-6})l_2 (repausationem habeat)　**12** τόσα TW°　χ. με εἰς ἄκρον T　καὶ] om P*B*†　ῥῖψαι αὐτὸν W°　**15** χειμάζομαι] T$B^{45-6}ll_2s$; χειμάζει με PA[B]*B*†s_2; με χειμ. W°: (ll_2s have two synonymous verbs)　τῇ] om T　**17** ἐγερεῖ $B^{45-6}l$　**18** ἀφησ. W°*B*†　οὖν] δὲ T　κατέπτηξε] + ταῦτ' ἀκούσας *B*s　καταλείψας δὲ T*B*　**19** πάλιν] om TW°*B*s　**20** βοᾶν TB^{45-6}; ἀναβ. W°: + πρὸς αὐτὸν *B*ll_2　πεπηρωμένε] PTs (see Note 38); πεπηλωμένε *B*l(s_2 'unclean'); ven λελωβημένον καὶ πεπηρωμένον (sic ap. Rosw.); inueterate dierum malorum l_2; om A[B]W°　ἀνάξιε] + καὶ T*B* (A[B]txt)　**21** tr τ. γῆς and τ. οὐρ. W°$B^{45-6}l_2$　θεομαχεῖν W°　**22** πῶς] + οὖν W°

τὴν σὴν ὑπηρεσίαν; στύψας οὖν καὶ τοῦτον ἀφῆκε. καὶ διαλεχθεὶς τοῖς λοιποῖς πᾶσι τὰ πρὸς τὴν χρείαν ἀπολαμβάνεται τὸν Εὐλόγιον καὶ τὸν λελωβημένον καὶ λέγει αὐτοῖς· Μὴ περιστραφῆτε μηδαμοῦ, ἀπέλθετε· μὴ χωρισθῆτε ἀπ' ἀλλήλων, ἀλλ' ἢ εἰς τὴν κέλλαν ὑμῶν εἰς ἣν ἐχρονίσατε. ἤδη γὰρ ἀποστέλλει ὁ θεὸς ἐφ' ὑμᾶς. ὁ πειρασμὸς γὰρ οὗτος συνέβη ὑμῖν ἐπειδὴ ἀμφότεροι περὶ τὸ τέλος ἔχετε καὶ στεφάνων μέλλετε ἀξιοῦσθαι. μὴ οὖν ἄλλο τι ποιήσητε, καὶ ἐλθὼν ὁ ἄγγελος μὴ εὕρῃ ὑμᾶς ἐν τῷ τόπῳ. θᾶττον οὖν ὁδεύσαντες ἦλθον εἰς τὴν κέλλαν ἑαυτῶν. καὶ ἐντὸς τεσσαράκοντα ἡμερῶν τελευτᾷ ὁ Εὐλόγιος· ἐντὸς δὲ ἄλλων τριῶν ἡμερῶν τελευτᾷ ὁ λελωβημένος. |

Χρονοτριβήσας δὲ ὁ Κρόνιος ἐν τοῖς περὶ τὴν Θηβαΐδα τόποις κατῆλθεν εἰς τὰ μοναστήρια Ἀλεξανδρείας. καὶ συνέβη τοῦ μὲν τὰ τεσσαρακοστὰ ἐπιτελεῖσθαι, τοῦ δὲ τὰ τρίτα παρὰ τῆς ἀδελφότητος. ἔμαθεν οὖν ὁ Κρόνιος καὶ ἐξέστη· καὶ λαβὼν εὐαγγέλιον καὶ θεὶς ἐν μέσῳ τῆς ἀδελφότητος διωμόσατο ἀφηγούμενος τὸ συμβὰν ὅτι Τῶν λόγων τούτων ὅλων ἑρμηνεὺς

4, 5 s (add. 17177): 'Do not turn anywhere, but go; and do not separate from one another, but return to your cell in which you lived long.'

15 See Note 39.

PTW°ll_2ss_2

1 *τοῦτον*] + *τοῖς ἐπιπλήκτοις λόγοις Bl* (mordaci sermone) *ἀφῆκε*] + *τούτους Bs* **2** *ἐπιλαμβ.* W°: + *πάλιν Bl* **3** *τὸν λελ. καὶ τὸν Εὐ.* T **4, 5** *μὴ περιστρ.... ἐχρονίσατε*] thus s (see above) s_2(*B*) **4** *μὴ περιστρ.... ἀπέλθετε*] om l_2 *μηδαμοῦ*] + *ἀλλ' B*(ss_2) *ἀπέλθετε*] om l: + *εἰς τὸν τόπον ὑμῶν* P; *μετ' εἰρήνης B*: + *καὶ* W° *ἀπ' ἀλλήλων*] *B* inserts a clause **5** *ἀλλ' ἢ...ἐχρονίσατε*] om P *ἀλλ' ἢ*] TW° (om *ἢ*); *ἀλλ' ὑποστρέψατε B* (ll_2ss_2) *εἰς ἣν ἐχρονίσατε*] om l_2 **6** *ὁ θεὸς*] + *τὸν ἄγγελον αὐτοῦ* P; *ἄγγελον* B^{45-6}; 'the end' s: txt TW°A^B*B*ll_2s_2 (l iam nunc enim ad uos dnūs deus mittet; l_2 incontinenter enim uisitat vos dnus *al* deus); (same use of *ἀποστέλλω* in *Vita Pachomii* passim) **7** *ὑμῖν συν.* T *τὸ*] om T **8** *μὴ οὖν...ποιήσητε*] om l_2s *καὶ*] TW°*B*; as if *μὴ* ll_2ss_2 (ne ueniens ang. non inueniat l_2); *ἵνα* P **9** *μὴ*] *οὐχ* W°; om P *τῷ*] + *αὐτῷ B*(l_2); 'your' ss_2 **10** *αὐτῶν* TW° *ἐντὸς*] + *δὲ* T (om *καὶ*) *τριάκοντα* B^{45-6}; *εἴκοσι τεσσάρων* A^B **11** *Εὐ.*] + *καὶ* (om *δὲ*) T *ἄλλων*] om l_2 *ἡμερῶν*] om T *τελευτᾷ*[2]] + *καὶ* W° **13** *δὲ*] *οὖν* W° *εἰς τοὺς π. Θ. τόπους* W°*B* **14** *τὸ μοναστήριον* W°A^B **15** *τοῦ μὲν*] $Tlss_2$; + *Εὐλογίου* PW°Bl_2 *τὰ*[1]] om T *τεσσαρακοστὰ*] W°Bll_2ss_2; *τριακοστὰ* PTA^B *τοῦ δὲ*] $Tlss_2$; + *λελωβημένου* PW°Bl_2 **17** *θήσας* W° *τῆς ἀδελφ.*] om T *ἀφηγησάμενος* TW°*B* **18** *τὸ συμβὰν*] *τὴν πρόγνωσιν τοῦ μεγάλου Ἀντ. περὶ αὐτῶν καὶ περὶ πάντων τῶν συμβεβηκότων* Bl_2 (quomodo omnia quae uenerunt Eulogio et leproso praedixisset beatus Ant.) *τῶν λόγων*] om W° *ἑρμηνεὺς*] + *ἐγὼ* W° **18—3** (p. 69) *ὅτι...αἰγυπτιστὶ*] om l_2

γέγονα τοῦ μακαρίου Ἀντωνίου, ἑλληνιστὶ μὴ εἰδότος· ἐγὼ γὰρ ἠπιστάμην ἀμφοτέρας τὰς γλώσσας, καὶ ἡρμήνευσα αὐτοῖς, τοῖς μὲν ἑλληνιστί, ἐκείνῳ δὲ αἰγυπτιστί.

Καὶ τοῦτο δὲ διηγήσατο ὁ Κρόνιος, ὅτι Ἐν τῇ νυκτὶ ἐκείνῃ διηγήσατο ἡμῖν ὁ μακάριος Ἀντώνιος ὅτι Ἐνιαυτὸν ὁλόκληρον ηὐξάμην ἀποκαλυφθῆναί μοι τὸν τόπον τῶν δικαίων καὶ τῶν ἁμαρτωλῶν. καὶ ἐθεασάμην μακρόν τινα γίγαντα μέχρι τῶν νεφελῶν, μέλανα, τὰς χεῖρας ἐκτεταμένας ἔχοντα ἐπὶ τὸν οὐρανόν, καὶ ὑποκάτω αὐτοῦ λίμνην ἔχουσαν μέτρον θαλάσσης· καὶ ἑώρων ψυχὰς ἀνιπταμένας ὡς ὄρνεα. καὶ ὅσαι μὲν ὑπερίπταντο αὐτοῦ τῶν χειρῶν καὶ τῆς κεφαλῆς διεσώζοντο· ὅσαι δὲ παρὰ τῶν χειρῶν αὐτοῦ ἐκοσσίζοντο ἐνέπιπτον εἰς τὴν λίμνην. ἦλθεν οὖν μοι φωνὴ λέγουσα· Ταύτας ἃς βλέπεις ὑπεριπταμένας ψυχὰς τῶν δικαίων αἱ ψυχαί εἰσιν αἳ εἰς τὸν παράδεισον σώζονται· αἱ δὲ ἄλλαι εἰσὶν αἱ εἰς τὸν ᾅδην ὑποσυρόμεναι, τοῖς θελήμασι τῆς σαρκὸς καὶ τῇ μνησικακίᾳ ἐξακολουθήσασαι.

(XXII) Διηγεῖτο δὲ καὶ τοῦτο ὁ Κρόνιος καὶ ὁ ἅγιος Ἱέραξ καὶ πλείονες ἄλλοι περὶ ὧν μέλλω λέγειν, ὅτι Παῦλός τις ἄγροικος γεωργός, καθ' ὑπερβολὴν ἄκακος καὶ ἁπλοῦς, ὡραιοτάτῃ ἐζεύχθη γυναικὶ κακοτρόπῳ τῇ γνώμῃ, ἥτις διελάνθανεν ἁμαρτά-

17 The text of s in cc. XXII, XXIII is contained in Tullberg's MSS A and B (*Paradisus* pp. 21—33). Cap. XXII exists in W°; but as W° and O are twin texts (see *Introd.* § 9) it seemed sufficient to cite O: any differences will be recorded after the List of Readings of W, at end of Text. On Paul the Simple see Note 40.

18—8 (p. 70) Soz. I. 13 (13) Καὶ Παῦλος ὁ ἐπίκλην ἁπλοῦς· ὅν φασιν ἄγροικον ὄντα καλῇ τὸ εἶδος γυναικὶ συνοικῆσαι· ἐπ' αὐτοφώρῳ δὲ αὐτὴν καταλαβόντα

PTW°lss_2

1 γὰρ] δὲ T   **2** τούτοις (om τοῖς) W°   **2, 3** τοῖς...αἰγ.] om T

PTW°l[l_2]s_2

4 καὶ τοῦτο to end of chapter is wanting in s: l_2 much interpolated   **4, 5** διηγεῖτο (bis) T*B*   **5** ὁ μ. Ἀντ.] om TW°   Ἀντ.] om *B*   **7** τινα] Pll_2; om TW°*B*   **9** λίμνην θαλ. μὴ ἐχούσης μέτρον W°   θαλ. before ἔχουσαν T*B*   **10** διιπταμένας W°   ὅσοι P   **12** παρὰ] ὑπὸ T   ἔπιπτον W°   **13** φωνή] + φησί W°   **14** ψυχὰς before ὑπεριπτ. W°   τῶν δικ. after εἰσιν TW°*B*   αἳ] καὶ T   **15** αἱ[2]] om T   **16** ἐξακολουθήσαντες W°

XXII (Περὶ Παύλου τοῦ ἁπλοῦ): PTOlss_2

17, 18 διηγεῖτο...ὅτι] om Ts   **17** διηγήσατο OB^{45-6} δὲ] om O   καὶ τοῦτο] Ps_2; om O*B*l   **18** τις] + ὀνόματι B^{45-6}ls   **19** ὡραιοτάτῃ] + τινὶ O   **20** ἥτις] om O   διέλαθεν T*B*†

νουσα ἐπὶ μήκιστον χρόνον. εἰσελθὼν οὖν ἐξ ἀγροῦ αἰφνίδιον ὁ Παῦλος εὗρεν αὐτοὺς αἰσχροπραγοῦντας, τῆς προνοίας εἰς τὸ συμφέρον ὁδηγούσης τὸν Παῦλον. καὶ γελάσας σεμνὸν ἐπιφωνεῖ αὐτοῖς καὶ λέγει· Καλῶς, καλῶς· ἀληθῶς οὐ μέλει μοι. μὰ τὸν Ἰησοῦν ἐγὼ αὐτὴν οὐκέτι αἴρω. ὕπαγε, ἔχε αὐτὴν καὶ τὰ παιδία αὐτῆς· ἐγὼ γὰρ ὑπάγω γίνομαι μοναχός. καὶ μηδενὶ μηδὲν εἰρηκὼς ἀνατρέχει τὰς ὀκτὼ μονὰς καὶ ἀπέρχεται πρὸς τὸν μακάριον Ἀντώνιον καὶ κρούει τὴν θύραν. ἐξελθὼν οὖν ἐρωτᾷ αὐτόν· Τί θέλεις; λέγει αὐτῷ· Μοναχὸς θέλω γενέσθαι. ἀποκρίνεται | ὁ Ἀντώνιος καὶ λέγει αὐτῷ· Ἐτῶν ἑξήκοντα γέρων ἄνθρωπος ὧδε μοναχὸς οὐ δύνασαι γενέσθαι· ἀλλὰ μᾶλλον ἄπελθε εἰς κώμην καὶ ἐργάζου, καὶ ζῆθι ἐργατικὸν βίον εὐχαριστῶν τῷ θεῷ· ὑπομεῖναι γὰρ τὰς θλίψεις τῆς ἐρήμου οὐ δύνασαι. ἀποκρίνεται ὁ γέρων πάλιν καὶ λέγει αὐτῷ· Εἴ τι ἂν με διδάξῃς ἐκεῖνο ποιῶ. λέγει αὐτῷ ὁ Ἀντώνιος· Εἴρηκά σοι ὅτι γέρων εἶ καὶ οὐ δύνασαι· ἄπελθε εἰ ἄρα θέλεις μοναχὸς γενέσθαι εἰς κοινόβιον πλειόνων ἀδελφῶν, οἵτινες δύνανταί σου τῆς ἀσθενείας ἀνέχεσθαι. ἐγὼ γὰρ μόνος κάθημαι ὧδε διὰ πέντε ἐσθίων καὶ τοῦτο λιμῷ. τούτοις καὶ τοῖς τοιούτοις ῥήμασιν ἀπεσόβει τὸν Παῦλον· καὶ ὡς οὐκ ἠνείχετο αὐτοῦ κλείσας τὴν

μοιχευομένην, ἠρέμα ἐπιγελάσαι καὶ ὅρκον προσθεῖναι ὡς οὐκ ἔτι αὐτῇ συνοικήσει· Ἔχε δὲ αὐτήν, πρὸς τὸν μοιχὸν εἰπὼν εὐθὺς ἐπὶ τὴν ἐρημίαν ἦλθε πρὸς Ἀντώνιον.

19—10 (p. 72) A and B are printed in full *Prol.* pp. 30—34.

PTOlss$_2$

1 *ἐπὶ μήκου[s] τῶν χρόνων* O   *οὖν*] + *ποτὲ B*†(lss$_2$)   *αἰφνιδίως* O   **2** *αὐτὴν αἰσχροπραγοῦσαν* Ols$_2$ **3** *καί*] + *θεασάμενος ταύτην μετὰ τοῦ συνήθους B*; cum eam ...cum alio iacentem uiro deprehendisset l; 'when he entered and saw them' s   *σεμνῶς* O   *ἐπιφέρει* T   **5** *ἔχε*] PTA^B Soz.; *ἔχεις* O*B*: + *καὶ* O   **6** *αὐτῆς*] s$_2$ breaks off to end of chapter

PTOls

6 *ὑπάγω*] + *καὶ* O*B*†(ls)   **7** *εἰρηκὼς*] + *ἀναχωρεῖ καὶ* T   **8** *ἐλθὼν* T   *οὖν*] + *ὁ ἅγιος* T; *ὁ μακάριος Ἀντώνιος* O*B* (al. *ἅγιος*, al. *μέγας*) s   **9** *ἐρωτᾷ αὐτὸν*] *λέγει αὐτῷ* T   *αὐτῷ*] *ἐκεῖνος* T: + *ὁ Παῦλος B*s   **10** *ὁ*] om O   *καὶ λέγει*] om TA^B *αὐτῷ*] P*B* (before *ὁ Ἀντ.*) s; om TOl   **11** *δύνασαι*] PA^{B38}*B*†ls; *δύναται* TOA^{B37}*B*†   *γενέσθαι* before *οὐ* TO*B*   **12** *ζῆθι*] *νῆθαι* (sic) O   **14** *πάλιν* before *ὁ* TO*B*   *αὐτῷ*] Ps; om TO*B*: (l ille)   **15** *ἐκεῖνο*] *τοῦτο* T*B*†   *ποιῶ*] PTA^B*B*$^{45-6}$s; *ποιήσω* O*B*†l   *ὁ*] + *ἅγιος* P   **16** *δύνασαι*] + *ὧδε εἶναι* P; + *μονάσαι* A^B*B*†; implere quod quaeris l: txt TO*B*†s   **17** *κοινόβιον*] + *εἴσελθε* TO*B*l; txt Ps   **18** *τῆς ἀσθ.*] om O   *ἀνέχεσθαι*] PT*B*†; *ἀνασχέσθαι* O*B*$^{45-6}$; *ἀντέχεσθαι* A^B; *ἀνέξασθαι B*†   **20** *ἠνείχετο*] PTA^B; *ἠνέσχετο* O*B*

θύραν ὁ Ἀντώνιος οὐκ ἐξῆλθεν ἐπὶ ἡμέρας τρεῖς δι' αὐτόν, οὐδὲ πρὸς τὴν χρείαν. ὁ δὲ οὐκ ἀνεχώρησε. τῇ δὲ τετάρτῃ ἡμέρᾳ χρείας αὐτὸν ἀναγκαζούσης ἀνοίξας ἐξῆλθε καὶ πάλιν λέγει αὐτῷ· Ἄπελθε ἐντεῦθεν, γέρων· τί με ὑποπιάζεις; οὐ δύνασαι ὧδε μεῖναι. λέγει αὐτῷ ὁ Παῦλος· Ἀμήχανόν μοί ἐστιν ἀλλαχοῦ τελευτῆσαι ἀλλ' ἢ ὧδε. περιβλεψάμενος οὖν ὁ Ἀντώνιος καὶ θεασάμενος ὅτι τὰ πρὸς τροφὴν οὐ βαστάζει, οὐκ ἄρτον, οὐχ ὕδωρ, καὶ τετάρτην ἔχει καρτερήσας νῆστις, Μήποτε καὶ ἀποθάνῃ, φησί, καὶ κηλιδώσῃ μου τὴν ψυχήν, εἰσδέχεται αὐτόν. καὶ τοιαύτην ἀνέλαβεν ὁ Ἀντώνιος ἐν ταῖς ἡμέραις ἐκείναις πολιτείαν οἵαν οὐδέποτε ἐν νεότητι. καὶ βρέξας θαλλοὺς λέγει αὐτῷ· Δέξαι, πλέξον σειρὰν ὡς κἀγώ. πλέκει ὁ γέρων ἕως ἐννάτης ὀργυίας δεκαπέντε μοχθήσας. θεασάμενος οὖν ὁ Ἀντώνιος δυσηρεστήθη καὶ λέγει αὐτῷ· Κακῶς ἔπλεξας· ἀπόπλεξον καὶ ἄνωθεν πλέξον· νήστει αὐτῷ ὄντι καὶ ἡλικιώτῃ ταύτην ἐπαγαγὼν τὴν σῆψιν, ἵνα δυσφορήσας ὁ γέρων φύγῃ τὸν Ἀντώνιον. ὁ δὲ καὶ ἀπέπλεξε καὶ πάλιν ἔπλεξε τοὺς αὐτοὺς θαλλούς, εἰ καὶ δυσχερέστερον διὰ τὸ ἐρρυτιδῶσθαι. θεασάμενος δὲ ὁ Ἀντώνιος ὅτι οὔτε ἐγόγγυσεν οὔτε ἐμικροψύχησεν οὔτε ἠγανάκτησε, κατενύγη. καὶ δύναντος τοῦ ἡλίου λέγει αὐτῷ· Θέλεις φάγωμεν ἄρτου κλάσμα; λέγει αὐτῷ ὁ Παῦλος· Ὡς

15—19 Soz. (14) *Πραότατον δὲ καὶ καρτερικὸν εἰς ἄγαν λέγεται τόνδε γενέσθαι τὸν ἄνδρα· ἀμέλει τοι καὶ γηραλέῳ ὄντι καὶ μοναστικῆς τληπαθείας* (al. *πολιτείας*) *ἀήθει, ἔτι γὰρ νέηλυς ἦν, παντοδαπαῖς πείραις προσβαλὼν Ἀντώνιος, ἐν οὐδενὶ ἀγεννῆ ἐφώρασε.*

PTOls

2 *ὁ*] *ὡς* T *δὲ*[2]] PA[B]; *οὖν* O*B*; om T **3** *ἀναγκαζούσης*] PO*B*†; *ἀναγκασάσης* T*B*†; *καταλαβούσης* A[B]*B*† *αὐτῷ λεγ.* TO **4** *ἐντεῦθεν*] PTA[B]; *ἔνθεν* O*B* *γέρον* T*B*† **5** *μεῖναι*] *εἶναι* O*B*[45–6] *ἀμήχανον*] *ἀδύνατον* A[B] *μοι*] *με* O **6** *ἀλλ' ἢ*] TO*B*[45–6]; *ἀλλ'* (om *ἢ*) P*B*†; *εἰ μὴ* A[B]; ls nisi **8** *τετάρτην*] + *ἡμέραν* OA[B]*B*[45–6] *καὶ*[2]] om O **9** *φησὶ*] om T *αὐτὸν*] + *τότε* *B*l (tandem) **11** *πολιτείαν* before *ὁ Ἀντ.* O; after *ὁ Ἀντ.* T *οὐδὲ* TO; *οὔτε ὅτε ἦν* A[B] *ἐν*] + *τῇ* T*B*[45–6] *θαλλοὺς*] + *ἐκ φοινίκων* *B*l (s, om s[an]) **12** *μέχρις* O*B*† **13** *ἐννάτης*] + *ὥρας* T *μοχθήσας*] PTO*B*[45–6]; *μόχθῳ πολλῷ* A[B]*B*†l (cum maximo labore) *οὖν*] *δὲ* T*B* **14** *δυσηρέσθη* O **16** *ἐπάγων* TO*B*† *σῆψιν*] sic PT*B*†; *σκέψιν* O; *στῦψιν* *B*[45–6]; *κόπον* *B*†; pondus ls **17** *τοὺς θαλ. τοὺς αὐτοὺς* T **18** *ἐρρυτιδῶσθαι*] PTO (*ἐρυ.* TO, and *-δεσθ-* O); *εἶναι αὐτοὺς ἐκ τῆς πρώτης πλοκῆς ἐρρυτιδωμένους* (*B*[45–6], al. *ἐρυσιδωμένους*) *B*: ('bent' *i.e.* 'wrinkled' ls) **19** *δὲ*] P; *οὖν* O*B*; om T **19, 20** *οὔτε ἠγανάκτησεν οὔτε ἐγόγγυσεν* (om *οὔτε ἐμικροψ.*) O **21** *ἄρτων*, om *κλάσμα* O

2026/08/18

08:39:45

mario

undefined

g

```
Top    -file-
Top-1 { --disableinterrupt-- }
Top-2 --@aborted--
Top-3 { --clearinterrupt-- --disableinterrupt-- (   )
        --exch-- 0 --exch-- --put-- --clear-- }
Top-4 --@aborted--
```

```
Top    -dict-
Top-1 //SharedFontDirectory
Top-2 -dict-
Top-3 -dict-
Top-4 -dict-
```